Propaganda for War

*How the United States Was
Conditioned to Fight the
Great War of 1914–1918*

by

STEWART HALSEY ROSS

I0191742

ProgRESSive

2009

Front cover: American artists created over 2,000 different propaganda posters during World War I. This portrayal of Germany as a depraved gorilla appeared in 1916, a year before America went to war. In 1939, Nazi Propaganda Minister Joseph Goebbels reprinted the poster with a new caption: "When they assaulted us 25 years ago, they wrote on their rotten slanderous poster: 'Destroy this mad beast—They meant the German people!'" *War Poster Collection, Manuscripts and Archives, Yale University Library.*

Library of Congress Cataloguing-in-Publication Data

Ross, Stewart Halsey.
    Propaganda for war : how the United States was conditioned to fight the Great War of 1914–1918 / by Stewart Halsey Ross.
    350 p. 0.8 cm.
    Includes bibliographical references and index.
    ISBN 0-7864-0111-7 (1996) 978-1-61577-141-7 (2009)
    1. World War, 1914–1918—Propaganda. 2. Propaganda, American—History—20th century. 3. World War, 1914–1918—United States. 4. United States—Politics and government—1913–1921. I. Title.
    D639.P7U67 1996
    940.54'88673—dc20   95-25927
                                         CIP

© 1996-2009 Stewart Halsey Ross. All rights reserved

No part of this book, specifically including the index, may be reproduced or transmitted in any form or by any means, electronic or mechanical, including photocopying, recording, or by any information storage and retrieval system, without permission in writing from the publisher.

Manufactured in the United States of America

Reprinted June, 2009 by ProgressivePress.com
PO Box 126, Joshua Tree, Calif. 92252

IN MEMORIAM

This reprint edition is completed
this Father's Day, June 14th, 2009,
on the 10th anniversary of the passing of
Paul Herman Walter Leonard
* 11/01/1910 — 6/13/1999 †
In remembrance of him,
of the lessons he passed down from History,
and in memory of his late sister
Thelma Eileen Leonard
* 9/10/1922 — 6/13/2009 †
Their lives were indelibly shaped
by the consequences of the Great War.

To the memories of my mother,
Shirley Schulman Cooper,
my father,
Louis Sylvan Ross,
and my father-in-law,
Irving Aduss

FOREWORD
to the Second Edition

By 1917, the year America entered the war in Europe, the enthusiasm that had marked the beginning of the conflict was waning. Implacable hatred for the enemy replaced fervor. When British troops were ordered out of their trenches to charge dug-in German machine guns, they went willingly, if reluctantly—like sheep to slaughter, critics said quietly. Not to do so meant facing a firing squad.

Following the disastrous offense ordered by French General Robert Nivelle in March and April at Verdun, large elements of the French army openly rebelled—refusing to obey orders, assaulting and even killing their officers, deserting by the hundreds in the dead of night. Paris was filled with disorderly troops, officers nowhere to be found. It was later called "the French mutiny," and details were covered up by an embarrassed nation—then and for the next 100 years. The archives are scheduled to be opened in 2017 (if then).

The morale of German soldiers in the front lines was certainly better than the *poilus* they faced, but British journalist Philip Gibbs reported that even the best German troops were affected by the murderous artillery fire. He wrote:

> There were some who could not be persuaded to stay in the trenches under those conditions . . . if they could see any chance of malingering. For the first time on our front the German officers could not trust the courage of their men, nor their loyalty, nor their sense of discipline.

At home it was a markedly different story. The French had always been self-sufficient in terms of agricultural productivity, and the war demanded little sacrifice from French citizens. The Paris government never imposed controls over food production or distribution, nor was it necessary to do so. Food was readily available and consumption actually increased throughout the war for the average Frenchman.

The situation was worse in England. In the years before the war England had imported some 60 percent of the food calories consumed by its population. U-boat depredations had gradually reduced these imports. Voluntary rationing was tried and when it proved ineffective, mandatory controls were applied. The result of the shortfall of food staples, for example, led to an increase of 25 percent in deaths from tuberculosis. While the British had to tuck in their waistlines, they never faced hunger.

It was the Germans and Austro-Hungarians who starved. By 1917, the Royal Navy's purposeful and vengeful food blockade had bitten deep. Before the war Germany had imported two million tons of fertilizers a year and six million tons of grain for fodder; those imports were cut off. The first food riots erupted in Vienna in May 1915 and in Berlin five months later.

The 1916 harvest was a disaster because of a wet and cold spring, and outright famine became widespread. Thousands lined up every day at soup kitchens. The diet of adults consisted of "war bread" containing little grain, fatless sausages, and a weekly allowance of three pounds of potatoes and a single egg. Horses and an occasional dog provided protein. For survival, the Germans relied on turnips and the cold, long winter of 1916-1917 was burned into the memories of the survivors as their infamous Rubewinter. Rickets, a debilitating bone disease among the young that left its victims deformed for life, a result of severe malnutrition, was endemic.

The war was being cast as a fight to the death by both sides, a struggle with the dark forces of evil. The hand-to-hand butchery in the trenches reflected the "no-quarter asked, none given" doctrine by the combatants. The biggest killer and maimer of all, artillery, extracted its deadly toll of thousands daily. The stakes were painted in harsh colors: survival, even to civilization itself. Rudyard Kipling declared savagely in a London newspaper:

> However the world pretends to divide itself, there are only two divisions in the world today—human beings and Germans.

No end was in sight.

The same technological advances that had made Europe capable of fighting such a war, also simplified the control of public opinion. Huge new literate populations spurred the growth of cheap newspapers. London alone had sixteen daily papers in 1914, the largest with a circulation of a million. Germany published four thousand newspapers, half of them dailies.

British public opinion was particularly well-conditioned for the war. For two decades leading up to the outbreak of the war, Germany's rapidly growing economic strength, and emergence as a naval power almost on a par with the Royal Navy, provoked anxiety in many of the most influential newspapers.

As author G.J. Meyer wrote elegantly in *A World Undone*:

> The Rupert Murdoch of the day, Alfred Harmsworth . . . owned a number of important papers aimed at different segments of the public. He used them to alert his readers to what he saw as the German menace, fostering, one of his competitors complained, "an anti-German frame of mind that takes no account of the facts.

The restrictive Defence of the Realm Act—the notorious DORA— was passed by Parliament less than one week into the war. It ensured that all war information originating in England or intended for publication in England was thoroughly scrutinized by growing legions of heavy-handed government censors. C. Hartley Grattan, American author of the postwar *Why We Fought*, concluded sarcastically that

> Honest, unbiased news simply disappeared from the American papers along about the middle of August 1914.

Sir Gilbert Parker, who headed the British group responsible for propaganda in America, kept his organization's work under cover until January 1918 when it was quietly disbanded. It had accomplished its mission—bringing the United States into the war on the Allied side. In an article in the March 1918 issue of *Harper's Monthly Magazine*, Parker told all. It made fascinating reading for Americans. Many came away feeling unclean. They had been raped and they swore it would never happen again. "Promises, promises," perfidious Albion would respond in 1939—and for a second time in a single generation, America would take up arms against those who sought to topple the British Empire.

ACKNOWLEDGMENTS

I sincerely appreciate the contributions to the manuscript by Arthur Walworth, World War I scholar and Pulitzer Prize–winning biographer of Woodrow Wilson. I am indebted to the staffs of the Norwalk Public Library and the Baker Learning Resources Center of Norwalk Community-Technical College for their cooperation during my research. I also must thank Yale University Library, Manuscripts and Archives, for the courtesies extended me, and particularly Judith A. Schiff, chief research archivist. To the Library of Congress, the National Archives, Harvard University's Baker Library, Princeton University's Seeley G. Mudd Library, the New York Public Library, the Connecticut State Library, and the Bridgeport Public Library, whose facilities and collections I used to advantage, my sincere gratitude. I owe a special debt of appreciation to the *New York Times* for that great newspaper's unmatched coverage of the World War I period, which I drew upon extensively.

My six adult children contributed in large and small measure to the book and I thank each of them: Cynthia, for her wise and understanding editorial suggestions throughout; Mark for his unstinting research; Karen, Robert and Jordan, for their attentiveness to one history lecture after another; and Larry, for being a smiling and caring observer. Judy, my wife and best friend, most of all, was a steadfast supporter and a patient listener over the extended period during which "the book" was practically all I talked about.

CONTENTS

INTRODUCTION

*I came to realize that the proper employment of propaganda is a real art.
... But not until the war was there a chance to see the enormous results
which properly directed propaganda can produce.*

Adolf Hitler, *Mein Kampf,* 1924

This book is about how the United States was conditioned to fight the
Great War of 1914–1918. Its focus is on the hypocrisies and deceptions of propaganda, and how the war was packaged, promoted, and sold to a gullible
nation as a holy crusade against evil.

Propaganda for war in the United States was not a new phenomenon.
Mass persuasion, in fact, closely attended the country's birth, with partisans
of independence and loyalists alike employing all the tools of communication then available to espouse their principles. Thomas Paine's pamphlet
Common Sense powerfully called for revolution at the same time that Sam
Adams, who believed that men were ruled by emotion rather than reason,
staged parades and fireworks on the Boston Common, burned effigies of
well-known enemies, and spread his radical gospel through his newspapers.
John Adams who would become America's second president, showed he was
a student of eighteenth-century public relations when he commented that
revolutionary propagandists "tinge the minds of people; they impregnate
them with the sentiments of liberty; they render the people fond of their leaders in the causes, and averse and bitter against all opposers."[1] Indeed, of all
the tracts inciting the colonists to armed rebellion, Thomas Jefferson's Declaration of Independence was perhaps the most effective propaganda.

During the Civil War, the Union and the Confederacy boisterously
traded lies and incredible atrocity tales. The abolitionist press exaggerated the
South's cruelties to slaves while the South defended its "peculiar institution"
as benign and paternalistic. Harriet Beecher Stowe's provocative, widely read
antislavery novel, *Uncle Tom's Cabin,* was Union propaganda; in 1863, when
Abraham Lincoln met Stowe in the White House, he is alleged to have
greeted her with, "So you are the lady who started the war!"

1

By the end of the nineteenth century, universal, compulsory free education in the United States was creating a nation of readers—easy, identifiable targets for communicators of all stripes, from advertisers peddling their wares, to publicity agents grinding their private clients' axes, to government propagandists. Newspapers and magazines proliferated to serve the new readers, and in 1898 the press agitation that fomented the war with Spain showed how almost overnight, print media could shape and mobilize American public opinion.

More ominously, the same educational system teaching literacy was also imbuing in students a narrow chauvinism. Every morning students pledged allegiance to their flag, the preeminent symbol of American nationalism. They sang their national anthem at assemblies and pored over history books depicting American achievements as the noblest among all countries. Graduates of America's schools grew up to become the patriotic mothers and fathers willing to send their equally patriotic sons to war.

Historian Arthur M. Schlesinger has written that education "occupies a central position with reference to all other provocations to war, for in so far as it embodies dangerous nationalistic prejudices, it is the means of disseminating them constantly to all the people. It is a seedbed of international discord for both present and future generations."[2]

As a result of these factors, for the first time in history, at the outbreak of the conflict in Europe in August 1914, propaganda immediately became a government-institutionalized element in the fighting of a war. Each belligerent recognized the need to stiffen the resolve of its soldiers in the trenches and of its civilians in the factories and on the farms, to undermine the morale of the enemy, and to influence public opinion in the neutral countries, the United States in particular.

One month into the war, on September 9, the *New York Times* wrote perceptively in an editorial that the European war deserved to be distinguished as "the first press agents' war," that "England, France, and Germany have long been aware of the value of press agents, and their use of bureaus to disseminate reports their Governments desire to have published, especially in the United States, is a new feature in the conduct of war. That these three nations should desire to have American favor is perfectly natural." However, in its projection for the future, that "no harm should come from this, as the good sense of the American people will compel the preservation of strict neutrality to the end," the *Times* proved to be far off the mark.

The first of two great propaganda wars on American soil, for the hearts and minds of supposedly evenhanded Americans, was between Great Britain and Germany. The British worked diligently to involve the United States as an active belligerent on its side while Germany sought vainly to maintain a precarious American neutrality. Both countries flooded America with war "news," pamphlets, books, speakers, movies, all presenting one-sided versions of the origins of the war and the righteousness of their cause. This struggle was unequal, for Americans were inextricably bound to their former mother country by both language and unspoken tradition. Moreover, this nation's print media—and powerful business interests committed to a German defeat—overwhelmingly sided with England and her allies. The hallmark of Britain's successful propaganda efforts were alleged German atrocities of gigantic proportions that strongly influenced naive Americans yearning for a chivalrous war from afar.

When Woodrow Wilson finally brought America into the fight in April 1917, a second propaganda onslaught was directed at Americans, this time run by their own leaders. The president, resolved to wage war "without stint or limit," established an organization euphemistically titled the Committee on Public Information. It was the first overt government propaganda agency in the nation's history. Its main objective was straightforward: to help unify the nation by justifying its involvement in the European war. To achieve this goal, the new propaganda office totally managed the news and intimidated dissenters. It rewrote modern world history in dozens of booklets printed by the tens of millions and distributed nationwide, lectured movie patrons nightly, and appealed to base emotions in hate-filled posters and advertisements. Patriotism and loyalty were the order of the day; "hyphenated" German-Americans, pacifists, and war protesters were to be distrusted, despised, jailed, and exported—and they were.

In the fall of 1918, as the shooting war in France was winding down, a third propaganda battle of sorts began in the United States. It was fought between a coalition of American government and powerful business interests and assorted "Reds" of every stripe. The new Soviet Union had left the war, signed a peace treaty with Germany, and proclaimed a radical form of government ballyhooed as a threat to the American way of life far worse than that from the Germans. Americans were promptly reconditioned to react with fear and hatred of the new "Hun," shaggy-haired, godless, bomb-throwing. What came to be called "the Great Red Scare" toppled of its own weight by the early 1920s, but left behind an insistent legacy of vicious anti–Soviet attitudes that persisted for much of the remainder of the century. Arguably, 1918, not 1945, marked the start of the Cold War.

Seventy-five years after Americans were assigned an alliterative "Beast of Berlin" (Germany's Kaiser Wilhelm II), they were given a "Butcher of Baghdad" (Iraq's president, Saddam Hussein) as the hated-enemy symbol for the 1992 Persian Gulf war. As before, Americans were charged with fighting an enemy "now" rather than "later," and the timeworn atrocities of "rape and pillage" made headlines. Crushing wartime news censorship by the Pentagon mocked America's press freedoms, and again, big-business communications media enthusiastically followed Washington's lead. Propaganda for war in the United States was alive and well in the last decade of the twentieth century.

Chapter 1

MYTHS AND LEGENDS

The amount of rubbish and humbug that pass under the name of patriotism in war-time in all countries is sufficient to make decent people blush when they are subsequently disillusioned. At the outset the solemn assertions of monarchs and leading statesmen in each nation that they did not want war must be placed on a par with the declarations of men who pour paraffin about a house knowing they are continually striking matches and yet assert they do not want a conflagration.

Arthur Ponsonby, *Falsehood in War-Time*, 1928

"William II, King of Prussia and German Emperor." The flattering, regal portrait of the monarch covered nearly the entire front page of the Sunday magazine section of the *New York Times*. The date was June 8, 1913, and the *Times* was commemorating the silver anniversary of the Kaiser's reign with five glowing pages. Under a page-wide banner—KAISER, 25 YEARS A RULER, HAILED AS CHIEF PEACEMAKER—the editors presented a charitable overview of recent German history for their readers.

> Twenty-five years ago, on June 15, 1888, the sudden death of the German Emperor Frederick, after one hundred days of reign, brought to the throne of the German Empire his son Wilhelm II, only twenty-nine years old, and looked upon as an autocratic and impulsive youth wrapped up heart and soul in military matters and thirsting for military glory. When, soon after his accession, he broke with Bismarck, the Iron Chancellor, making it perfectly clear that he intended to be sole master in Germany, the apprehensions as to what his reign might bring became graver and more widespread. Within his own dominions and abroad Wilhelm was considered a menacing force—a potential war lord.
>
> ...Now ... he is acclaimed everywhere as the greatest factor for peace that our time can show. It was he, we hear, who again and again threw the weight of his dominating personality, backed by the greatest military organization in the world—an organization built up by himself—into the balance for peace wherever war clouds gathered over Europe.
>
> ...And, on every hand, this is enthusiastically acknowledged by his contemporaries. In this twenty-fifth year of his rule eminent men here and abroad are intoning a chorus of praise to him as the great peace lord of the world.

5

The paragraph was meant as a brief history lesson for the paper's otherwise well-informed readers. Few Americans then had even a tiny grasp of European history. Europe was far away—especially for Midwesterners and Westerners—and its problems did not concern the United States. The U.S. State Department itself reflected this insularism. Three-time Democratic presidential aspirant William Jennings Bryan, now secretary of state, had been named to the highest-level cabinet post not because of his foreign-policy acumen, of which he had none, but because President Woodrow Wilson had been persuaded by his political advisor and confidant, Edward Mandell House, that he had to repay Bryan's pivotal support in the 1912 Democratic national convention. The administration's recent appointments to ambassadorial posts in the European capitals were also payments of political debts. Like the undistinguished cabinet members, these inexperienced diplomats would prove to be less than deft when they were plunged into the cauldron of the Great War.

On the inside pages of the special section, Hugo Muensterberg, the distinguished, German-born Harvard professor of psychology and history, addressed "the one characteristic feature" of the Kaiser, which, he suggested, "strikes every typical American as hopelessly contradictory." Muensterberg asked, "How is it possible that such a thoroughly modern man can indulge in such mediaeval views of the divine right of kings? How can a mind trained in the ideas of the engineer of to-day combine with them a belief in a mystical imperialism? How can a human being with such humor, insist on such pompousness of ceremony?" He summarized his analysis by suggesting that "in politics, in culture, in outward life, the Emperor is the realization of the deepest instinct of the German nation."

A year later, Muensterberg would be tagged with the hateful label of "hyphenate." He and his family would be ostracized and, like nearly all of his fellow nine million German-Americans, he would be watched for disloyal and unpatriotic acts. He stopped going to faculty meetings, "because," as he sadly told a young friend, "I do not wish to sit between two empty chairs."[1]

Arthur von Gwinner, chairman of Germany's mighty Deutsche Bank and a member of the Kaiser's influential *Herrenhaus*, and Austrian pacifist Alfred H. Fried, holder of the 1911 Nobel Peace Prize, shared a full page, enthusiastically describing their emperor's achievements during his reign. Financier von Gwinner packed his write-up with statistics: a population increase from 47 to 66 million, a tripling of hard-coal production, a quadrupling of pig-iron production, a tripling of foreign trade, a fivefold increase in savings-bank deposits. By any benchmark, these were impressive growth figures.[2] The arrogant German could scarcely wait to throw down his gauntlet in a parting challenge to American readers:

> Travel in Germany and you will hardly find such things as filth and misery such as you see in London, in Paris, and in most other capitals and coun-

Wilhelm II of Hohenzollern, soon after he became King of Prussia and Emperor of Germany in 1888, in a favorite pose. While the Kaiser loved pomp, he was also a man of considerable substance, by far the brightest and best educated of all of Europe's monarchs. *National Archives.*

tries. . . . Let me know whether you meet with beggars. The streets of the poor quarters in Berlin and practically all other German towns are well paved, cleaned, and lighted as those of the wealthy. Compare it with your other European capitals.

A "noted English authority," Lord Blyth, wrote warmly about Wilhelm as "the central factor of Germany's peaceful policy." He suggested that the Kaiser did not want war, "not only because peace will pay Germany better, but because he sincerely prefers peace for its own sake." He credited the Kaiser's policies to the influence and "unfailing wisdom" of his grandmother, Queen Victoria, and his "natural desire to follow the lead of his illustrious uncle, King Edward."

"A veteran diplomat," who chose to remain anonymous, directed his article to women readers of the *Times*, reviewing the kaiserin's role as loving mother and grandmother as well as supportive and understanding wife. The article's saccharine headline evoked its contents: "No Other Consort of a Prussian Ruler Ever Wielded Such a Beneficent Influence Over Her Husband, or Made Such an Impression Upon the People, by Whom She Is Regarded with Profound Affection."

There was a tiny publicity slipup on the page, however, scarcely noticeable to most readers. One of the photographs showed two of the empress's young grandchildren at martial play—Prince William with a toy rifle on his shoulder, unmistakably goose-stepping, and Prince Louis Ferdinand, saluting. Certainly, this was a carelessly selected illustration from Germany's viewpoint, since Germany's peaceful intentions rather than its military traditions were the focus.

More familiar to the *Times'* readers was Andrew Carnegie, American steel tycoon, builder of libraries, and lately pacifist of international acclaim.[3] He had first met the Kaiser in 1907, when he had been invited to attend the German emperor's annual sailboat regatta off Kiel. Carnegie, in his contribution to the *Times* commemoration, reported that he had "never enjoyed a visit more" and that the Kaiser was "a remarkable man indeed, alert, earnest, affable, a man with a mission which he labors earnestly to fulfill, a born ruler of men." He concluded his nearly full-page peroration almost religiously: "The civilized world this day bows reverently before you, peace preserving Emperor of Germany, and offers its thanks and congratulations. We are all your admiring loving debtors. May it be your favored lot long to be spared and pass in venerable old age into the dim beyond revered of all men, your hands still unstained." Another noted American, Dr. Nicholas Murray Butler,[4] president of Columbia University and director of the Carnegie Endowment for International Peace, suggested that Wilhelm II, had he not been born a prince, would "have been chosen monarch—or Chief Executive—by popular vote of any modern people among whom his lot might have been cast."

It was the bold front page, however, that attracted most attention. Next to the large portrait of the regal, confident-looking Kaiser were five congratulatory statements, each with a facsimile signature of its author.

First in order came ex-president Theodore Roosevelt, himself a winner of the Nobel Peace Prize for his mediation efforts ending the Russo-Japanese War eight years earlier. Roosevelt gruffly thanked Wilhelm for his "help in bringing about the Peace of Portsmouth . . . a real help to the cause of international peace." The two world leaders were remarkably similar in character: articulate, strong-willed, flamboyant, militaristic. Both shared an interest in and regard for U.S. Navy Captain Alfred Thayer Mahan's jingo theories on the importance of naval power; the U.S. already had a powerful fleet and Germany was rapidly building Europe's second largest to counter the Royal Navy's dominance. Roosevelt's eldest daughter, Alice, who had dined with the Kaiser shortly after her marriage to Nicholas Longworth in 1906, observed that he "was alert, very friendly, and seemed interested in every imaginable topic. He asked us many questions about America; he wanted to hear our impressions of our visit to London, and of our trip to the Far East. He seemed to have the Yellow Peril, as it was called in those days, very much on his mind."[5] Reports from others show that the two world leaders professed a liking and respect for one another, at least publicly.[6]

The next front-page tribute was from former president William Howard Taft, who by temperament was far better suited than Roosevelt to talk about peace.[7] Taft wrote that "the truth of history requires the verdict that, considering the critically important part which has been his among the nations, he has been, for the last quarter of a century, the greatest single individual force in the practical maintenance of peace in the world."

There followed the views of three other far less eminent commentators: Great Britain's Duke of Argyll, Germany's Count Johann von Bernstorff, and another Englishman, Sir Gilbert Parker.

Argyll said nothing about peace in his short profession of goodwill. Instead, he concentrated on the Kaiser's close family ties to the British crown, imputing his worthy traits to his mother, Vicki, Queen Victoria's favorite daughter. "Her clear mind and wide discernment," the duke wrote, "enabled her to place all matters in their true perspective. Her son inherited her gifts." The editors identified Argyll as the brother-in-law of King Edward VII, a familiar figure to at least some Americans until his death three years before.[8] Though his subjects had affectionately called him "Edward the Peacemaker," a strong case could be made that Edward strove during his brief reign not for peace but for Great Britain's hegemony in Europe at the expense of Germany. Despite the fact that his father had been a German and that his mother had never been able to rid herself of her German accent, Edward (who also spoke English as if he were a born German) was antagonistic to Germany and especially to his nephew, Wilhelm II. Many observers credit Edward as initiator of the program to diplomatically isolate Germany immediately upon the death of Victoria in 1901, one of the background factors contributing to the outbreak of the war.

Some readers who knew the genealogy of Europe's royal families might have wondered why the recently crowned British king himself, George V, had not sent along a congratulatory note to his first cousin, the Kaiser. But it was not like King George to expose himself to the limelight, directly or indirectly. The dyspeptic, nervous little monarch apparently had a difficult enough time preparing himself to read his annual message opening Parliament. He much preferred to shoot grouse in the country, perhaps his one talent, than be involved in matters of state.[9] It is unclear whether George V harbored an active hatred of Germany, like his father, or was merely jealous of the dynamic Kaiser and Germany's rapid rise as a world power. Once England went to war against Germany, Colonel Edward M. House, America's most important foreign diplomat, reported that Britain's king was "the most bellicose Englishman that I have so far met."[10] In 1917, in a ludicrous attempt to rid the royal family of its Germanic taint, George officially changed his name from Saxe-Coburg-Gotha to Windsor and anglicized the names of his relatives in the court. Seventy-two years later a loyal subject presented a charitable view of the name-changing—that "It was an imaginative, well-executed stroke and a brilliant exercise in public relations."[11]

The next tribute was from von Bernstorff, German ambassador to the United States. The urbane, astute diplomat, acknowledged by many as the dean of the Washington diplomatic corps, had worked diligently to improve generally sour German-American relations since coming to Washington in 1908. He understood the importance of American public opinion to his mission—and he knew how to influence it. Indeed, it is likely that von Bernstorff himself broached the idea for the special section to *Times* staffers, and may even have suggested contributors and offered the prestige of his office in soliciting articles. He was comfortable working with newspapermen in both Washington and New York City and maintained the respect of most of the press for his integrity right up to February 1917, when Wilson broke diplomatic relations with Germany.

Parker, bylined "Novelist and Member of Parliament," was the last to offer a brief tribute for the Kaiser. The questions of who had selected him for a front-page position in the company of two former presidents of the United States, and why, remain unanswered. Parker's contribution, which was noteworthy for its swagger, gave strong clues to the powerful propaganda role he was to assume shortly:

> The highest praise that I can offer concerning the Emperor Wilhelm II, is that he would have made as good a King of England as our history has provided, and as good a President of the United States as any since George Washington.
>
> It was said of the Emperor Wilhelm that he was medieval in his war spirit, but he has proved himself to be a modern keeper of the peace. He was declared to be reckless, and that the worst that can be said of him after twenty-five years is that he is impulsive. The world has never been hard upon men of impulse who are not at the same time reckless and selfish, and the Emperor Wilhelm is neither of these.
>
> When he became Emperor, Germany—and Prussia particularly—was rigid, narrow, and pedantic in all too many respects. Under his enlightened tolerance, and broad-minded guidance she has become—even Prussia has become—resilient, absorptive, and almost impulsively adaptable.
>
> The world owes Emperor Wilhelm a debt of gratitude. He might have found cause to reap advantage from European embroilment of his own making, but he has proved himself among the most civilized, internationally patriotic of rulers.

Damned with faint praise—and too many adjectives! A patronizing attitude toward Americans can also be detected, an approach Parker would perfect later on. But Parker was much more than a pedant with a flair for exaggeration. In August 1914, he would drastically change his official views of Emperor Wilhelm II, Germans, and Germany. At the outbreak of war, Parker was picked to head the American section of Great Britain's official propaganda agency directed at neutrals, located at London's Wellington House. The reporters and editors of the *New York Times*, Carnegie, Butler, Roosevelt and Taft would later also modify their opinions. Ex-president Roosevelt, in fact, would become the most shrill of all of America's arch Germanophobes.

There was room at the bottom of the front page for a short article dealing with the king of Italy. Victor Emmanuel II's mildly supportive comments—by attribution, since the king "while most democratic in his life does not permit interviews with himself and does not give direct statement to the press"—were entirely appropriate, for in 1913 Italy was still a treaty ally of Germany and Austria-Hungary. When the war broke out in August 1914, however, Italy elected to remain neutral, invoking a clause of the pact under which the signatories were not bound to joint action unless the war was "defensive." Italy then actively sought the most lucrative prospective postwar spoils from the two belligerent alliances, finally joining the war on the side of the Allies in May 1915.[12] While there was a substantial bloc of Italian-Americans in big cities on the East Coast, Italy did little noticeable propaganda work in America, perhaps never quite able to overcome the stigma of having transparently sold her support to the highest bidder.

What about Germany's principal ally, Austria-Hungary? Why had no important diplomatic figure from the crumbling dual monarchy, so soon to be at the heart of the crisis that would plunge Europe into war, been willing to show solidarity and wish the Kaiser well on his silver jubilee? Wilhelm was known to have a warm regard for 83-year-old Emperor Franz Joseph and relations between the two countries were steadfast.[13] Perhaps von Bernstorff had not contacted the Austrian ambassador to Washington, but that would have been a surprising oversight on the part of the public-relations minded German. It was more likely that Austria's overseas information apparatus was too slow-moving to meet the deadline of the *Times*, for a year later—when prompt attention to publicity opportunities was of far greater importance— it took the Austrian ambassador six months to prominently get his and his nation's views before the American people.[14]

A few *Times* readers might have expected a warm note from another of the Kaiser's first cousins, Czar Nicholas II, Emperor of all the Russias. The two maintained a frequent, superficially fraternal correspondence, signing their letters Willie and Nicki—up to the outbreak of war. Wilhelm, however, knew Nicholas for what he was—weak, uninformed, dim-witted.[15] The last czar was dominated by an equally ignorant wife, compounding Russia's miseries with her paranoia. Alexandra was a former Danish princess who remembered Prussia's defeat of her native land in 1864—and by association detested the Kaiser for it. The German emperor also took into account Russia's perpetual foreign-policy goal of gaining access to the Mediterranean from the Black Sea through the Turkish straits—by diplomacy, if possible, but more likely by an opportunistic war. Germany had worked long and hard to woo the Turkish Empire into an alliance, and thus would actively support Turkey's defense of its strategic waterway. In addition, czarist Russia in 1913 was unarguably the most backward, harshest nation in Europe, with little to gain by a one-shot publicity gesture in an American newspaper. Just as Russia would later attempt no organized propaganda campaign in the United States once the war broke out, except for a feeble effort to conciliate America's antagonistic Jews, she shunned publicity beforehand.

Nor was it to be expected that republican France would be represented in the June 8 *New York Times*. Wilhelm had no royal cousin there. More significant, the French had nurtured a hatred for Germany since 1871, when Prussia defeated France and took the provinces of Alsace and Lorraine as indemnity. At the highest levels in the French government there remained a spirit of *revanche*; France was determined to retake the two lost provinces.[16]

Pre–World War I America was the heyday of newspaper journalism. It would not be until 1923 that broadcast radio would make its appearance in the United States and "electronic" media would begin to challenge the monopoly of the press. In 1913 the nation boasted an astonishing total of nearly 20,000 daily and weekly newspapers. Of the dailies, 175 were published in cities with populations of over 100,000. These principal newspapers, which communicated news of national and international as well as local or sectarian interest, made up the two chief U.S. press associations which cooperated in the exchange of news: the Associated Press and United Press International.

Newspapers were also cheap. Recently invented typesetting machines and high-speed rotary presses had sharply reduced printing costs. The typewriter was a speedy new tool for reporters, and global news-gathering organizations fed streams of information into newsrooms via telegraph and submarine cables. Advertising was a growing factor and revenues from this source meant that publishers no longer had to depend on the newsstand price to maintain profits. Intense competition in the large cities also helped keep prices low. Nearly all of America's big-circulation dailies cost only one cent, Monday through Saturday.

Furthermore, America was increasingly a literate society, a direct result of universal, compulsory free education. Adults were able to read, wanted to read, and could afford to read—not only newspapers but a proliferation of magazines and books. Free libraries were spreading throughout the country in large cities and small, stimulated by the philanthropy of America's wealthy.

The result of all this was an almost unnoticed communications revolution that paralleled the more boisterous industrial revolution of the nineteenth century. Scarcely appreciated was its corollary: public opinion could be molded more quickly than ever before—in fact, at an astonishing rate when put to the test. In the short weeks between the assassinations of Archduke Ferdinand and his wife in Sarajevo in late June and England's declaration of war against Germany in early August, the populations of Europe's largest countries, generally friendly toward one another, were readied psychologically for the brutalities to come.

The *New York Times* was then, as it is today, America's most prestigious and influential newspaper. With its local competitors it formed the powerful clique of "great New York papers" whose syndicated news stories and articles were published in small-town papers across the country. These included Joseph Pulitzer's *World,* which once the war broke out became so supportive of the president's policies that it was disdainfully referred to as "Wilson's organ";[17] Charles Dana's *Sun*; Horace Greely's *Tribune*; William Gordon Bennett's *Telegram*; and latecomer William Randolph Hearst's outspokenly anti-British *American.*

As Harold D. Lasswell observed in his assessment of propaganda in the Great War,

> There is no doubt about the superb qualifications of newspapermen for propaganda work. The stars in the propaganda firmament during the world war were mostly journalists. . . . Newspapermen win their daily bread by telling their tales in terse, vivid style. They know how to get over to the average man in the street, and to exploit his vocabulary, prejudices and enthusiasms. . . . They are not hampered by what Dr. Johnson has termed "needless scrupulosity." They have a feeling for words and moods, and they know that the public is not convinced by logic, but seduced by stories.[18]

The *Times'* thick Sunday edition of June 8, 1913, was a good value at five cents, and it can be assumed that most of its readers, on their day off, leisurely read it section-by-section. Editorial "slant" was a function not only of the content of the story itself but also of its location within the paper, the size of its headline, and the day it was run. Editors who wished to push a feature story thus made sure the story appeared in a Sunday edition, particularly in the well-read special sections.

By any measure, then, the *Times'* beneficent coverage of Wilhelm II's anniversary was worthwhile publicity for Imperial Germany and its Kaiser. For Ambassador von Bernstorff, regardless of the extent of his involvement with the paper's editors, it was something of a personal triumph.

The Kaiser correctly foresaw the dangers of an anti–German bias in America. Such a leaning was, in fact, an inclination toward Germany's European adversaries. Thus, from the turn of the century until well into the war, when it was clear that Woodrow Wilson and America were irreversibly committed to Germany's defeat, the Kaiser worked continuously to regain the

American goodwill toward his country that had existed during the Franco-Prussian War in 1870-71, but not since.

Promptly after Roosevelt succeeded to the presidency in 1901, Germany conferred a medal on him as a token of the Kaiser's esteem. In 1902, Wilhelm invited Roosevelt's daughter Alice to christen his new racing schooner that he had purposefully commissioned from an American naval architect and a shipyard in New Jersey. His brother, Prince Henry, was present at the launching, and followed up the ceremonies with a whirlwind tour of America. In 1904, the Kaiser shipped a statue of Frederick the Great to Washington, and it was dedicated with appropriate fanfare in front of the Army building.[19]

Wilhelm established a program of exchange professors between U.S. and German universities to promote German viewpoints among opinion leaders in America. "Roosevelt" and "Harvard" chairs were established at the University of Berlin and corresponding German chairs at Columbia, Harvard, and other major U.S. universities.

Nevertheless, all of Germany's prewar public-relations efforts proved futile. For it was not so much lukewarm American-German relations that favored Great Britain—it was England's steadfast diplomacy to placate America's growing international interests. Indeed, England was fully aware that the United States had used Canada as a hostage for British good behavior, particularly since the end of the Civil War. The victorious Union army was then the world's most powerful, and America had just hurdled western Canada to acquire Alaska.

After 1895, when President Grover Cleveland stunned England with an ultimatum over a minor boundary dispute between Venezuela and British Guiana that nearly led to war, the British had bent over backwards to settle every potential conflict that arose between the two countries. Alone among the European powers, England supported America during the Spanish-American War. In 1901, negotiations over English rights in a canal through Central America ended with a treaty that gave the United States a free hand to build an isthmian canal. A year later, England agreed to a peaceful settlement of its Venezuelan debt. England even sided with America over a disputed Alaskan boundary. Most important of all, there was the common language that bound America to England. By 1914, a third war between the English-speaking peoples was scarcely possible.

But a war among the heavily armed European powers was becoming almost a certainty by 1914. Europe was divided into two opposing formal coalitions: Germany, Austria-Hungary, and an uncertain Italy, the Triple Alliance, formalized in 1882; and France and Russia, the Dual Entente, dating from 1894. After abandoning her turn-of-the-century "splendid isolation," England signed a treaty with emerging Japan in 1902 binding the two countries to come to each other's assistance in case either was attacked by two or more powers.

Then in 1904, England established a secret *entente cordiale* with her former traditional enemy France, acknowledging France's suzerainty in Morocco in exchange for France's recognition of Britain's dominance in Egypt. Britain's foreign secretary, Sir Edward Grey, extended an earlier verbal agreement between the two countries which provided that under certain circumstances, in case of an attack on France by a third power, England would protect the northern coast of France with its fleet. There was but a single document binding the two nations: a letter from Grey to French ambassador Paul Cambon promising, in the event France were seriously threatened, to negotiate on the question of common action. Finally, in 1907, England patched up her outstanding differences with Russia in classic imperialistic style. In Tibet, both nations agreed to seek no advantage; in Afghanistan, Russia recognized British suzerainty; in Persia, Russia was given a sphere of influence in the north and Great Britain a sphere in the south. By then, England was the de facto third member of what became the Triple Entente.

There had been a series of serious diplomatic crises starting right after the turn of the century—what has been called the period of "European anarchy"—that threatened the fragile peace. In 1905, there was the first disagreement between Germany and France over Morocco, the "Algeciras affair"; in 1908, the "Bosnian affair" between Austria-Hungary and Russia; in 1911, the second Moroccan crisis at Agadir, again between Germany and France; and the two "Balkan Wars" which broke out in 1912 and ended in 1913.

Then came the match for the conflagration: the assassinations of Archduke Franz Ferdinand, the Austria-Hungarian heir apparent, and his wife, on June 28, 1914, in Sarajevo, Bosnia, during a state visit. It was precisely as Otto von Bismarck, Germany's former chancellor, had predicted: "Some damned foolish thing in the Balkans" would ignite the next war.[20]

At the outbreak of war, Germany almost overnight faced a generally hostile U.S. press, particularly the New York dailies that carried so much weight. England's first, telling act of war, early on the morning of August 5, was to cut the two underwater telegraph cables connecting Germany to America, hamstringing communications to these papers in the crucial early days when Americans were making up their minds over the big question of the moment: which of the belligerents started shooting first?

As historian Harry Elmer Barnes observed in his assessment of the war,

> This favorable attitude of the American press toward the Entente Powers was an enormous advantage to the latter. We were made to feel that the Entente was fighting the cause of the small and weak nations against the ruthlessness of a great bully. We were inevitably led to believe that the War had been started through the deliberate determination of Germany to initiate her alleged long-cherished plan to dominate the planet, while the Entente had proposed diplomatic settlement from the beginning and had only taken up arms in self-defense with the utmost reluctance. This theory

of the German provocation of the War and the German lust for world dominion was played up in the newspapers ... until the danger from Germany struck terror into the hearts of Americans.[21]

Of all the enduring myths about Germany that had their origins in the propaganda of World War I, none has persisted longer and with more intensity than that of unique "German militarism" throughout history. If there were, in fact, any validity to this thesis, objective studies of historical data regarding numbers of wars fought, sizes of armies and navies, and military expenditures, for example, would be expected to reflect this supposed German aggressiveness. In fact, such studies show quite the opposite.

One estimate has established that in the nearly half a millennium between 1480 and 1940 there were some "2,600 important battles involving European states." Of these, France participated in 47 percent, Germany (Prussia) in 25 percent, and England and Russia in 22 percent each. During the same period, there were 278 wars among the principal states in Europe. England, France, Spain and Russia topped the list, being involved in 28 percent, 26 percent, 23 percent, and 22 percent, respectively. Austria was fifth, at 19 percent, and Germany (Prussia) tenth, at 8 percent, the same as the Netherlands. Denmark was the most "pacific," involved in only seven wars.[22]

Another study credits Germany (Prussia), among all European nations, as being least warlike, historically having had the "lowest percentage of years with war." As most rational thinkers might expect, the author of this study concluded that the "war burden shifts from country to country in the course of time" and that "there are no consistently peaceful and consistently militant countries."[23]

A further historical analysis compares involvement in wars by Europe's major powers in the century from Waterloo to Sarajevo. This study showed, not surprisingly, that Great Britain led the list, with ten—for how else was the British Empire created? Russia followed with seven, France with five, and Austria and Germany (Prussia), with three each. And in August 1914, contrary to the myth that the Germany army was the largest in Europe, the numerical strengths of both the Russian army and the French army were greater than that of the German army.[24]

As for military expenditures in the years just prior to the outbreak of the war, the "peace-loving" Triple Entente nations clearly outspent the "militant" Triple Alliance nations, as the table on page 17 shows.[25]

The prominent British pacifist Edmund Dene Morel suggested that such "figures tell their own tale. They reduce to absolute absurdity the legend of a Germany arming to the teeth in order to overawe her innocent and peaceable neighbours."[26] Observing that Germany was "commonly regarded as an exceptionally aggressive nation," Bertrand Russell, the eminent philosopher and also a noted English pacifist, wrote in the July 1915 issue of the *Atlantic Monthly*,

Military Expenditures, 1900 to 1913
(millions of pounds sterling)

	Army	Navy	Total
Russia	636.8	173.4	810.2
France	464.0	196.4	660.4
Great Britain	390.1*	499.5	889.6
Triple Entente total	1490.9	869.3	2360.2

*Not including 178 millions in extraordinary expenditures in the Boer War.

	Army	Navy	Total
Germany	551.5	214.4	765.9
Austria-Hungary	282.5	46.2	328.7
Italy	193.7	95.0	288.7
Triple Alliance total	1027.7	355.6	1383.3

This is no doubt true of their spirit, but when we come to inquire into their acquisitions, we find that in recent years their gains of territory have been insignificant in comparison with those of England and Russia, and approximately equal to those of France. Since 1900, we [Great Britain] have gained the Transvaal and the Orange Free State, we have consolidated our position in Egypt, and we have secured a protectorate over Southern Persia and its oil wells. The French, meanwhile, have gained about four-fifths of Morocco, and the Russians, though they have lost a small portion of Manchuria, have gained more than half of Persia. The Germans in the same period, have gained only a not very valuable colony in West Africa.[27]

Americans, especially the Calvinist resident of the White House, demanded a chivalrous, law-abiding war. The nation continued to embrace romantic images of war, carryovers from recent victorious conflicts: tides of brave infantry, galloping cavalry, wheeling cannons, Rough Riders charging up San Juan Hill, Admiral George Dewey surgically annihilating the Spanish fleet in Manila Bay. Combat was expected to be honorable, civilians and property protected, and neutral nations exempted from perils. When such "civilized" behavior was not forthcoming, the cry of atrocity was raised.

Germany's *casus belli* was that France, Russia, and England had encircled her and were preparing to attack. As a nation with no easily defended borders, Germany claimed to have been forced to strike first—to invade Belgium and then France out of military necessity, before Russia's enormous armies could move ponderously into eastern Germany. Indeed, Germany's expected swing through Belgium in the event of war, based on the Schlieffen Plan[28]—which England used as its pretext to declare war against Germany—was an open secret among Europe's diplomats and military theorists.

It was the British version, however, that prevailed in the United States—that England went to war to defend "independent and perpetually neutral" Belgium,[29] that Germany was the undoubted aggressor, that the Entente nations were simply defending their borders, and that the militaristic, wanton "Huns" waged war contrary to international law and the unwritten laws of humanity.[30]

For the whole world to read and judge, each of the belligerents published in distinctively colored bindings its own "official documents" relating to the origins of the war. Great Britain was first off the press with its *Blue Book*, containing 160 diplomatic documents. It was followed immediately by Germany's *White Book* with 27 documents. There was also Russia's *Orange Book*, Belgium's *Gray Book*, Serbia's *Blue Book*, and Austria-Hungary's *Red Book*. It was not until November 1914 that France finally published its *Yellow Book*, apparently using the extra few months to develop what most historians later agreed were the most "creative" interpretations of the facts among all the versions.

No sooner had war broken out than the American section of Britain's propaganda machine, now headed by Sir Gilbert Parker, went into full swing. Parker's group, which grew rapidly to over fifty publicity specialists, had a straightforward goal: to help drag America into the war on the side of the Allies. When lies were called for, Parker lied glibly; and when atrocities were found to play well in the press, Parker created enormous German barbarities. Most important, Parker and his team at Wellington House went about their propaganda work quietly—so discreetly, in fact, that few in America, and until near the end of the war only a handful even in Parliament, knew that the British government had a formal propaganda apparatus trained on the U.S.[31]

Two young Britons, the Washington correspondent of the London *Times*, Arthur Willert, and the head of British military intelligence in the United States acting under the guise of a purchasing agent, Sir William Wiseman, played vital propaganda roles from inside America. At first the two directed a band of well-financed "publicists," promoting and helping fund every pro–British and anti–German cause they could uncover. The facile Wiseman quickly outgrew his early responsibilities and by the time America was an active belligerent had become a trusted advisor of Colonel Edward M. House and one of the favored few who had the confidence of a wary Woodrow Wilson. He took advantage of his closeness to America's two most powerful men to energetically lobby for Britain's views of the postwar world. Indeed, no other foreigner had a more important and long-lasting influence on America's foreign policy during the war—and immediately after.

By contrast with the well-placed and efficiently organized British, the Germans tried to make do in the United States with von Bernstorff and a pickup team of propagandists in New York City, at first headed by an articulate former German colonial secretary, Bernhard Dernburg. The patriotic services of idled publicity people from the Hamburg-Amerika steamship line, foreign-affairs personnel, and stranded diplomats were enlisted and a German Information Service was set up in Manhattan. A daily "fact sheet" was mailed to America's press and opinion leaders, and stridently pro–German weekly newspapers in English were published. A fluent young German-American poet and writer and a prominent American journalist with ties to Woodrow Wilson and an anti–British bent, were put on the German payroll. The handful of prominent U.S. professors who outspokenly supported Germany were pulled together. All who could, wrote books and newspaper and magazine articles and gave talks presenting Germany's views of the war. Unstinting support for Germany also came from the nearly 500 German-language newspapers throughout the East and Midwest, and from the two-million-strong National German-American Alliance.

Berlin never set up an equivalent to the American department of Wellington House. Except for ample funds and a steady flow of German-language propaganda material, the German propagandists in the United States got little formal help from overseas. And, unlike the cautious, smoothly functioning British, the Germans were unable to keep their propaganda work quiet—as much a result of their own ham-handedness as of brazenly non-neutral U.S. Secret Service surveillance.

The Great War was promoted from the beginning by the Allied Powers as a holy crusade against the forces of evil—a principle vastly embroidered for its own population by the United States when it went to war in April 1917.

Charles A. Beard lucidly described this mythmaking in his classic work, *The Rise of American Civilization*:

> In their work of "educating the United States" the [Entente] propagandists soon discovered that the American people were more easily moved by stories of atrocities than by the folios of Red, White and Yellow books packed with carefully selected diplomatic documents, issued by the belligerents in their own defense. ... With a view to perfecting the technique of Entente propaganda, a complete official thesis was evolved for the guidance of those who needed a creed to support their emotions. It ran in the following form: Germany and Austria, under autocratic war lords, had long been plotting and preparing for the day when they could overwhelm their neighbors and make themselves masters of the world. England, France and Russia, on the other hand, all unsuspecting, had pursued ways of innocence, had sincerely desired peace, and made no adequate preparations for a great cataclysm. ... To further their ends, the story for babes continued, the Germans had hacked their way through Belgium, a small and helpless country whose neutrality had been guaranteed by all the powers in their fond desire to safeguard the rights of little countries; and in cutting their way through this defenseless kingdom, the Germans had committed shocking deeds, crimes against humanity, offenses not justifiable in the name of war, horrors not usually incident to armed conflicts. To crown their infamy, so ran the Entente articles of faith, the Germans did what no other Christian people would do, namely, employ the submarine, a new instrument of warfare, sending cargo, crew, and passengers alike to the bottom of the sea. Embellished in many details,

embroidered with rumors and ghastly stories, this Entente war creed was pressed_upon the people of the United States with such reiteration and zeal that in wide and powerful circles it became as fixed as the law of the Medes and Persians. To question any part of it in those spheres was to set one's self down as a boor and a "Hun" and, after 1917, as a traitor to America besides.[32]

The Allied interpretation of the origins of World War I was based on the notion of Germany's "sole guilt."[33] It built the self-perpetuating legend that destroyed any chance for the nonvindictive peace that Woodrow Wilson at first championed but lost during the Paris Peace Conference, distorting the judgment of a whole generation of diplomats.

One month into the war, nearly every newspaper in English in the United States was editorially parroting England's propaganda line. Tainted news stories and feature articles of imaginary battlefield successes, biased concepts of the war's origins, and atrocity sensations were on the front pages. Pamphlets and books by Great Britain's familiar novelists, poets and diplomats were rushed to printers. Personal letters signed by well-known Englishmen were mailed regularly to America's opinion makers. Celebrities and lecturers crossed the Atlantic to meet the nation's social elite, to balance bone-china tea saucers and cups on their laps, and to declaim against the "Hun."

The Germans did their propaganda best, countering the one-sided media coverage with their own newspaper and magazine publicity, promotional literature, direct mail, motion pictures, and speakers—but never on the scale nor of the consistently high quality of the British effort.

The propagandists from overseas, both English and German, knew their targets well. There were segments of the heterogeneous American population initially predisposed to support Germany—or to oppose England or Russia. There were America's "hyphenated" German-Americans, some 9 percent of the population, centered mainly in the Midwest, with strong ties to the fatherland. There were perhaps half as many Irish-Americans, nearly all strongly pro–German or anti–British. There were far fewer Jews, but all, affluent and poor alike, hated czarist Russia and the virulent anti–Semitism they had fled. Many Americans loved the music of Beethoven, Bach, and Wagner, and esteemed German *Kultur*; this was especially so on college campuses, where many of the top professors were German-trained.

There were pacifists who were against all wars; anarchists who preached overthrow of all governments; militant trade unionists like the Industrial Workers of the World, with similar goals; and socialists who saw the war in Europe starkly as one among greedy capitalists out to establish a new twentieth-century hegemony. There were also the Progressives who had twice helped elect Wilson to the presidency and who correctly foresaw that America's entry into the war would mean the end of their hard-won political gains. There were a few Americans who had already accommodated to their president's immediate call for neutrality and would stubbornly cling to this ideal.

And, finally, there was a tiny minority of the well-informed who understood the fundamentals, that the war was due not to a single cause but to a critical mix: the balance-of-power alliance system, an untrammeled arms race, chauvinistic nationalism, imperial rivalry, and—the root cause of all major wars— economic competition. The majority of Americans, however, were of English origin and, consciously or not, inclined toward the Entente powers.

America's press bias and public opinion reaction were reinforced by Germany's early military successes. The well-worn themes of German "militarism" and "expansionism" were exemplified by its invasion of neutral Belgium and the German army's rapid march on Paris. The occupying army's sometimes cruel treatment of Belgian civilians and the destruction of property along the route of its advance were considered proofs of German inhumanity. The German army was particularly vengeful against the Belgian *francs-tireurs* who waged guerrilla warfare, yet Germany was unable to convince Americans— who nurtured legends of their own Minutemen irregulars—that armed civilians operated outside the protection of international law. British propagandists worked over the "poor little Belgium" theme throughout the war, milking it for every possible American tear. The highlight of this emphasis was the infamous Bryce Report, aimed mainly at America but distributed worldwide. It detailed alleged gruesome atrocities by the German army during the early weeks of fighting in Belgium.

Other German "atrocities" were thoroughly exploited by Parker's opportunistic propagandists. In May 1915, without warning, a German submarine torpedoed and sank the British passenger liner *Lusitania*. More than 1,200 civilians died, including 128 American citizens. The outcry in the United States was hysterical—an example of German terrorism striking close to home. At the same time, sober analysts wondered how the fastest liner then in Atlantic service could have been successfully attacked by a U-boat—and why the giant ship sank so quickly. Others asked why Americans should not be forbidden to book passage on British ships.

Another example of atrocious German conduct was the execution by firing squad of nurse Edith Cavell, a British national who headed a hospital in occupied Belgium. Cavell had been convicted by a German military tribunal of helping Allied soldiers escape, a war crime punishable by death. At the trial, she admitted her guilt. In the days following her execution, British propagandists transformed the nurse into a national heroine and martyr—the English equivalent of France's Joan of Arc.

Until America came into the war, there were few lulls in Britain's atrocity propaganda. The heavy toll on merchant shipping exacted by U-boats during 1915 and 1916 included numerous Allied passenger liners sunk with U.S. citizens aboard, providing regular opportunities for the British to cry murder on the high seas. "Eyewitness" survivors of submarine attacks were landed in New York as promptly as possible to describe to anxious reporters the details of their ordeals. A new propaganda claim became popular, that sadistic U-boat crews routinely shelled lifeboats. Hospital ships had also become a favorite target of U-boat commanders, according to news stories originating in Great Britain.

While Woodrow Wilson publicly exhorted Americans to be neutral, in his private conversations he leaned from the start toward the Allied cause, abetted by his strongly pro–Ally aides (particularly his chief confidant, House), nearly all of his cabinet, and every one of his ambassadors. The staunchest Anglophile of all was Walter Hines Page, America's minister in London, who strove unceasingly, even conspiratorially, to draw America into the war on the Allied side.

Independent of the government, but working toward war with Germany, were powerful freelance forces: newly formed jingo societies financed by manufacturers and bankers standing tall for America's global pretentions; a famous general pushing "preparedness" and his own agenda for the presidency; and an almost paranoid ex-president Roosevelt, the loudest-voiced pro-war partisan of all, spewing venom at both Woodrow Wilson and the Kaiser. And there was the inexorable rise of fury against "foreign enemies" in the United States fired by hate-filled propaganda, particularly against the "hyphens"— German-Americans, Austro-Americans, Irish-Americans (but not Franco- or Italo-Americans). "Hyphenates" had been used for many years in the United States and had been neutral in tone, but by 1917 the term had turned pejorative. The hyphenated American had come to be seen as an individual with divided loyalties and hence as un–American.[34]

The president was keenly sensitive to U.S. public opinion. He supposedly held at bay for as long as he could the growing forces calling for war against Germany because he was uncertain the nation was ready. It was publication of Germany's secret "Zimmermann Telegram" in March 1917, suggesting that Mexico, with German and Japanese help, move north to retake its lost lands in the event of war between Germany and the United States, that finally got the support of the regions bordering Mexico. Absurd though it was, the German foreign minister's proposal was no less moral than the secret treaties already signed by the Allies to apportion conquered enemy territories among themselves. Nevertheless, the subsequent furor over what many considered Germany's monumental duplicity created what Wilson hoped was the near unanimity of public opinion he thought he needed. And he had another provocation: the resumption of unrestricted submarine warfare by Germany the previous month. In mid–March, three American ships were torpedoed, with loss of life. Whether these sinkings were the incidents that finally pushed the president over the edge is not known; the only certainty is that it was Woodrow Wilson who put America into war.

On April 2, 1917, Wilson addressed the joint session of the Congress he had brought back to Washington from recess, asking for an immediate declaration of war against Germany. Five days later, he unceremoniously signed the document.

With America at war, Wilson created by executive order America's first propaganda agency, the Committee on Public Information (CPI). Its euphemistic title was calculated to convey the very essence of a republic; nowhere appeared the distasteful term "propaganda." To give the organization the high-level credence it would surely need to fend off expected domestic attacks on restrictive censorship—not to mention charges of political partisanship—three of its members were from the president's cabinet, and all, like Wilson himself, were trained lawyers. The fourth, its chairman, George Creel, was a journalist of modest repute with a penchant for controversy. While some historians casually credit him with being a "muckraker"—a crusading, progressive journalist—CPI's chairman did not quite make the grade. Creel was far more a "muckslinger," less willing to support his contentions with facts than to capture his readers with sensationalism. He was an opportunist, most of all—the very personification of a fast-growing breed of American huckster, the public relations counsel.

Operating fast and loose, as was his stock in trade, CPI's chairman single-handedly organized a public-relations and advertising program of gigantic proportions. He hired journalists, advertising practitioners, artists, and scholars for his communications crusade to "hold fast the inner lines," becoming at the same time one of the nation's most powerful men during a critical time in its history. One of only a very few counselors heeded by the reclusive Wilson, Creel had the president's ear and unfailing support, for the scholar-historian turned politician in the White House had by 1917 become a thoroughgoing propagandist in his own right. While Wilson and Creel were almost diametrically opposite personalities, the two nevertheless worked harmoniously to further the idealistic president's wartime and immediate postwar goals.

The Committee on Public Information not only helped unify American public opinion, its incessant drumbeat for conformity fed an exploding national intolerance of political dissent. Americans who earlier had opposed the nation's entry into the war—including Progressives who were strong backers of Wilson, and even socialists—felt it was their duty to support the war once America was a belligerent. Arguably, some of them considered their actions eminently sensible, especially in light of the ruthless crackdown on opposition to the war. Many later proved to have been "closet" opponents of the war, for in the congressional elections of 1918, in the secrecy of the polling booth, they soundly repudiated Wilson and his Democratic Party. Soon after, when Wilson needed his old Progressive supporters most to help him push through the Congress the Versailles peace treaty and the League of Nations, they were nowhere to be found.

The president himself was caught up in the maelstrom of chauvinism he had helped foment and publicly led the charge against war critics, introducing or strongly supporting one restrictive ordinance after another, either by design or default. He pushed hard for passage of the most repressive anti-espionage and sedition acts in the nation's history. He laced his speeches with unambiguous criticisms of pacifists and hyphenates. He passively went along with his postmaster general's aggressive censorship of antiwar publications. When Russia left the war, Wilson did everything he could to bring the new Soviet Union back into the conflict. He first tried anti–Soviet propaganda from inside St. Petersburg; and, when that did not work, dispatched 7000 American troops to support the antirevolutionaries.

As passions cooled after the war, the gigantic lies created by Great Britain's and America's propaganda were one by one exposed to the light. England did not go to war to defend the neutrality of Belgium and the "honor" of Great Britain; England went to war because of an unwritten agreement to come to the aid of France if France went to war against Germany. The Bryce Report that purportedly proved systematic, organized German brutality in Belgium was nearly all hokum; practically all of its "evidence" would be thrown out of any court of law as worthless. There has never been a shred of evidence that German soldiers cut off the hands of Belgian boys. Atrocities supposedly routinely committed by U-boat commanders were wild exaggerations; no less an authority than the commander of U.S. naval forces in the European theater during the war said so. Von Bernhardi, Nietzsche, and Treitsche, who preached a warlike Germany, were never the household names in their country as British and American propagandists insisted; the noisy Pan-German ultrachauvinists also had only a negligible influence on official German foreign policy.

A calm assessment of the hysteria in the United States—associated with sabotage and sedition by presumably ubiquitous German agents and spies— showed only a handful of indictments and fewer sentences. Scarcely a year after the Armistice a renowned New England judge declared that it was his best judgment that "more than 99 percent of the pro–German plots never existed...."[35] A U.S. ambassador's sensational disclosure of a Potsdam Crown Council meeting on July 5, 1914, to ready Germany for the war to come a month later was a crude hoax with far-reaching consequences. We now know that unrestricted submarine warfare, the use of which by Germany was the proximate cause for America's entry into the war, was also practiced by the U.S. Navy from December 7, 1941, on[36]—and was so admitted by the United States in Nuremberg in 1945. "Sole German guilt," a cornerstone of Allied propaganda, no longer held water once the immediate prewar correspondence between conniving Russian and French diplomats was made public by a mocking Soviet Union. Indeed, a strong case could be made, if guilt had to be apportioned, that Russia's hands were bloodiest, for that nation was the first to mobilize its vast armies, and in 1914 mobilization was war. Even America's 32 months of "neutrality" became suspect when the powerful pro–Allied biases at the highest levels in the government, business, the press, and the clergy were viewed objectively in the years following the Armistice. Indeed, while Woodrow Wilson earnestly tried to keep America out of the war, he had nevertheless decided in 1914 that Germany must not be allowed to win the war. But he—and America—could not have it both ways.

A disillusioned America, its crusade to "make the world safe for democracy" proved a hollow deception by the vindictive Treaty of Versailles, turned away from Europe and Woodrow Wilson's League of Nations, the world's best hope for future peace. The seeds had been planted for the next world war; they would germinate in 20 years.

Chapter 2

THE BRITISH

Great Britain entered the World War with nothing that could even remotely be termed an official propaganda department. She finished the struggle with the best developed and probably the most effective organization devoted to propaganda of any of the belligerent nations. ... Building in part on the precedents of the unofficial propaganda experience of the past, but also doing a great deal of skillful pioneering of their own, the able men whom Mr. Masterman and his successors gathered together accomplished one thing which history must not overlook. They revealed once and for all that official propaganda, dextrously handled and adequately financed, is one of the most potent instruments of modern warfare.

James Duane Squires, *British Propaganda at Home
and in the United States, from 1914 to 1917*, 1935

Well before 11:00 P.M. on August 4, 1914, as Great Britain's ultimatum to Germany demanding immediate withdrawal of its troops from Belgium was expiring, and with Germany already at war with France and Russia, an English ship with an unusual silhouette had slipped her cable and gone to sea. The vessel's surreptitious mission had been planned two years before by the Committee of Imperial Defence. The destination was a precisely charted location in the North Sea off the German port of Emden. It was there that five underwater cables ran out from the shore and snaked southward through the English Channel. One went to Brest in France, one to Vigo in Spain, one to Tenerife in the Canary Islands off Africa, and two, the most important, went west to New York City via the Azores.

The ship was the four-year-old, 1,013-ton *Telconia*, a specialized cable-layer. She was an easily maneuverable 213 feet long, ideal for her close-to-shore assignment that night. Her experienced crew was skilled in cable retrieval, for the nature of submarine cable laying and cable maintenance demanded the equipment and capability to grapple the sea bottom to retrieve parted or malfunctioning cables. Indeed, her owner was the Telegraph Construction and Maintenance Co., Ltd. By early morning on August 5, when Great Britain was officially at war with Germany, the *Telconia* had snagged

27

the five cables, one at a time, and hauled them aboard. Each was cut and the ends dropped over the stern. Britain's first offensive action of the Great War was done—with neither gunfire nor casualties—and the ship returned to port.[1] The only remaining cable link available to Germany was a Liberia-to-Brazil section, jointly owned by Germany and the United States. In 1915, the British cut this cable, too, after persuading its American owners that such action was in the best interest of the Allied cause.

England was chief among the world powers to rely on these underwater cables. British-owned cables efficiently bound together its enormous empire and its strategically located naval bases and coaling stations—Gibraltar, Malta, Alexandria, Aden on the route to India; Singapore and Hong Kong in the Far East; Cape Town, Freetown, Mombasa in Africa; and Halifax, Bermuda, Jamaica, St. Lucia in the western Atlantic and Caribbean.[2] *Lloyd's Register of Shipping* of 1914 listed a total of 56 cable-laying ships, 27 of which were English or under the direct control of England—certainly in keeping with her imperial needs. In 1900, the French, then still smarting from their colonial facedown with England at Fashoda in the Sudan, were not far off in their assessment of the worth of Great Britain's global cable-communications network: "England owes the influence in the world perhaps more to her cable communications than to her navy. She controls the news, and makes it serve her policy and commerce in a marvelous manner."[3]

The tiny size of the British cable-cutting mission belied the scope of the defeat dealt to Germany. The action had taken place precisely when U.S. public opinion was being formed about which country had started the war. The *New York Times* of August 6 reported the cable cutting, and pointed out that "until direct cable service is restored, all word of happenings in Germany must pass through hostile countries—Russia on the east, France on the west, and England on the north." The same news story also included the reaction of Austria-Hungary's acting consul general, who said, "I cannot tell you how much I regret the cutting of the cable; it is with apprehension that I look forward to the next two or three weeks. ... The cutting of that cable may do us great injury. If only one side of the case is given, as may happen, if only the English cable is left, prejudice against us will be created here."[4]

Throughout the war, Germany thus had to resort to Guglielmo Marconi's new and unreliable "wireless" or the slow mails to get its messages west across the Atlantic. Both were compromised by lack of security. As early as the end of 1914, British naval intelligence was able to intercept and promptly decode practically all German radio messages, including military communications, and the Royal Navy routinely stopped neutral vessels on the high seas and opened mail coming from or going to Germany. Finally, the two German-owned radio stations on the Atlantic coast close to New York City, in Sayville on Long Island and in Tuckerton in New Jersey, were taken over and operated by the U.S. Navy, severely restricting their use by the Germans.

Thus from the opening of hostilities—and throughout the war—the British and their allies had a monopoly on rapid communication with America. Nearly all the war "news" that appeared in American newspapers came from London or Paris, tainted with the obvious bias of its origins and rigorously censored at the source. The restrictive British Defence of the Realm Act—the notorious DORA—was passed by Parliament less than one week into the war, and insured that all information originating in England or intended for publication in England was thoroughly scrutinized by growing legions of censors. As a result, U.S. news correspondents in England were effectively barred from sending home any news not favorable to the Allied cause. What they chose to copy from British newspapers was either predigested "information" or out-and-out lies. Most reporters on the fighting fronts traveled with British or French forces, since that was the only way they could promptly transmit their stories home, heavily censored as they were.

One American observer concluded that "honest, unbiased news simply disappeared out of the American papers along about the middle of August, 1914."[5] Johann von Bernstorff, Germany's ambassador to Washington and a keen student of public relations, expressed his frustration this way: "It all turns on which side gets the news in first; for the first impression sticks. Corrections are generally vain, especially as they appear as a rule in small print and in inconspicuous places."[6]

The near absolute control of the news by the British—and thus indirect control of America's press—had a vital corollary, for through this monopoly their propaganda could be effectively anonymous. Unlike the Germans, who had to publish new magazines and set up a news-information agency, and who tried to buy existing American papers, the British quietly worked their influence through existing American media. Only the Germans, Americans came to believe, were trying to subvert U.S. public opinion. As early as February 2, 1915, the influential *New York World* editorially commented on what was gradually becoming an act of faith in the United States: "Germany is the only country engaged in this war which has officially undertaken to manipulate American opinion. It is the only belligerent which maintains a lobby in the United States to incite public sentiment against other belligerents with which we are friendly."

While individual patriotic Englishmen reacted overnight to the need for presenting to America England's view of the origins of the war and for damning Germany's,[7] it took scarcely a month longer for a formal propaganda apparatus to swing into action. The British recognized the importance of public opinion in the neutral nations, the United States in particular, and, not surprisingly, their first propaganda organization was targeted at the uncommitted.

Prime Minister Herbert H. Asquith chose his close friend Charles F.G.

Masterman to build a propaganda bureau.[8] Masterman had been an author of some note and a journalist on the staff of the *Daily News* before he entered politics and became a member of Parliament. At the outbreak of war, Masterman was under-secretary of the Home Office and also chairman of the National Health Insurance Joint Committee, located in a London office building close to Buckingham Palace known as Wellington House. Masterman set up his headquarters there.

According to Ivor Nicholson, a Wellington House staffer, from the beginning Masterman was under no delusions about the thanklessness of his patriotic assignment. He cautioned his group that not only would they have to labor in secret, but that they could expect criticism and be unable to defend their work. Furthermore, Masterman said that it was unlikely that anyone would receive credit or even acknowledgement for his services. According to Nicholson, "This prophecy was amply fulfilled."[9] Masterman kept an equally low profile after the war, as if his public-relations work had somehow been discreditable. His obituary in the *Times* of London on November 18, 1927, was vague about his wartime efforts and an important bibliographic directory, *Who Was Who, 1916–1928*, had only seven words about his job during the war in an otherwise comprehensive sketch of the Rt. Hon. Charles Frederick Gurney Masterman: "Director of Wellington House (Propaganda Department) 1914–18." Nicholson also pointed out that Masterman, like his later American counterpart, George Creel, was mostly on his own. Asquith "was quite content to leave the British official propaganda in the hands of Mr. Masterman ... and it does not appear that the Prime Minister or his colleagues took a deep and constant interest in the work of Wellington House."[10]

Masterman's first wartime conference was attended by such internationally famous British authors as H.G. Wells, Arnold Bennett, Sir Arthur Conan Doyle, John Galsworthy, Thomas Hardy, John Masefield, George Trevelyan, and G.K. Chesterton. The latter three had earlier been fellow journalists with Masterman on the *Daily News*. Two others, also renowned men of letters, Sir Arthur Quiller-Couch and Rudyard Kipling, did not attend, but "sent messages offering their services."[11]

Masterman selected a fellow M.P., Sir Gilbert Parker, to head the group responsible for propaganda in America, by far the most powerful neutral to be wooed and, hopefully, won, with its giant smokestack industries, its productive Midwest granaries, its mountains of cotton, its wealthy banks. While America would quickly become a vital supplier of munitions, few in England in 1914 yet looked to America as a financial resource, and fewer still viewed America's population of 100 million as a military fount. An American army fighting side by side in France with the English and French was then a preposterous concept. By early 1916, however, England and France would be on the brink of bankruptcy; from then until the Armistice, the Great War would be financed almost entirely by the United States. And fresh American doughboys in France in 1918 would help to turn the tide against the war-weary Germans and bring victory to the Allies.

Parker was apparently an easy choice for Masterman. A Canadian by birth, Parker had traveled extensively in the United States and had cultivated a wide circle of American acquaintances before settling in England. He had been a member of Parliament since 1900 and was knighted in 1902 in recognition of his popular novels. In 1915 he would be made a baronet and a year later appointed a member of the Privy Council. Sir Horatio Gilbert George Parker was a spinner of tall tales, and not a particularly gifted one, according to one source that reviewed his first of 36 books, *Pierre and His People* (1892), a novel of the Canadian northwest. The reviewer wrote, "It is doubtful whether he had more than a glimpse of the prairies, let alone of the remote north; certainly the geography, the flora and the fauna, are exceedingly hazy, the characters unconvincing, and the plots and incidents sensational."[12]

Parker's fundamental objective was to bring America into the war on the side of the Allies. He would do this by tying America and Britain to a common cause—the defeat of a dangerous, aggressive Imperial Germany. A first step was to point the finger of guilt at Germany (and Austria-Hungary) for starting the war. Another strategic propaganda building block was the bold lie of German expansionism in the Americas. The British had recent first-hand experience of how violently America reacted to prospective violations of its hallowed Monroe Doctrine.[13] A sure-fire ploy to gain America's active support was to stress that Germany would certainly cross the Atlantic if it won the war in Europe, an argument used effectively by the British again in their successful propaganda efforts early in World War II.

Americans would also have to be convinced that there could be no negotiated peace with Germany short of total Allied victory and that England, France, and Russia were, in fact, fighting America's war. Once the United States was actively a belligerent, the nation's public opinion would be directed to accept nothing less than "unconditional surrender." Other tactical communications objectives evolved, to mesh with the war's shifting strategic needs. And, as the propaganda tempo built up, propaganda based on a semblance of reasoning gave way to propaganda of fear and hatred. German soldiers and sailors were accused of committing literally "unspeakable" crimes, and atrocity propaganda soon became the linchpin of Wellington House's overall efforts.

Little of Parker's work seems to have been haphazard. He based his communications efforts on the best market intelligence he could obtain, using as many sources as were available, so he could frame his messages for maximum impact. He corresponded with his "many friends" in America, detailing Great Britain's interpretations of the great issues of the moment, often humbly asking for their opinions. He thoroughly investigated the views of America's opinion leaders—publishers, editors, politicians, clergymen, educators. He read America's most influential newspapers and magazines. The dozens of prominent Britons he sent to America to lecture as propagandists were briefed before they left on how to hew to the current "line." They were even more thoroughly debriefed on their return, so that Londoners would be able to apply their firsthand experiences.

The thoroughly market research–oriented Parker also tried to measure the results of his work as he went along. A confidential weekly newsletter, *The American Press Resume*, was compiled in Washington by Kenneth Durant, an American on the Wellington House payroll, who selectively condensed and analyzed what he considered pertinent editorial material from major-city newspapers across the country. It can be assumed that Parker considered his newsletter not only a source of useful feedback for himself and his staff but also as tangible proof of his work, and thus an effective internal political tool to defend his decisions and so, possibly, to advance his career.

Parker, as he had been enjoined to do, kept quiet[14] until March 1918, almost a year after America had entered the war and his own "American department" had been disbanded.[15] By then, Parker felt unconstrained enough to describe the full extent of his previous operations. In an article in the March 1918 issue of *Harper's Monthly Magazine*, he spoke directly to the Americans he had worked so diligently to mislead.

> Practically since the day war broke out between England and the Central Powers I became responsible for American publicity. I need hardly say that the scope of my department was very extensive and its activities widely ranged. … The work was one of extreme difficulty and delicacy… [We were in] constant touch with the permanent correspondents of American newspapers in England … [and] frequently arranged for important public men in England to act for us by interviews in American newspapers. … Among these distinguished people were Mr. Lloyd George (the present Prime Minister), Viscount Grey, Mr. Balfour, Mr. Bonar Law, the Archibishop of Canterbury … and fully a hundred others.
>
> …We supplied three hundred and sixty newspapers in the smaller States of the United States with an English newspaper, which gave a weekly review and comments of the affairs of the war. We established connection with the man in the street through cinema pictures of the Army and the Navy, as well as through interviews, articles, pamphlets, etc.; and by letters in reply to individual American critics, which were printed in the chief newspaper of the State in which they lived, and were copied in newspapers of other and neighboring States. We advised and stimulated many people to write articles; we utilized the friendly services and assistance of confidential friends; we had reports from important Americans constantly, and established association, by personal correspondence, with influential and eminent people of every profession in the United States, beginning with university and college presidents, professors, and scientific men, and running through all the ranges of the population. We asked our friends and correspondents to arrange for speeches, debates, and lectures by American citizens … we had our documents and literature sent to great numbers of public libraries, Y.M.C.A. societies, universities, colleges, historical societies, clubs, and newspapers.[16]

Few Americans appear to have read Parker's comprehensive article in *Harper's*—in particular, those U.S. senators who participated in the German propaganda hearings that began in the fall of 1918. Those hearings were conducted in a surreal atmosphere—as if British propaganda aimed at influencing American actions had never existed.

Parker also saw to it that the prominent Americans he lured to England were lavishly entertained by London society, and were invited to the most exclusive clubs and to the great estates of the British Empire's most affluent. Such social propaganda made the already pro–Ally guests into even stronger advocates—and into active missionaries of the Allied cause when they recrossed the Atlantic.

Direct-mail was an important communications medium, and Parker's staff culled from *Who's Who in America* what the *Times History of the War* unqualifiedly stated were "200,000 names" of influential Americans. A typical form letter, on Sir Gilbert's personal letterhead (20, Carlton House Terrace, London, S.W., England), machine-stamped 17 MAR 1915 and addressed Dear Sir, shows Parker's deft and solicitous touch:

> I am well aware that American enterprise has made available reprints of the official papers relating to the present European war; but the original British prints of these publications may not be accessible to those persons of influence who would study them for a true history of the conflict. I am venturing to send to you under another cover several of these official documents. I am sure you will not consider this an impertinence, but will realize that Britishers are deeply anxious that their cause may be judged from authoritative evidence.
>
> In common with the great majority of Americans, you have, no doubt, made up your mind as to what country should be held responsible for this tragedy, but these papers may be found useful for reference, and because they contain the incontrovertible facts, I feel you will probably welcome them in this form.
>
> My long and intimate association with the United States through my writings gives me confidence to approach you, and I trust you will not think me intrusive or misunderstand my motive.
>
> [signature][17]

Other Englishmen were also happy to lend their names—and business cards—to the patriotic mailings to America. Among the American-published pamphlets read by the author 75 years later, four—*General Smuts's Message to South Wales*, *The Economic Weapon in the War Against Germany*, *Convicted out of Her Own Mouth—The Record German Crimes*, and *The Conflict for Human Liberty*—remarkably still retained their little inserts, "with the compliments of Professor W. Macneile Dixon (University of Glasgow)," one of Parker's principal staffers.[18]

Effective enclosures enhance direct mail, and Wellington House had many excellent propaganda pieces from which to choose. Best was the Oxford series of "historical" booklets—easy-to-read, pocket-size pamphlets rarely longer than 24 pages. They were written by Oxford University history faculty and authorities in related fields; even the Bishop of London put his name on one. The common denominator for authorship were credentials that bespoke authenticity and credibility, for the contents were creative interpretations of modern European history. The most persuasive of these propaganda pieces successfully masked their biases. They covered almost every conceivable aspect of the war—a pamphlet, so to speak, for everyone, Briton and American alike.

The *New York Times Book Review*, in its first "Bibliography of the European War," on November 29, 1914, listed 107 new or reissued titles of works which fit its definition of war literature, included the first seven Oxford pamphlets.[19] "Above all they are controversial books," according to the prefatory writeup:

> The British and Germans have made a specialty of controversy, writers of each nation seeking to show, through many pages of argument, that England or Germany, as the case may be, has been utterly right in everything throughout, while Germany or England, as the case may be, has been absolutely wrong to the last detail of international happenings. ... Most of the volumes from the pens of Americans have taken the view opposed to that of Germany on the rights and wrongs of the war. The case of Belgium seems in many instances to have been the chief factor in determining the American viewpoint.... Of books which have caused discussion, the works of Treitschke and Bernhardi have undoubtedly aroused the widest comment and argument.

Four months later, in an updated bibliography, there were 172 new titles and 30 additions to the Oxford series.[20]

By war's end, 87 Oxford pamphlets had been produced, all of which were distributed in the United States. Parker wrote four: *Is England Apathetic?* (1915), *The United States and This War* (1915), *What is the Matter with England?* (1915), and *Two Years of War* (1916). Masterman wrote two: *After Twelve Months of War* (1915), and *The Triumph of the Fleet* (1916). Prime Minister Asquith had his name on five, and eight more were signed by members of his cabinet: Arthur Balfour (three), Sir Edward Grey (three), and David Lloyd George (two). It can be assumed that Wellington House staffers served as ghostwriters for the busy politicians whose names were on the pamphlets. Walter Hines Page, U.S. ambassador to England, also authored a booklet, *The Union of the Two Great Peoples*, published in 1917. The wildly Anglophilic Page, a former editor and publisher, and Woodrow Wilson's favorite letter-writer, needed little prompting for his propaganda effort, nor apparently any literary help.

These propaganda pieces were sent over to the United States in bulk for distribution by the many pro–British (or anti–German) organizations that had sprung up, mostly homegrown but many covertly financed by the British. James Duane Squires's landmark 1935 study of British propaganda in America contained a list of propaganda pieces shipped to America between 1914 and 1917 which he believed to be "fairly complete." It included nearly fifty "British Official Documents" and over 200 unofficial ones. The unofficial documents, almost always produced and funded by the government's propagandists, typically appeared with commercial imprints to convey a sense of objectivity. Squires appropriately assessed Parker's direct-mail work as seeming to originate with "a kindly, friendly Englishman, who more or less was doing only his simple duty by his many American friends in sending them his literature, and inviting their observations on it or on the war in general."[21]

While few in England were supposed to know about Masterman's work, Geoffrey Dawson, the young and newly appointed editor of the *Times* of London, England's most powerful newspaper, nevertheless uncovered some of the details of Wellington House operations. In a letter to his reporter in Washington, Arthur Willert, on December 9, 1915, Dawson wrote acidly, "To my horror I discovered that that ass and self-advertiser Gilbert Parker was supposed to be in charge of American public opinion here.... You probably realize that Masterman is the official head of this precious organization.... Asquith steadily refuses to answer any questions about Masterman's activities."[22] Articles by Parker's big-name writers were easy to place in America's top magazines and newspapers, for most of America's editors were pro–Ally and would grow more partisan; even they were influenced by the persuasive British propaganda they published. Books, too, were hurriedly completed, for U.S. publishers had discovered a huge market for texts on the war.

Sir Arthur Conan Doyle, a practicing physician and Boer War historian before he became world famous as the creator of Sherlock Holmes, had been stridently anti–German in the immediate prewar years. At the outbreak of the war, the "skilled student of military operations as well as the ingenious devisor of plots ... no less an intense patriot than a clear and logical thinker," dusted off a short treatise that he had published the year before, "Great Britain and the Next War." It was reissued in hardcover and rushed into print in the United States. The new edition was not bashful about Conan Doyle's intended readers: "His summing up of German motives and German plans is particularly valuable to Americans in light of after events."[23]

The thin, 48-page book was aimed at countering retired German general Friedrich von Bernhardi's controversial *Germany and the Next War*, first published in Germany in 1911. Von Bernhardi made a splendid target for British propagandists. While England, like every world power, had ultra-chauvinistic military officers who preached an interpretation of the Darwinian code, only Germany had a militarist who wrote a book with such transparently jingo chapters as "The Right to Make War" and "The Duty to Make War." Conan Doyle, like so many British propagandists after him, made von Bernhardi his chief foil: "Every one of his propositions I dispute.... These results are that he, a man whose opinion is of weight and a member of the ruling class in Germany, tells us frankly that Germany will attack us the moment she sees a favorable opportunity."[24] In his book von Bernhardi referred to the Royal Navy's infamous bombardment of Copenhagen in 1807 without a declaration of war, citing it as a prime example of "perfidious Albion."[25] This apparently struck a sensitive nerve in Conan Doyle, who wrote that "It must be admitted that the step was an extreme one, and only to be justified upon the plea of absolute necessity for vital national interests.... It is not an exploit of which we need be proud, and at the best can only be described as a most painful and unfortunate necessity."[26]

Viscount James Bryce, historian, scholar, and former ambassador to the United States, also got into print quickly. While he was, at first, familiar only to the Washington diplomatic corps and to the nation's wealthy "400" with whom he had curried favors, he would become one of the most famous Englishmen of all during the war years as chairman of the Committee on Alleged German Atrocities. In the meantime his 16-page booklet, *Neutral Nations and the War*—another product specially packaged for Americans—was Bryce's opening volley as a propagandist. He attacked "the school of Treitschke and Bernhardi: their hatred of peace and arbitration, their disregard of treaty obligations, their scorn for the weaker peoples," summing up the major propaganda themes that would play so well in the American press. And, like every thoughtful British propagandist, Bryce was careful to sugarcoat his presentation by patronizing the Americans his booklet was intended for. "America," he wrote, has "twice withdrawn their troops from Cuba, which they could easily have retained. ... They have resisted all temptations to annex any part of territories of Mexico."[27]

Few of the world's poets could command the front page of a New York City newspaper for one of their works. But Rudyard Kipling, of "white man's burden" and *Jungle Book* fame, managed to. The *New York Times* of September 2, 1914, allotted two columns to a blatantly propagandistic poem by Great Britain's poet laureate, headed "RUDYARD KIPLING CALLS FOR BRITONS TO STAND UP AND MEET THE WAR." Two years later, following the naval battle of Jutland of May 31–June 1, 1916, the *New York Times* accorded to the patriotic poet/novelist-turned-war correspondent a series of four more front-page columns. Kipling's tales of daring, gallantry, and self-sacrifice, titled "Destroyers at Jutland," were in the finest traditions of the Royal Navy.

Classical scholar and writer Gilbert Murray published a collection of 13 of his best essays and addresses on the war just after America entered as a belligerent. Murray was able to say in his preface that two events had recently occurred, "so vast and beneficent, at least in their present appearances, that hitherto one had hardly dared to pray for them."[28] One was the Russian Revolution; the other was the entry of America into the war. Murray professed he hated war, "not merely for its own cruelty and folly, but because it is the enemy of all the causes that I care for most, of social progress and good government and all friendliness and gentleness of life, as well as of art and learning and literature." He claimed that he had vigorously opposed the British policy of war in South Africa and had been "either outspokenly hostile or inwardly unsympathetic towards almost every war that Great Britain has waged in my lifetime."[29] The book included an article written in September 1914, "How Can War Ever Be Right?" that appeared as Oxford Pamphlet No. 18; a 1915 speech, "Herd Instinct and the War," reprinted in the *Atlantic Monthly*; and "The Sea Policy of Great Britain," also reprinted in the *Atlantic*, that was specifically a rejoinder to an article in the magazine written by American Arthur Bullard. Threequarters of a century later, Murray's propaganda remains lucid and persuasive, rifled directly at its principal target, America's intellectual community. It was effective, responsible, credible—the hallmarks of the best of British mass persuasion.

Of all the brilliant and internationally famous British writers who vigorously supported the war effort with their pens, none contributed more than H.G. Wells. By 1914, the prolific, versatile Wells had already published eleven "fantastic and imaginative romances" (later to be called science fiction), including *The Time Machine, War of the Worlds, The First Men in the Moon,* and *The Invisible Man,* which continue to be popular eight decades later. He had also published twelve other novels, six nonfiction books with social and political themes, three collections of short stories, and even two children's books. His *Anticipations of the Reaction of Mechanical and Scientific Progress Upon Human Life and Thought,* published in 1902, projected the transportation, cities, social order, and wars of the coming century with remarkable perspicacity—and had established Wells as a respected seer.

During the Great War, Wells published five propaganda books. The first, in 1914, *The War That Will End War,* was a collection of brief, hastily written essays. Wells clearly targeted Americans as his audience to enlist their immediate support. He wrote that England looked particularly to the United States to play a role in the pacification of the world for which the whole nation was working. Wells suggested first that Americans need not "fire a single shot or load a single gun." Then he changed his tune, dangling an alluring bait: only if the United States "came in" would America "have a voice in the final readjustment and set their hands to the ultimate guarantees." In a chapter titled "An Appeal to the American People," Wells concluded his call for American intervention eloquently, stating that in this war "the influence of your States upon its nature and duration must needs be enormous, and at its ending you may play a part such as no nation has ever played since the world began.... It is not for ourselves we make this appeal to you; it is for the whole future of mankind.... Already the wounds of our dead cry out to you."[30] Later, Woodrow Wilson would idealistically picture his postwar role in precisely such a light.

In quick succession came *What Is Coming?—A European Forecast* and *Italy, France, and Britain at War*. In the former book, Wells was more interested in the future than the present. Remarkably—some 30 years before the fact—he referred to the development of atomic energy and its likely uses. The latter book was based on his admittedly reluctant tour of the warfronts: "I avow myself an extreme Pacifist. I am against the man who first takes up the weapon.... I do not merely want to stop this war. I want to nail down war in its coffin." Self-proclaimed pacifist he may have been, but Wells was first a loyal Englishman with a patriot's job to do: "I hate Germany, which has thrust this experience upon mankind, as I hate some horrible infectious disease. The new war, the war on the modern level, is her invention and her crime."[31]

Wells's most powerful propaganda text was his novel *Mr. Britling Sees It Through*, a stiff-upper-lip vision of John Bull at war. The book struck a respondent emotional chord on both sides of the Atlantic and the publisher could scarcely keep up with demand; first published in September 1916, the book was reprinted the same month, twice in October, four times in November, and twice in December. An editorial in the *New York Times Book Review* of November 5, 1916, purred enthusiastically: "So far-reaching has been the significance of Mr. Wells' war novel ... that we find it regarded even at this early date as something in the nature of a historical document." The story Wells related was his version of the beginning of World War I and its impact on one family and its patriarch in a London suburb. Its central figure is a distinguished philosopher of sorts, who at first is perplexed by the war, then gradually came to understand its meaning, finally becoming a critic of his own country for what he sees as its bureaucratic bungling—and a critic of America for its neutrality.

The highlight of the book is its ending. Britling, who has lost his son on the battlefields of France, writes a long letter to the German parents of his son's former tutor, who has also just been killed. In this letter, Wells, speaking through Britling, eloquently builds a persuasive case for British righteousness. He asks, "What are we fighting for? Do you know? Does anyone know?" He then gives his answer, that "it is you and I who must stop these wars, these massacres of boys." As to which country was "most to blame" for the war, it was, "quite plainly and simply," Germany—and "there must be no mistake between us on this point."[32]

Wells later began to have misgivings about the rightness of the crusade he had so strongly defended and, alone among Great Britain's famous-writer propagandists, put some revisionist views on paper while the shooting was still going on. Soon after the new Soviet government's disclosure, in early 1918, of the "secret treaties" among the Allies agreeing on the division of the spoils of war, Wells published *In the Fourth Year: Anticipations of a World Peace*. He was by then plainly disillusioned and he wrote that "while we talked about this 'war to end war,' the diplomatists of the Powers allied against Germany were busily spinning a disastrous web of greedy secret treaties, were answering aggression by schemes of aggression, were seeing in the treacherous violence of Germany only the justification for countervailing evil acts.... The Russian revolution put a match to that pile of secret treaties and indeed to all the imperialist plans of the Allies; in the end it will burn them all."[33] Just after the Armistice, with the embers of war not yet cooled, the indefatigable Wells collaborated with eight other British publicists, including Bryce and Murray, on a book promoting the League of Nations.[34]

In 1934, in his autobiography, Wells shed light on "when the first effectual destructive tap came to my delusion." He recalled seeing a royal proclamation and that what had struck him was "the individual manner of the wording. King George was addressing 'my people.' There was no official 'we' and 'our' about it." Wells wrote that he "had been so busy with the idea of civilization fighting against tradition" that he had gotten used to "the liberal explanation of the monarchy as a picturesque and harmless vestigial structure." When he abruptly realized that England's monarch had placed himself at the head of his people, it "was like a bomb bursting under my nose. ... So long as you suffer any man to call himself your shepherd, sooner or later you will find a crook round your ankle.... We were fighting for 'King and Country' and over there they were fighting for 'Kaiser and Fatherland'; it was six of one and half a dozen of the other."[35]

Perhaps even more effective propaganda than Wells's *Mr. Britling Sees It Through* was another fictional account, *Christine*, by an obscure author, Alice Cholmondeley. Harold D. Lasswell, one of the doyens of World War I propaganda analysis, wrote that the book "was plausible, well-written, and utterly devastating." After the war, Lasswell related, "more than one member of the German propaganda service" told him that they considered *Christine* "the best piece of propaganda work gotten out by the Allies during the course of the War."[36]

The tale is based on a purportedly authentic collection of sensitively written letters sent by a young and impressionable English violinist to her mother from Germany, where she has gone to study. The heroine's letters begin in late May 1914. The first letters reflect her enthusiastic anticipation of life and art in Germany, but step by step she is "enlightened" about the realities of Germans and their harsh civilization. When she takes her first walk alone, she discovers that Germans are rude—policemen in particular—and that men and boys purposely bump her. At her boarding house, the talk is always about immaculate Berlin and filthy London, and she is held personally responsible for the Boer War. She is restricted by arbitrary regulations and not allowed to practice on the Sabbath. Germans are haughty and the Prussian caste system onerous. Children commit suicide at a high rate in Germany because they are overworked in school. She meets a pregnant woman who prays for a son so that she can be the mother of a soldier. Christine becomes engaged to a young German officer whose musical aspirations were stifled by his rigid society, but her marriage is stopped by her fiancé's commanding officer. Germans celebrate the approach of war and there is frenzied rejoicing over the declarations of war with Russia and France. Finally, there is a "great dull roaring, as of a multitude of wild beasts who have been wounded" when England declares war against Germany. Christine tries to escape internment, but is stopped at the border and forced to wait in the sun for two hours. She catches pneumonia and dies in Germany in August 1914.[37]

Christine included no atrocities, no biased views of modern European history, no tirades against the Kaiser. Rather, the book was simply a skillfully calculated baring of a narrow interpretation of the "German character," sufficient to establish the vast gulf separating the Anglo-Saxon tribe from the Teutonic tribe, and so to justify the killings.

Lasswell summarized the book by writing that the facts about German life were "floated in a wave of gush about music and mother" and reported that *Christine* had "a tremendous circulation among women and school children in Allied and neutral countries." He suggested that it was "typical of the circumstantial-sentimental type of thing which can be placed in the fiction columns of a woman's magazine or in the book stalls."[38]

Alone among Great Britain's famous men of letters to maintain some measure of objectivity and historical perspective was Irishman George Bernard Shaw. From before the outbreak of the war through the drawn-out deliberations in Paris and after, Shaw, a socialist, was, as he remained, a flamboyant critic of what he called "Capitalist morality." He wrote:

> I have no ethical respect for modern Capitalist society, and therefore contemplated the British, German, and French sections of it with impartial disapproval. I felt as if I were witnessing an engagement between two pirate fleets, with, however, the very important qualification that as I and my family and friends were on board British ships I did not intend the British section to be defeated if I could help it.[39]

According to Shaw, fundamental to the conflict was balance-of-power diplomacy, which he called "conquistadoresque foreign policy," shared equally among Europe's great powers. Shaw also ridiculed Great Britain's claim to rule the seas as another contributing cause: "morally monstrous and practically childish. ... A claim on the part of any one Power to dominate the naval armaments of all other nations and treat the oceans and the Mediterranean as its own peculiar territory, needs only to be stated to appear utterly outrageous to everyone except the claimants."[40] Shaw's principal contribution to a balanced understanding of the war and its antecedents was his appropriately titled "Common Sense about the War," an article some 34,000 words long, which the *New York Times* published in full in three installments, November 15, 22, and 29, 1914. He summarized his case this way:

> 1. The war should be pushed vigorously, not with a view to a final crushing of the German army between the Anglo-French combination and the Russian millions, but to the establishment of a decisive military superiority by the Anglo-French combination alone....
>
> 2. We cannot smash or disable Germany, however completely we may defeat her, because we can do that only by killing her women; and it is trifling to pretend that we are capable of any such villainy. Even to embarrass her financially by looting her would recoil on ourselves. ... The word after the fight must be *sans rancune*; for without peace between France, Germany, and England, there can be no peace in the world.
>
> 3. War, as a school of character and a nurse of virtue, must be formally shut up and discharged by all the belligerents when this war is over.
>
> 4. Neither England nor Germany must claim any moral superiority in the negotiations. Both were engaged for years in a race for armaments. Both indulged and still indulge in literary and oratorical provocations....
>
> 5. Militarism must not be treated as a disease peculiar to Prussia. It is rampant in England....
>
> 6. It had better be admitted on our side that as to the conduct of the war there is no trustworthy evidence that the Germans have committed any worse or other atrocities than those which are admitted to be inevitable in war or accepted as part of military usage by the Allies....
>
> 7. ...We must remember that if this war does not make an end of war in the west, our allies of today may be our enemies of tomorrow as they are of yesterday, and our enemies of today our allies of tomorrow as they are of yesterday; so that if we aim merely at a fresh balance of military power, we are as likely as not to negotiate our own destruction.

Shaw's anti-establishment article was also published in England, where it provoked an immediate storm of protest. He was called "Mr. Bernhardi Shaw" by a leading newspaper; Christabel Pankhurst, the country's leading suffragette, labeled him "frivolous, inconsistent, destructive, and unprofitable"; Robert Blatchford, editor and M.P., asked whether Shaw's "pernicious pamphlet" had passed the censor, calling its author "a bumptious merry-Andrew, hungry for more notoriety" and urging Britons not "to listen to his cracked laughter and his reckless slanders and perversions of truth. Go way, George Bernard Shaw. Go and hide your shame."[41] Author Arnold Bennett, in a special to the *New York Times* on November 17 titled "The Nonsense about Belgium According to Bernard Shaw," said that Shaw's article was "the talk of the town, and it deserves to be.... [It] is so objectionable in its flippancy, in its perversity, in its injustice, and in its downright inexactitude as to amount to a scandal. Mr. Shaw has failed to realize either his own importance or the importance and very grave solemnity of the occasion. The present is no hour for disingenuous, dialectical bravura."

Others treated Shaw differently. Herman Ridder, publisher of New York's influential German-language daily, *Staats Zeitung*, in an editorial on

November 18, employed far less sophisticated language in his review of "Common Sense About the War." Ridder wrote that "after a hundred days of English explanations, distortions, and hypocrisies ... it remained for an Irishman to permit himself the luxury of telling the truth. ... The position adopted by Mr. Shaw is a distinct step forward. ... Of course, Mr. Shaw will not be taken seriously in England. ... Mr. Shaw will be read, and it amuses me to picture the 'upholders of little nations' and the 'defenders of democracy and civilization of Europe' choking with impotent rage at the playwright who has dared to speak what they have striven so hard to forget."[42]

Shaw continued his jibing, sarcastic analyses throughout the war. He ridiculed Britain's propaganda associated with Germany's invasion of Belgium: "The overwhelming sensation of the first months of the war was the devastation of Belgium not only by the German invasion, but by the Belgian and British defence." As for the atrocity stories brought over by Belgian refugees, "which they soon had to supplement liberally from their own imagination, so great was the demand for them," Shaw mockingly maintained that in his own neighborhood there was "a young Belgian warrior, convalescing from his wound," who described how "a beautiful woman, with her hands chopped off at the wrist, had held up the bleeding stumps and said, 'Avenge me, brother.'"[43] Shaw wrote astutely that "the violation of Belgian neutrality by the Germans was the mainstay of our righteousness; and we played it off on America for much more than it was worth. I guessed that when the German account of our dealings with Belgium reached the United States, backed with an array of facsimiles of secret diplomatic documents discovered by them in Brussels, it would be found that our own treatment of Belgium was as little compatible with neutrality as the German invasion."[44]

Shaw scoffed at the excessive patriotism of many of his fellow writers and at what he called "nonsense" about neutrality: "Neutrality is utter humbug. ... There is no such thing as a breach of neutrality, because there is no such thing as neutrality."[45] Not all of Shaw's barbs were lighthearted; he got serious when it came to Great Britain's often wretched treatment of its "Conshys"[46]—although America would later treat its conscientious objectors more cruelly. He was at his iconoclastic best, in tones that recalled professor of phonetics Henry Higgins in his 1912 play *Pygmalion*, in a passage calling for the abolition of compulsory military service,

> and with it the end of all the need ... of young women presenting young civilians with white feathers and singing "Oh we don't want to lose you; but we think you ought to go," which had a specially irritating effect in its cockney form of "Ow wee downt wornt—to le-oose yew—bat we thinkew orter gow." I remember making a private note that in war time only the most perfect speakers should be allowed to sing war songs.[47]

Political cartoons were powerful communications tools during World War I, as they remain today, and Wellington House actively exploited them.

As the author of a 1919 survey of wartime cartoons observed, "Editorials are read by few, news stories by more, feature articles by more, headlines by more, and perhaps cartoons by most of all. Because they contrast with the printed material surrounding them, they stand out; they require little thought for their complete digestion."[48] The most flagrantly anti–German cartoonist of all was Louis Raemaekers, a Dutch newspaper cartoonist for Amsterdam's *Telegraaf*. The British made the most of his obscene work. Raemaekers, practically unknown in the United States at the start of the war, quickly became a celebrity when his vicious caricatures of the Kaiser, the crown prince, and Germans in general as inhuman beasts were first exhibited in London in December 1915. Raemaekers was received by Prime Minister Asquith, who no doubt told him how much his work was appreciated. The French, too, recognized his value, presenting him with the Cross of the Legion of Honor, "the most fitting recognition of his genius and his services in the cause of freedom and truth."[49] When America was in the war, Raemaekers came to Washington to show off his latest wares in a special exhibit.[50]

Wellington House saw to it that collections of Raemaekers' work were published in book form in the United States. First, in 1916, there was *Raemaekers' Cartoons*, a collection of 148 "with accompanying notes by well-known English writers." The introduction, written by Francis Stopford, editor of *Land and Water*, included a virtual eulogy to this wholly unremarkable cartoonist, who, in fact, contributed so much to the myths of German violence and inhumanity. The British propagandist wrote preposterously that "Louis Raemaekers will stand out for all time as one of the supreme figures which the Great War has called into being. His genius has been enlisted in the service of mankind, and his work being entirely sincere and untouched by racial and national prejudice, will endure; indeed, it promises to gain strength as the years advance. When the intense passions, which have been awakened by this world struggle, have faded away, civilization will regard the war largely through these wonderful drawings."[51] Astonishingly, according to Stopford, Raemaekers was a man of peace: "It has been said that no man living amidst these surging seas of blood and tears has come nearer to the role of Peacemaker than Raemaekers." Stopford also took advantage of the opportunity to encourage "unconditional surrender" to Americans, a theme which, by 1916, had become one of the latest wartime goals of Great Britain: "God grant that it [peace] not be long delayed, but it can only come when the enemy is entirely overthrown and the victory is overwhelming and complete."[52]

Asquith signed his name to "An Appreciation from the Prime Minister," the final preamble to the cartoons. The preamble continued the "no peace without victory" harangue and included, for good measure, a gentle poke at American neutrality: "Mr. Raemaekers' powerful work gives form and colour to the menace which the Allies are averting for the liberty, the civilization, and the humanity of the future. He shows us our enemies as they appear to the unbiased eyes of a neutral, and where his pictures are seen determination will be strengthened to tolerate no end of the war save the final overthrow of the Prussian military power."[53]

A second volume, of 108 different cartoons, titled *Kultur in Cartoons*, also with accompanying notes by well-known English writers, was published in the U.S. in 1917.[54] This collection was even more grotesquely anti–German than the earlier one. In 1918, as might be expected from the methodical British propagandists, there was yet another volume, appropriately titled *America in the War*.[55] This time, the Committee on Public Information contributed to the contents, and each full-page cartoon was faced with a page of commentary by such distinguished patriots as Postmaster General Albert Sydney Burleson, the prominent rabbi Stephen W. Wise, Senator Henry Cabot Lodge, former secretary of war Lindley M. Garrison, former ambassador to Germany James W. Gerard, the noted journalist Ida M. Tarbell, William Jennings Bryan, arctic explorer Robert E. Peary, and the composer John Philip Sousa.

This final collection included cartoons dealing with Raemaekers' by-then-familiar theme of German atrocities, showing U-boats shelling lifeboats and torpedoing hospital ships, and inhumane treatment of wounded prisoners-of-war. One cartoon illustrated the "intended" annexation of America by the Germans. Most, however, focused on the American home front, and were accurate reflections of the wartime United States. There was a long selection from George Creel's 1916 presidential-campaign book, *Wilson and the Issues*, and several of the celebrities' commentaries bear Creel's mark, if not his name.[56] In all the volumes, the cartoons themselves are horrible depictions of an inhuman enemy, but the accompanying descriptive "analyses" are often more extreme. That Americans accepted such interpretations is clear testimony to the anti–German hysteria that had already been established in the United States.

The Germans reacted vigorously to Raemaekers' cartoons, trying unsuccessfully to suppress their distribution. A price was even put on the cartoonist's head should he ever venture across the border into Germany, and he was charged in the Dutch courts of endangering the neutrality of Holland. In 1918, Count von Hertling, Germany's ex-chancellor, referring to the effectiveness of Allied propaganda, said that "when a result was not obtained by the spoken or written word it was achieved by pictorial representations—productions of absolutely devilish fantasy, from which one turns with horror and disgust. But the result had been attained. A hatred has been raised among enemy populations against the Central Powers and particularly against Germany."[57]

Considerably more far-reaching in its influence on America than the Wellington House propaganda barrage directed at public-opinion leaders was the scattershot campaign aimed at all Americans. No less a propaganda expert than Adolf Hitler later defined the obvious target: "At whom should propaganda be directed? At the scientific intelligensia, or the less-educated masses? It must be aimed perpetually at the masses alone. ... All propaganda must be popular in tone, and must keep its intellectual level to the capacity of the least intelligent among those at whom it is directed."[58]

To this end the lecture circuit in the United States, a popular communications medium of the period, was thoroughly exploited by the British. There were already in place promotional-minded lecture bureaus only too happy to book speakers from overseas who would relate their personal experiences, the more grisly the better. These lectures drew large audiences. If the lecture was free, costs were covered by a covert British subsidy; often, admission was charged, drawing profits for both the promoters and the speakers (and their cause). The J.B. Pond Lyceum Bureau, for example, was the exclusive manager of British Army Captain A. Radclyffe Dugmore. In an illustrated four-page, two-color brochure—a propaganda piece in its own right—Pond promoted Dugmore in his "Fighting It Out" speech as "one of the most interesting figures among the war lecturers announced for the season of 1917–18." Dugmore's prewar lecture, "Stalking Africa's Big Game with a Camera," apparently had qualified him as a person with "rare ability as an entertainer." Since then, he had been gassed in the battle of the Somme and "disabled for all further active service." Among the topics to be covered in his speech were "poisoned candy dropped from German aeroplanes for our children and germ filled candy." According to the brochure, Dugmore could also still be engaged to deliver his famous earlier lecture on African wildlife.[59]

One of the fundamental objectives of wartime propaganda is the portrayal of the enemy as a violator of accepted principles of warfare and humanity. As early as the first week of the war, news reports from Europe published in American newspapers began to log outrages by the German army. These first reports seemed tentative and the actions portrayed by German troops not particularly atrocious. The originators—French propagandists to start with, before the British arrived on the continent—were still unsure how to handle the presentations and how far to stretch the truth. American newspaper editors were equally ambivalent. The following are typical of the German-atrocity headlines and news stories published by the *New York Times* during the first month of the war. Each was given a prominent position in the newspaper.

August 8
DANISH CHILDREN SHOT?
Said to Have Been Executed Because They Cried
"Vive la France!"

PARIS ... Twelve Danish children who were on a German train going to the frontier, carried away by the imprudence of their youth and the fervor of their young hearts, shouted 'Vive la France!' They were immediately dragged out of the train, and four of them were picked out and shot.

August 10
GERMANS, HE SAYS, SHOT REFUGEES
Student's Affidavit Tells of Murder of Five Near the Frontier

August 11
ASSERT GERMANS BURNED A VILLAGE
Outrage in Belgium Reported by Paris Papers—Those Trying to
Put Out Fire Shot
The Eclair Says That Any Captured Frenchman is Regarded as a
Traitor and Executed

August 13
CHARGE CRUELTIES BY GERMAN TROOPS

PARIS. [Report of a French commandant at Mézières:] On Aug. 10 I visited
the wounded soldiers belonging to the Chasseurs in hospital here. Adolphe
Gomes, Member 842 of the First Company, told me that when lying
wounded during the retreat of his company on Aug. 8 he saw a German
horseman finish off French wounded with his revolver.

By the third week in August, the British had gotten into the act:

August 22
BRITISH PROTEST AT GERMAN ACTS
Declare That Rules of War Under the Hague Treaty
Are Being Violated
And Call the Shooting of Non-Uniformed Men in Belgium
a Reversion to Barbarism

LONDON. ... What nothing justified were promiscuous looting and drunken
murders—acts not only contravening specific Hague regulations, but leading straight back, if condoned, to the worst barbarism which the laws of war
are devised to eliminate.

August 28
GERMANS BURN AND SACK LOUVAIN
Non-Combatants Were Slain, Say Unconfirmed Reports from Holland

By September, the atrocity stories had grown bolder and less equivocal:

September 1
BOYS WITH HANDS CUT OFF
PARIS. Mrs. Herman H. Harjes, wife of the Paris banker, who, with other
American women, has been deeply interested in relief work, today visited
the North Railroad Station and was shocked by the sight she saw among
the Belgian refugees. ... "I saw boys with both hands cut off, so it was impossible for them to carry a gun."

The tale of Belgian boys with hands chopped off by Germans, whether
or not the purported intent was to ensure they would never become soldiers
to fight Germany, was a popular fable embraced by Allied propagandists.[60]
Many other imaginative examples were developed for appeal to a worldwide

audience whose tastes varied from ecclestiastical to prurient. Among them: the famous altarpiece wantonly thrown by a German officer into the flames of the burning Louvain library, the crucified Canadian soldier, the women whose breasts were cut off after being ravished, the German corpse factory where glycerine was distilled from the bodies of dead German soldiers, the deliberate bombing of hospitals and machine-gunning of ambulances, and other horrors "too terrible to relate" (and then described in detail). As the historian and politician Arthur Ponsonby later wrote, "War is, in itself, an atrocity. Cruelty and suffering are inherent in it. Deeds of violence and barbarity occur, as everyone knows. Mankind is goaded by authority to indulge every elemental animal passion. But the exaggeration and invention of atrocities soon becomes the main staple of propaganda."[61] Indeed, as another postwar commentator observed, 'The one true and perfectly authenticated 'atrocity' in the World War, and the situation which produced by far the greatest suffering and death among the civilian population was the illegal blockade of Germany, continued for many months after the Armistice.... It could be justified only on the ground of weakening Germany and lessening future German competition through the death of some 800,000 German women and children.[62]

It was German military successes on the land and seas, however—their rapid drive through Belgium and their subsequent occupation of the country, and their sinking of the *Lusitania* nine months later, that gave Britain its two most enduring propaganda opportunities. German clumsiness in executing British nurse Edith Cavell for treason in October 1915 was a third.

Since England's avowed reason for going to war was Germany's invasion of neutral Belgium, there were high stakes in keeping that issue on the front pages. The British worked diligently to build and maintain an image of Belgium as a tiny, defenseless country attacked and ravaged by a monster aggressor. Belgium was a natural "underdog," always Americans' weak spot. This propaganda theme of "poor little Belgium" played so well in the press for the British that it remained the dominant one throughout the war, both in the United States and in England. Few Americans knew or cared to remember that Belgium's former king, Leopold II, had a record of colonial pillage and brutality second to none in his personally owned and operated 900,000-square-mile Congo Free State from 1885 to 1908.[63] And no Americans yet knew of the prewar military discussions held between a supposedly neutral Belgium and England and France. When the German army occupied Brussels in September 1914, secret official documents were discovered in the archives of the Belgian government that clearly incriminated Belgium as an active party to Allied war plans. As early as January 1906, according to the papers, the military attaché of the British legation in Brussels had discussed with the chief of the Belgian general staff joint steps to be taken by Belgium,

Great Britain, and France in the event of a war with Germany. A plan was adopted that called for the landing of two British army corps in France, the troops, in turn, to be transported to the most advantageous area of Belgium for operations against the Germans. The documents also indicated that the Belgian ambassador to Germany in 1911 knew about the covert schemes and was opposed to them. In a report to the Belgian minister for foreign affairs, he asked why similar preparations had not been made with Germany to repel an invasion by the French and British. In 1912, a further series of official conversations were held, refining the original plan, this time calling for some 160,000 British troops to be landed in Belgium, even if Belgium did not ask for assistance.

The first formal atrocity propagandists were the Belgians themselves. Working feverishly—considering the wealth of written declarations and affidavits they claimed were gathered—the Belgians cataloged dozens of "authentic" atrocities by the onrushing German troops. A comprehensive report was written and a prestigious committee rehearsed for a presentation to those who could do their country the most good. The select committee included the principal representatives of the country's three major political parties, to reflect the eclectic nature of the Belgian democratic monarchy: Emile Vandervelde, Socialist; Paul Hymans, Liberal; and Louis de Sadeleer, Conservative. Belgium's minister of justice, Henry Carton de Wiart, was the spokesman, to add the necessary pinch of judicial credibility.

En route to the United States, the delegation made a two-day publicity and good-will stopover in London. On September 1, 1914, de Wiart previewed his American presentation at a reception given the commissioners by King George V. Among the supposedly authenticated German atrocities described by de Wiart was one particularly gruesome example, based on a statement from a "reliable man": "At Diest a mother and her daughter of twelve were shot to death, a young man was bound to a tree and burned alive and two were buried alive with their heads downward."[64] The mission also related its atrocity stories to Sir Edward Grey, the foreign minister, and, in the interest of solidarity, to the French and Russian ambassadors, before taking a steamer to New York.

While the Belgian delegation was still on the high seas, a radio message from Berlin was received by the Associated Press in New York and printed on the front page of the *New York Times* of September 7. The message originated from German military headquarters in Aachen (Aix-la-Chapelle), and was signed by five American news correspondents: Roger Lewis of the Associated Press, Irvin S. Cobb of the *Saturday Evening Post* and *Philadelphia Public Ledger*, Harry Hansen of the *Chicago Daily News*, and James O'Donnell Bennett and John T. McCutcheon of the *Chicago Tribune*.

In spirit we unite in rendering German atrocities groundless, so far as we are able to. After spending two weeks' with and accompanying the troops upward of 100 miles, we are unable to report a single instance unprovoked.

We are also unable to confirm rumors of mistreatment of prisoners or of non-combatants with the German columns. This is true of Louvain, Brussels, Luneville, and Nantes, while in Prussian hands.

We visited Chateau Soldre, Sambre, and Beaumont without substantiating a single wanton brutality. Numerous investigated rumors proved groundless. Everywhere we have seen Germans paying for purchases and respecting property rights, as well as according civilians every consideration.

After the battle of Barse, we found Belgian women and children moving comfortably about.

The day after the Germans had captured the town of Ste. Marie, we found one citizen killed, but were unable to confirm lack of provocation. Refugees with stories of atrocities were unable to supply direct evidence.

Belgians in the Sambre Valley discounted reports of cruelties in the surrounding countries.

The discipline of the German soldiers is excellent, as we observed.

To the truth of these statements we pledge our professional and personal word.

Certainly, the reporters had observed only a tiny portion of the actions of German soldiers, nor was it established how closely they were supervised by their hosts. Significantly, however, none of the five ever repudiated the statement, although Cobb later modified his views after America was into the war.[65]

Dr. Hendrik Willem van Loon, who had spent four months on the German front in Belgium for the Associated Press, declared in a January 1915 interview with New York's leading German-language newspaper "that the reports about German atrocities were indecent lies, probably manufactured in London, and that the Belgian people were incensed at the charge that they had spread such tales."[66] There would be other respected American eyewitnesses to the actions on the fighting fronts in the summer and fall of 1914 who also repudiated German atrocity stories, but they were no match for the torrent of British propaganda coming from Europe into the United States.

On September 16, the Belgian delegation met with Woodrow Wilson and de Wiart was able to present his report. The report's brief summary strummed nearly every heartstring: "Peaceful inhabitants were massacred, defenseless women and children were outraged, open and undefended towns were destroyed; historical and religious monuments were reduced to dust, and the famous library at the University of Louvain was given to the flames."[67] One can detect a fine English literary hand in the effective choice of words and the simple metaphors, pointing to the likely editorial role played by Wellington House in honing the final report for American consumption. Great Britain had much to gain by a successful Belgian propaganda mission to the United States. Nor would it be the last time that Englishmen served the common propaganda cause as expert translators, editors, and ghostwriters for their non-English-speaking allies.[68] De Wiart also gave the president samples of so-called dumdum bullets, "explosive" cartridges he claimed were used by the Germans. This "hard evidence" was counterpropaganda to the Kaiser's note of September 7 to Wilson accusing French and English troops of using dumdums, which were forbidden by international law.[69] In the note, Wilhelm II had also protested what he called the Belgian government's inciting of its civilian population to guerrilla warfare and atrocities. The Germans called these Belgian guerrillas *francs-tireurs* (French sharpshooters). Their sniping from concealed positions outraged the very proper German military, who, according to international law, had the right to shoot them. More than any other factor, it was the *francs-tireurs* who drove the German army to reprisal hostage taking and organized shooting of Belgian civilians.[70]

Wilson's guarded public response to the Belgian presentation was that of a skeptical trained historian and a cautious politician, still anxious to project his nation's neutrality. He said that the report and the dumdum bullets would receive his "most attentive perusal and thoughtful consideration.... It would be unwise, it would be premature, for a single government, however fortunately separated from the present struggle, it would even be inconsistent with the neutral position of any nation which like this has no part in the contest, to form or express a final judgment."[71] Wilson used some of the identical phrases in his fence-straddling reply to the Kaiser's protest, implying that the U.S. government had no intention of taking part in any controversy arising between the belligerents over the conduct of the war—at least in those early weeks of the war.

A 120-page booklet reproducing the entire Belgian report was printed and broadcast nationwide through Wellington House's rapidly growing number of distribution channels. The report would also serve as an excellent model upon which an expanded report of alleged atrocities by the Germans in Belgium would be prepared, this one exclusively by the British.

Emile Vandervelde's English-born, wealthy, and well-connected socialite wife promptly followed her husband across the Atlantic. She, too, would tell Americans all about German atrocities. According to her memoir, the idea for her propaganda tour came from a reporter from the *New York World*, who suggested she go to America to enlist the sympathy of American women and children for "the poor Belgians." Mme. Vandervelde, like her husband, also stopped off in London on her way to New York to take advantage of the public-relations opportunity. She addressed a meeting of England's prestigious Eighty Club, attended by "many well-known American women ... much touched by the speaker's heart-rending stories," according to a *New York Times* report of September 2, before being given a regal send-off by Queen Mary. Despite the fact that her autobiography established that she had personally seen none of the supposed German atrocities she came to America to talk about, in it Mme. Vandervelde proclaimed, "I felt convinced that I ought to try to enlist the sympathies of the American people, by telling them, as an eyewitness, something of the horrors which had taken place in Belgium. By so doing I might perhaps be able to influence public opinion."[72]

Mme. Vandervelde's mission was anything but a private venture. Her trip was sanctioned by her queen and she recalled that she was given $150,000 for her expenses. She pointed out that after she had "already collected about $150,000" in donations in the United States the Belgian prime minister asked her to go on to Brazil and Argentina for further fund-raising. She declined, she said, on the advice of former president Roosevelt and British ambassador Sir Cecil Spring-Rice. She claimed she obtained donations of over $300,000 for Belgian Relief during her six-month tour, more than compensating her government's investment in her extravagant tour of duty. One measure of Mme. Vandervelde's apparent dedication to the worth of her adopted nation's cause was her enforced celibacy. As she frivolously described in her memoir, "Men did not try to make love to me. I suppose they realized that being in mourning, very much upset about what was going on in Europe, and very hard worked with speaking all over the country, any advances would have been discountenanced immediately."[73]

Wellington House worked quickly on its own Belgian atrocities project. At its heart were over 1,200 depositions made by individuals recounting acts of atrocity by German soldiers. Most of the depositions were made in England by Belgian refugees who had crossed the channel. The balance were made by British and Belgian soldiers who had been stationed in England or France. The final report piously pointed out that "the depositions were in all cases taken down in this country by gentlemen of legal knowledge and experience, though, of course, they had no authority to administer an oath. They were instructed not to 'lead' the witnesses or make any suggestions to them, and also to impress upon them the necessity for care and precision in giving their evidence."[74] No mention was made that many, if not most, of the barristers sent out to scour the British countryside for cooperative refugees could neither understand nor speak Flemish, the language then spoken almost universally by the Belgian people.

In addition to the statements, there were diaries supposedly taken from dead or captured German soldiers. The report stated that "it appears to be the custom in the German Army for soldiers to be encouraged to keep diaries and to record in them the chief events of each day. They were described as "the most weighty part of the evidence, because they proceed from a hostile source and are not open to any such criticism on the ground of bias, as might be applied to Belgian testimony."[75] In light of the obvious propaganda potential of such material to the enemy, one wonders why German soldiers were not forbidden to keep diaries.

By mid–December 1914 the data were nearly all assembled. For what would officially be titled *Report of the Committee on Alleged German Atrocities*,

Asquith also named a prestigious committee. Its chairman was a man with impeccable credentials. He was Viscount James Bryce, noted scholar and author of a massive two-volume history of the United States called *The American Commonwealth* that he had published in 1888. On the centenary of the book's publication, a noted American historian called Bryce's book "incomparably the best 19th-century study of the United States, excepting always the even more remarkable earlier work of Alexis de Tocqueville."[76] Bryce had also been ambassador to the United States from 1907 to 1913, and while in the United States had traveled all over the country, speaking at colleges and impressing audiences with his erudition. In 1923 Abbott Lawrence Lowell, president of Harvard, dedicated his book *Public Opinion in War and Peace* "To The Memory of My Guide, Counsellor and Friend, Viscount Bryce." British journalist Arthur Willert, who knew Bryce well and had closely observed

Viscount James Bryce, internationally respected British scholar, historian, and former ambassador to the United States, was chairman of his nation's famous committee that cataloged supposed German atrocities in Belgium. Could such a noble man, pressured by wartime exegencies, affix his name to a collection of lies? *Author's collection.*

his conduct in America, described his role this way: "As a peripatetic advertisement for the United Kingdom he was unequalled."[77]

Lord Bryce had been a student at Heidelberg University, had received honorary doctorates from other German universities, and had been awarded the *Pour le Merite*, the highest honor Kaiser Wilhelm II could bestow on a foreigner. According to one source, he had been a neutralist until the outbreak of war, sympathizing with German rather than French aspirations and considering Russia the main menace to England on the continent; and as late as July 1914, he was strongly opposed to any moves that would involve England in a European war. When Germany invaded Belgium, however, Bryce avowedly changed his stance, convinced there was "no alternative but to fight and fight to the end."[78]

Could such a noble man be swayed by simple patriotic exigencies? Most Americans thought not. Wellington House's *American Press Resume* of May 27, 1915, reported that "even in papers hostile to the Allies, there is not the slightest attempt to impugn the correctness of the facts alleged. Lord Bryce's prestige in America put scepticism out of the question, and many leading articles begin on this note." On June 7, an enthusiastic Masterman wrote to congratulate Bryce on his success, saying that the report had "swept America" and that "even the most sceptical declare themselves converted, just because it is signed by you!"[79]

Bryce had six distinguished supporting members on his commission. Four were knights[80]: Sir Frederick Pollock, noted jurist and law historian, and Sir Edward Clarke, Sir Alfred Hopkinson, and Sir Kenelm Digby, eminent barristers. Two were writers: H.A.L. Fisher, historian and vice-chancellor of the University of Sheffield (and later Bryce's adoring biographer), and Harold Cox, editor of the *Edinburgh Review*. British historian Trevor Wilson claims that "only Cox ... seemed ready to probe the evidence thoroughly, even at the risk of finding it inconclusive."[81] But Cox was overruled by his peers and he willingly signed his name to the document.

Twelve years after the report was published, Fisher defensively (and ponderously) referred to Bryce's chairmanship as a task "devolved on him than which none could have been more repugnant to a man of his sensitive nature and political antecedents. ... To some minds the Bryce Report gave pleasure, as supplying evidence of barbarities which might serve to steel the resolve of the Allied nations and to impress the uncertain and wavering conscience of the Neutrals. ... Bryce never considered the enquiry from any such angle. He was not concerned in finding propaganda against the Germans."[82]

The report, some 30,000 words long, was an organized compilation of the "best" of the depositions, with editorial analyses.[83] When it was made public simultaneously in London and Washington on May 13, 1915, the *New York Times* obediently reproduced it in full, with a damning headline, "GERMAN ATROCITIES ARE PROVED, fiNDS BRYCE COMMITTEE," and a series of subheads that included key words and phrases calculated to support the report's conclusions:

> Not Only Individual Crimes, but Premeditated Slaughter in Belgium
> YOUNG AND OLD MUTILATED
> Women Attacked, Children Brutally Slain, Arson, and Pillage Systematic
> COUNTENANCED BY OFFICERS
> Wanton Firing on Red Cross and White Flag; Prisoners and Wounded Shot
> CIVILIANS USED AS SHIELDS
> Proof That Belgians Did Not Fire on Germans at Louvain
> —Germans Received Kindness

In a ruled box at the top of the first page was a synopsis of the "Findings of the Committee" for those too busy to read all the details:

> 1. That there were in many parts of Belgium deliberate and systematically organized massacres of the civil populations, accompanied by many isolated murders and other outrages.

2. That in the conduct of the war generally innocent civilians, both men and women, were murdered in large numbers, women violated, and children murdered.

3. That looting, house burning, and the wanton destruction of property were ordered and countenanced by the officers of the German army, that elaborate provision had been made for systematic incendiarism at the very outbreak of the war, and that the burnings and destruction were frequent where no military necessity could be alleged, being indeed part of a system of general terrorization.

4. That the rules and usages of war were frequently broken, particularly by the using of civilians, including women and children, as a shield for advancing forces exposed to fire, to a lesser degree by killing the wounded and prisoners, and in the frequent abuse of the Red Cross and the White Flag.

The report pointed out that the Committee was especially impressed by the character of the outrages committed in the smaller villages. Many of these were exceptionally shocking...."

> In Malines: One witness saw a German soldier cut a woman's breasts after he had murdered her.
>
> In Hofstade: Two young women were lying in the back yard of the house. One had her breasts cut off, the other had been attacked.
>
> In Sempst: The corpse of a man with his legs cut off, who was partly bound, was seen by another witness, who also saw a girl of seventeen dressed only in a chemise and in great distress. She alleged she had been dragged into a field, stripped naked and violated.
>
> In Eldwyt: A man's naked body was tied up to a ring in the wall in the back yard of a house. He was dead, and his corpse was mutilated in a manner too horrible to record.
>
> In Boort Meerbaek: A German soldier was seen to fire three times at a little girl of five years old. Having failed to hit her, he subsequently bayonetted her.
>
> In Haecht: Several children had been murdered. One of 2 or 3 years old had been nailed to the door of a farmhouse by its hands and feet, a crime which seems almost incredible, but the evidence for which we feel bound to accept.
>
> In Eppeghem: The dead body of a child at 2 was seen pinned to the ground with a German lance.

Other examples listed included these:

> A lance-corporal in the Rifles ... states that they entered a house in a small village and took ten Uhlans prisoners and then searched the house and found two women and two children. One was dead, but the body was not yet cold. The left arm had been cut off just below the elbow. The floor was covered with blood. The woman's clothing was disarranged. The other woman was alive but unconscious. Her right leg had been cut off above the knee. There were two little children, a boy about 4 or 5 and a girl of about 6 or 7. The boy's left hand was cut off at the wrist and the girl's right hand at about the same place. They were both quite dead.
>
> ... Another took his bayonet and fixed it and thrust it through the child.

He then put the rifle on his shoulder with the child upon it, its little arms stretched out once or twice.

At Louvain, at Liège, at Aerschot ... there is evidence that the troops were not restrained from drunkenness, and drunken soldiers cannot be trusted to observe the rules or decencies of war, least of all when they are called upon to execute a preordained plan of arson and pillage. From the very first, women were not safe. At Liège, women and children were chased about the streets by soldiers. A witness gives a story, very circumstantial in its details, of how women were publicly raped in the market-place of the city, five young German officers assisting.

The *Times'* editorial of the same day referred to the members of the Bryce Commission as "men of high character and standing [that] sufficiently attest the trustworthiness of the findings now reported." The editorial concluded that "the detailed accounts of murder, torture, mutilation, and outrage given by the committee make dreadful reading, they are shocking, they would be altogether beyond belief were they not so well attested. This is the German military policy of frightfulness." To anticipate questions some *Times* readers might ask concerning the "coincidence" of the report's publication a week after the *Lusitania* sinking, the editorial smugly pointed out that the document had been completed several weeks before and mailed to the United States for release on May 13. One still wonders if, indeed, the completed report had not been withheld for a suitably propitious release date to increase its effectiveness; if so, it would typify thoughtful British coordination of their propaganda efforts for optimum effect on American public opinion.[84]

None of the committee members went to Belgium, nor did any of them talk to the refugees and the other witnesses. While the depositions understandably omitted the names of Belgian witnesses with relatives still in Belgium, to forestall possible reprisals, the names of British soldiers who had testified were also omitted. Regarding the actual depositions themselves, the report stated that the original documents would be held in the custody of the Home Department and would be available for reference after the war. One historian subsequently pointed out that "Twenty years later exhaustive searches in the foreign office and home office failed to reveal any traces of these documents."[85]

The Bryce Report touched another important base: it denied the existence of Belgian *francs-tireurs*. It stated that the German government had sought to justify their severe actions by invoking military necessity and excused them as retaliation against civilians shooting at German troops. In fact, according to the report, no proof had ever been given that such firing ever occurred. The Belgians, too, said there never were any such people as *francs-tireurs* in 1914, although their argument might have been better accepted had they admitted to some limited sniping by civilians as understandable reprisals to severe measures by their occupiers. That nation's formal report stated preposterously that "in truth there are not, and there never were any francs-tireurs in Belgium. ... The Commission of Inquiry, after minute inquiry, has not succeeded in discovering a single case which displays the participation of the civil population in hostilities."[86]

Still beating the tom-toms of anti–German propaganda years after most reputable historians had discounted the integrity of the Bryce Report, commission-member H.A.L. Fisher cumbersomely concluded his patriotic analyses by writing that "in its broad findings the Report has not been and will not be overthrown. Its influence on public opinion all over the world [it was translated into 27 languages], even in so distant a place as Teheran, but more especially in America, was very great, for it exhibited with great moderation and unanswerable force the evil consequences which may ensue from a malign theory of conduct held by a military caste to whom war seemed to have become a sort of sacred mission."[87]

The Germans promptly prepared a formal response to the Belgian Commission of Inquiry and the Bryce Report with *The White Book of May 1915*. All their testimony was claimed to have been taken under oath, in an attempt to discredit at least one glaring defect in the Bryce Report's methodology. As might be expected, this counterpropaganda effort threw the blame for German violence against civilians on the Belgian guerrillas:

> The Belgian civil population fought against the German troops in many places in the provinces of Liège, Luxembourg, Namur, Hainault, Brabant, East and West Flanders. The fights were of a particular dreadful character in Aerschot, Andenne, Dinant, and Louvain.... Men in all stations of life—workmen, factory owners, doctors, teachers, even priests, not to speak of women and children—were arrested with weapons in their hands.... Germans were fired on from houses and gardens, roofs and cellars, fields and woods. The methods of fighting employed by the civilian population were absolutely incompatible with the universally recognized rules of international law.[88]

The German report also responded to specific atrocity charges made by the Belgians. For example, at Aerschot, the clash with civilians occurred not because German officers "attacked the honour of the Burgomaster's family," but "because the commanding officer was shot." At Dinant, it was not "peaceful inhabitants" who were innocent victims of German arms but "treacherous attackers" of German soldiers. In Louvain, "the burning torch was applied by German troops only when bitter necessity demanded it" and confined to that part of the city in which armed civilians fought German troops.[89] Thoroughgoing British censorship saw to it that few copies of the *White Book*—and no associated publicity—ever appeared in the United States until the war was over.

France was not to be denied, and in 1915 published its own formal atrocity study, *Germany's Violation of the Laws of War*. This document contained ten chapters with 121 specific examples, drawn from reports by French soldiers, sworn statements by French civilians, proclamations and orders by German commanding officers, and the ubiquitous "genuine diaries" and letters of German soldiers captured on the battlefields. The chapters covered seemingly every conceivable transgression: violation of the neutrality of Luxembourg and Belgium; violation of the French frontier before a declaration of war; killing of prisoners and wounded; looting, arson, rape, and murder; violations of the Geneva Convention; use of forbidden bullets, burning liquids, and asphyxiating gases; bombardment of fortresses and unfortified towns without notice; destruction of buildings consecrated to religion, art, science, and charity; treacherous methods of warfare; and cruelties inflicted on the civil population. The intent of the report was to prove that the German outrages were not simply the individual acts of fiendish soldiers but a deliberate policy of the German government and the German army. Diaries outlined formal orders to loot, to shoot wounded, and to take no prisoners. One of the highlighted German atrocities was the burning of a Red Cross hospital in Gomery, Belgium, in which some 300 wounded died and doctors and nurses were either individually killed by German officers or executed in groups.

Wellington House recognized the propaganda value of the creative French effort, translated it, added a special introduction aimed at American readers, and saw to its prompt publication and distribution in America. A *New York Times* book review on January 2, 1916, suggested that "any one who is still inclined to discount the reports of German atrocities in Belgium and France, or at least to wait for proofs, will find the proofs in abundance in this volume." The introduction, viciously anti–German, also replayed for its intended readers the Allied theme of "no peace talks": "As a matter of deliberate and predetermined policy the German Government and the German army have persistently sanctioned the systematic violation of the Geneva and Hague Conventions. It is this all-important fact, herein set forth and proved, which completely justifies the Allies in their proclaimed determination not to sheathe the sword nor to listen to any proposals of mediation, until the power of German militarism shall have been finally overthrown. ... Until she is utterly broken and repentant, there can be no safety for the lives and property of non-combatants by land or by sea."[90]

Those able and willing to dispute the atrocity stories were few. In a magazine article published one month before America entered the war, United Press correspondent William G. Shepherd related his experiences on the war fronts. He had covered the invasion of Belgium, was one of the few newsmen to witness the second battle of Ypres, and was the first American reporter permitted at the British front in France. Shepherd—who prefaced his criticism of atrocity reporting in Belgium by stating that his sympathies were strongly pro–Ally and that "humanity will gain more from an Allied victory than from German success"—was critical of both newspaper readers and newspaper editors at the outbreak of war. He wrote, "The American public read a mass of rot in those days in its daily allotment of war news. It did not know the difference between the truth and the lie; neither did the editors. ... War is the faker's opportunity." Shepherd also commented that fakers generally did no harm, but that their reports of German atrocities in Belgium "produced serious results."[91]

Philip Gibbs, a well-respected British war correspondent, in his detailed military history of the conflict, wrote, "Greedy was the appetite of the mob for atrocity tales. The more revolting they were the quicker they were swallowed. The foul absurdity of the 'corpse-factory' was not rejected any more than the tale of the 'crucified Canadian' (disproved by our own G.H.Q.) or the cutting off of children's hands and women's breasts, for which I could find no evidence from the only British ambulances working in the districts where such horrors were reported."[92]

In 1944, George Creel self-righteously pointed out that as chairman of America's Committee on Public Information during the Great War he had "refused to give the Brice [sic] Report official circulation. The charged mutilation of women, and the tale about the crucifixion of a Canadian soldier were such obvious fabrications that the later report of Ambassador Brand Whitlock and Herbert Hoover were also disbelieved or else doubted."[93] Some years earlier, at a college student's convention, Creel had blithely told his audience that "we fooled you kids the last time with all that nonsense about German soldiers bayoneting Belgian babies. It wasn't true."[94] Indeed, Wellington House had so effectively promoted its Bryce Report that anything that America's Committee on Public Information might have done, had it been created before April 1917, would have been superfluous.

Lord Bryce returned to the subject of atrocities in October 1915, in a speech in the House of Lords that called attention to the forced relocation of Christian Armenians by the Moslem Turkish government and the attendant starvation and killing of the deportees. This time, Bryce was on somewhat firmer ground, for later peacetime studies established that there had been deaths and killings on a large scale. One source declared that "out of the total Armenian population in Turkey (about 1,800,000), one-third escaped deportation, one-third was deported, and one-third massacred."[95]

Wellington House promptly saw the propaganda value of exaggerating this genocide, especially in the United States—to counter current German reports from Poland detailing Russian atrocities against the Jews in that country. The propaganda would be far more effective, it was reasoned, if the responsibility for the Armenian killings was shifted to Turkey's ally, Germany. Bryce once again put his prestigious name on a major propaganda report focusing on the cruelty of Germans. This time Bryce's "ghost" for the project was a young Oxford don, Arnold J. Toynbee, who had joined Wellington House in May 1915 to avoid having to enlist in the army. Toynbee would become the best-known and most respected British historian of this century.

In his early days at Wellington House, Toynbee had honed his skills in what he called the "Mendacity Bureau," by writing propaganda articles for American publications. He then turned to the writing of the latest Bryce report, *The Treatment of Armenians in the Ottoman Empire, 1915-1916*, which was 700 pages long. His biographer described it as "a scholarly compilation, however ugly its subject matter," adding that "the accuracy of Toynbee's account of the destruction of the Armenians has never been questioned." Toynbee also wrote two short propaganda pamphlets related to his newfound area of expertise: *Armenian Atrocities: The Murder of a Nation*, published in 1915 with Bryce named as author, and in 1917, *The Murderous Tyranny of the Turks*, with a preface by Bryce but identifying Toynbee as the writer.[96]

Toynbee's diligent work produced comparatively little press coverage in the United States, though a Committee on Armenian Atrocities was formed, and its report—based on sources that were "unquestioned as to veracity, integrity, and authenticity"—was a page-one story in the *New York Times* on October 4, 1915. The "eminent Americans" who had compiled the report suggested that the atrocities were "unequalled in a thousand years." But the massacres of Armenians by Turks faded from the front pages, as if there was scarcely anything newsworthy about a 300-year-old religious conflict.[97]

Nearly a year passed before German "inhumanity" on a large scale was back on the front pages. In July 1916, Wellington House expressed shocked indignation over the German "deportation" of some 20,000 French civilians in occupied northern France. Beginning in April, German authorities had forcibly moved mostly men—but often families, too—from industrial areas to agricultural districts within France to help grow food. The French were paid a small wage and could also supplement their meager rations. Aside from the by-then-routine charges of German brutality from the British, the white slavery and concubinage that supposedly accompanied the moves were added to spice the news stories. Later that fall, a plan for the compulsory removal of some 400,000 Belgian farm and factory workers to Germany—bonafide deportation, not just relocation—went into effect. The growing shortage of food and other supplies as a result of the British blockade, along with distrust of a hostile civilian population at the rear of its army, prompted the German decision. The outcry in the Allied press was instantaneous, and the "poor little Belgium" theme got a renewed lease on life in the United States. The deportations were trumpeted as "slavery," as bad or worse than the earlier atrocities by German soldiers. A storm of formal diplomatic protest was unleashed against the Germans, first from the Pope, then from major neutrals, and finally from the United States. There were well-organized protest meetings in New York, Boston, Philadelphia, and Baltimore. By the end of 1916 German authorities had conceded that the advantages of enforced labor were proving to be illusory and that by abandoning the program they would deprive their enemies of a propaganda forum. On March 2, 1917, an imperial order halted further deportations and called for the repatriation of those already deported. Repatriation was completed by mid–July.

Undoubtedly, individual vicious acts were committed by German soldiers as they fought their way through Belgium, especially in response to resistance by the *francs-tireurs*. Direct reprisals against these civilian guerrillas, including hostage-taking and shooting, were also organized by the highly disciplined German army as part of a campaign of *Schrecklichkeit* (frightfulness) that was a concept of the nineteenth-century Prussian military strategist Karl von Clausewitz. As a result, over 5,000 Belgian civilians were estimated to have been killed by the Germans in 1914.[98] However, this estimate, by a Belgian historian ten years after the war, did not distinguish between those civilians killed unintentionally by German artillery, for example, and those executed.

For perceived military necessity or, less often, for revenge, every army *sometimes* shoots its prisoners, the wounded included. Every army *sometimes* pillages and rapes. Because a naval commander's first priority is *always* the safety of his ship and crew, and *sometimes* for revenge, some submarine commanders of every navy have *sometimes* fired on lifeboats, just as some surface-ship captains have *sometimes* left enemy sailors to drown. But the calculated fiendishness and depravity of German soldiers and sailors and their officers detailed in the well-publicized reports by the Allies that so inflamed American public opinion were, in fact, the calculated and depraved lies of British propagandists. That Americans, not yet belligerents, swallowed these preposterous tales is a measure of the power of propaganda.

If the Bryce Report was later called the most powerful and enduring example of World War I propaganda, it was the sinking of the *Lusitania* and "unrestricted submarine warfare"—the torpedoing of merchant vessels without warning—that would be burned into the minds of Americans as the most outrageous of all German atrocities. Woodrow Wilson would pointedly call U-boats "outlaws" in his April 2, 1917, speech asking Congress for a declaration of war against Germany.

In August 1914, international law decreed that submarines must conform to what were called "cruiser rules," which had evolved and been progressively codified by the world's maritime powers since the 1600s in a humanitarian attempt to distinguish wartime combat vessels from noncombatants on the high seas. The rules, which applied to naval ships or commerce raiders encountering suspected enemy merchant vessels, in effect represented a common law for sea war. Specifically, it was understood that an enemy merchant ship must be stopped, visited, and searched to establish its identity, cargo, and ports of destination. Only then could the raider put aboard a small "prize crew" to sail the captured ship and its cargo to a friendly port, temporarily interning the ship's crew and passengers; or take aboard the entire ship's complement and then sink the ship. It was considered a breach of cruiser rules, and hence of international law, simply to allow the crew and passengers to take to the ship's lifeboats before the ship was sunk. If these gentlemanly rules of war were somehow to work, it was incumbent upon merchantmen to passively submit to stopping, boarding, and searching. If the merchant ship elected to make a run for it, or if she mounted guns as a potential threat to the cruiser, it was understood she forfeited her status as a noncombatant and became the equivalent of a man-of-war.

Cruiser rules had been first promulgated at a time when all commerce raiders were surface vessels. During World War I the German submarine would become the most important commerce raider. The very nature of the tiny *Unterseeboot* meant that, even with pacific targets, U-boats could scarcely meet the letter of the law, let alone the spirit. Submarines could stop and search, but carried no extra sailors to serve as prize crew. Nor did their cramped quarters allow for extra passengers. Moreover, whenever a U-boat commander brought his vulnerable craft to the surface, it was temporarily in jeopardy—to ramming or even to a small, hidden cannon. Nevertheless, U-boat commanders could—and generally did, at the beginning of the war— give crew and passengers time to enter lifeboats before they sank commercial vessels, usually by gunfire to conserve their small store of expensive torpedoes.

Prior to the outbreak of the war, First Lord of the Admiralty Winston Spencer Churchill had been confident that the Germans would not use their submarines to sink British merchant ships "without challenge or any means of rescuing the crews." In 1913, retired admiral Sir John Fisher, who would later return to active duty as first sea lord, had predicted otherwise. In the event of war, he said, the German *Hochseeflotte* (High Sea Fleet) would use its submarines against British commerce—and U-boats could not be expected to adhere to the cruiser rules.[99]

Before the war, the German navy itself had not considered its submarines as serious commerce raiders. Early-model German submarines, like those of the rest of the world's navies, were slow and notoriously unreliable, and poor sea-keeping qualities limited their range. They seemed best suited for defensive reconnaisance patrols, the closer to a friendly shore the better. Once hostilities began, however, a group of bold and resourceful U-boat commanders demonstrated to their top brass, and other navies as well, the offensive capabilities of the submarine. On September 22, 1914, a lone U-boat of obsolete design torpedoed and sank, in rapid succession, three British armored cruisers—a stunning defeat for the Royal Navy. It was a harbinger of what was to come: newer U-boats would be faster on the surface, would stay underwater longer, would have extended range, mount heavier deck guns, and carry more torpedoes.

The first British merchantman sunk by a U-boat was the steamer *Glitra* on October 20, 1914. The U-boat commander had scrupulously observed the cruiser rules: he had surfaced, fired a warning shot from his deck gun to halt the ship, launched a boat with a few sailors to visit and obtain information on the ship's identity, cargo, and destination, gave sufficient time for the crew to lower their lifeboats, and then opened the ship's sea cocks to sink her. The submarine even towed the ship's lifeboats toward the nearby Norwegian coast. From that date almost to the last month of the war, the submarine threat to Great Britain's ocean lifelines was unrelenting. While the threat waxed and waned, a function more of the ongoing diplomacy between the United States and Germany than of the capabilities of the growing U-boat arm or the effectiveness of British antisubmarine warfare, U-boats came extremely close to choking off shipping into the British Isles, which would effectively have won World War I for Germany.[100]

At the height of the first intensive German submarine campaign in early 1915, nearly 200,000 tons of British shipping were going to the bottom each month. In April 1917, two months after Germany resumed unrestricted submarine warfare with a large fleet of modern U-boats, 881,000 tons of Allied shipping were sunk, the highest monthly total during the war. Losses ran about ten ships per day, or a loss rate of some 10 percent per month, a level of destruction with which neutral shipping and new construction could not hope to keep pace. These levels decreased as ocean convoys began in the summer of 1917, but even as late as August 1918, German submarines sank some 250,000 tons of shipping. Tight British Admiralty censorship throughout the war kept top secret the enormous shipping toll and the critical danger it posed to the Allied war effort itself. By war's end, German submarines had sunk 4,837 Allied ships of some 11 million tons; 178 German submarines were sunk during the war, most lost to mines. America lost 80 ships totaling 340,000 tons.[101]

The German submarine war against merchant shipping got underway in earnest in February 1915, when Germany publicly announced a war zone around the British Isles. The note presented by German ambassador Johann von Bernstorff to the U.S. State Department on February 5 was unambiguous:

> The waters surrounding Great Britain and Ireland including the whole English Channel [are] to be a war zone. On and after the 18th of February 1915 every enemy merchant ship found in the said war zone will be destroyed without it being always possible to avert the dangers threatening the crews and passengers on that account. Even neutral ships are exposed to dangers in the war zone, and in view of the misuse of neutral flags ordered on January 31 by the British Government and of the accidents of naval war, mistakes will not always be avoided and they may be struck by attacks directed at enemy ships.[102]

Germany staunchly defended its submarine "blockade" as retaliation for England's blockade of its ports, a blockade the Royal Navy would maintain, its screws tight, for nearly a full year after the signing of the Armistice.

Churchill was quick to capitalize on the diplomatic and propaganda opportunties presented by the German U-boat offensive against commerce. In his personal interpretation of World War I, Churchill was not unwilling to credit his own contributions to ultimate victory. He wrote that "the first British countermove, made on my responsibility ... was to deter the U-boat from surface attack. The submerged U-boat had to rely increasingly on underwater attack and thus ran the greater risk of mistaking neutral for British ships and of drowning neutral crews and thus embroiling Germany with other Great Powers."[103] Of the "other Great Powers," the one Churchill had in mind for "embroiling" was the United States. His Admiralty sent out orders to ensure that German submarines henceforth were forced to attack submerged and thus to sink without warning. Among the new procedures: merchant captains must disregard a surfaced U-boat's order to heave to and must "engage the enemy" by ramming or with gunfire; under no circumstances must a ship surrender to a U-boat; it was mandatory for captains immediately to radio their positions as soon as attacked by submarines; in submarine waters, ships were to fly the flag of a neutral country (unofficially the flag to fly was the Stars and Stripes) or no flag at all; names and ports of registry on hulls were to be painted over.

As early as February 3, 1915, the *New York Times* carried an announcement from the British publisher of a shipping magazine:

> To the Captain, officers, and crew of the first British merchant vessel, other than an armed cruiser, which succeeds in sinking a German submarine, The Syren and Shipping Gazette will present the sum of £500.... The idea of a merchantman's deliberately attacking a war vessel may seem rather bold, but it must be remembered that the submarine is the most vulnerable craft afloat and she carries on her operations under conditions of great difficulty.

"Q-ships"—disguised merchantmen with concealed guns and Royal Navy gun crews—were sent out to plod along normal trade routes as easy targets, to entice U-boats to the surface and then to engage them in unequal gunfights. These decoy vessels flew neutral colors, had smoke apparatus aboard to simulate fire, and carried cargoes of wood in sealed compartments to make them difficult to sink. Their crews were even rehearsed to jump into lifeboats to feign abandoning of the ship. There were also inflammatory orders that "white flags should be fired on with promptitude and that crews of captured German submarines be treated as criminals, not as prisoners-of-war." One observer reported that Churchill himself suggested that survivors of U-boats "be taken prisoner or shot—whichever is most convenient."[104]

Churchill also correctly analyzed the strategic impact on Anglo-American relations of the German submarine blockade. He wrote that "the German announcement threatening neutral as well as British merchant ships had altered the whole position of our controversies with America. Sir Edward Grey, aided and guided by [U.S. ambassador] Page, was enabled by processes of patience, tact and conciliation, to sustain our position without quarreling through the whole of March and April: and in May an event occurred which was decisive."[105]

By May 1, 1915, when the *Lusitania* left New York for Liverpool on its fateful last voyage, most German submarine commanders were far more cautious about surfacing and sinking merchant shipping with their cannons. Their response to England's aggressive antisubmarine tactics was to attack underwater and unobserved, using torpedoes, precisely as Churchill had anticipated. In fact, U-boat captains had been given specific rules to follow when conducting anticommerce predations:

> The first consideration is the safety of the U-boat. Consequently, rising to the surface in order to examine a ship must be avoided for the sake of the boat's safety, because, apart from the danger of a possible surprise attack by enemy ships, there is no guarantee that one is not dealing with an enemy ship even if it bears the distinguishing marks of a neutral. ... Its destruction will therefore be justifiable unless other attendant circumstances indicate its neutrality.[106]

In the meantime, Wellington House had sharpened its propaganda skills on the first incidents on the high seas involving U-boats and U.S. citizens. On March 29, an American passenger, Leon Chester Thrasher, drowned along with 110 other passengers and crew when the *Falaba*, a 5,000-ton British cargo–passenger liner, was torpedoed and sunk. According to the front-page story in the *New York Times* on the following day, survivors claimed that their ship's captain had been given only five minutes to get his passengers and crew into lifeboats, but while they were being lowered, a torpedo was fired, "striking the engine room and causing a terrific explosion."

Later statements of the ship's surviving officers, and the cargo manifest itself—neither of which were released in full until 1965—are clearly at variance with the story that appeared in American newspapers. According to these records, the U-boat commander first gave the *Falaba*'s master ten minutes to abandon ship, then another ten minutes, and finally a last three-minute extension, during which time the *Falaba* was radioing for assistance. As the last extension was running out, a British trawler came over the horizon, and the submarine sent a torpedo into the ship. Thirteen tons of munitions in her cargo holds blew up, causing the "terrific explosion" that killed so many of her passengers.[89]

Just five days before the *Lusitania* was sunk, the U.S.–owned oil tanker *Gulflight* was struck by a torpedo, but not sunk. Two of her crew jumped overboard and were drowned and later that day her captain died of a heart attack. These were the first Americans to die aboard a U.S. ship as a result of a U-boat attack, and would be the last until after the United States broke off diplomatic relations with Germany in February 1917.[107] The British version was that the U-boat attack had been that of a murderous buccaneer, flouting the cruiser rules as always. Again, logs of the ships involved reveal a much different story. The U-boat had encountered the *Gulflight* being convoyed into a nearby port by two Royal Navy patrol boats, which had suspected her of refueling a U-boat known to be in the vicinity. The submarine commander had surfaced and ordered the convoy to heave to. One of the patrol boats then tried to ram, forcing the submarine to dive. The U-boat then fired a torpedo into the *Gulflight*. According to the submarine's log, only then did the commander see the American flag on the stern of the tanker, and he abandoned the attack. A corollary of the cruiser rules was that a noncombatant vessel in the "protective custody" of men-of-war was a legitimate target.

Kapitanleutnant Walther Schwieger's dispassionate log of the sinking of the *Lusitania* (see Chapter 3), first published in 1920 in the French magazine *L'Illustration*, can be assumed to be generally accurate, and after three quarters of a century, the *U-20* commander's brief record remains one of the few uncontroversial elements in the far-reaching disaster at sea that changed world history. The sinking raised numerous questions, some of them unresolved until decades after the war, some still unanswered. Many of the official answers provided at the time were inspired by the needs of the war and the opportunities for propaganda raised by the tragedy.

The *Lusitania* was the fastest ship then in Atlantic service, rated at more than 24 knots. How could it have been intercepted by a submarine with a maximum speed on the surface of only about 12 knots, and about half that when submerged? Soon after the war began, in a supposed economy move by its owners, Cunard, the *Lusitania*'s crew was reduced and six of the ship's boiler's were taken out of service, reducing her top cruising speed to 21 knots. During the last minutes of her final voyage, however, she was running at only 18 knots while her captain was taking a navigational fix on the visible headlands. Further, the ship was running a dangerously straight course for the nearly half hour required for the bearing. When Captain William Turner was asked at the formal inquiry why he had not been zigzagging as he approached Ireland, as his orders had specifically called for, his remarkably naive reply was that he understood that he should zigzag only after he saw a U-boat's periscope.

Was the *Lusitania* an ordinary passenger liner, as the British steadfastly insisted, or, as the Germans claimed, was she an auxiliary cruiser—an armed one, to boot—of the Royal Navy? In 1903, a formal agreement had been concluded between Cunard and the British Admiralty to build two large, 24–25 knot liners to Admiralty specifications, which included the capability of carrying 12 six-inch cannons. They were the sister ships *Mauretania* and *Lusitania*, both launched in 1906.[108] Colin Simpson, in his study of the episode, asserts that in May 1913, as part of Churchill's war-preparedness program, the *Lusitania* was dry-docked in Liverpool for secret refitting work, including installation of gun rings and magazines. According to Simpson, following the outbreak of war, the big liner was again dry-docked, this time to have her armament installed, and "on September 17 she entered Admiralty fleet register as an armed auxiliary cruiser, and was [so] entered into the Cunard ledgers."[109]

After the sinking of the *Lusitania*, the British Admiralty and Cunard emphatically and repeatedly denied the liner was armed, and paraded dozens of survivors who testified they had seen no guns. Captain Turner swore she was unarmed, as did Dudley Field Malone, collector of the Port of New York.

Two major diving expeditions on the vessel have been reported, the first in 1962 by John Light when his underwater photographs of the wreck revealed the superstructure ripped open (not damaged by the torpedo), other demolitions, and cables and chains—all pointing to earlier "salvage" operations reputedly by the Royal Navy.[110]

Why did the giant *Lusitania* take an immediate sharp list and sink in only 18 minutes? The *Titanic*, which had struck an iceberg, presumably tearing a 300-foot gash in her hull under the waterline, stayed on an even keel and afloat for more than two and a half hours.[111] Schwieger, on the same war patrol in which he sank the *Lusitania*, found he had to use a second torpedo to sink a much smaller steamer. Captain Turner himself at first acknowledged to the press that there had been only one torpedo hit, which was followed almost immediately by an internal explosion. Did the torpedo trigger the rupture of the ship's high-pressure steam boilers and steam lines or ignite coal dust in her bunkers? Or did it detonate munitions in her cargo holds?

The British at first denied that the passenger-carrying *Lusitania* doubled as an ammunition ship. The cargo manifest established otherwise: 4,200 cases of rifle cartridges and 1,250 cases of 3.3-inch shrapnel shells, along with sundry contraband and foodstuffs. The cartridges contained some 11 tons of gunpowder, which the British said would burn but not explode. They also insisted that the artillery shells were not filled with gunpowder and hence were harmless.[112] But Light discovered during his dives "a huge split in the hull opposite where the torpedo struck whose everted edges suggested an internal explosion greater than any torpedo could cause"—and forward of the boiler rooms which the British pinpointed as likely sources for the secondary explosion.[113]

In 1995, Robert D. Ballard, famous for his underwater investigations of the sunken liner *Titanic* and Germany's World War II battleship *Bismarck*, made known his team's findings during extensive surveys and photographic analyses of the *Lusitania* wreck in *Exploring the Lusitania*. Where Light had indicated a "huge, gaping hole" where the secondary explosion ostensibly occurred, Ballard wrote that he found none. As for munitions exploding, Ballard was unequivocal, contradicting what many historians now accept as the probable cause for the ship's rapid sinking. "One thing we are sure of: if any contraband had been stowed away in the magazine, it didn't explode. ... If it held munitions, they were not the cause of the secondary explosions that sank the ship.[114] Ballard also rejected exploding boilers as a principle cause of the sinking. Instead, his firm conclusion was that the erupting torpedo ignited a volatile mixture of coal dust and oxygen in a starboard coal bunker, resulting in "a massive, uncontrollable explosion, a tidal wave of fire that rips through the ship's deck and blasts it way through the side of the hull."[115]

Secretary of State William Jennings Bryan knew the *Lusitania* was a munitions ship. Senate anti-war leader Robert M. La Follette, in a speech five months after America was at war, claimed that "four days before the *Lusitania* sailed, President Wilson was warned in person by Secretary of State Bryan that the *Lusitania* had six million pounds of ammunition aboard, besides explosives, and that the passengers who proposed to sail on that vessel were sailing in violation of a statute of this country, that no passenger shall travel upon a railroad train or sail upon a vessel that carries dangerous explosives. And Mr. Bryan appealed to President Wilson to stop passengers from sailing on the *Lusitania*." For this statement by one of its members, the U.S. Senate endeavored to impeach La Follette. Malone was again questioned about the ill-fated liner's last cargo and he confirmed La Follette's allegation. But America was at war—and the whole matter was quietly swept under the rug.

Did the Admiralty know all along that the *Lusitania* was steaming into an area that sheltered at least one German submarine? There can be no doubt of that fact. During the previous weeks, U-boats had been very active off the Irish coast. Furthermore, intelligence on the general whereabouts and operational status of most of the *Hochseeflotte*'s submarines had been submitted daily to the Admiralty since the end of 1914 by "Room 40," the British naval intelligence unit responsible for intercepting and decoding German radio communications. By early 1915, "Room 40 knew the total strength of the U-boat fleet, the rate at which it was growing, the number of U-boats at sea or in port, losses, and, in most cases, the size of the fleet in any particular area."[116]

Why had the Royal Navy not sent out a naval escort to protect the *Lusitania* during her final approach to St. George's channel and into Liverpool? In the House of Commons following the sinking, Churchill explained that the policy of the Admiralty was for merchantmen to look after themselves. The available destroyers were required to guard the troop transports crossing the channel. But on May 1 there was a flotilla of destroyers in the port of Milford Haven, several hours' steaming distance from the western approaches of the Irish coast. They were there to escort ships carrying important cargo into Liverpool, and had escorted an eastbound U.S. horse-transport just the week before. The light cruiser *Juno*, the largest naval vessel in the area, had been on patrol at that time, ostensibly to escort the *Lusitania*, but on May 5 was signaled to return to Queenstown.

Why was the *Juno* again recalled, this time on the afternoon of May 7, after Area Commander Vice-Admiral Sir Henry Coke had dispatched her in response to distress signals from the sinking liner? At first, the Admiralty denied that the *Juno* had been recalled, issuing a cover-up story that the cruiser had been delayed by a submarine attack. Then it defended its recision of Coke's order by emphasizing that the cruiser was of obsolescent design and particularly vulnerable to torpedoes. If Coke's order had held, the *Juno* would have been the first major rescue vessel on the scene, probably saving hundreds of lives. But First Sea Lord Fisher, at the Admiralty, had other priorities; as for First Lord of the Admiralty Churchill, he was far away from the action, on a surreptitious mission to France ostensibly to discuss the military situation with the British high command. The British propagandists' version, of course, was quite different. Not only had the Germans ruthlessly sunk an unarmed passenger liner but their submarines had lain in wait at the scene to torpedo ships on mercy missions. Dramatic tales of periscopes, torpedoes, and close brushes with disaster were given to the American press by officers of British merchantmen who had arrived in Boston and New York the week following the sinking of the *Lusitania*. The officers claimed they had taken the *Lusitania's* S.O.S. and had steamed to the area, only to be driven away by what they were sure were many lurking U-boats.

What about the *Lusitania's* master? How did his acts of commission and omission contribute to the disaster? A lone ship's best defense against submarine attack was speed, the faster the better, and every ship captain understood this fundamental. Turner unconvincingly defended his less-than-top-speed run off the Irish coast, testifying under oath during the formal investigation that he did so "to secure the ship's arrival outside the bar at Liverpool at about four o'clock on the morning of the eighth, when the tide would serve to enable her to cross the bar into the Mersey at early dawn." Turner's general orders called for him to stay well offshore from the headlands where U-boats were known to lurk. Amazingly, Turner brought the *Lusitania* close inshore to a well-known promontory along the Irish coast for the "precise four-point bearing" he claimed he needed to establish his exact location. Unaccountably, too, during the foggy early morning hours, Turner had sounded his powerful foghorn, an audible beacon that carried for miles— certain to attract a surfaced, hunting U-boat. Turner, it must be concluded, commanded the *Lusitania* as if there was no war going on—almost as if his every action was calculated to put his ship into maximum danger.

The final report of the Mersey Commission investigating the sinking, made on July 17, 1915, stoutly supported the government. By carefully preselecting witnesses from among the many survivors, the commission was able to arrive at appropriate findings, chief among which was that there was no internal explosion of any sort, except that directly resulting from "at least two torpedoes." As for the captain,

> was his conduct the conduct of a negligent or of an incompetent man? ... The conclusion at which I [Lord Mersey] have arrived is that blame ought not to be imputed to the captain. The advice given to him ... was not intended to deprive him of the right to exercise his skilled judgement in the

difficult questions that might arise from time to time in the navigation of his ship. ... He exercised his judgement for the best. ... The whole blame for the cruel destruction of life in this catastrophe must rest solely with those who plotted and with those who committed the crime.[117]

Was the *Lusitania* sinking a German atrocity or was the sinking a tightly held conspiracy—one of the most audacious and successful propaganda strokes engineered in the twentieth century? A major diplomatic objective of the British was to bring America into the war; purposefully putting the *Lusitania* into maximum jeopardy would have served that strategic objective.[118]

There were also astonishing high-level diplomatic conversations in London the morning of the sinking. Woodrow Wilson's unofficial emissary, Colonel House, first talked to Foreign Minister Grey, then to King George V—conversations that House himself considered extraordinary. In his diary of that date, House recorded that he and Grey had discussed the war and U.S. intervention. "We spoke of the probability of an ocean liner being sunk, and I told him if this were done, a flame of indignation would sweep across America, which would in itself carry us into the war." Later that morning, in Buckingham Palace, according to House, the king also spoke, "strangely enough, of the probability of Germany sinking a trans–Atlantic liner and of the consequences of that act. I said to him much of what I had said to Sir Edward Grey. Then George V said: 'Suppose they should sink the *Lusitania* with American passengers aboard?'"[119]

The next day, House recorded in his diary that the king wanted to talk to him again, and again the subject was the *Lusitania*. "He said he had been struck by the fact that two hours after we had discussed the possible sinking of a trans–Atlantic liner, mentioning the *Lusitania* as being perhaps the unfortunate ship, she was sunk. He had spoken of it to the queen as a strange coincidence. He also thought it was strange that I had said such an instance might provoke the United States into war and he was wondering what I thought of it today."[120]

Poster No. 97, one of many printed by Great Britain's parliamentary recruiting committee, is almost a laundry list of alleged German atrocities: "Wanton sacking of Cities and Holy Places; the murder of thousands of innocent Civilians; the flinging of vitriol and blazing petrol on Allied Troops; the killing of our Fisherfolk and desertion of the drowning; the infliction of unspeakable torture by poison gases on our brave troops at Ypres; poisoning of wells in South Africa; ill-treatment of British prisoners; assassination of our Wounded." And at the top of the poster, in bright red: "COLD-BLOODED MURDER! Remember Germany's Crowning Infamy, The Sinking of the Lusitania with Hundreds of Women & Children."[121]

Later in 1915 Wellington House reacted as expected to another atrocity opportunity, this one a result of monumental diplomatic stupidity on the part of the Germans. At dawn on October 12, Edith Cavell, a nurse of British nationality in occupied Belgium, was executed by a German firing squad. She had been tried before a five-judge military tribunal and found guilty of aiding the escape of Allied soldiers.

Nurse Cavell had earlier been a matron of a teaching hospital for nurses in Brussels and played a role in the establishment of the Belgian nursing service. When German troops crossed the Belgian frontier, Cavell helped organize an underground escape organization for wounded British, French, and Belgian soldiers. By the time of her arrest, she had helped over 200 such troops to return to their lines through Holland, as she admitted at her trial.

When Brand Whitlock, U.S. ambassador to Belgium, learned of the death sentence, he tried to secure a pardon. He later reported that "when the Kaiser heard of the murder of Miss Cavell, he was furious; demanded all particulars, issued orders, took measures, and so on."[122]

She was, after all, a woman in a man's war, and chivalry demanded better than the Germans seemingly were willing to give. Her violent death was every propagandist's dream come true. According to the attending British clergyman, on the eve of her execution she gave her message to the world: "This I would say, standing as I do in view of God and eternity, I realize that patriotism is not enough. I must have no hatred or bitterness towards anyone."[123] These charitable words, almost certainly the product of the creative writers in Wellington House rather than a frightened nurse about to be shot to death, were made as much of as Lord Nelson's dying ones at Trafalgar. Nurse Cavell was portrayed as both saint and martyr. Parker's organization would properly judge that Cavell's execution did more to increase pro-war sentiment in the United States than any single incident except the invasion of Belgium and the *Lusitania* sinking.

After suggesting that "whatever may be our sympathy with the woman, whatever feeling of horror the shooting of a woman by a file of soldiers may arouse," an editorial in the *New York Times* of October 23 pointed out that Edith Cavell had flagrantly violated the provisions of military law under which she operated. It quoted Article 102 of the Instructions for the Government of Armies in the United States, issued as General Order No. 100, dated April 24, 1863: "The law of war, like the criminal law regarding other offenses, makes no distinction on account of the difference of sex concerning the spy, the war traitor, or the war rebel." The *Times* editorial then removed any ambiguity its readers might have inferred by concluding that "it is because of this very act of the Germans at Brussels and because of countless other acts of like kind, all the fruit of of the stern, blind German devotion to the ruthless ideas of militarism and State power, that the civilized world has turned against Germany, unsparingly condemns, detests the ideals she seeks to obtain by such inhuman practices, and hopes and fervently prays for defeat in arms, lest by triumph her unspeakably horrible ideals should come into dominance and the hands upon the clock of civilization be turned back a thousand years."

On October 31, the magazine section of the *New York Times* reserved its first three pages for an article by one of its favorite contributors, James M. Beck, "The Case of Edith Cavell—A Reply to Dr. Albert Zimmermann, Germany's Under Secretary for Foreign Affairs." Zimmermann had issued an official apology which nevertheless expressed surprise that the shooting of an English nurse and the trial of several women in Brussels for treason had caused a sensation. Beck, for readers who might have forgotten, was proudly introduced as "one of the leaders of the New York Bar ... the author of the most widely read article written since the war began, entitled: 'The Dual Alliance vs. The Triple Entente,' which was subsequently expanded into a book called *The Evidence in the Case*, pronounced by a distinguished publicist to be 'the classic of the war.' After its publication in the *New York Times* this article was reprinted in nearly every language of the civilized nations and over a million copies of it were published." Beck, a persuasive pro–Entente propagandist, made the most of the occasion. After flaying German cruelty over and over again and scorning Zimmerman's apology, he skillfully interwove purported American interests into his presentation. "There is one aspect of the tragedy," Beck wrote, "which especially concerns the honor and dignity of the United States and should receive its swift and effectual recognition. Her secret trial and hurried execution was [*sic*] a studied affront to the American Minister at Brussels, and therefore to the American nation. ... It would be incredible, if the facts were not beyond dispute, that the request of the United States for a little delay was not only brutally refused, *but that our Legation was deliberately misled and deceived until the death sentence had been inflicted.*" Therefore, according to Beck, the fate of Miss Cavell was as much America's concern as was that of the *Lusitania*. Beck concluded by imploring the women of America, "will you not honor the memory of this martyr of your sex, who for all time will be mourned as was the noblest Greek maiden, Antigone, who also gave her life that her brother might have the rites of sepulture? Will you not carry on in her name and for her memory those sacred ministrations of mercy which were her lifework?"

The Germans later charged the French with having executed three of their nurses for similar activities: Margaret Schmidt and Ottile Voss in 1915 and Felicie Pfaadt in 1916.[124] In 1917, the celebrated Dutch dancer Mata Hari was executed by the French, having been tried and found guilty of spying for the Germans.

One British historian summed up Cavell's execution by writing that "before Nurse Cavell's execution, the American authorities had done their utmost to secure a remission of the death sentence—at a time when many in Britain did not expect that it would be carried out. Propaganda, in short, had little to do with the American response to Nurse Cavell's death. However justified the German authorities may have felt in their conduct, they had clear warning that powerful forces in the USA took a different view, and that to shoot Nurse Cavell would be to outrage these forces."[125]

A British biographer asked rhetorically, "Was Edith Cavell's execution justified?" Notable Englishmen were quoted, who, in the 1930s, all agreed that she had been treated fairly by the Germans—but, in fact, had betrayed her privileged position as a nurse. A. Duff Cooper, M.P. and later Minister of Information during World War II, said bluntly: "If ever a woman was justly executed according to the rules of warfare, Nurse Cavell was. She used her position to get soldiers back to Britain."[126]

After the war, Cavell's remains were returned to England amid much pomp and circumstance, crowned by a memorial service in Westminster Abbey. Befitting her status as a war heroine, a statue was erected in London, opposite the National Portrait Gallery. On its pedestal was engraved for posterity the place and time of her execution and a condensed version of a compassionate nurse's supposed final words:

EDITH CAVELL
BRUSSELS
DAWN
OCTOBER 12
1915
PATRIOTISM IS NOT ENOUGH
I MUST HAVE NO HATRED OR
BITTERNESS FOR ANYONE

Not all British propaganda appealed to base emotions. England's "declaration of sympathy with Jewish Zionist aspirations" in November 1917, which came to be called the Balfour Declaration and set the stage for the founding of the state of Israel 31 years later, was made to appear, on the surface at least, as humanitarian in spirit. In fact, the cautiously ambiguous statement was a bold and dramatic propaganda stroke with specific targets in mind, created not by any of London's propaganda offices but by England's highest-level officialdom.

During discussions in the cabinet in October 1917 over the objectives of the proposed declaration of support for a "national home for the Jewish people" in Palestine, "Balfour did not think it necessary to dwell on the larger aspects of the Zionist question, nor did he say anything about strengthening the resistance to French pretensions in Palestine or about the long-term advantages to be expected from a British association with the Zionists. He chose to rest his case for the declaration mainly on its value as propaganda."[127] Foreign minister Balfour's intended targets were Jews in Russia and the United States. He pushed for the declaration's prompt approval and announcement, concerned that Germany might preempt England's move with a formal pro–Zionist declaration of its own—despite Palestine then being part of Turkey, a sensitive ally of Germany.

Perhaps the most compelling reason of all for making the announcement in the late fall of 1917 was London's anxiety—and Washington's and Paris's as well—that the new Bolshevik government in St. Petersburg would take Russia out of the war, permitting Germany to move troops from the eastern to the western front. It was vainly hoped that, with a sufficiently strong incentive, Russian Jews, whom the British considered strongly pro–Zionist, might throw their weight against the Bolsheviks and somehow prevent the separate peace with Germany that loomed. In fact, the Balfour Declaration and the associated British propaganda had no discernible impact on Russia's Jews, for the Allies' worst-case scenario promply occurred. Russia left the war and then signed a peace treaty with Germany in March 1918.

The British were better able to exploit the propaganda value of their official support of Zionist aspirations in the United States. In 1917, there were about three million Jews in America, most of whom were recent immigrants from eastern Europe, primarily Russia, where they had been cruelly treated. These newcomers, unassimilated or partially assimilated, had not forgotten England's alliance with the czarist Russia they had fled. They had been anti-Russian at the start of the war, and even after America entered the war they remained lukewarm in their attitude toward England. There was also a small minority of wealthy and influential Jews of German ancestry with emotional ties to the fatherland. Many of these Jewish German-Americans were initially powerful supporters of the German cause.

The British, however, overestimated Jewish power in the United States. There were few Jewish banking houses of size and the Jewish vote was a political factor in only a few states. There was also the erroneous perception that Jews, holding a disproportionate number of positions as newspaper publishers and editors, shaped U.S. public opinion to their own needs. Nevertheless, Zionists in America, as elsewhere, enthusiastically and publicly embraced British support for their cause. It can be assumed also that the non-Zionist majority of Jews in the United States at least moderated their antagonism toward the British Empire as a result of the Balfour statement. The declaration was considered a sufficiently powerful new propaganda tool that the Department of Information in London promptly added a new Jewish section, staffed principally by British Zionists.

If Balfour had dangled the image of a new home for the Jews as a propaganda ploy, Prime Minister David Lloyd George supported Zionist aspirations in Palestine for another reason. He had a debt to settle, a moral *quid pro quo* of sorts, with Dr. Chaim Weizmann. Weizmann, a brilliant organic chemist and fervent Zionist, had developed a process to produce acetone—a necessary element in the manufacture of the explosive cordite—from corn rather than from wood, which had to be imported from America. According to one account, when Weizmann turned down Lloyd George's offer of a knighthood in recognition of his service to the empire, he asked instead that Great

Britain reward him by supporting the creation of a Jewish state.[128] In 1948, when the state of Israel came into existence, Weizmann was elected president of the Provisional Government, and then in 1949 first president of the new state.

Complementing Parker's official work at Wellington House in London was covert propaganda spread in America. Unlike the German propagandists in the United States, whose activities were closely monitored by American intelligence agents, vigorously exposed in the press and harassed at every turn, and probed in depth immediately after the Armistice by a U.S. Senate Subcommittee, British agents effectively cloaked themselves in invisibiliy.

There were, of course, the formally recognized diplomatic officials, chiefly the ambassador and his aides, many doubling as gatherers and transmitters of "intelligence" of all sorts. The British ambassador was career diplomat Sir Cecil Spring-Rice, who had been secretary at the Washington embassy during the Benjamin Harrison and second Grover Cleveland administrations. In 1886, he had been best man at Theodore Roosevelt's second wedding and later formed close friendships with other important Republicans, including Senator Henry Cabot Lodge and former secretary of state John Hay.

Once the war began, Spring-Rice proved less than well suited to the requirements of his stressful job, often showing the strain with undiplomatic outbursts of temper. House recorded in his diary his frequent exasperation in dealing with the moody Briton. In October 1915, for example, after an acrimonious exchange, House concluded that Washington was "no place for a nervous and delicate Ambassador. It was unfair to him and us." Two months later, after an hour-and-a-half talk with Spring-Rice, House wrote that he had never seen him "more entertaining, affectionate, and reasonable." This prompted some second thoughts: "How can I go to London and demand his head? I am trying to think of some way to save him, and it will probably result in some modification of the President's, Lansing's, and my wishes to have him recalled."[129]

British journalist Sir Arthur Willert was a caustic critic of Spring-Rice in his private wartime correspondence. But in his memoirs many years later, he made a remarkable *volte-face*, in the best patriotic traditions of the British Empire:

> Thus began [in 1914] four years of as happy a relationship between ambassador and newspaper correspondent as can ever have existed. ... The dispatches and letters I sent home during the labyrinthine controversies that strained Anglo-American relations while America was neutral in the First War could never have been written without the help of the ambassador's knowledge of international law and the apperceptive speed with which he unraveled the essential from the unessential. ... Looking back at it all, I wonder whether Spring-Rice's success does not entitle him to be considered as, perhaps, the last ambassador to shape vital policy at home by the cogency of his argument and by his personal influence.[130]

If Spring-Rice knew details about Wellington House and Willert's extracurricular activities, or if he himself had been involved in clandestine propaganda, there is no hint of it in the two volumes of his published corre-spondence.[131] Remarkably, there is not even a mention of Sir William Wiseman, who, from mid–1916 until Spring-Rice was replaced by the far more competent Lord Reading in January 1918, usurped nearly all his diplomatic responsibilities.[132]

Royal Navy Captain Guy Gaunt, the British naval attaché, was also on the scene when war broke out. Despite his close ties to British naval intelligence and his covert propaganda work, Gaunt shows up often in House's diary. Gaunt initially was a trusted conduit for secret information between House's Manhattan apartment, London, and the British Embassy in Washington. Gaunt also played the role of knowledgeable interpreter of British reaction to American diplomatic notes. A measure of the esteem in which House held Gaunt is given by this entry in House's diary on May 6, 1916: "I told Gaunt that he reminded me of Bernstorff, inasmuch as he had courage and good temper and viewed matters like a sportsman. I wish Gaunt was British Ambassador and that Bernstorff was Minister for Foreign Affairs in Berlin. It is my intention to suggest to the British Government that they handsomely recognize Gaunt's service during the war."[133]

Neither of House's wishes came to pass. In fact, House would soon quietly promote another for Spring-Rice's job. Gaunt's effective work in America was recognized by Great Britain, however, for he was knighted in 1918 and retired as vice-admiral the same year. In his memoir, Gaunt, as might be expected, had little to say about his covert wartime work in Washington and New York, where he—like his German peers—had an office in lower Manhattan overlooking New York harbor, the better to observe ships entering and leaving the port. Gaunt did, however, touch briefly on the important relationship he had with fellow Australian John Revelstoke Rathom, publisher of the wildly Germanophobic *Providence Journal*. Gaunt wrote that he "arranged to give him the 'low-down' ... and I wouldn't be responsible for its complete accuracy, so long as it counteracted the 'dope' supplied to the Press by Dr. Fuehr, Count Bernstorff's propaganda merchant. There was to be a simultaneous publication in the *Times* and *Providence Journal*."[134]

Two other men, however, stand out as the principal directors of British propaganda on American soil: Arthur Willert, the brilliant Washington correspondent for the *Times* of London (he was knighted in 1918), and Sir William Wiseman, who, in the guise of a purchasing agent, was chief of British intelligence (M.I.6) in the United States.[135] The two worked together intimately. Willert wrote seven books, including two that deal with World War I—*The Road to Safety: A Study in Anglo-American Relations* and *Washington and Other Memories*—plus numerous articles that catalogued his long journalistic and diplomatic career. His writings touch but gingerly, however, on his wartime years in the United States. Wiseman, on the other hand, published nothing of his World War I activities. He commented during an interview in

1959 that "he'd been tempted to write an autobiography but felt even at this date that he might print something that would hurt someone or hurt England's foreign relations."[136]

Willert, 32 years old in 1914, had been Oxford-educated and joined the staff of Great Britain's most powerful newspaper, the *Times*, in 1906. After overseas assignments in Paris and Berlin, he was named chief Washington correspondent in 1910. His service in that high-profile job lasted until 1920, and was interrupted only in 1917-18, when he was secretary of the British war mission for his "chief," Lord Northcliffe. For a time he represented a new and overt Ministry of Information under the new ambassador to Washington, Lord Reading. In July 1918, Willert was back nearly full time as Washington editor, but still doing the propaganda work he obviously relished. Painted on his office door under "The Times, London" was the euphemistic title, "The British Pictorial Service."

Willert later parlayed his talents as a communicator and his wartime experiences in Washington into more clearly defined diplomatic positions. In 1921, he left the *Times* to become press officer and head of the news department of the British Foreign Office.[137] In that capacity, he was a member of the U.K.'s delegation to the Washington Naval Conference in 1921-22, the London Economic Conference in 1924, the London Naval Conference in 1930, and the Geneva Disarmament Conference in 1932-34. He lectured in the United States during the 1930s and maintained a close relationship with President Franklin D. Roosevelt, with whom he had worked in wartime Washington more than twenty years before. At the outbreak of the Second World War, Willert again became a propagandist, this time formally, as head of the Ministry of Information Office for the Southern Region, one of twelve subdivisions set up by Great Britain for administration purposes. He held that post until 1945.

A journalist, especially a foreign correspondent, is only as good as his sources. By 1914, Willert had cultivated useful contacts with many of America's most powerful political figures of both parties, particularly those in Washington who influenced U.S. foreign policy. State Department officials who could give him the inside information he sought included Secretary of State Bryan, counselors Lansing and Polk, and, of course, Colonel House. He had become a perspicacious observer of American domestic politics and public opinion, as his in-depth reports back to London clearly show. He had also adapted his Oxford English to the idiom of America, at least in his writing. Just before the 1916 election, for example, he wrote to his editor, "The public is almost 'war mad.' The Kaiser, in particular, has 'got their goat.' It is the spirit of the sheriff's posse out on a cold night, a determination to make the object of their hue and cry pay for lost sleep and wet feet."[138] Few Englishmen then knew what a sheriff's posse was, and fewer still would have used the term. Aside from the mixed metaphors—a posse is always on horseback, and thus unlikely to get wet feet—one wonders if Willert's associates in London quite knew what he was talking about.

Three weeks into the war, Willert was being primed for other, more "serious" work. On August 27, Geoffrey Dawson, editor of the London *Times*, wrote to him that circulation was "enormous. It has more than doubled since the war began and is steadily going up. ... Your serious work will come a little later. Meanwhile it is vitally important that you should remain at your post and keep us informed both publicly and privately."[139] Prompted by Dawson, Willert offered his services to the British Embassy. He wrote articles for American magazines, including "The British Case," published along with Bernhard Dernburg's "The German Case" in *The World's Work*. When Raemakers's infamous anti–German cartoons were first published in the United States, Willert wrote the supporting text for them.

By September, Willert was reporting to London that American public opinion was unquestionably on the side of the Allies, that the "nagging" should stop, that "we have got that support now." A month later, he reinforced his point: "It is fair to say that feeling here is anti–German rather than pro-British. Belgium and the scrap of paper have clinched it." The same month Northcliffe sent an encouraging cable: "You grumble at being marooned in Washington but, as a matter of fact, you are doing a very great service for the Empire."[140]

Willert's correspondence with Dawson in the winter of 1914–15 is filled with his sensible interpretations of how Britain should wage the propaganda war in America:

> We are convinced and our American friends agree that dignity and reticence is our chief card. ... I have formed pretty definite conclusions about the question of publicity. ... Avoid the appearance of organization as much as possible. It should be made continually clear that we are not commercially jealous of Germany ... that we don't intend to dismember and cripple German civilization. The Bernhardi type of Pan-Germanism, its paganism, its cynicism, should be shown up whenever possible.[141]

In November 1914, Willert prepared a memorandum for the British Foreign Office covering the forthcoming "publicity work" to be done in America, arguing that it "ought to be educational and not controversial." He pointed out that in the United States contradiction was "of slight journalistic value." What counted, Willert wrote, showing the depth of his understanding of America and Americans, was "sensational statement," not "sober corrections," and that the first requisite was "to keep green the memory of German guilt of the war and to prevent Americans from modifying their first impressions that the war is one of peaceful Democracy against armed Autocracy." Willert recommended that British propaganda should "consist of carefully chosen documents and pamphlets putting the basic issues of the war in their true perspective." Most urgent "for the moment," Willert wrote, was to decide how to distribute the propaganda literature. He suggested that he be responsible, using "the comprehensive machinery" at his disposal, and that the materials appear to originate from the *Times*. Willert concluded with a "tentative list of targets":

1. The 20,000 newspapers, daily and other, published in the United States.
2. Public libraries.
3. Lawyers' offices, so far as addresses are obtainable.
4. Universities.
5. School teachers (addresses obtainable from State authorities).
6. Hotels.
7. Clubs (male and female).
8. Reading and smoking cars on railway trains (The Times, for instance, distributes 70 copies of the Weekly Times to the N.Y. Central R.R. alone).
9. Waiting rooms of doctors and dentists, etc.[142]

Willert, however, underestimated the value of atrocity propaganda. In March 1915, he wrote to Dawson that he knew about the upcoming Bryce Report but felt that "such atrocity tales are discounted."

Willert's correspondence shows that Northcliffe's *Times*—and Northcliffe himself—played a direct role in British propaganda efforts, almost from the start of the war. In a December 1914 letter to Willert, Dawson boasted that the French *Yellow Book* "had to be turned from rather a tangle into a triumph." Whether it was a triumph or a transparent propaganda tract depended on one's viewpoint. In fact, many historians now agree that the *Yellow Book*, of all the belligerents' published apologias, was the one most filled with lies and forgeries. Edmund von Mach, Harvard professor and German propagandist, devoted three consecutive weekly news columns in the *Boston Evening Transcript* to the debunking of Dawson's pride and joy. Nevertheless, von Mach appreciated the British newspaper's editorial work, for he recorded sarcastically that "The book is delightful reading."[143]

At the start of the war, Lord Northcliffe was uniquely well-positioned to contribute his personal animosities, his staff, and his money to his nation's patriotic efforts. While still plain Alfred Harmsworth in 1896, he had published diatribes against Germany and her Kaiser in his newly acquired *Daily Mail* in response to Wilhelm II's supportive telegram to President Paul Kruger of the Transvaal.[144] Discovering that this newfound anti-German theme helped sell newspapers, the *Mail* later that year published a series of articles, "Germany As She Is," that focused on the dangers from England's newest commercial and military rival. In 1897, Harmsworth followed up with another series of articles under the pejorative title "Under the Iron Heel." They "described forts on the island of Heligoland that no one could photograph, and lumpy private soldiers who would obey orders like machines," as well as a German emperor with few redeeming characteristics:

> Between the walls of acclamation came riding the Kaiser. A man of middle age, sitting constrainedly and bolt upright; a dead yellow skin, hard-

pencilled brows, a straight, masterful chin, lips jammed close together under a dark moustache pointing straight upward to the whites of his eyes. A face at once repulsive and pathetic, so harsh and stony, so grimly solemn. ... He looked like a man without joy, without love, without pity, without hope. He looked like a man who had never laughed, like a man who could never sleep. A man might wear such a face who felt himself turning slowly to ice.[145]

By the time Harmsworth bought the *Times* in 1908, he was the undisputed king of London's Fleet Street and had been elevated to the peerage, taking the title Lord Northcliffe. Militant imperialism was on the march in Great Britain, and Northcliffe took it upon himself to proclaim the British Empire's greatness and to warn of the dangers that threatened her from Middle Europe. That same year, the Royal Navy launched the world's first all-big-gun battleship, the *Dreadnought*, which heated up the naval race between England and Germany. Northcliffe fervently believed that God and history had ordained that Great Britain rule the seas, and as much of the contiguous lands as possible—and, to the best of his great ability, worked tirelessly to communicate this homily to all of the English-speaking world.

Working for Northcliffe, Willert was not above tailoring his dispatches to fit the changing needs of his own nation's and America's foreign policies. For example, he later confessed that "during the waiting period between Bernstorff's dismissal and the declaration of war I had on the whole exaggerated in The Times the importance of the embryo war plans then under discussion. I did this to meet House's desire that The Times should try to curb British impatience with American slowness."[146]

There is evidence that Willert culled from his collected papers material that showed that British propagandists were trying to drag America into the war. In his surviving correspondence with Dawson, Willert tips his hand only twice as far as the kind of "organization" he was developing and its makeup. On December 31, 1916, he writes, "I have got the establishment of a publicity bureau in my hands," and on February 13, 1917, "We have got the skeleton of a good organization. The salient thing about our plan is that it will involve purely unofficial machinery. Its membership would probably be Wiseman, the head of the Intelligence people here; Norman Thwaites, one of his assistants; Murray Allison, Ian Beith, myself, and perhaps Granville Barker."[147]

Willert had nothing but praise for the team members. Wiseman, he wrote, "is one of those rare Englishmen who thoroughly understand and get on with Americans. He is on excellent terms with the people who really count and, what is more remarkable, has managed to get for himself a powerful position without offending any of our compatriots. I have worked a good deal with him lately. ... He would be the head of the committee and a better one we could not find." Norman Thwaites, a former companion-secretary of Joseph Pulitzer, the idiosyncratic publisher of New York's *World*, "is a thoroughly good and competent fellow, knows journalism thoroughly, and is popular in newspaper circles." Murray Allison "is doing effective work with Raemaekers' cartoons and is most energetic and full of ideas." Ian Beith "is lecturing and writing here and has made himself extremely popular." Granville Barker "is also lecturing and helping generally."[148]

One particular document in the Willert collection sheds light on the broad extent and some of the details of British sub-rosa activities prior to America's entrance into the war. It is Pomeroy Burton's comprehensive "Publicity Report" of April 28, 1917, to John Buchan, the newly appointed head of foreign propaganda in the reorganized Department of Information in London. Burton, one of Northcliffe's chief aides and formerly the city editor of the *New York World*, arrived in America, as Willert put it, "with a mandate from Northcliffe and the Prime Minister to report upon propaganda. His scheme, to a great extent the joint product of himself, Wiseman and myself, was just completed when the Balfour Mission arrived [on April 22] and it gave the New York publicity office its pattern."[149]

While the report was essentially a proposal for "an active publicity campaign in the United States," with America into the war there were strong hints of what the small but elite propaganda team of Willert-Wiseman-Thwaites-Allison-Beith-Barker had already accomplished. Existing patriotic organizations, "whose special aim is the enlightenment of the American public," had been one of Willert's main targets, and "definite arrangements with several of the best of these societies" had been made. "They are glad to link up with us because we can furnish them with precisely the material they most desire, now that America is in the war, and they in turn provide us with a superb distributing agency." The Vigilantes, a jingo organization of writers and journalists, was described in the report as "by far the most important distributing agency of the lot." More important was Willert's comment that "I have helped them to shape their organization and raise their working capital."[150] One wonders how many other "patriotic" American organizations, friendly newspapers, and cooperative book publishers were supported by British capital.

Among these pro–British U.S. book publishers, none could have been more Anglophilic in 1917 than George H. Doran, if his company's long string of stridently anti–German books and pamphlets are any measure of his views. In a letter to the Committee on Public Information's George Creel on September 10, 1918, concerning a newly published Doran book that was being criticized as not sufficiently anti–German, Doran pulled no punches as to where he stood—and profits be damned:

> As you know, I have aimed to be violently pro–Ally and anti–German, during the entire period of the war. A book which we have recently published, called *Ten Months in a German Raider*, is now under censure by some very patriotic gentlemen. ... Will you have one of your most expert editors read it, and if there is the slightest suggestion of aid or comfort to any enemy anywhere I will immediately withdraw the book.[151]

Burton's report considered a recent letter from Doran, presumably to Willert, that was "so interesting and to the point" that Burton included it in its entirety. Doran suggested that "America is not a tractarian country, and we pay little or no attention to pamphlets." Instead of the free booklets distributed by Wellington House, which he criticized as ineffective, he recommended cheap books "stating exactly the things which Britain would like to have presented to the American public." He said he would properly promote such books, adding that the advertising "would be worthwhile propaganda in itself." The letter showed Doran not only as understanding the role of the book publisher as propagandist but as being a shrewd businessman as well. He concluded, scarcely veiling his misplaced altruism, "that London is spending a great deal of money and I should like to see it spent in directions which would be productive and effective."

Doran backed his words with deeds, promptly publishing, among others, *Hurrah and Hallelujah: The Teaching of Germany's Poets, Prophets, Professors and Preachers—A Documentation.* The book was supposedly written by a Dane, J.P. Bang, professor of theology at the University of Copenhagen, "in the spring of 1915." Books by "neutrals" were particularly sought after by the British, for their messages would supposedly be unbiased. But the careful reader of *Hurrah and Hallelujah* wonders if, in fact, the book had not been written by an Englishman. It carried a copyright of 1917, but with an introduction dated February 1917. It is scarcely possible that Doran could have translated and printed the book so soon after his letter to Willert of March 22. The introduction was bylined by an English novelist, Ralph Connor, who recited for the reader the by-then-standard litany of anti–German harangues. It was the final chapter in the book, however, so pro–British that it could not have been written by someone who was not an Englishman, that is a tipoff to the book's likely Wellington House origins.

As he had promised to the British, on the back covers of his many nickel and ten-cent war pamphlets Doran advertised "Important Books of the Day," from $1 to $2.50, with provocative titles like *The Crime, I Accuse, The German Terror in France, The German Terror in Belgium, The German Fury in Belgium,* and *The Great Crime and Its Moral.* Emphasis was on atrocities, for Doran, like newspaper publishers, had discovered what the public would pay to read.

The Burton plan for propaganda, according to its author, was written at his request by Willert, "than whom no one more clearly understands the scope and effect of the German propaganda work which had been done in the United States." It was divided into four main sections: News, British Effort Here, American Effort Here, and Private Work.

As for "News," the report was detailed and unambiguous, showing complete understanding of American newspaper publishing practices. For example, it was recommended that the "afternoon war bulletin service" be moved up by two hours, enabling "every morning newspaper in the United States to get all the war news into all the editions, country and city." Other suggestions included "lifting of the lid" on censorship of war news, injecting more human interest in news stories, and improving relations with "the best" (presumably pro–British) American correspondents.

The "British Effort Here" covered a War Book Branch under Doran, a Lecture Bureau, films, exhibitions, books, pamphlets, cartoons, war pictures, postcards, maps, and all other "Legitimate Propaganda Material." It was recommended, for example, that lectures, which had previously been given "to society circles in the large cities," should instead by directed at "the masses." Bazaars and exhibitions, "done most earnestly and well on a small scale," should be expanded. It was made clear that at these activities there was quite no substitute for the war-wounded: "I would suggest that if an injured American aviator, no longer fit for service, could be procured, it would add greatly to the attraction." The English already had almost three years' experience in stimulating patriotic fervor; presumably they had discovered that amputees and the blinded would draw best.

According to Burton's plan, arrangements needed to be made for the free use of *Punch* magazine's war cartoons in American newspapers, without concern for copyrights. The lawsuits already begun by *Punch* for copyright infringements against the *Philadelphia Bulletin* and the *Chicago Herald* were not only "short sighted and unpatriotic—[but] idiotic, and should be stopped at once."

The "American Effort Here" was to be "linked up closely with and largely guided by the British Effort branch, but not openly so, the whole idea being to have it under the direction of Americans and all its materials disseminated through purely American channels." This propaganda would be distributed through such jingo organizations as the American Defense Society, the National Security League, and the National Committee for America.

Burton obviously relished the opportunity to criticize the organized propaganda work already accomplished by Wellington House and other formal London-based offices. He warmed to his task as he went along, writing that

> there is overwhelming evidence that such publicity work as had been done here by the British has been badly done. The scattered work done here in the direction of distribution of pamphlets, special articles, exhibitions and lectures, has really made no impression, and so far as Wellington House, the War Office, the Foreign Office and the Admiralty (the four branches in London which have up to now regulated all publicity matters here) are concerned, they might have saved a lot of money by doing nothing—the results would have been the same.

In fact, neither Wiseman (who had far bigger fish to fry), nor Willert, nor newcomer Burton were in a position to assess the overall results. Indeed, America had been drawn into the war, meeting the principal objective of Great Britain's formal propaganda campaign in the United States.

As for enemy propaganda, Burton's comments were also exaggerated and self-serving. He wrote that "the German propaganda, with its direct wireless news service, its constant contact with newspapers small and great and in all languages throughout the country, its organized driving power showing in a hundred different ways, though resented by the more intelligent classes, still had a cumulative effect even among those classes, while among the masses of working people there is no doubt whatever that its effect has been very great and far-reaching."

There was also this short paragraph, inserted as a hand-written addition to the typed rough draft, presumably by Willert:

> It looks now as if Washington is not going to help much in this [publicity program] direction, at first, at any rate. The President's appointment of a publicity director of very limited experience who is, according to present plans, to be surrounded and advised, not by practical newspaper men but by departmental heads and their "expert" subordinates—does not augur well for a steady flow of the kind of informative publicity which is so urgently needed now in every section of this great country.

The "publicity director of very limited experience" referred to was George Creel, who, while he might appear to be "surrounded" by high officials, would take advice from no one but Woodrow Wilson. Willert later worked with Creel and others on the Committee on Public Information. On February 22, 1918, Willert cabled Northcliffe, "I am on quite good terms with Creel."[152]

Three quarters of a century later, the Willert-Wiseman-Burton report stands as an excellent synthesis of goal-directed psychological warfare. Its framework is even appropriate for a late twentieth-century propaganda organization. Only the electronic media would now have to be added: radio, television, and the Internet.

From time to time, when his auxiliary functions as head propagandist permitted, Willert fed Dawson feature articles dealing with American politics for publication in the *Times*. Each was carefully crafted to support British foreign policy goals, yet correctly interpretive for use by England's diplomats. On August 14, 1918, he forwarded two such articles "by the courtesy of W. [Wiseman] ... on U.S. after-the-war policy." In his cover letter, Willert wrote that "we must be prepared to find that the President will stand very much aloof in the peace discussions and will be inclined to act as an arbiter rather than as an ally and that American policy promises to be very liberal not only regarding trade matters but in such things as the freedom of the seas. The moral I would draw from this is that in preliminary discussions especially about trade matters, it is up to us to do what we can to meet the American view so that we may have American sympathy and trust in other things."[153]

In all of Willert's books published after the war, he carefully circumscribed the role of British propaganda in America, hewing to the unwritten code of discretion for people like himself. However, he did finally acknowledge that "the British machine in America ... developed ... from an old-fashioned and understaffed Embassy into an immense and multifarious business organization by the end of the war."[154]

Sir William Wiseman arrived in the United States in December 1915, at age 30, in the uniform of an army captain. He had just been appointed head of British military intelligence in America, using as his cover the Ministry of Munitions' American and Transport Department. For the next three and a half years, Wiseman played an increasingly influential role in American foreign policy decision-making, becoming at the same time the most powerful foreign voice in Washington.

Before the war, Wiseman, the tenth holder of a baronetcy that went back to 1628, had spent two years at Cambridge. After working as a reporter for the *London Daily Express*, he traveled to Canada and Mexico, where he began a career in real estate and banking. In 1914, Wiseman had been a lieutenant in the artillery; he was then transferred to the infantry and promoted to captain. In Flanders a year later, he was gassed and sent home to recuperate. He was subsequently chosen by British military intelligence to work in the United States. An "old shipmate" of his father had recommended him for the post, certainly not then considered critical for the war effort.

During 1916, Captain Wiseman's espionage—and counterespionage—duties were as broad and creative as he could make them. It can be assumed that at first Wiseman diligently performed the routine covert tasks expected of a head intelligence agent in a neutral country during wartime, directing what almost certainly was a large force of clandestine operatives. It is clear that he collaborated with Willert on various propaganda projects, but the specifics of these activities during his first year in the United States remain obscure, for Wiseman, like Willert, removed from his collected papers what he considered incriminating documents.[155]

If Wiseman's early clandestine propaganda work in the United States remains a mystery, from December 17, 1916, when he first met House, until near the end of the Paris peace conference in June 1919, Wiseman became "the spy who came out of the cold." During this latter two-and-a-half-year period, he was on intimate terms with House, the man who kept World War I's most complete, highest-level diary. Wiseman understood, as did nearly everyone in Washington, that to reach President Wilson meant first to gain House's patronage. Wiseman thus set out to ingratiate himself to House, flattering him and giving him the admiration of a protégé. Wiseman's youth was on his side, for the 57-year-old House came to treat him like the son he never had. In turn, Wiseman later said, he regarded House "almost as a father."[156] Too, Wiseman's title was an asset, for House coveted his associations with the rich and famous and undoubtedly was flattered at having a baronet of the British Empire close to his elbow. More important, House, an unofficial diplomat himself, was looking for a new back-door communication link with England following the British government's reorganization and the dismissal of Foreign Minister Grey, House's prior close contact with London. Wiseman's discretion and supposed high-level contact with the foreign office in London appealed to the Texan.

Wiseman described his first meeting with House, in December 1916, this way, modestly outlining his function:

> Spring-Rice wished to make a confidential communication to Colonel House, and asked me to convey his message personally. The message itself was of no particular importance, but the talk I had with Colonel House convinced him that I should be a sympathetic and discreet channel of information. From that day until the time that the United States came into the war, I was confidential intermediary between Colonel House and the British Ambassador. ... I also communicated to the Foreign Office, through my Chief in London, certain information and suggestions which Colonel House thought they ought to have.[157]

In a letter he wrote to Wilson five weeks after he first met with Wiseman, House said that Wiseman "is in direct communication with the Foreign Office and that the Ambassador and other members of the Embassy are not aware of it." House went on, exuberantly, "I am happy beyond measure over this last conference with him, for I judge he reflects the views of his government."[158] In fact, Wiseman, before he met House, had not been in regular "direct communication with the Foreign Office," as he apparently had intimated to House, nor were his views necessarily those of his government's. But Wiseman was playing for large stakes and if he had purposefully misled House to gain entry into the inner sanctum of American political power—Woodrow Wilson himself—the prize was certainly worth the gambit.

It was also in House's self-interest to commend Wiseman to the president, thereby enhancing Wiseman's stature in London. House arranged the first meeting between the two men in a conspicuous environment: a State Department reception in honor of the Russian ambassador, in June 1917. Two witnesses to the event recorded versions of the meeting. Gordon Auchincloss, House's son-in-law and then an assistant to State Department Counselor Frank Polk, observed that "the President went around the room in about 3 minutes and then stopped to talk to Sir W. for about 15 minutes."[159] Willert, unmistakably proud of the success of his close collaborator, recalled the occasion this way:

> Instead of treating him to the perfunctory sentence or two usual to such introductions, the President talked with him for nearly half an hour, and then desisted only because he was pried loose by his entourage. Onlookers were astonished and mystified. Who was this unknown young man, obviously English, whom the President had singled out for his attention? ...The Diplomatic Corps in Washington was shaken to its gossipy foundations.[160]

Two weeks later, Wilson invited Wiseman to the White House for dinner, and then met with him privately for more than an hour. Wiseman kept notes of this first interview with the president, and he promptly relayed them to London. Many more secret cables based on his discussions with Wilson and House would follow, the early ones directed to his military intelligence chief and later communications, as his prestige grew, to the Foreign Office. This first private meeting was wide-ranging and confidential, setting the pattern for the future and covering such topics as former ambassador to Turkey Henry Morgenthau's covert mission to meet with Turkish leaders; the huge U.S. naval shipbuilding program, which was causing anxiety in the Admiralty; the problem of competing demands among the Allies for money and supplies from America; Wilson's concern about low French morale; and House's pet idea of a secret Anglo-American naval treaty, which Wilson said he opposed.

What is remarkable is that the president of the United States was talking about high-level foreign policy matters with a young Englishman with no formal credentials from the British Foreign Office. Obviously, House had done his missionary work well. Also, according to Wiseman's biographer, "His well-bred manners and sense of propriety recommended him to House and Wilson, both rather punctilious men. In many ways Wiseman was a young House with an Oxbridge accent."[161] Wiseman would draw himself close to Wilson as the months passed, a good listener who—like the succession of British diplomats who would pass through the White House—was also careful to butter up the president. Following Wilson's war message to the Congress, House was undoubtedly pleased to inform him that Wiseman had commented that "if Shakespeare had written the address it could not have been more perfect."[162]

It was not long before Wiseman's unique position as diplomat extraordinaire was recognized by Great Britain's political hierarchy. Lord Northcliffe, who had come to America in June 1917 as head of a British mission to coordinate war activities, cabled to Churchill a month later that he had "long believed war can only be won from here. The position is most difficult and delicate. Sir William Wiseman ... is the only person, English or American, who has access to Wilson and House at all times. ... The Administration is entirely run by these two men."[163] Wiseman also moved physically closer to House, the better to communicate, as these two cables show:

London, August 4, 1917, Wiseman to House:
I am offered an apt for the winter, 7th floor, 115 E 53d St. Do you think it is unwise for us to be in the same building?

New York, August 4, 1917, House to Wiseman:
An apt in the same bldg will be a pleasure and convenience and without objections.[164]

In August 1918, Wiseman arranged to spent his vacation at Magnolia, Massachusetts, the frail House's summer retreat from New York City's summer heat and humidity. He played tennis and golf with Gordon Auchincloss, and talked with House. Wilson appeared, apparently unexpectedly, the day after Wiseman arrived. Wiseman reported to London that the president had been "delighted" to find him there and "insisted on my remaining with the party." Few American politicians or foreign diplomats were privileged to talk with the reclusive, distrustful president—even in Washington—much less spend a vacation discussing plans to redraw the map of the world. According to Willert, Wiseman had become "so well trusted by the American leaders that could they have had their way, he would have been appointed British Ambassador when Spring-Rice was recalled early in 1918."[165]

Wiseman's biographer concluded an assessment of his role as influential foreign-policy advisor, trusted intermediary, and industrious communicator by writing:

> His initiative ... helped ease the financial crisis, stream-lined British representation in the United States, brought Reading over as ambassador. His advice led to House's trip to Europe in late 1917 that helped determine the extent of American participation in the international war bodies. His recommendations fashioned the British approach to Wilson for troop amalgamation, and his report from Europe to Wilson and House prompted the steps to be taken to circumscribe Pershing's responsibilities. His restrained emphasis on the necessity for some sort of United States action in Russia undoubtedly affected the change in attitude by House in this matter, and advice from him and Reading moderated British pressures on Wilson for intervention.[166]

Yet Wiseman, seemingly the smooth, precise operative, was not always successful. The propaganda mission to St. Petersburg that he personally orchestrated from New York was a botch, almost humorous in its naiveté. It failed not only because its objective was far too ambitious, but also because of Wiseman's selection of its inept leader. Wiseman apparently had begun to think about such an expedition soon after America entered the war, after receiving alarming intelligence information from London that Alexander Kerensky's provisional government was being endangered by "revolutionary pacifists." German intrigue and propaganda in Russia were supposedly focused on bringing about a separate peace between the two countries. This specter of Soviet "pacifism" at first frightened, then haunted, the Allies, for if Russia left the war the German army could safely transfer its forces in the east to the stalemated western front. Such a move could, it was feared, tip the military balance and win the war for Germany. It should be recalled that the British Balfour Declaration of November 2, 1917, had as one of its objectives the wooing of Russian Jews, most of whom the British rightly considered to be strongly Zionist. The Allies would soon send in armies—American, British, French, and Japanese—to fight the peace-promoting Bolsheviks. The intention was initially to bring them back into the war against Germany, then later to try to destroy their new political and economic order.

Meanwhile, Wiseman attempted to keep Russia in the war, with House's

understanding support, by sending a five-man team into St. Petersburg—
somehow, first, to "expose present German intrigues and their undoubted
connection with the late reactionary Government. Second, to persuade the
Russians to attack the Germans with all their might and thus accomplish the
overthrow of the Hohenzollern dynasty and autocracy in Berlin." These objectives would have been a tall order for any five agents; for Wiseman's amateurs,
they were unattainable. Their leader was W. Somerset Maugham, a relative
of Wiseman's by marriage, and one of the very few famous British authors
who elected not to write propaganda. In 1914, Maugham was too old and too
short to enlist, but, according to his biographer Ted Morgan, "Maugham
wanted to do his bit. He could have stayed in England, like Lytton Strachey
who knitted mufflers ... or like Shaw and H. G. Wells who wrote letters to
editors about the end of Prussian militarism."[167] Instead, the French- and
German-speaking Maugham joined the Red Cross as an interpreter with an
ambulance unit in France. He was then impressed into British intelligence as
an unpaid agent in neutral Switzerland, where his fame as a writer would—
in theory, at least—gain him access to enemy secrets. His covert work there
had been sufficiently undemanding as to allow Maugham time to write a
comedy between trips across Lake Geneva into France to file his reports and
pick up new instructions.

Wiseman's selection of Maugham was casual: the peripatetic ex-spy had
been in New York City when the decision was made to organize the project,
just after America entered the war. Maugham, while professing his limitations
as an intelligence agent, nevertheless patriotically agreed to take on the assignment. At the end of July, with $21,000 for expenses from Wiseman, Maugham
sailed from California to Tokyo and Siberia, and went overland to St. Petersburg. By September, Maugham and his four co-conspirators[168] had established contact with Thomas Masaryk, Czechoslovakia's future president. With
Masaryk's help and some of Maugham's money, a Slav press organization was
set up to distribute anti–German propaganda. Before the end of September,
Maugham had concluded—and so reported to Wiseman—what was obvious
to nearly every foreign observer then in St. Petersburg, that the Kerensky
government was losing popularity and would soon topple. Arguably, this conclusion was the highlight of Maugham's two-and-a-half-month tour of duty.
In early November, Maugham left Russia under orders from Wiseman to
report to London for a personal presentation of his findings. He also had the
transcript of an October 30 interview with Kerensky that projected the Bolshevik overthrow of his government days later. Preposterously, Maugham later
went on record as saying he believed that had his puny efforts been begun
earlier, he might have turned the tide of history.

Wiseman was also active in London and Paris after the Armistice, acting as high-level chaperon and public-relations executive for American dig-
nitaries, particularly Woodrow Wilson. He also sought to restrict press

coverage of the peace deliberations, as the following then-secret memorandum illustrates: "The President's Secretariat [to the peace conference] will consist of Gordon Auchincloss, Hugh Frazier and George Creel. Creel, however, will be well controlled by the other two. I also spoke to House about the danger of any American press campaign during the Conferences. He is entirely opposed to anything of the sort."[169]

Wiseman's relationship with House paid valuable postwar dividends for him. He joined the international banking firm of Kuhn Loeb and Company in New York City, becoming a partner in 1929. He maintained warm ties with his mentor and benefactor from Texas, as Wiseman's extensive correspondence with House shows, until House died in 1938. During World War II, according to one source, Wiseman "was to show that he had not lost his old touch." In 1940, he acted as an intermediary between German officials in the United States ostensibly anxious to arrange peace with both Downing Street and the White House. Wiseman purportedly obtained "a great deal of information about Germany, much of which was proved to be both accurate and valuable."[170]

In 1951, the state of Texas, to commemorate the special relationship between one of its most illustrious sons and a titled Englishman, made Wiseman an honorary citizen of Texas. Wiseman's obituary in the 1963 *Brittanica Book of the Year* identified him precisely but with a discreet British understatement: "British diplomat (b. Feb. 1, 1885—d. New York, N.Y., June 17, 1962), head of the British intelligence unit in the U.S. during World War I."

England marked the centenary-plus-one of the birth of Kaiser Wilhelm II in 1960 with a remarkable British Broadcasting Corporation radio tribute to the man so universally villified two generations before. In it, the Kaiser was absolved from the charge of personal war guilt, and distinguished British peers, who had met him at the height of his power and during his post-war exile, testified to his abilities, integrity, and charm. Emphasis was placed on his love of England and his deep attachment to Queen Victoria, his grandmother. The program's narration stated that "Misfortune did not sour him. On the contrary, he died of old age without bitterness to those who had foully slandered him."[171] In a critical article based on the broadcast, British historian F.J.P. Veale wrote that the program "is both historically important and politically significant. It is noteworthy both for the facts which it disclosed and for the facts which it discreetly omitted to mention. Quite correctly it stated that the "Wicked Kaiser Myth" was believed without question in Great Britain for ten years after 1918, and that it is still widely believed by the ignorant. But it made no reference to the fact that this belief was the product of an officially inspired campaign of lies fabricated on an unprecedented scale.... Nevertheless this broadcast remains memorable because it demonstrates so strikingly what little reliance can be placed on the durability of even the most unanimous verdicts of contemporary opinion."[172]

If some of England's noblemen could forgive the Kaiser's supposed transgressions after so many years had passed, at least one still harbored the powerful myths of sole German guilt for the Great War. He was diplomat Sir Arthur Willert, who had contributed so mightily to the fiction as a propagandist. In a 1953 retrospective, Willert—exposing his deeply ingrained chauvinism—referred to Germany as "a congenital aggressor,"[173] to the war as "the Kaiser's,"[174] and to "the war upon freedom started by Germany in 1914."[175]

Chapter 3

THE GERMANS

In the two and a half years between the outbreak of war and the rupture between Germany and America the sums paid out from official funds for propaganda work in the Union ... did not, all told, exceed a million dollars. That is surely only a small fraction of what England and France have expended during the war in order, in spite of very thorough preparation in peace time, to win over American public opinion to their cause. ... The thirty-five to fifty million dollars which, according to the statements of our enemies, were swallowed up by German propaganda in the United States belong, therefore, to the realm of fable.

Johann von Bernstorff, *My Three Years in America*, 1920

If Kapitanleutnant Walther Schwieger was surprised that the tall, four-funneled passenger liner outlined in his periscope was not zigzagging, as would be expected of a British ship in submarine waters, there is no record of his taking the time to discuss the aberration. From the moment his pilot tentatively identified the target—either the *Mauretania* or her sister ship, the *Lusitania*—the captain of *Unterseeboot-20* had been concentrating on the course that would bring his slow-moving submarine into position to intercept the enemy.[1]

Since arriving at his assigned station two days before, close off the southern coast of Ireland in the busy Irish Channel that led to the giant port of Liverpool, the terminus for most of England's transatlantic traffic, Schwieger had sunk a small schooner and two large steamers. In the previous week *U-30*, operating in the same area, had also been successful, sinking five merchantmen and torpedoing, but not sinking, the U.S. tanker *Gulflight*. *U-20*'s patrol sector was a productive hunting ground for German submarines in the spring of 1915 and remained so throughout the war. The Royal Navy had been stunned by early U-boat successes against their men-of-war, in particular the sinking of three cruisers in less than two hours by a lone submarine the previous September, but remained blissfully unconcerned about their potential as commerce raiders.

It would be more than a year before the British Admiralty would seriously organize and deploy forces to fight what ultimately became the crucial naval battle of the war—that waged in the North Atlantic between German submarines and British merchant ships carrying food, weapons, and the raw materials needed to fuel the Allied engines of war.[2] Meanwhile, the western approaches to Queenstown in Ireland and north through St. George's Channel to Liverpool were patrolled by only a ragtag collection of obsolete navy ships, too few in number and commanded and manned by second-tier crews. England's principal naval concerns were on the other side of the British Isles, in the North Sea and the English Channel, where there was based its mighty Grand Fleet with modern warships and the best crews. The German *Hochseeflotte*, above all, had to be bottled up in its ports of Emden and Wilhelmshaven.[3] Of equal importance was escort duty for the streams of troop transports and hospital ships that shuttled back and forth across the English Channel, bringing fresh recruits and soldiers back from leave to the slaughter in the trenches in one direction, the seriously wounded and Tommies returning home for leave in the other.

The third day of *U-20's* patrol dawned foggy. The submarine cruised on the calm surface, charging batteries. Schwieger was making his way west and north, back to base. His fuel supply was approaching a critical level and he had only three torpedoes left. By late morning, the sun had begun to burn off the fog and visibility steadily improved.[4]

Schwieger's log reported the sighting by a lookout of a black smudge of smoke on the northeastern horizon at 1:20 P.M.[5] It rapidly grew into a large steamer that was steering toward Galley Head, one of the prominent headlands on the southern Irish coast used as a visual navigation reference point for ships in transit. *U-20* dove to periscope depth and began her fateful stalk. The log continued laconically, as might be expected from an experienced submarine commander: "2:35 P.M. The steamer turns starboard, takes a course to Queenstown and thus makes it possible a drawing near for the firing. Up to 3:00 P.M. ran at high speed in order to get a position up-front."

The *Lusitania* loomed like a black cliff in the reticle of Schwieger's periscope, less than half a mile away, cleaving the sea directly in front of *U-20*. Schwieger had made a perfect approach and could scarcely miss from the point-blank range. He wrote:

> 3:10 P.M. Pure bowshot at 700 metres range, G-torpedo 3 metres depth adjustment, angle of intersection 90°, estimated speed 22 knots. Shot strikes starboard side right behind the bridge. An unusually heavy explosion takes place with a very strong explosion cloud (cloud reaches far beyond front funnel). The explosion of the torpedo must have been followed by a second one (boiler or coal or powder?). The superstructure right above the point of impact and the bridge are torn asunder, fire breaks out, and smoke envelops the high bridge. The ship stops immediately and heels over to starboard very quickly, immersing simultaneously at the bow. It appears as if the ship were going to capsize very shortly. Great confusion ensues on board; the

R.M.S. *Lusitania*, in New York harbor, as the great Cunard liner departed for Liverpool on May 1, 1915, on her last voyage. Few knew she doubled as a munitions ship, carrying, in addition to her 1,959 passengers and crew, tons of small-arms ammunition and highly explosive fused shells. *National Archives.*

> boats are made clear and some of them are lowered to the water. In doing so great confusion must have reigned; some boats, full to capacity, are lowered, rushed from above, touch the water with either stem or stern first, and founder immediately. On the port side fewer boats are made clear than on the starboard side on account of the ship's list.

Schwieger continued to observe the mortally stricken liner through his periscope, and may have clicked off in his mind a series of impressions he had not detailed in his log. He may have established more precisely the spot where the torpedo struck, using the splintered No. 5 boat on the starboard as a reference. He had aimed more amidships, which meant the *Lusitania* had been steaming more slowly than estimated. Perhaps Schwieger was again surprised, for he knew that the *Lusitania* was capable of speeds better than 24 knots. Why had her captain not rung up maximum speed? "The ship blows off [steam]," he wrote in his log. "On the boat the name 'Lusitania' becomes visible in golden letters. The funnels were painted black, no flag was set astern. Ship was running 20 knots."

It could be expected that Schwieger knew of the secret British Admiralty order that their merchantmen fly a neutral's flag—an accepted *ruse de guerre*, and so ardently claimed by the English—when close to the British Isles, for a copy of these orders had fallen into the hands of the German navy. But it can be assumed that he had not known that on a recent eastbound passage of the *Lusitania*, a different master had run up the Stars and Stripes during his approach to Liverpool.[6]

Schwieger may not have noticed the rows of open portholes; those on the starboard side already underwater from the list were taking in hundreds of tons of seawater every minute. If he had, he would again have been shocked by yet another obvious breach of wartime seamanship by the well-respected naval enemy.[7]

The U-boat commander observed the confusion on the lifeboat deck of the sharply heeling ship and noted that the ship's lifeboats had been swung out on their davits, the only apparent acknowledgement by the *Lusitania*'s master of a submarine threat. If Schwieger had known, he might also have wondered why the ship's captain had held but one perfunctory lifeboat drill during the voyage—and that only for the mostly inexperienced crew. Schwieger probably also noted that many of the passengers in the few lifeboats being launched and those who were already in the water were either without lifejackets or had them on improperly. Was this because of panic—or was it, incredibly, the first time the passengers had tried to don them?

The log continued: "Since it seems as if the steamer will keep above water for only a short time, we dived to a depth of 24 metres and ran out to sea. It would have been impossible for me, anyhow, to fire a second torpedo into this crowd of people struggling to save their lives."[8]

Eighteen minutes after the torpedo had struck—and moments after the ship rolled ponderously to port as if trying to right herself—the bow of the 755-foot-long *Lusitania* struck the sea bottom some 300 feet below. Before the stern went under, the vessel rolled back to starboard and settled onto her starboard side on the ocean floor. Of the 1,959 passengers and crew aboard the ship when she had steamed majestically down the Hudson River and through the Narrows of New York harbor six days earlier, 1,198 were mutilated by the two explosions, trapped inside, or drowned. Among the dead were 128 American men, women, and children. The day was May 7, 1915.

As far as the U-boat captain was concerned, there was little more to be said of the *Lusitania* and he concluded his brief narrative by writing that "the wreck must lie off the Old Head of Kinsale, lighthouse bearing 358° true, 14 sea miles off in 90 metres of water. The shore and lighthouse are clearly seen."

Schwieger turned his submarine west and called up maximum underwater speed to avoid what he knew would be an avenging flotilla of patrol boats. When safely out of the area, he surfaced and shaped a course that would take *U-20* north past the Hebrides, northeast above the Shetlands, and then southeast into the North Sea and home, retracing his outward-bound voyage. He had earlier recorded in his log that he had elected to return the long way around the western side of Ireland, rather than take the shorter passage up through the Irish Sea and the narrow North Channel, where previously *U-20* had run into heavy patrol activity. Schwieger certainly would not attempt passage through the shortest route, the English Channel and the Straits of Dover, known to be infested with minefields and anti-submarine nets.

Schwieger first re-established radio contact with his base at Emden on May 12 as *U-20* entered the North Sea some 200 miles from the German coast, about the maximum range of submarine radios at that time. His message: "Have sunk one sailing vessel, two steamers, Lusitania." *U-20* received a prompt reply from the commander of the High Sea Fleet: "My highest appreciation of the commander and crew for success achieved of which *Hochseeflotte* is proud and my congratulation on their return." Schwieger later signaled that he had used only one torpedo to sink the liner, perhaps because he might still have been puzzled as to why his target had gone down so quickly. Finally, he was ordered to bring his submarine into port at Wilhelmshaven, not Emden.

All of these radio messages were promptly decoded by the British and used in their propaganda efforts to counter German foreign-office statements that the commander of *U-20* had acted contrary to orders—which he had not. The German Admiralty had issued a general declaration of a war zone around the British Isles effective February 18, 1915, and *U-20*'s captain had specific orders, when he left on war patrol on April 30, to attack "transport ships, merchant ships, warships." In addition Schwieger, like all U-boat commanders at that period of the war, was operating under general orders that gave him the discretion to sink ships that appeared to be neutral but which might be disguised enemy vessels. He had the authority to sink these latter ships with or without warning.[9]

In Germany, there was general satisfaction over Schwieger's skillful exploit, in the press, among prominent educators, and by ordinary civilians. On May 8, the prestigious *Berliner Tageblatt* reflected that there was "no one in Germany who does not with deepest regret learn of the fact that with the sinking of the *Lusitania* so many civilians were compelled to offer their lives as a sacrifice to the operations of the war. But, at the same time, one dare not for a single moment overlook the fact that they perished as a result of English pride and English irresponsibility as well their own indifference."[10]

Also on the eighth, the *Muenchner Neueste Nachrichten* referred to the newspaper warning that had appeared in American papers on the day the *Lusitania* sailed. Its editorial concluded that "if anything can add to the tragedy of the circumstances of these sacrifices, it is the fact that they were warned as no one had ever been before ... and they were deceived through the conscienceless effort of the English Admiralty, the English shipping interests. ... It is our opinion that it is no more than the simplest duty and responsibility of the American officials to support the warnings of the German ambassador ... against taking passage ... on ships of nations at war with Germany."[11]

One day later, the *Berliner Neueste Nachrichten* expressed less sorrow for the loss of life and a far more martial spirit, writing that "the torpedoing of the giant British liner *Lusitania* fills us with satisfaction in spite of the fact that it brings to mind the gruesome fate of the *Titanic*. Now finally, the firm of Wilson and Grey will realize that we will no longer be deterred by anything and are determined to go on in full, bloody earnestness. An Anglo-Saxon newspaper claims that now Woodrow Wilson must act since so many citizens of free America have found a watery grave. Should he crave action with us, just let him begin."[12]

Der Lusitania-Fall, a collection of German public opinion concerning the sinking of the *Lusitania* was published later in 1915, and focused on reactions of German college professors. Many recorded their views that the liner was an auxiliary cruiser of the Royal Navy and, therefore, armed or not, she could legitimately be sunk without warning.[13]

Mary Heaton Vorse, an American journalist, was in Germany immediately after the sinking of the *Lusitania*. She overheard conversations like the following, in a German cafe:

> "As for me," said one woman, "I have no pity for those people on the *Lusitania* at all. Why should they travel on a munitions ship? People who travel on munitions ships must expect to be blown up."
> … A tall man with jowls and huge mustaches joined the group, wiping his mouth. "Well, they blew up the *Lusitania*," he said cheerily, "a good job. Our U-boat commanders are keen fellows." Everybody nodded and murmured approval.
> … From the north to the south, I heard not one word of pity or mercy to the victims of the *Lusitania*. People repeated over and over, "Well, it serves them right! Traveling on a munitions ship."[14]

The German ambassador to the United States, Count Johann von Bernstorff, recorded that he learned of the fateful assassinations in Sarajevo while dining at the elite Metropolitan Club in Washington on June 28, 1914. While von Bernstorff considered the incident "very serious" and "peace-menacing,"[15] he nevertheless did not change his summer vacation plans, and left on schedule for Germany the following week.

Von Bernstorff had been ambassador since 1908, following the untimely death of his predecessor, Baron Hermann Speck von Sternburg. Von Sternburg's tour of duty had been marked by warm ties with President Theodore Roosevelt. He had become a member of Roosevelt's intimate "tennis cabinet," clambered over Washington's rugged Rock Creek Park with the vigorous chief executive, and affectionately called the president Teddy. Roosevelt, in turn, called him Specky. Von Sternburg had overseen the establishment of exchange professorships at the leading universities of both countries, glowed with pride as his wife formally unveiled in Washington a statue of Frederick the Great sent by the kaiser,[16] and presided over other goodwill gestures that seemed to

Count Johann von Bernstorff (hat in hand), Germany's ambassador to the United States, en route to Europe after being given his passports in February 1917. Von Bernstorff worked diligently to keep America out of the war, but could not prevent his country's resumption of unrestricted submarine warfare, the proximate cause for America's entry into the war. *National Archives.*

presage ever more cordial relations between Imperial Germany and the United States.

Like von Sternburg, von Bernstorff had an American wife, spoke English flawlessly, and understood Americans and America. He averred that poker was his card game and baseball, the quintessential American pastime, his favorite spectator sport. Indeed, von Bernstorff, like von Sternburg before him, represented a new breed of young, modern German minister, appointed to his post not only to negotiate treaties but to project a benign, friendly image of his increasingly powerful country. Von Bernstorff was tall and thin, always immaculately groomed, careful to appear at all times like the aristocrat he was. He was descended from a distinguished Saxon family, and his father had been Prussia's ambassador to England when von Bernstorff was born in London in 1862.

Von Bernstorff, who had been consul-general in Egypt when he was named ambassador, recalled an enthusiastic send-off by the Kaiser. He wrote that the Kaiser had talked animatedly about America and "more especially regarding his friend Theodore Roosevelt," who would later deeply disappoint him. The new ambassador was told to emulate his predecessor "and travel about a great deal" in the United States, and to "make myself at home in all circles of American society."[17]

Missionary work by Germany to improve the generally cool relations between the two governments had begun much earlier. From a friendly attitude toward Germany during the Franco-Prussian War of 1870–71, in which Germany was believed to have fought defensively against the attacking French, American public opinion had turned hostile following three diplomatic incidents. The friction began in the Samoan Islands in the Pacific in the late 1880s. There, a drawn-out dispute over control of the islands, pitting U.S. colonial interests against those of Germany (and of England, as well), was interpreted in America as evidence of Germany's frantic imperialistic drive.

Then, in 1898, the public accepted as fact the report that a German naval squadron in the Philippines, commanded by Vice-Admiral Otto von Diederichs, had interfered with the American fleet following Admiral George Dewey's victory over the Spaniards. According to one source, "during the whole period of the Spanish-American War, American sentiment was unanimous in its criticism of Germany's policy and methods of action at Manila. Never had the United States and Germany come so near the severance of diplomatic relations as during the Dewey-Diederichs episode."[18] The British, who also had a fleet in Manila Bay at the time, took advantage of the propaganda opportunities that arose from the American-German dispute to influence U.S. public opinion. Another interpreter of the incident wrote that "Diederichs repeatedly complained that Captain Chichester [commander of the Royal Navy squadron in the Philippines] and other British officers, as well as the British consul, were circulating vicious anti–German rumors and that the English newspapers of Eastern Asia picked up these reports and embroidered them."[19] These colored newspaper accounts, which were corroborated by Hong Kong–based U.S. Vice-Admiral E.H. Seymour, found their way into the American press. Important British newspapers subsequently kept up the anti–German drumbeat by reprinting German newspaper articles critical of American actions in Manila. This practice became so pervasive that the U.S. ambassador to Germany, Andrew D. White, reported that British newspapers and news agencies were prepared to publish "everything which could arouse prejudice in the United States against Germany, and that one of them, on at least one occasion, resorted to the invention of fictitious news for this purpose."[20]

The last serious diplomatic event came in 1902. When Germany (and Great Britain) tried to collect legitimate debts from Venezuela by threatening military action, President Roosevelt sternly warned Germany against such reprisals, which he considered infringement of America's Monroe Doctrine.

Germany's next step, according to those Americans who put stock in the noisy declarations of Germany's militant Pan-German League, would be the founding of colonies in South America and a direct threat to the economic and military security of the United States.

Through no fault of his own, Ambassador von Bernstorff was unable to sustain close personal ties with Roosevelt's two successors. With William Howard Taft, his relations were formal, although there were two instances when Taft let diplomatic custom go by the board: when he invited von Bernstorff to join him in his Pullman on a trip to his home in Ohio, and when the president appeared unexpectedly at the German Embassy, where a ball was being held in honor of his daughter.

Like nearly all political officeholders, U.S. and foreign, the German ambassador was able to maintain only narrowly prescribed contacts with the circumspect Woodrow Wilson.[21] Von Bernstorff focused his energies elsewhere. As an ambassador, he had a seat in the diplomatic gallery of the House and the Senate, and he established steady, friendly contacts with those congressmen and their appointees who hailed from sections of the country with large German-American voting blocs. His charm and impeccable demeanor assured him invitations to Washington's most important social events. By 1914, many in the nation's capital considered von Bernstorff the dean of the foreign diplomatic corps. He was not only welcome within the State Department, but respected and well liked by his peers, and sought out by the press. Eight American colleges awarded honorary degrees to the popular German minister.

Secretary of State Robert Lansing later recalled that

> Count Johann von Bernstorff, the German Ambassador, was a man of marked ability, and in all my intercourse with him I found him an affable though dangerous antagonist. He was a master of the art of diplomacy and concealed his thoughts and feeling with great skill. I felt that it was always necessary to be on my guard in talking with him and to be extremely cautious in whatever I said because I knew he would take advantage of the least slip of the tongue and utilize it later. With him it was always a duel of wits. …I never really trusted him. I knew that he plotted to cause a break between the President and me. I felt he was sly and exceptionally clever, that he would go to any lengths to gain his end. Take it all together Count von Bernstorff was a dangerous man and required constant watching.[22]

After war broke out, and particularly following the sinking of the *Lusitania* when the threat of war between the United States and Germany loomed large, the German ambassador worked tirelessly in Washington to maintain diplomatic relations between the two countries. He understood far better than anyone in the *Wilhelmstrasse* that Germany's resumption of unrestricted submarine warfare meant war with America, and insistently communicated his concerns to Berlin.[23] Most of all, von Bernstorff strove to support initiatives, both American and German, for a negotiated settlement of the conflict, for he had come to believe that otherwise Germany was certain to lose the war. He later wrote that before the war "no one in Germany had thought it possible that the Union would have to be reckoned with as a factor, much less a decisive factor in a European war."[24]

In Berlin in the first week of August 1914, von Bernstorff was hurriedly briefed by the Foreign Office and, presumably, by the espionage bureaus as well. He was "to enlighten the Government and people of the United States on the German standpoint,"[25] a mission scarcely different from the one he had been assigned in 1908. This time, however, the stakes were incomparably higher. He would now wear two hats for Imperial Germany: principal diplomat in Washington and nominal head of a propaganda organization he was charged to build in the United States. Von Bernstorff was assigned additional staff for his embassy and ordered to return to Washington as soon as possible.

Unlike England's propaganda effort, with its London-based Wellington House directorate, Germany's propaganda campaign aimed at Americans relied mainly on a small, informal, but well-financed organization that von Bernstorff set up in New York City. There was also no Reich equivalent of Great Britain's ultranationalist newspaper tycoon, Lord Northcliffe, to organize and fund a supplementary, personal propaganda organization. While German propaganda work would be done in the hustings through direct-mail, pamphlets, books, motion pictures, and speakers, the main thrust was to try to tell Germany's side of the story to the "great New York newspapers" that had such a powerful influence on national public opinion.

Von Bernstorff wrote retrospectively that

> it was naturally to be expected that public opinion in the United States would be overwhelmingly on the side of the Entente. This was indeed the case, to an unexpected extent, as a result of the violation of Belgian neutrality. ... The German-Americans asked for no more than unconditional neutrality. This was also the aim of German policy through its representatives in America. We never hoped for more.[26]

Not all of the cards were stacked against Germany. There was, first of all, a substantial population of German Americans, nearly 10 percent of the nation's total, by far the largest non–English ethnic minority. The U.S. Census of 1910 listed 8,262,618 people in the United States who had checked off Germany as their country of origin. Some two and a half million of these had been born in Germany, and nearly four million were born in the United States of parents born in Germany. There were influential German-American populations in many of the country's biggest cities—in New York and in the Midwest, in such cities as Chicago, Cincinnati, Cleveland, Columbus, Dayton, Des Moines, Milwaukee, and St. Louis. When the European war began, these German-Americans, many well educated and affluent, firmly backed the

German cause. One observer wrote, "Blood ties, and sympathies grounded in a perfectly natural emotional basis, determined the policies and affected the thinking of the majority of German-Americans."[27]

The most well-respected of this pro–German element in the United States at the start of the war was a tiny handful of distinguished university professors who had been born or educated in Germany, had traveled there, or who had otherwise come to respect German *Kultur*. Chief among them were Hugo Muensterberg and Edmund von Mach, both at Harvard, the nation's most prestigious university, and John William Burgess of Columbia University.

Muensterberg a Berlin native, at Harvard since 1902, had been an exchange professor at the University of Berlin. By 1914, Muensterberg had already written 15 books on psychology and history that had been published in America, starting in 1899. The *New York Times* considered his views on the war important enough to give him a full news column in the issue of Sunday, August 9: "SAYS CRISIS FORCED KAISER TO FIGHT; His Duty Required It, Asserts Muensterberg, Who Holds Russia Responsible. APPEALS FOR FAIR PLAY; Calls It Primarily a 'Moral Conflict' Where Slavs and Germans Confront Each Other."

In *The War and America*, which he published soon after the outbreak of the war, Muensterberg argued that the Russians were the villains. He wrote that the war was between Russian barbarism and Western culture, specifically German *Kultur*, and that Germany was serving the cause of humanity by fighting Russia. He pointed out that France wanted Alsace and Lorraine and England coveted the German African colonies. He predicted that the next great war would be between Russia and England, with Japan on the side of Russia. Japan, Russia, and Mexico would attack the United States. England, Germany, and the United States, therefore, should unite.

Muensterberg understood the new role of propaganda. He wrote:

> The first days the newspapers were filled with cablegrams from Germany's foes. Incredible rumors of German atrocities, highly-colored reports of Germany's evil intentions, falsehoods about the German people and the German leaders, were thrown into the editorial offices from the English cables. The Germans had no chance. ...This at once gave to public opinion a vivid impulse against Germany, and this first impulse of the crowd worked havoc in the editorial rooms. The average American reader has no idea how much anti–German feeling is infused into the so-called facts which are sent over the ocean. He sees that the news is dated from Vienna or Berlin and he does not know that most of the American correspondents on the continent for many years have been Englishmen who never saw America.[28]

Muensterberg also used his prestige to communicate directly with the president. In November 1914, he wrote to Wilson complaining about the obvious skew of U.S. foreign policy to the detriment of Germany. He heavy-handedly pointed to the "submission of the administration to England's wishes" and "interpretations and decisions which help the Allies only," and he threatened that the large, influential, and traditionally Democratic "German, Swedish, Jewish and Irish vote" might well desert the party in future elections.[29]

The politician and scholar in Wilson took Muensterberg's charges seriously. He immediately asked for clarification: "I have received and read with a great deal of surprise your letter. Certainly no administration ever tried more diligently or watchfully to preserve an attitude and pursue a line of conduct absolutely neutral. I would consider it a favor if you would point out to me what are considered the unneutral acts of which this administration is thought to have been guilty."[30]

The Harvard professor responded with another persuasively critical letter, adding further details and giving former history professor Wilson the German viewpoint:

> All cables sent by and received by wire pass uncensored, while all wireless news is censored. ...The policy of the administration with regard to the holding up, detaining and searching of Germans and Austrians from neutral and American vessels is a reversal of the American policy established in 1812. ...The United States permits the violation by England of the Hague Convention and international law in connection with conditional and unconditional contraband. ... Many of the complaints refer more to the unfriendly spirit than to the actual violation of the law.[31]

Muensterberg's second letter obviously impressed the president, for he sent it along to State Department counselor Robert Lansing asking him for "a memorandum ... of the answers and comments that might be made upon his statements. Here at last is a very definite summing up of the matters upon which German anti-administration feeling in this country is being built up, and perhaps it would be wise to take very serious note of it. The case they make out is *prima facie* very plausible indeed."[32] On December 9, Lansing replied at length, hitting out at both Muensterberg and Bernhard Dernburg, Germany's unofficial propaganda spokesman, for what he considered to be interference in the foreign affairs of the United States. Lansing wrote:

> Muensterberg is a German subject. [In fact, he was a naturalized U.S. citizen] ... These two foreign writers have severely criticized this government's conduct of its foreign affairs, have made charges unfounded in fact or in law, have distorted the truth, and have bitterly assailed the President and the Department of State for alleged injustice to Germany and undue friendliness for the cause of the Allies. In pursuing this campaign of misrepresentation and vilification they have done so by means of addresses and publications which have been widely circulated throughout the country relying upon the freedom of speech and of the press guaranteed to the people by the Constitution.[33]

Lansing then refuted item-by-item Muensterberg's charges of U.S. favoritism. In his transmittal letter, he urged against a presidential reply to Muensterberg, whom he called a German agent. To do so, he cautioned, would give him and his government unwarranted credibility. Wilson followed Lansing's recommendation and let the matter drop.

Von Mach, like Muensterberg a naturalized U.S. citizen, began his pro-German propaganda work with a series of 30 weekly articles for the *Boston Evening Transcript*, one every Wednesday from October 14, 1914, to May 5, 1915. His columns were billed as "The German Viewpoint." Until the *Lusitania* was sunk—and "the German viewpoint" was no longer credible—von Mach reported that there was no pressure on him "to lessen his freedom of expression" and that his articles were printed "as he had written them."[34]

After the loss of his newspaper forum on May 7, 1915, von Mach collected his articles in book form, under the title *Germany's Point of View*. The purpose of the book, according to its author, was "to go to the root of things, and to explain, if possible, why those who had not lost faith in Germany differed from many of their fellow citizens in their interpretation of the relative merits of the causes of the several belligerents."[35] He admitted that there was a prejudice against Germany because of her rapid rise as a world power, with a huge army and a fast-growing navy, but argued that militarism was not so serious in Germany as in France or Russia—or as England's navalism. Germany wished for no new territory and no unwilling citizens. She wanted to develop her colonies and her home commerce to meet the needs of a fast-growing population.

The book's 32 chapters covered such subjects as the neutrality of Belgium, the German constitution, Alsace and Lorraine, the French *Yellow Book* (three chapters), Germany's food supply, the German army, English "calumny," and Sir Edward Grey (also three chapters). Like Muensterberg's, von Mach's book was a reasoned, unemotional analysis of the war, intended to appeal to educated, informed Americans.

Von Mach's magnum opus was his 1,200-page *Official Diplomatic Documents Relating to the Outbreak of the European War*, published in 1916. It contained, among its other materials, photographic reproductions of official editions of the government documents published by Austria-Hungary, Belgium, France, Germany, Great Britain, Russia, and Serbia. Von Mach tried to establish his credibility as an objective historian in the book's Introduction, where he discussed government "collected documents":

> In Great Britain these documents are often printed on large sheets of white paper, loosely bound, called "White Papers." If the documents are very important, they are later reprinted in pamphlet form, and are then called by the color of their cover, "Blue Books."
>
> In America the British Blue Book won the greatest favor, not only because it became known first but also because of its inherent worth. Its dispatches

are well written, and sufficiently numerous to tell a consecutive story. The book is well printed, provided with indexes and cross references, and represents the most scholarly work done by any of the European Governments.

The German White Book, on the other hand, contains few dispatches, and these only as illustrations of points made in an exhaustive argument. Such a presentation can be convincing only if one has confidence in the honesty of the author. There can be no doubt that as a source book for study the British Parliamentary Papers are superior to the German Papers....[36]

If von Mach sometimes feigned objectivity, the views of John William Burgess were never below the surface; the Columbia professor indulged his anti–British animosities with zeal. Burgess had been educated in Germany and claimed he knew Heinrich von Treitschke intimately. Burgess recalled in his memoir that during the summer of 1871 he had taken time off from his studies to watch the victorious German army make its triumphal entrance into Berlin. He wrote that "it was the most magnificent manifestation of power which the world had ever furnished. I had never seen the march of the Grand Army of the Republic through Washington six years before, and in me, as an American who had taken part in the battle for the Union, this roused far deeper feeling; but as a manifestation of power, I had never and have never, seen anything to equal this march of the victorious Germany army."[37]

His antagonism toward what he considered Great Britain's hypocritical pretenses went back at least as far as 1887. He recalled then visiting one of England's "magnificent ducal estates" and discussing the British economic system with his host and agreeing that one pillar of Great Britain's strength was its free trade between her colonies and other countries, because there was no manufacturing and commercial competitor. But suppose some successful competitor should arise? "We should have to shut them out by law or destroy them by force," was the frank reply by the landlord, Burgess wrote.[38]

In 1897, according to Burgess, there was little indication of war between America and any other country in the world. "But soon, stories of Spanish atrocities in Cuba began to be circulated in the United States, and the shrewd observer" had enough evidence "that the British trick of atrocity invention was in the game and that ... Great Britain was desirous of involving the United States in a war with Spain or some other power, ... We knew the potency of this weapon in British hands, and we knew that if the British statesmen had resolved to create a war between the United States and some European power they would find it no difficult task."[39]

Burgess was subsequently honored as the first exchange professor between the United States and Germany, inaugurating the Roosevelt professorship at the University of Berlin in 1906. The Kaiser who was intimately involved in all phases of the U.S.-German educational program and even attended lectures given by his scholarly American guests, later conferred upon him the prestigious Order of the Prussian Crown.

By 1914, Burgess was universally recognized as the nation's leading political scientist. His credentials were impeccable: Ph.D., J.U.D., LL.D., former professor of constitutional and international law, dean of the faculties of Political Science, Philosophy, and Pure Science, and founder of the School of Political Science, all at Columbia University. His *Political Science and Comparative Constitutional Law*, published in 1890, was a well-respected scholarly work that justified America's and the Teutonic races' "manifest destiny" based on their superior talent for government.

Burgess needed little incentive to pick up his anti–British cudgel once the war broke out in 1914. He wrote strongly worded articles for newspapers and magazines, lectured often, and published two books, *The European War of 1914* and *America's Relations to the Great War*. In the first, Burgess lamented the wave of anti–German hysteria in the United States and erroneously prophesied that it was bound to disappear, for "who is so blind as not to perceive at a glance that the united triumph of the Autocrat of the Land and the Autocrat of the Sea means their domination of the world, and what have the Germans ever done to us to deserve abuse at our hands?"[40] He listed the proximate cause of the war as English ambition in the East, with the ultimate causes to be found in the deep contrast between Germany and England. The entire system of England was aristocratic and based on the exploitation of colonies, according to Burgess, while Germany was truly democratic, without a poor and suppressed lower class. German militarism was no threat to the United States, he insisted, while English navalism, as in the past, was a perpetual menace.

The final chapter, "The German Emperor," which had earlier been published on the editorial page of the *New York Times*, was an attempt to counteract "the monumental caricature of biographical literature" in the United States "concerning the physical, mental, and moral make-up" of the Kaiser. Burgess said he had known Wilhelm II for nearly ten years and had observed him in many different situations, "at Court and State functions, at university ceremonies and celebrations, at his table, and by his fireside surrounded by his family, when in the midst of his officials, his men of science, and personal friends, and, more instructive than all, alone in the imperial home in Berlin and Potsdam and in the castle and forest at Wilhelmshohe." As for his appearance, "the Emperor is an impressive man physically. ... I saw him once seated beside his uncle, King Edward VII and the contrast was very striking, and greatly in his favor." The Kaiser "is also an exceedingly intelligent and highly cultivated man" and "always appeared to me most deeply concerned with the arts of peace."[41]

The second war book Burgess wrote focused on what he correctly interpreted as American hypocrisy: that in fact, if not in law, America was not neutral. As far as he was concerned, "Germany's submarine program was entirely legal and proper when tested by the requirements of the *lex talionis*, a well established branch of international law." As for Britain's declaration closing the North Sea, the U.S. government's protest, "or rather remonstrance ... is a document not calculated to fan American pride into a consuming flame. Its flattery of Great Britain is without foundation in truth, and passes the limit between courtesy and servility. Its cry for relief is a wail of weakness."[42]

The German propagandists dug as deeply as they could into their limited resources of authors of repute, especially those without German-sounding names, to write books espousing the German cause. One they came up with, Frank Harris, the controversial and much-traveled Irish-born journalist, playwright, biographer, novelist, and writer of erotica, probably should have been left to his own devices. His 1915 treatise, *England or Germany?* was so filled with a jumble of loose "facts" and the author's heavy-handed prejudices against England that it was apparent to any reader, with or without a comprehensive understanding of modern European history, which side had paid for his services.

Harris drew chiefly on his creative writing talents. He told his readers that he had spent nearly 25 years in England and only five in Germany, and, therefore, could be objective. Harris purposefully spared no sacred cow, ludicrously writing that

> many years ago, the late Cecil Rhodes told me of his intention to bring University students from all the colonies and from America and Germany to Oxford. I could not help laughing, the scheme seemed to me fanstasically absurd. Fancy bringing real University students down to a high-school like Oxford. ... "No, no, Rhodes," I cried, "if you want to do good, send hundreds of English students from Oxford and Cambridge each year to some German university, and come to think of it, you might send a hundred members of Parliament, too, and half a dozen Ministers. Then, indeed, you might in time help to achieve the impossible and make of England a modern state.[43]

A *New York Times* book review of May 30, 1915, properly concluded that "Mr. Harris seems to have had no good reason for this publication."

By far the best—and most objective—of all the German-financed propaganda books was Edwin J. Clapp's scholarly, thoroughly documented *Economic Aspects of the War: Neutral Rights, Belligerent Claims, and American Commerce in the Years 1914–1915*. Clapp was an American economics professor at New York University. His lectures on England's interference with American commerce had attracted the attention of Heinrich Albert, one of the principal German propagandists in the United States. Albert paid Clapp $3,750 to write *Economic Aspects of the War*, which was based on his college lectures, and then gave him an additional $11,500 to print 7,500 copies and $4,000 more to promote sales of the book.[44]

As a vigorous defender of American rights as a neutral and of the sanctity of international law, Clapp was not reluctant to call down a plague on the houses of both belligerents: "London announced that vessels carrying cargoes to and from Germany ... would be subject to seizure. This was the culmination of the British lawlessness. The culmination of the German lawlessness was the *Lusitania* horror."[45] He also upheld the U.S. sale of munitions to the Allies, stating that Germany had sold arms to belligerents in the past, and the Krupps had grown rich as a result.

Clapp levelled his most powerful broadsides at the British. America must assert its rights and immediately put a stop to England's illegal detention of its cargoes, he contended. It was in America's power, and he insisted it was her duty, to restore international law on behalf of the neutral world. He wrote: "When both belligerents are breaking the law and each is claiming the acts of the other as justification, the pressure of neutrals must be applied to the one which refuses to join in a return to law and order. Our problem is to compel that joint acceptance of a compromise which we proposed in our note to the belligerents in February. Germany is ready for acceptance; the pressure must be applied to England."[46]

There is much useful information on one of the most fundamental aspects of World War I in Clapp's fact-filled book. Unfortunately, the author's close association with the German cause marred the credibility of his work in the immediate postwar years. Clapp's name surfaced in July 1918 during the Federal government's well-publicized investigation of the purchase of the *New York Evening Mail* in 1915 by the German government. He acknowledged that he had been the writer of many of the *Mail's* strongly anti–British editorials before the U.S. entered the war, but denied that he had known of the paper's financial ties to Germany.

A dynamic and thriving German-language press in the United States served the nation's German-literate population. There were daily and weekly newspapers, trade and professional magazines, religious publications, and German-society papers of all kinds. A comprehensive study of the history of German-language newspapers and periodicals in the United States lists a grand total of about 5,000 such publications (which came and went), beginning with the first issue of the first German-American newspaper, the Philadelphia *Zeitung*, on May 6, 1732.[47]

In August 1914, the German-reading population of New York City had its choice on newsstands of no fewer than eight dailies, five weeklies, two Sunday papers, and one semi-monthly. Wisconsin—with the biggest German-language press of any state in the Union—had 89 daily and weekly newspapers published in German for its German-Americans.[48]

In the early months of the war, there was rapid growth in circulation and revenues of all the German-language press, which paralleled that of American newspapers in general. The *New Yorker Staats–Zeitung* was America's leading German-language newspaper. Over 80 years old at the outbreak of the war, it had been in financial difficulties and had been considering changing to the English language before its wartime revival. The Chicago *Abendpost* had the largest circulation of the German newspapers in the Middle West.

The major editorial focus of these newspapers before August 1914 had been two perceived threats to the German-American way of life: prohibition and woman suffrage. Once the war was underway, these papers, while continuing their anti-dry and anti-suffrage drumbeats, overnight embraced another cause—the fatherland's. Almost without exception, they accepted and staunchly defended the German government's official explanations of the origins of the war and its progress. Furthermore, because nearly every English-language newspaper in the country was seen to be in the Allied camp, the German-language press was doubly impelled to present the German side. Neither subsidies nor bribes from the German propagandists, as were later alleged, were required to spur on their support.

Nevertheless, the propaganda value to Germany of the strongly supportive German-language press in the United States can be considered to have been minimal, for the papers went to the wrong people. Those who could read German already inclined toward the cause of their native land. Almost none of America's uncommitted could read German. Some of the German-language newspapers, recognizing this, began to print their more important articles in English, urging their regular readers to pass along the paper to their English-speaking friends.

The Lutheran church in America, with about 6,000 congregations across the country, also bound together Americans of German descent. Many of these churches conducted their services in German for their German-American congregants, and their German-trained pastors were outspoken in their support of the German cause. One such pastor, addressing his congregation in the name of his synod, presumably echoed the views of a majority of his fellow German church leaders when he said,

> We should no longer look as silent spectators on the conflict of political truth and social righteousness, but enter the arena in full sight of friend and foe, and with the talents which we possess serve the bold champions of the German cause as well as we are able. Too long already have we ... lain inactively in well-protected trenches as little more than passive spectators of the conflict .... Heretofore our efforts at reform were confined to the tranquillity of the church and the limited circle of the congregation. But from now on we propose to help in shedding the rays of German truthfulness, German honor, and German loyalty, among the masses as far as we are able.[49]

By far the most dominant unifying force for German-Americans, however, was the National German-American Alliance. Founded in 1901, and chartered by Congress in 1907, by 1914 the organization boasted more than two million members and branches in 40 states. It was the largest ethnic organization of its kind in American history.

Membership in the Alliance was limited to U.S. citizens, for a principal objective of the organization was to promptly make citizens of newly arrived German immigrants and thus be able to rally an enfranchised constituency in support of its goals. The programs of the Alliance, like those of other ethnic groups, were mainly cultural: promoting the study of the native language and emphasizing the home country's contributions to the history of the United States in the nation's public schools. The German-American Alliance expected that the new citizens would take an active interest in community as well as national affairs, and would "practice their civic duty, with regard to the ballot box, fearlessly and according to their own consciences." These new citizens would also pursue, according to the organization's constitution, such "aspirations and interests as are not inconsistent with the general weal of the country and the rights and duties of good citizens; for the protection of the German element against 'natavistic attacks'; and for the promotion of sound, amicable relations between Americans and the old German fatherland."[50]

"Natavistic attacks" could be read as assaults by prohibitionists and woman suffragists—for, in fact, these twin demons were the Alliance's raison d'être. Germans in the United States had always vigorously opposed the concept of prohibition. As far as German-Americans were concerned, the Woman's Christian Temperance Union, the Prohibition Party, and the militant Anti-Saloon League were attacking their social customs and their rights as Americans—literally, their heritage.

In 1900, when the Prohibition Party began an aggressive campaign against alcohol, it found an ally in the woman suffrage movement—and German-Americans had another target at which to focus their fury. Rigidly patriarchal German-Americans believed that the woman's place was in the home and not in the voting booth. If prohibition was directed against the rights of the individual, then woman suffrage represented an attack against the very foundations of traditional German concepts of the family organization.

In the same camp with the German-American Alliance were the wealthy American brewers, nearly all of German extraction. These big businessmen saw clearly the specter of an alcohol-free America and worked assiduously, both overtly and covertly—and unsuccessfully, as it turned out—to overturn the prohibitionists' bandwagon.[51] In 1913, for example, a brewers' and liquor dealers' group, hiding behind an organization called the National Association of Commerce and Labor, contributed $12,000 to the Alliance. These funds were used to prepare and distribute anti-prohibition literature and to pay expenses for speakers who would rail against prohibition. A lobbying committee was also set up in Washington, its funds coming from the brewers.

At the outbreak of war, the Alliance, wholeheartedly behind the cause of the fatherland, supported the German propaganda effort in every way possible. The Alliance published propaganda pamphlets and distributed them free, sponsored speakers from Germany, and held rallies to oppose arms shipments to the Allies. The Alliance funded the speaking tour of Dr. Eugen Kuehnemann, noted exchange professor from Breslau University, who "traveled over 107,600 miles in the United States, spoke in 137 cities in 34 states and the District of Columbia, and gave 121 speeches in English and 275 in German, and was heard by about 213,580 people."[52] During the presidential election campaign in 1915, the German-American Alliance strongly campaigned for Wilson's opponent, Republican Charles Evans Hughes. The defeat of Hughes was a serious blow to the prestige of the Alliance. Once America was into the war, the Alliance's days were obviously numbered.

In January 1918, Senator William Henry King introduced a bill to repeal the Alliance's charter, and a subcommittee of the Senate Committee on the Judiciary was appointed to look into the wartime activities of the organization. Hearings were conducted between February and April 1918, with a supporting commentary in the press reflecting the anti–German attitudes expressed in the hearing room. Theodore Roosevelt, for example, in a speech delivered to the Republican State Convention of Maine, offered his particular views of loyalty as the investigation was winding down. He bellowed, "Men of German blood who have tried to be both Germans and Americans are not Americans at all, but traitors to America and tools and servants of Germany against America. Organizations like the German-American Alliance have served Germany against America. Hereafter we must see that the melting pot really does not melt. There should be but one language in this country—English."[53]

On July 2, 1918, the Congress unanimously voted to repeal the act of 1907 which had granted the Alliance's charter. This officially put the National German-American Alliance out of business.

From the start of the war, much of Germany's propaganda in the United States was counter propaganda. The Germans were forced into a defensive, reactive approach to the avalanche of propaganda themes of the British. Two principal issues that had to be addressed immediately were Germany's violation of Belgium's borders and its chancellor's careless reference to an 1839 Belgian neutrality treaty as a "scrap of paper."[54] The Germans first tried to rationalize their invasion of "perpetually neutral" Belgium by offering proof that by August 1914 the Belgians had already violated the spirit of the treaty by fortifying the Belgian-German border, but not the Belgian-French border, and that both England and France had conspired with Belgium for this purpose. After they entered Brussels in September, the Germans were able to flaunt captured government documents that revealed secret pre–1914 military understandings between Belgium and England.[55]

Also to be addressed were the German army's hostage taking and shooting of civilians in Belgium, the supposedly wanton destruction of property during the early fighting in that country, and militant pan–German themes, such as those expounded by the jingo ex-general Friedrich von Bernhardi in his book *Germany and the Next War.*[56] And soon would come the enormous German "atrocity" burdens of the *Lusitania*, the Bryce Report, and nurse Edith Cavell.

The German propagandists also had to contend with the lurid and exaggerated picture, painted by some anti–German American authors, of a colossal scheme, hatched by the superpatriotic Pan-German League and financed by the Imperial German government, for world domination by Germany and her allies. According to such Germanophobes, pan–Germanism was more than simply that country's brand of chauvinism, but a dangerous cult unique to Germany, combining imperialism, militarism, and nationalism.

A leader among these critics of Germany was U.S. history professor Roland G. Usher. His *Pan-Germanism*, published in 1913, became the bible of America's anti–German disciples. To the uncritical reader, the book appeared to be a scholarly work. It was, however, filled with generalities and scantily supported statements; there were practically no references, nor even an index. But Usher was a persuasive writer. As a friendly reviewer in the *New York Times* of March 16, 1913, wrote "of his remarkable study," Usher "examines [Pan-Germanism] with great care, patience, and acuteness." Sprinkled throughout, however, were the anti–German polemics that became so popular in the United States once the war broke out. Usher wrote that the Germans aimed "at nothing less than the domination of Europe and of the world," that the vital factor in the international situation was "the aggression of Germany," and that pan–Germanism was "an offensive movement directed against England, its object, the conquest of the English possessions in the Mediterranean and in Asia."[57]

Usher was an early discoverer of von Bernhardi, "a man whose undoubted attainments and learning compel the respect of his enemies, and whose following in Germany is large in numbers and influential in character."[58] Usher correctly referred to von Bernhardi's book as "undoubtedly, the baldest and frankest statements of Germany's 'rights' to be found." More important, Usher betrayed his extreme British bias to anyone who had not already reached such a conclusion when he listed the *Fortnightly Review*, by nearly every objective measure one of the most rabidly anti–German periodicals in all of England, as the source for the "best statements in English" on the subject "during the last two or three years ... some of which are certainly semi-official."[59]

The Pan-German League was, indeed, a strident and noisy jingo group, intent on spreading its gospel of German cultural and racial superiority. It had a long and specific agenda.[60] Like similar organizations in other countries, its demands were certain to come into conflict with the interests and beliefs of other nations. However, the Pan-German League's supposed impact on political decision making at home and reports of its vast overseas propaganda efforts were wild exaggerations. There is no evidence that the League broadcast "millions of pamphlets" in numerous foreign languages, nor did there ever exist a "great Pan-German plan" by which German influence should be spread from Hamburg to the Persian Gulf.

To a lesser degree, the British were also involved in counterpropaganda, monitoring the propaganda activities of their enemies so as to be able to react effectively. In 1917, before America entered the war, a secret report was completed by the British War Office's intelligence division. It was written by Peter Chalmers Mitchell and covered German propaganda worldwide. Mitchell claimed that he had studied "between two and three thousand books and pamphlets of Enemy origin" and had compiled "the most condensed and comprehensive summary of German War-Literature."[61] He summed up the four principal themes developed by "the more serious [German] propagandists" and candidly assessed their impact on Americans:

> 1. Contrast between the strong and peaceful progress of Germany as compared with the violent methods of her adversaries—This form of propaganda has undoubtedly been effective. It is plain there has been much that was violent, aggressive and oppressive in the past history of England, France and Russia. It should be pointed out, however, in forms suitable for all classes of readers, that Germany, although a late arrival in the field, has done her best to make up for lost time. 2. Germany poses to America as engaged entirely in self-defence—The territorial aspirations that she states in her own country should be proclaimed in America .... Germany speaks with two voices; a peaceful voice for America, a violent and aggressive voice for her own country. 3. Veiled threats and bribes to America, especially with regard to Japan—Undoubtedly the fears of the West and the Middle West, with regard to Japan, make a good basis for German propaganda; but it must be insisted that Germany is just as ready to make friends with Japan against America as vice versa, that, in fact, she is purely selfish. 4. The moral basis of German Kultur and the theory of duty to the State—With regard to this, it should be pointed out that this spirit is essentially different from the free choice and responsibility of the individual conscience which are the basis of American liberty. ... The essential American idea is that every human being in questions of right and wrong must be free to follow the dictates of his own conscience.[62]

Mitchell concluded his analyses of German propaganda in the United States by writing that "the vigor and success of pro–German propaganda in the United States has apparently been under-estimated.... If, as seems possible, America is going to be driven into the war, more by force of events than in accordance with a definite moral judgment, a most difficult position will arise. New propaganda restating the case of the Allies from the beginning, and taking very full cognizance of the German case, instead of merely repeating our point of view, will be most necessary."[63]

Whenever the German propagandists were able, they struck back with embellished atrocity tales of their own, particularly relating to the actions of

Russian troops. The *New York Times* of September 3, 1914, carried a story from the German Embassy about "Russian horrors" in East Prussia: "The Russians cut off the breast of a mother and impaled her five children on a fence. Four Cossacks ravished a woman while they handcuffed her husband and forced him to be a witness."

The Germans claimed violations of international law by all of Germany's enemies, especially the Belgian civilian snipers, the *francs-tireurs*; loudly called attention to England's illegal and indiscriminate blockade which was starving German women and children; and heaped scorn on the use of non-white colonial troops by both the French and English. There was the well-publicized case of a Royal Navy "atrocity" on the high seas, involving the British muleship *Nicosian*, the Q-ship *Baralong*, and a U-boat sunk by the *Baralong*'s guns. Six of the submarine's survivors were alleged to have been killed while they were still in the water and six more unarmed U-boat crewmen hunted down and shot when they took refuge aboard the abandoned *Nicosian*.[64]

Many of the popular themes of the most effective German propagandists, however, were correct—if exaggerated—analyses of recent world history. Britain's earlier transgressions against America were stressed. While America was still a colony, according to the German viewpoint, England plundered and oppressed her; the War of 1812 was a result of English attacks on American neutral commerce, and in that war, as in the Revolutionary War, England armed "savages" to fight Americans; during the Civil War, while purporting to be neutral, England actively helped the Confederacy.

German propagandists portrayed Great Britain in the current war as using the conflict to destroy what had been a flourishing German-American trade and thus establish the postwar economic preeminence of the British Empire at the expense of the United States. Morally, England's illegal blockade to starve the civilian population of Germany was presented as so evil as to justify Germany's U-boat reprisals. Great Britain's interference with neutral commerce, arming of merchant ships, mine laying in the open seas, and abuse of neutral flags were blatant violations of international law and the hallowed concept of freedom of the seas.

On the positive side, the Germans vainly tried to defend what they believed to be the superiority of their *Kultur* and education, their nation's historic mission to advance civilization, the humanity and discipline of their army and navy, and the order they said they had brought into their colonial possessions.[65] In the Atlantic Ocean off the British Isles, so the Germans trumpeted, German submarines were fighting America's War of 1812 all over again.

Individual Germans were also sincerely convinced that the war had been thrust on their country through the envy of England, the revanchist dream of France, and the territorial greed of Russia. They believed that these forces had combined to isolate Germany and restrict her legitimate expansion.

Germany was a nation with no easily defended borders and therefore needed a powerful army. Furthermore, Germany had been encircled by the Entente powers, a straightforward military threat to her security. The war was, therefore, a defensive one for Germany.

The Germans continually sought "fair play." As early as the third week of the war, Germany's chancellor addressed a plea directly to the American people and America's press for evenhanded treatment, pointing out that "Germany is completely cut off from the rest of the world, and can neither send out news nor receive it. The Empire is therefore unable to defend itself against the falsehoods propagated by the press of the hostile countries. It can only defend itself by its deeds. The German people will be profoundly grateful for every effort to disseminate the real truth."[66]

Nearly two years later, Germany's foreign minister, Gottlieb von Jagow, emphasized this same theme in a Berlin interview with an American reporter. He pleaded that "all Germany wants is fair play. Let the American papers give the people all the news; let Americans pass judgement with all the facts in their possession, that is all that Germany asks, but please try to accord us what you must surely admit we deserve, and that is simple justice." Von Jagow supported his contention of one-sided U.S. press coverage with an example:

> When our Zeppelins attack London, which is a fortified city defended with cannon, full of soldiers and prepared as far as it can be to resist attack by land or air, the American papers teem with the most vitriolic articles about the "Huns." When the airmen of the Allies attack absolutely unprotected German towns and villages without one cannon or one soldier in them and kill old men, women, and children, your papers are either silent or else they give a carefully expurgated account, without bitter criticism.[67]

As the tactics of the German propagandists in America shifted from week to week to respond to British initiatives or to focus on one newsworthy topic or another, their two fundamental strategies remained fixed: to stop the flow of munitions and critical raw materials to the Allied powers that were keeping England and France in the war and, above all, to keep America out of the conflict.

The planning, execution, and financing of most of Germany's U.S. propaganda took place through what the Germans themselves came to call their "propaganda cabinet" in New York City. The cabinet consisted of under a dozen German nationals, German-Americans, and anti–British Americans. Chief among them, in addition to von Bernstorff, were Dr. Bernhard Dernburg, Dr. Heinrich F. Albert, Dr. Karl Alexander Fuehr, George Sylvester Viereck, and William Bayard Hale. Military Attaché Captain Franz von Papen and Naval Attaché Captain Karl Boy-Ed, while part of the group, were less concerned with influencing United States public opinion than with directing their energies on aggressive and clandestine—and sometimes illegal—operations.

Dernburg, a successful banker and a former secretary of state of the Colonial Office, and Albert, of the Ministry of the Interior, had passed through U.S. customs along with von Bernstorff on August 23, 1914. Fuehr was the former interpreter of the consulate-general in Japan and had been unable to return to Germany because of the British blockade. Viereck was a brilliant young German-American poet and author anxious to serve the cause of the fatherland. Hale was a caustically anti–British American journalist with a score to settle with Woodrow Wilson.

This cabinet worked out of four offices. Three were clustered together in lower Manhattan: the Hamburg-Amerika Lines building at 45 Broadway, von Papen's office at 60 Broadway, and the German consulate at 11 Broadway. One was at 1123 Broadway, further uptown, and also served as headquarters for the German Red Cross Commission to the United States. The German-American Club and the Manhattan Hotel, both near Central Park, were generally used for meetings, which were held once or twice a week. Whenever von Bernstorff took the train from Washington for an overnight stay to participate in these meetings, the meetings were held instead at his suite in the elegant Ritz-Carlton Hotel.

The Germans lost little time in organizing their propaganda efforts. Von Bernstorff kicked off Germany's newspaper campaign with an interview in the *New York Times* that was published on August 30. The feature story, which occupied the entire front page of the well-read Sunday magazine section, was accompanied by a bemedalled portrait of the envoy in formal diplomatic attire. Von Bernstorff skillfully—and diplomatically—wove into his statements every main propaganda argument he could muster at that early point in the war:

> I have no wish to criticize England, but in every detail of this crisis her actions have amazed me. ... Her cutting of the cables was symptomatic of what clearly is a determination that, when it shall suit the purposes of Germany's enemies, America shall be misinformed not only concerning the causes of the war, but concerning the day to day events of the great contest. ... I cannot but believe that England's extraordinary action in drawing an Asiatic yellow race into the European struggle between white men will do much with the people of this country. ... Upon Russia we lay all the blame. Every person in Germany, from the Emperor down to the humblest of our citizens, is convinced that the war was brought about by Russia as a means to the accomplishment of her Pan-Slavic aims. ... Two false impressions seem to exist widely here. One is that Germany brought on the war, which is regarded as good reason for general condemnation. The other is that Germany willfully violated the neutrality of Belgium, and this is regarded as a just cause of righteous indignation. ... The sympathies of the American people all should be with Germany. You went to war with Spain when your naval ship, the *Maine*, was blown up in Havana Harbor. We went to war only after

our frontier had been crossed by hostile and armed forces from Russia, France, and England....

By September 1914, there was a functioning German Information Service working out of midtown-Manhattan offices, headed by Fuehr with the help of former Hamburg-Amerika Line publicity agent Matthew B. Claussen. The information service's principal product was a daily "fact sheet" that was mailed to over 500 newspapers across the country and to influential officials. The masthead included the statement that "its contents come only from reliable sources, chiefly the press of the European capitals. The authority for every story is clearly indicated. In view of the British censorship of war news, it is believed that in this sheet will be found an invaluable supplement to the regular news reports enabling papers to give a more comprehensive picture of events. We shall be glad to supply photographs, mats or cuts of any illustrations appearing in the sheet, upon request, by mail or telegraph."[68]

The bulletin carried translations of news stories and articles from leading newspapers and magazines in Germany, reprints of favorable articles from the U.S. press, excerpts from books, comments on war news, cartoons, and interviews with noteworthy observers who had just returned from the battlefronts. Much of Fuehr's up-to-date information came through a newly formed wireless link, the Trans-Ocean News Service, which connected Nauen, Germany, with Sayville, Long Island.

Working closely with pro–German publishers and printers in the United States, Fuehr's busy office printed hundreds of documents in English—newly created books and pamphlets, previously existing material translated from German, even outdated anti–Belgian pamphlets authored by British writers Edmund Dene Morel and Arthur Conan Doyle. Fuehr's files later showed that he had received from Germany nearly 4,000 separate articles, pamphlets, books, and similar printed materials, of which he had translated some 1,500.

Early in 1915, Fuehr organized the American Correspondence Film Company to import German movies from the war fronts and distribute them to motion-picture houses across the country. By the end of the year, Fuehr reported to von Bernstorff that as a result of his office's initiatives, "our opponents now seem to have recognized the effectiveness of this propaganda"[69] and were exhibiting their own war films.

Fuehr also took the time to write and publish a book of his own, *The Neutrality of Belgium*, that responded to the most pressing propaganda challenge facing the Germans. The book gave a detailed and accurate historical overview of the origins of the quintuple treaty of 1839 that established Belgium's "perpetual" neutrality, assessed the changing European political climate by the turn of the century, and stoutly put the onus on Belgium for its patently non-neutral military discussions with Great Britain that began in 1906. Fuehr's thesis was that Belgium and England had secretly worked together during peacetime to prepare for military cooperation in a coming war and thus Belgium had forfeit her neutral status "according to the rules of international law." While certainly biased, the well-documented book was nevertheless a reasoned, generally nonpolemical treatise filled with many unassailable facts that challenged the validity of England's loudly proclaimed indignation over Germany's "breach" of Belgian neutrality.[70]

Under the direction of Fuehr, the German Information Service managed to survive unimpaired until diplomatic relations were broken in February 1917. Until then, it continued to send out its fact sheet, kept tabs on American public opinion, and did its best to keep the news coming over the wireless from Germany. Two new English-language publications were also put into service: a weekly magazine-size newspaper, *The Fatherland*, featuring strongly pro–German (and anti–British) articles and editorials—most quite rational—and a similar biweekly called *The Vital Issue*. The latter shortly became a weekly and was renamed *Issues and Events*, with much more astringent editorial material.[71] Both were available on selected newsstands in many big cities and by subscription through the mail.

American opinion makers could thus observe firsthand—and literally catalog—much of the German propaganda directed at them, for every daily bulletin from the German Information Service literally carried the stamp of the Imperial German government. And from August 1915 on, following the *World*'s sensational exposé of the contents of Dr. Albert's briefcase, which unequivocally tied *The Fatherland* to the German payroll, few looked upon the new pro–German newspapers as other than official German propaganda organs. Such a transparent approach to mass persuasion, contrasted with the invariably quiet, covert methods used by the British, would haunt the Germans. Nearly all Americans, from Woodrow Wilson on down, would fervently come to believe that only the Germans were trying to subvert U.S. public opinion.

The Germans recognized, of course, the limitations of a national stamp on all their propaganda. What was needed chiefly was an existing, respected New York City newspaper of large circulation that could be bought and its editorial policies cautiously tilted in the direction of the new owners. In June 1915, the Germans quietly bought the *New York Evening Mail*, but its overly enthusiastic anti–British stance earned its new owners small propaganda return on their investment of $1.4 million.[72]

Promptly organized after August 1914 were numerous "embargo" and "peace" organizations directly or indirectly in consonance with Germany's two principal strategies—to stop the flow of munitions to the Allies and to keep America out of the war. Nearly all had properly euphemistic titles—and most were financed and otherwise abetted in greater or lesser degree by the German government.

The most important of these were the American Neutrality League, professing to support neutrality by opposing arms exports; the American Embargo Conference, its function defined in its title; the American Independence Union, advocating independence of England through American neutrality; the Friends of Peace, an umbrella group that stood foursquare against munitions traffic on humanitarian grounds; and the American Humanity League and the American Organization of Women for Strict Neutrality, both urging an end to the manufacture and export of munitions. More blatantly pro–German was the Literary Defense Committee, whose major function was the printing and distribution of propaganda materials; by the end of 1915, it reported that it had distributed more than one million such pieces. The Germans also set up an organization called Labor's National Peace Council, whose purpose was to organize labor within the munitions industries and thus disrupt production. A small German University League was also established, enlisting pro–German college professors in Germany's cause.

The Germans worked closely with Irish immigrants—there were about four million in the United States—and financially supported the movement for Irish independence from Great Britain. Von Papen recorded in his memoirs that early in the war he had been introduced to Sir Roger Casement, a leader of the Sinn Fein organization, and met with him frequently in New York City. Von Papen claimed to have been the one who recommended to Casement that he go to Berlin to present his views on how his followers might contribute to an Allied defeat.[73] The most vigorously anti–British Irish were members of the militant American Truth Society. Its raucous voice was *Bull*, a monthly magazine started in 1916 that was filled with brazen cartoons and punishing editorials. *Bull*'s editor, and president of the society, was Jeremiah O'Leary, a busy lecturer. He was accurately labeled by the British as "a copious propagandist of a crude, popular, but effective kind."[74] An early 1917 issue of *Bull* listed its circulation at 200,000. During the Senate propaganda hearings in late 1918, chief government witness A. Bruce Bielaski admitted that "just how much the German Government assisted in financing the American Truth Society has never been fully developed." He said that there were records of "the transfer of some $10,000 ... on the books of Kuhn, Loeb & Co.," but admitted that the society had collected a "good deal of money in small amounts.[75]

O'Leary had made national headlines during the 1916 elections when he sent a telegram to the president saying that because of Wilson's non-neutral acts, O'Leary and other Irish-Americans were unable to vote for him. Wilson responded angrily: "I would feel deeply mortified to have you or anybody like you vote for me. Since you have access to many disloyal Americans and I have not, I will ask you to convey this message to them."[76]

Once America entered the war, *Bull*'s second-class mailing privileges were revoked, effectively killing the publication. In his legal deposition seeking to bar *Bull* from the mails under the new Espionage Act, Postmaster

General Burleson threw the book at O'Leary. He claimed that *Bull*'s mission and activities were designed

> to breed discontent with the conduct of the war ... [to] cast suspicion and discontent upon the motives of the United States in entering and prosecuting the war; to create a general spirit of hostility with respect thereto; ... to wilfully make or to convey false reports or false statements with intent to interfere with the operation or success of the military or naval forces of the United States, to promote the success of its enemies ... to cause insubordination, disloyalty, mutiny and refusal of duty in the military or naval forces of the United States ... and to cause antagonism and resistance among the people with respect to enlistment, execution of the draft and the sale of bonds to raise revenues to carry on the war. ...[This] constitutes in effect the advocating of treason, insurrection, and forcible resistance to the laws of the United States.[77]

In November 1917, a federal grand jury indicted O'Leary, the managing editor, and the business manager of *Bull* for violations of the Espionage Act, charging the three with conspiracy to bring out "insubordination, disloyalty, mutiny, and refusal of duty" among U.S. armed forces personnel.[78]

If the German ambassador was the titular, though informal, head of propaganda operations in the United States, the chief spokesman during the early months of the war was Dr. Bernhard Dernburg. He soon was referred to as "the Kaiser's mouthpiece" by the often-mocking New York press. Nevertheless, the press was impelled to prominently cover his addresses and statements, as much because of the eloquence and logic of his arguments as for his controversial stances, which helped to sell newspapers.

Dernburg had entered the United States as an accredited representative of the German Red Cross. According to von Bernstorff, however, his main job was to negotiate loans to pay for prospective purchases of war materials. When the Germans found that the Wilson administration, in its early efforts to project a spirit of neutrality, forbade American loans to any of the belligerents, Dernburg, apparently insufficiently occupied with his Red Cross duties and unable to return home because of the British blockade, sought alternative patriotic service. Von Bernstorff recalled that "as Dr. Dernburg was thus an unwilling prisoner in New York he began to write articles on the world-war for the daily Press. He had a gift for explaining the war in a quiet, interesting manner, and particularly for setting out the German standpoint in a conciliatory form. His propaganda work therefore met with extraordinary success."[79] An article in the magazine *The World's Work* in 1915, after he had left the United States, said this of Dernburg:

> Editors welcomed his letters to the press and his magazine articles. Invitations from non–Germanic sources began to pour in for addresses to men's clubs and popular forums, Dr. Dernburg even becoming the guest of honor at banquets, where he frequently spoke with great felicity. He did not waste

much time in talking to the converted—the German-speaking part of America; he went mainly for the "native American" contingent.[80]

It is unclear whether Dernburg became a propagandist by default or whether he had been expressly assigned that mission by the Foreign Office in Berlin, which knew about his capabilities as communicator and administrator. What is certain is that, until he intemperately defended his country's sinking of the *Lusitania* in a talk in Cleveland on May 8, 1915, and was forced to leave America, he did far more for Germany's cause in the United States than any other individual. A measure of Dernburg's impact on U.S. public opinion was one reaction of the British government. An April 21, 1915, story in the *New York Times* dealing with Dernburg's peace proposals cited the grudging credit given him by the British for his success as a diplomat: "Hitherto it has been the habit of the British press to sneer at German diplomacy. A new note is struck in some quarters today. This is a direct result of Dr. Dernburg's activities.... The *Star* says, notably: 'In the United States Dr. Dernburg is conducting a very able campaign for the capture of American opinion. We ought not to belittle his propaganda.'"

Others applauding his performance were his rival propagandist, Arthur Willert, and U.S. publisher Oswald Garrison Villard. In October 1914, Willert commented to his editor, "So far I have managed to checkmate all of Bernstorff's moves. Dernburg is a far more subtle customer."[81] Villard, publisher of *The Nation* and the *New York Evening Post*, and no friend of Germany in 1915, wrote that "the German cause has had numerous advocates, of whom the ablest is unquestionably Doctor Bernhard Dernburg ... whose years of residence in New York have apparently made him understand the best method of appealing to the American public."[82]

Early in his career, Dernburg had spent several years as a junior banking clerk with the Wall Street firm of Ladenburg, Thalmann & Co. before returning to Berlin to become a clerk in the Deutsche Bank of Berlin. He moved ahead rapidly, becoming a director in 1901. When the bank formed a trust company to salvage bankrupt businesses, Dernburg was promoted to its head. In 1906, his successes at reviving insolvent businesses came to the attention of Chancellor Bernard von Bulow. Germany's moribund colonies needed an infusion of new vitality, and Dernburg was offered the colonial secretaryship. As the new colonial minister, the liberal-minded Dernburg discarded traditional German diplomatic formalities to obtain firsthand information. He toured each of Germany's far-flung colonies in Africa and the Pacific and traveled through America's southern states to learn about cotton as a potential cash crop, particularly for German East Africa. He instituted broad reform programs that corrected previous abuses of the native populations, improved living standards, and helped promote economic self-sufficiency. According to one report, "In a few months Dr. Dernburg had become the most powerful man in von Bulow's cabinet ... and shone as a stump speaker."[83]

In 1914 in America, Dernburg was prepared to call not only on his political and diplomatic acumen but on his skills as both speaker and public-relations executive, although his use of the American idiom was not always flawless. Dernburg must have elicited understanding smiles from Americans when he declared in one speech that his country had been "forced to draw quickly when she saw her enemies reaching for their hip pockets,"[84] although he would have been more effective referring to holsters rather than hip pockets.

Dernburg was always careful to point out that his comments

Bernhard Dernburg was the most productive propagandist for the German cause in the United States until he intemperately defended the sinking of the *Lusitania* and was forced out of the country. *Author's collection.*

were those of a "private person," that he did not pretend to express official sentiments, but that he was sure his opinions were shared by nearly all Germans. In fact, Dernburg took on the role of government spokesman, sometimes usurping the role of von Bernstorff.

An acknowledged yardstick of the success of any publicity campaign, then as today, is the "ink" it generates in the media. By that measure alone, Dernburg was a resounding triumph. Using the *New York Times* as a benchmark, from early September 1914 to late June 1915, when he sailed for Germany under relentless pressure by American media, scarcely a week went by without publication of his letters, prominent news stories dealing with his talks, and editorial responses to his—and Imperial Germany's—views of the European war. Dernburg was a news maker, and the *Times* and other newspapers followed him and apparently faithfully reported what he said wherever he went. While the *Times* was unswervingly anti–German, its editors nevertheless gave the German propagandist a regular forum for his controversial views and typically treated him respectfully, as exemplified in an editorial on December 5, 1914, "Dr. Dernburg's Argument":

> Dr. Dernburg's presentation of the German case in the current number of *The North American Review* is marked by the qualities which he, almost alone of the swarm of German propagandists and apologists let loose in our land, seems able to show. It is temperate in tone and quite clear of offensive imputation. It essays to deal with the facts of history and to find an explanation of the course pursued by each of the Powers in the forces that history discloses rather than in the wickedness of one or another set of rulers and the virtues of another set.

Dernburg was introduced to the readers of the *New York Times* on Sunday, September 6, 1914, in a page-long interview under the headline "GERMANY PREPARES FOR UNPARALLELED SUFFERING; Herr Dernburg, Head of Her Red Cross and Recently Colonial Secretary, Tells of Plans for Mitigating the Horrors of the Greatest War." His interviewer was lavish in his praise, writing that Dernburg "spoke with authority and insight. ...He knows this country well, and declares himself proud that he secured here his business education. ... He has been a figure of considerable eminence in the European financial world. ...He is best known to Germany, however, as a philanthropist and promoter of advanced sociological science, which explains his deep interest in the work of the Red Cross."

In the interview, Dernburg stated that his mission to America was "that of a confident suppliant, pleading the cause of humanity. ...My own home is now a hospital. My family is living in the basement. The balance of the structure is devoted to the sick and wounded." He then took advantage of the publicity opportunity to cover far more ground than his Red Cross work. He vigorously defended his country's colonial policies and, in particular, his stewardship of Germany's colonies in Africa. Dernburg admitted that when he took office as colonial secretary, Germany's overseas affairs were "rather muddled." But he had worked diligently, he said, to put things right. He said he was "the first Colonial Secretary of any European country to go to Africa. It was not an easy journey; it had none of the peculiarities of a pleasure jaunt. I penetrated 800 miles from the coast, spending thirty-one days, practically on foot. ...Was Germany brutal with her colonies?" he asked rhetorically.

> No! Was it brutality or elevated civilization which led us to send to Africa for the relief of suffering native populations the celebrated Dr. Koch, who discovered the cholera bacillus and the dread secret of the sleeping sickness? ...After Koch's discovery we called in Ehrlich, the discoverer of salvarsan, who helped to stop the progress of the plague. ...This was not the work of the "mailed fist," was it? Can the world believe that it was done by the same men capable of such atrocities as those with which my countrymen have been credited in Belgium?

Dernburg invoked America's racial prejudices and attacked England and France for "bringing into Europe to help them in their fight against us the uncivilized from India, and rank[ing] as their allies the yellow Japanese!" Those two countries, he also said, "are denouncing us for cruelties which never have occurred" and, at the same time, "fighting side by side with Russia, whose treatment of the Jews they have just left off proclaiming and condemning." Dernburg concluded by emphasizing that Germany was "not at war because of any greed for anything belonging to our neighbors. Germany was very busy and utterly contented with her own affairs when she was forced into this unjustifiable war."

In this first important newspaper interview, Dernburg had no opportunity to present the generally accurate, if one-sided, interpretations of modern European history that would become his stock in trade. Nor was he able to probe all of Germany's important propaganda themes. Dernburg would do all of this later, with remarkable eloquence and persuasive force—discreetly balancing defence of his country, attacks against his country's enemies, and attempts to stay on the best of terms with his hosts.

In March 1915, Dernburg's wife arrived in New York to join her husband, and was promptly enlisted in the propaganda campaign. In a full-page article, "Women of Germany, and the War," published in the March 20th *New York Times* magazine section a week after her arrival, Mrs. Dernburg targeted the sensibilities of American women by focusing on home front support of the wounded. The interviewer, however, was able to dig out her political views as well, regarding Germany's enemies, France, Russia, and England—especially England:

> We regard the English as cousins of the Germans. ... We German women are offering up our husbands, our children, the best of all we have in a war for existence. ... For England, the war is a piece of business. ... England's course in the war we resent bitterly with the hatred such as only one member of a family can have for another, the hatred of the same blood. ... We cannot hate very hard, we Germans, but we can despise.[85]

Dernburg also involved himself in the acquisition of a New York City daily newspaper that would serve Germany's interests. In March 1915, he analyzed all of New York City's major dailies in a comprehensive report to von Bernstorff that, in its thoroughness and clarity, reflected its author's many talents. Dernburg included in his report in-depth financial data and the profitability of specific morning and evening papers (undoubtedly available to him through his former Wall Street contacts), estimated costs, and circulation figures. He referred to prohibition and the wealthy brewers "who command almost illimitable capital." Dernburg showed his exasperation at his foreign office's lack of foresight in not having acquired a bonafide U.S. newspaper before the hostilities. He closed by pointing out the cardinal requirement of any newspaper purchase: that "the transaction would have to be handled with the utmost delicacy. No suspicion of the influence behind it should be allowed to reach the public. And the newspaper world is like a sounding-board."[86]

On April 2, the *New York Times* titled an editorial "Dr. Dernburg justifies the Sinking of the *Falaba*," with quotes that would be echoed almost word-for-word five weeks later over the sinking of another British ship: "Dr. Dernburg expressed 'regret personally' for 'the loss of innocent lives' when the British merchant ship *Falaba* was sunk by a German submarine's torpedo, but he says that the act was 'perfectly justifiable. All the passengers had ample warning that by taking passage in the steamship they would expose themselves to danger.'"

On May 8, the day after the sinking of the *Lusitania*, Dernburg was in Cleveland, Ohio. Instead of his planned address, he had a hastily prepared handout that responded to the day's most important news event for the unusually large press contingent on hand. He faced a hostile group of reporters who undoubtedly interrogated the veteran publicist with more rancor than he had yet experienced. Dernburg summarized his interpretation of the disaster this way:

> The fact is that the *Lusitania* was a British war vessel under orders of the Admiralty to carry a cargo of contraband of war. The passengers had full warning, first by the German note to England in February, second, by advertisement. Germany wants to do anything reasonable so as not to make the United States or its citizens suffer in any way. But she cannot do so unless Americans will take necessary precautions to protect themselves from dangers of which they are cognizant. ... I can only say that any ship flying the American flag and not carrying contraband of war is and will be as safe as a cradle. But any other ship, not so exempt, is as unsafe as a volcano—or as was the *Lusitania*.[87]

Back in New York, two days later, Dernburg was cornered by reporters in his hotel. He expanded on his inflammatory defense of the sinking, implying that Americans could not be considered neutral if they insisted in traveling on British ships within the German war zone. Germany was "not to blame" in the sinking the *Lusitania*, he said. "It is a catastrophe of war. ...The Cunard Line is responsible. ...The British Admiralty is equally, if not more, responsible, for permitting innocent American travelers to be used as shields on a ship that was nothing more or less than an auxiliary cruiser and contraband carrier." Concerning submarines, Dernburg pointed that since the war began they had become recognized weapons of war and that England was building them as fast as she could. He took a calculated swipe at Bethlehem Steel's clandestine construction of submarines for the Royal Navy—which was contrary to U.S. law—by pointing out that Great Britain was "having them built here, and shipping the parts to Canada to be put together. And England intends to use them when she has the opportunity against German ships."[88]

Von Bernstorff recorded his reaction to Dernburg's too-candid remarks, writing that "I had, therefore, no other resource but to advise him to leave the country of his own accord. He would probably have been deported in any case, and his continued presence in America could no longer serve any useful service. ...The sea was raging and demanded a sacrifice."[89]

Indeed, the sea was violently agitated. America's reaction to the

Lusitania's sinking was hysterical. The disaster was reflected in the biggest, blackest newspaper headlines in New York newspapers since the early days of the war, and editorials blazed with fury. The *New York Times'* lead editorial of May 8, "War by Assassination," insisted that "there must go to the Imperial Government at Berlin a demand that the Germans shall no longer make war like savages drunk with blood." The editorial used one superlative after another: "In the history of wars there is no single deed comparable in its inhumanity and horror. ...Germany has wantonly and without provocation [used] dastardly assassination methods. ...[This] transcends in atrocity anything our Government could have apprehended ... exhibiting a degree of brutality which is commonly associated with madness."

Other leading New York City newspapers were equally loud in their condemnation of the dastardly deed:

> The *Herald*: The civilized world stands appalled at the torpedoing of the *Lusitania*, with the terrible loss of life. ...If ever wholesale murder was premeditated, this slaughter on the high seas was. ... It is a time of gravity in American history unmatched since the Civil War.
>
> The *Sun*: That it was premeditated we know; that it was reckless of innocent non-combatant lives we are sure; and "dastardly" is the word on millions of American lips this morning.
>
> The *Journal of Commerce*: The attack on the *Lusitania* was not war. It was simply attempted murder ... plain and unqualified piracy.
>
> The *Tribune*: The nation which remembered the sailors of the *Maine* will not forget the civilians of the *Lusitania*!
>
> The *World*: We recall no other instance in which a great nation has deliberately elected to become an outlaw. Civilization might better perish than to survive on the terms that Germany offers to mankind.

New York's clergymen had a full day to prepare sermons for their expectant congregants, and on May 9 followed the lead of the press of the city, deploring the "crime" but avoiding a call for war. All strove to describe the sinking in fresh phrases: "a brutal and inhuman act," "not piracy but organized murder," "a crime against civilization," "unbelievably savage," "abhorrent even to the standards of bloody war," the work of "a nation drunk with power," and an "act not to be condoned." But true to their calling, many then turned the other cheek: "Go to war? No, let our brother, Germany, be unto us as a heathen, one who has cut himself off from the congregation." ... "This is an hour for lamentation, but not for anger—an hour for grief, but not for madness. There is no more reason to go to war with Germany today than there was yesterday. ...We should reaffirm our love of peace and our faith in reason and good will...." "There is no reason for a rupture. Let us see to it that there will be no rupture unless the other fellow starts it. There is no reason why we should go to war."[90]

Ex-president Theodore Roosevelt also weighed in with his warlike views, saying he expected the United States to take action "without an hour's unnecessary delay," although he was not specific as to the action he meant. He said, seeking to come up with a catchy phrase, that "the sinking of the *Lusitania* was not only an act of simple piracy, but it represented piracy accompanied by murder on a vaster scale than any oldtime pirate had ever practiced before being hung for his misdeeds."[91]

Americans in the Far West, 3,000 miles from the influence of the East Coast's Anglophile press, were more sanguine about the torpedoing of the *Lusitania*. They were led by California's most powerful newspaper, the *San Francisco Chronicle*, which had taken a sharply different editorial tack from New York's papers. On May 8, it credited Germany with scoring "her largest individual triumph in the war on British commerce. ...The largest lesson of the *Lusitania* is one for the United States, and it is the reiterated truth that for defense purposes the dreadnought is junk. ...Our people have had ample warning, and should know that when they step aboard a British ship they are consigning themselves to the protection of a nation which at present can offer very little security for those at sea." The experience of David F. Houston, the secretary of agriculture, who was in Los Angeles when the *Lusitania* was sunk, reflected this strong regional insularity. He reported that after he had learned about the sinking he had breakfast with a group of local officials and was surprised there was only a few minutes' discussion concerning the tragedy—"Nor did any reporter of any local paper seek to interview me on the matter, and no citizen brought it up during the remainder of my stay in the West, which lasted several weeks."[92]

A May 12 editorial in the *New York World* summarized editorials from 100 leading American English-language newspapers:

> Of these, seventy-three spoke in terms of horror and detestation of the crime itself, consideration of the probable American attitude being secondary. Fifteen counseled patience and reliance upon the President to uphold American interests and honor. Seven discussed military and other considerations, having already expressed their views of the moral aspects of the case. One article was plainly written before the loss of life was known. Two may be described as "on the fence." Two only, one in Milwaukee and one in Atlantic Highlands, New Jersey, took the German view of the von Bernstorff "warning" and of the grim necessities of war as mitigating German responsibility.

On June 13, Dernburg sailed for home from New York. When asked by the reporters on deck if he had any final comments to make, he replied that his feelings for America were "absolutely unchanged. I have been treated everywhere with undiscriminating nicety except on one occasion, which I do not wish to refer to." "Was it about the Lusitania?" "Yes." "Do you take exception to the attitude of the United States on what you had said in Cleveland after the sinking of the Lusitania?" "Exactly: that is what I meant, but I do not resent it. I hope this struggle will soon be over, honorably for all, and that is all I have to say."[93]

The *New York Times* gave Dernburg an understanding send-off in an editorial the following day. It said the fact that Dernburg would be remembered "chiefly, if not wholly, for the very worst of his several mistakes—what he said about the sinking of the *Lusitania*—is perhaps somewhat more natural than just. Compelled by his position to plead on the wrong side of a very bad case, he was precluded from expressing the feeling of horror which he presumably shared with other civilized people, and he had to endure judgment, not as counsel for his client, but as a human being. The situation was one to earn something of sympathy for an intelligent and well-intentioned man, but the circumstances were all against him."

The *New York Herald*, one of the most outspokenly anti–German newspapers in New York City, treated Dernburg's departure less formally:

> So, blessings on his going! He has been slow to pass!
> He has put his foot so often in his mouth of sounding brass
> That a few of us would like to stand outside the woodshed door
> When the Kaiser leads him thither to even up the score.

As Dernburg scuttled away from the limelight, von Bernstorff appointed Dr. Heinrich F. Albert to head the propaganda cabinet in Dernburg's place. Albert then proceeded to commit a blunder of such proportions as to permanently undermine the entire structure of the German propaganda apparatus in the United States. The details of the unprepossessing attaché's conspicuous carelessness on Saturday afternoon, July 24, 1915—and what has come to be called "the case of the purloined briefcase" or "the minister without portfolio"—have captivated students of propaganda and espionage ever since.

Albert had entered the United States at the end of August 1914 as the commercial attaché of the German Embassy. Unable to negotiate public business, Albert turned to more discreet activities in support of his country's cause, becoming at first official paymaster for Germany's diplomatic and consular representatives—and their activities, both overt and covert, legal and illegal—in the United States. He had a joint bank account with von Bernstorff in the Chase National Bank in Manhattan which often totaled several million dollars. Until the contents of his famous briefcase gave him worldwide notoriety, Albert lived quietly in New York City, prudently masking his important financial activities. Those who knew Albert gave him high marks for his knowledge of U.S. economics.[94]

Albert is also credited with being the mastermind behind by far the most ambitious of all the German clandestine operations in the United States to staunch the flow of ammunition to the Allies. It was his plan to set up, from scratch, a complete munitions manufacturing facility—without revealing its German ownership. Vital machine tools and raw materials were to be bought up, munitions contracts negotiated (but never filled), and high wages paid so as to cause labor unrest in nearby plants. The scheme, as conceived, was intended to deny other munitions makers both the machinery and the materials needed to produce ammunition for the Allies.

The dummy operation was called the Bridgeport Projectile Company and was located in Bridgeport, Connecticut. Construction work on the facility began in April 1915, with "operations" scheduled to begin in September. Before Albert's plan was rudely exposed on the front pages of the *New York World*, about $3.5 million had been spent on the project. Von Papen had exulted that the Aetna Powder Company's entire production through the end of 1915, some five million pounds, had been tied up:

> Every firm in the United States making machine tools, hydraulic presses and rolling mills for the manufacture of war material was given enough orders by our company to keep them occupied at full capacity for a couple of years at a maximum rate of delivery. When the Allies settled their price difficulties in the spring of 1915 and started to place their orders, they found that all the contractors with the equipment to build the necessary factories were fully booked with orders. Our secret had been well kept.[95]

Equally successful, from Germany's standpoint, were efforts to corner the U.S. market on carbolic acid, used to manufacture trinitrotoluol and other high explosives. Two existing New York City chemical companies under German management, Heyden Chemical Works and the Bayer Company, were contracted to buy large quantities of carbolic acid which, in turn, were converted into pharmaceutical preparations sold in America and exported to neutral countries. According to von Bernstorff, this undertaking "was eventually closed down after making considerable profits for the Imperial Treasury. In the same way, for some time, all the bromine coming on to the market, the products of which were used to manufacture and increase the density of [poison] gas, were bought up."[96]

During the later Senate hearings dealing with German propaganda, Professor Albert Bushnell Hart testified that Albert was "the Machiavelli of the whole thing apparently. I met him in Cambridge once or twice. He was the finest gentlemen you ever saw. He was such an exquisite gentleman that it lost its effect." Senator Knute Nelson replied, to laughter among his colleagues: 'He was like the man that Byron described when he says 'He was the mildest-mannered man that ever scuttled ship or cut a throat.'"[97]

The most authoritative version of what Albert did—and did not do—on a muggy summer's day on Manhattan's Sixth Avenue "El" comes from former treasury secretary William Gibbs McAdoo. McAdoo was involved in the incident because the U.S. Secret Service was an agency of the Treasury Department, and on May 14, 1915, by executive order, he had been authorized to conduct surveillance of German Embassy personnel and German-American "suspects."

In his memoir, published 16 years later, McAdoo wrote that it was Secret

Service Agent Frank Burke who "picked up" Albert's briefcase. In the account which McAdoo asked Burke to put down in writing, Burke related that he and a fellow agent had been shadowing German-American propagandist Viereck whom they knew. They followed Viereck and a "conspicuously German" individual (whom they did not know) as the pair left 45 Broadway in lower Manhattan. Viereck and his companion boarded an uptown train at the Rector Street station, and were trailed inconspicuously by the American agents. Burke wrote that "the unknown man carried a large, heavily stuffed brief-case. From that, and also from the general manner and appearance of the stranger, I came to the conclusion that he was a man of rank and importance in German circles. I could get nothing from their conversation, because it was in German, which I do not understand."[98]

After a more careful study of the unknown man's saber-scarred face, Burke said he recalled a description of Albert by a customs attorney that fit the stranger: "six feet one inch in height, fifty years old, and of about one hundred and ninety pounds in weight." The same lawyer had told Burke that Albert "was the most important representative of the German government in the United States. I came to the conclusion that Viereck's companion was Dr. Albert."

When the train stopped at the 23rd Street station, Viereck got off, followed by Burke's fellow agent. Burke continued to keep his eye on the briefcase, which Albert had wedged between himself and the side of the train. At the 50th Street station, Albert, who had apparently nodded off to the rhythm of the swaying train, hurriedly got up and left the train, absentmindedly leaving his bulging briefcase behind. Burke continued: "When I saw that he had left his brief-case, I decided in a fraction of a second to get it. ... I picked it up and started for the front door. Dr. Albert was then trying to get back into the car through the rear door. I could see, from the corner of my eye, that he was having some difficulty. A very fat woman was planted in the door; she was evidently asking something of the guard, while Dr. Albert tried to push by her."

Burke related that from the train platform he observed that Albert came "pouring out in a hurry," apparently "greatly disturbed." According to Burke's story, "there were enough passengers alighting from the train to give me a little cover. The Doctor was between me and the stairs, and I did not dare to start for the street at that moment. I went to the wall of the station, and pretended to light a cigar, striking one match after another, and blowing them out, with the brief-case against the wall, partly covered by my coat." Albert then rushed down the stairs to the street. Burke followed cautiously, and saw Albert "some distance out in the street where he could get a better view of pedestrians, with panic written on his face. Almost immediately he discovered me with the bag and dashed in my direction."

Burke then described a foot race for a fast-moving trolley car. When he jumped on, Burke told the conductor that the man running after him "was crazy ... and if he got on the car, he would cause trouble. Certainly the wild-eyed appearance of the Doctor corroborated my statement and the conductor called to the motorman to pass the next corner without stopping so the nut could not get on."

Having eluded his pursuer, Burke concluded his story to McAdoo by saying he phoned his chief, William J. Flynn, "who came in his machine, and we drove to the office, where a glance at the contents of the bag, though much of it was in German, satisfied me that I had done a good Saturday's work."

According to McAdoo's account in his memoir, Flynn telegraphed him in Maine, asking for an immediate meeting. Flynn arrived at McAdoo's summer home the next day, with the contents of Albert's briefcase.[99] After he had "spent the afternoon and evening looking over the captured documents," McAdoo came to the conclusion that they were of "immense importance." He wrote that "while they did not furnish any basis for legal action, yet they showed plainly enough that illegitimate activities were going on; that our neutrality laws were being grossly violated. I saw an opportunity to throw a reverberating scare into the whole swarm of propagandists—British and French as well as German—and I decided that this could be done most effectively through publicity."

President Wilson and Colonel House next had the opportunity to skim through the materials from Albert's briefcase. They agreed with McAdoo that the American people should be made privy to what they considered dastardly—albeit legal—German activities. In fact, many of the plans and programs discovered among Albert's papers were perfectly legitimate and were only reprehensible when presented in the garish, exaggerated form in which they appeared to the public. The best medium to use for exposure, it was decided, was the administration's favorite newspaper, the *New York World*, and the individual to handle the matter with the required discretion was Wilson's favorite newspaperman, Frank I. Cobb, the paper's chief editorial writer.

On Monday, July 26, a tiny classified advertisement appeared in the *New York Evening Telegram*: "Lost:—On Saturday, on 3:30 Harlem Elevated train, at 50th St. station, brown leather bag, containing documents. Deliver to G. H. Hoffman, 5 East 47th St., against $20 reward."[100]

The only restriction put on Cobb was that the source of the "scoop" not be revealed, for, in fact, the U.S. Secret Service had brazenly committed an act contrary to international law by stealing the briefcase of an accredited foreign national. Indeed, Woodrow Wilson, by collaborating in a blatantly anti–German action, showed unambiguously where his sympathies lay.

Cobb and his team of editors had plenty of time to sift through and organize their cornucopia, gather photographs, and plan their presentations. On Sunday, August 15, the *World* broke the news of German perfidy in its patently sensational way, which harked back to the "yellow journal" days of the

Spanish-American War. The front page carried a huge four-line headline, followed by oversize subheads:

HOW GERMANY HAS WORKED IN U.S.
TO SHAPE OPINION, BLOCK THE ALLIES
AND GET MUNITIONS FOR HERSELF,
TOLD IN SECRET AGENTS' LETTERS.
Chancellor, Ambassador, Financial Agent and Bankers Chief Figures in
Vast Scheme Revealed in Documents Obtained by The World—Fatherland
Financed, Author Fox's[101] Expenses Paid, Plans Laid to Buy Press Association and Otherwise Control News of the War
COST PUT AT $2,000,000 A WEEK
BERNSTORFF DRAFT $1,100,000.
Big Arms Plant and Powder Works, Which Outwardly Dicker with Allies,
Secretly Owned by Germany and Preparing to Deliver Munitions Sept. 1—
Edison's Supply of Carbolic Acid Taken Over for Shipment—Plan to Buy
Wright Plant Considered—Poison Gas Supply of Allies Crippled—Strikes
in Munitions Plants Fomented."

A large, unflattering picture of Viereck, staring out, head-in-hands, also graced the front page. Underneath was a photostat of a statement to Albert, dated June 20, "For June—$1750, of which I received—$250, Leaves a balance of $1500." Next to it was a photostat of a letter to Albert of the same date, signed by Viereck, which concluded, secretively: "Will you please O.K. this and I shall then send my secretary for the cash. I am sending this letter by boy as for obvious reasons I do not wish it [to] go through the mails." There was also a translation of an incriminating letter in German from Albert to Viereck, of July 1, that included the following:

From the moment when we guarantee you a regular advance, I must—
1. Have a new statement of the condition of your paper.
2. Practice a control over the financial management. In addition to this, we must have an understanding regarding the course in politics which you will pursue, which we have not asked heretofore.

As Viereck later wrote,

A veritable box of Pandora, Albert's portfolio unloosed every half-hatched plan of the Germans. Germany appeared in the act of buying up munition plants surreptitiously to prevent shipments to Europe. She was discovered stirring up Southern interests to advocate an embargo on arms unless Great Britain consented to take cotton off the contraband list. There were sinister suggestions of strikes in munitions plants. Germany's good faith in her relations with the United States were seriously impugned by the advice of one of Albert's correspondents, a German official, to delay the shipment of chemicals and dyestuffs badly needed by American manufacturers, even if Great Britain should permit them to pass the blockade, in order to exert pressure on the American Government.[102]

For four more days, the *World* followed up with more details and more provocative headlines: "Passport Plot Traced by U.S. to Doors of German

Embassy; Chancellor Saw Great Benefit in the Good Dispatches of Fox; American Arms for Germans—Attempts to Handicap Allies; Plans for Big Press Bureau Drawn Up for Government; Agent's Letter Declared General Walkout in Detroit, Cleveland and Cincinnati Munitions Plant Could be Arranged for $50,000; Capt. von Papen Submitted a Plan to Shut Off From the Allies the Only Open Supply of Chlorine He Found; Anti-Arms Campaign Promoted by Chancellor and Ambassador; Cabinet Soon to Take Up Proof of German Intrigue; Germany May Recall Officials Who Have Directed Propaganda." There was even a facsimile copy of the "status of contract" with the Bridgeport Projectile Company as of June 30, 1915. "Mug shots" of all the German "conspirators" were plastered on front and inside pages: von Bernstorff, von Papen, Boy-Ed, Hale, the feckless Dr. Albert—even Chancellor von Bethmann-Hollweg, for good measure.

On August 19, the last day the ongoing story made the front page, the *World*'s lead story shifted smugly to "proof of German intrigue" and to the authenticity of the documents: "No attempt to question the authenticity of the documents printed by The World has been made by Count von Bernstorff, Financial Director Albert, or any of the other officials who in furtherance of the German official programme have been promoting its secret undertakings. Berlin has been equally silent."

George Sylvester Viereck occupied a unique niche within the propaganda cabinet. He was editor and publisher of the German propagandists' most effective communications medium, *The Fatherland*. He was an indefatigable essayist and defender of the German cause and, along with William Bayard Hale, the group's interpreter of American public opinion.

Viereck was well suited by temperament and experience to his wartime role. He had come from Munich, Germany, to New York City in 1896 as a boy of 12, the son of a political writer and publicist for German-American causes. His father, who had been a member of the Reichstag, was reputed to be a bastard son of Kaiser Wilhelm I, and George Sylvester later embraced this tenuous family tie to the Hohenzollerns as a subliminal reason to support Wilhelm II's Reich.

Viereck attended New York public schools and was graduated from the College of the City of New York in 1906. During his precollege years, Viereck published poems in German and English in American newspapers and magazines. In 1904, his first book of poems, in German, was published. Once out of college, Viereck became a whirlwind. In rapid succession he wrote a book of plays in English, published his first novel, and then completed a critically acclaimed book of poems in English under the title *Nineveh*. He translated Schiller's *Joan of Arc* into English for a memorable Harvard Stadium performance by Maude Adams, lectured on American poetry at the University of Berlin as a self-styled "exchange poet," and authored his first book with a political theme, *The Confessions of a Barbarian.* The book was based on his first visit to Germany, and he presented to his German-American readers his positive impressions of Germans and their society, at the same time defending his own strong ties to America. By this time, the prolific and versatile Viereck was being hailed by some literary critics as a new *Wunderkind.*

Viereck's literary successes triggered a demand for him as a public speaker for German-American causes. In 1908, only 24 years old, he addressed a huge audience in Columbus, Ohio, on "German Day," under the auspices of the National German-American Alliance. The title of his speech, delivered in German, was "Why German-Americans Oppose Prohibition." While acknowledging that he was personally not a drinker—"I don't think that in my whole life I have drunk more than one barrel of beer, nor, to avoid misunderstandings, more than a quarter of a gallon of whiskey"—he told his enthusiastic audience that an important reason for the "spread and the persistency of Germany culture and customs" was unquestionably a "gladhearted interpretation of life." Viereck concluded his peroration that German-Americans opposed to prohibition were fighting for significant principles, "not for beer."[103]

In 1910, to promote a plan to stimulate cultural exchanges between the United States and Germany, thereby fostering goodwill, Viereck enlisted the support of ex-president Theodore Roosevelt. In turn, Viereck backed Roosevelt in the 1912 presidential election, going to the extent of writing a special poem for the Bull-Mooser, "Song of Armageddon," and reading it to New York audiences.

By August 1914, Viereck in addition to being a celebrated poet and author on both sides of the Atlantic, was a journeyman editor and publisher. He had worked as a staffer for four years on his father's German-language monthly and as associate editor of *Current Opinion.* He had been publisher and editor of his own German-language magazine, and then publisher and editor of an avant-garde literary magazine in English called *The International.*

It was as editor of *The Fatherland,* however, that Viereck would gain notoriety—and long-term enmity in the United States. The idea for *The Fatherland* appears to have originated not with the German Embassy, as was alleged over and over during the war years, but with four friends at dinner shortly after the outbreak of the war—Viereck, Alfred Lau, Hans Hinrichs, and Dr. Virgil Coblentz. According to Lau, he (Lau) told the group that he had written a letter to the *New York Sun* pleading for fair play for Germany, but the letter had not been published. Viereck countered that he would print the letter in *The International,* but Lau recalled telling him,

> Who in hell reads *The International?* or words to that effect, as *The International* had a very limited circulation (highbrow). ... We decided then and there to print a new magazine. We each contributed $50—and the same night went to the New York Athletic Club and wrote telegrams to leading German writers, professors, and people who could support us financially. So

The Fatherland was actually started in the N.Y.A.C. which later became one of the leaders in pro-war and anti–German sentiment. …The name, I am sure, was invented by a fifth friend, F. A. Borgemeister.[104]

The first issue of the five-cent periodical, which had an initial print run of 5,000 copies, was on New York City newsstands on August 10, 1914. These copies were apparently gobbled up, and 10,000 additional copies were printed. This second run was turned over to idle German reservists in New York awaiting ships to take them to Europe, who peddled them on the streets, newsboy-style. According to Viereck, "The following week's edition had jumped to 15,000 copies, without meeting the demand. It rose to 25,000, then to 50,000, to 75,000 and 80,000 copies. … There were hundreds of thousands who wanted to read the other side of the great conflict, conscious that for some reason or other the American press had failed in its mission and had become the special pleader of a cause espoused by Japs, Senegalese, Cossacks, Indians and the riff-raff of creation nominally fighting for civilization."[105]

Viereck let his readers know exactly where the publication stood—with the seals of Germany and Austria-Hungary in red and black on the cover and the slogan "Fair Play for Germany and Austria" on the masthead. He wrote in an editorial that the purpose of *The Fatherland* was "to place the German side of this unhappy quarrel fairly and squarely before the American people. To review, week by week, the actual events of the war, so far as they can be authoritatively ascertained. To review, week by week, the attitude of the American press, to combat, as far as lies within our power, the misstatements and prejudices of the Slavophile and the German-hater, to point out discrepancies and to protest against injustice towards a race that has rightfully earned the sympathy and admiration instead of the jealousy of the so called civilized world for its industry, its art, its philosophy, and its humanity." The first issue featured a lead article by Muensterberg and a provocative poem by its editor lauding Wilhelm II as a "prince of peace."[106]

The Fatherland and its successors, *Viereck's: The American Weekly* and *The American Monthly*,[107] were used from time to time as forums by the very few distinguished U.S. professors who supported Germany's cause: Muensterberg, von Mach, Burgess, Kuno Francke of Harvard, and William Shepherd of Columbia. Dernburg, Hale, and other members of the propaganda cabinet also contributed essays and articles, as did England's Bertrand Russell and other antiwar and pro-embargo figures, including U.S. senators William J. Stone and Robert M. La Follette.

Most of all, *The Fatherland* was a product of the editor's experience and of his persuasive writing. Viereck published long, biting editorials, book reviews, letters from readers, excerpts from antagonistic articles that had appeared in American publications and sarcastic rejoinders (typically written by Viereck himself), a regular column called "Behind the Scenes at the Capitol," stories about U-boat and Zeppelin successes, and anti–British cartoons.

Viereck's father, Louis, authored articles on the scene in Germany as a staff correspondent. Favorite targets were the National Security League and Theodore Roosevelt. There were beer advertisements from Piel Brothers, Budweiser, and Wiedemann Brewing, and advertisements for pro–German books from Viereck's Fatherland Corporation. His publishing company— amply funded not only through Albert's budget but also through von Bernstorff's, Fuehr's, and Dumba's[108]—printed and distributed thousands of English-language article reprints, pamphlets, and books, and distributed official German publications.

Viereck had few scruples when it came to attacking what he conceived as the nation's pro-Entente "establishment" and its spokesmen. He referred to Dr. Charles W. Eliot, president-emeritus of Harvard University, as "sleek old Eliot, who bartered away his reputation and the prestige of his university for a five-foot bookshelf." Secretary of State Bryan, "silly and dishonest," became "Sir William," because his daughter was married to a captain in the British army. Fellow bard Percy MacKaye, who had written a pro–Ally poem, was disposed of as a "very poor poet and a worse dramatist and his feeble quacks will not disturb the European equilibrium." Woodrow Wilson was the "weak-kneed sophist in the White House."[109]

But these personal diatribes were not regular editorial fare. Viereck had plenty of legitimate pro–British, anti–German, and "preparedness" targets to shoot at and much to communicate without seeking out unnecessary controversy. Reading 80-year-old issues of *The Fatherland*, the author easily credits it with being a reasonable, effectively written, even powerful voice of dissent. Its barbed criticisms were certainly not always constructive, and its unwavering support of the Central Powers was often overly enthusiastic.[110] Yet, the passage of time has smoothed the rough edges of the publication's editorial stance—that the United States had no fundamental quarrel with Germany and no overwhelming reason to go to war.

Viereck was always willing to lay his views on the line. Late in 1914, Cecil Chesterton, editor of London's *New Witness* and younger brother of the author G.K. Chesterton, challenged Viereck to a formal debate on the war. The two matched wits and traded "facts" on the stage of a packed theater in Manhattan on January 17, 1915. According to a *New York Times* story the following day, "Mr. Chesterton, short and pudgy and with an accent truly English, was in good form and handled his side of the question without gloves." Viereck, too, was apparently in fine fettle. His opening remarks flattered his opposite as England's "most able champion." Then he turned to sarcasm: "His speech scintillates with epigram. He takes logic and tosses it up into the air like a juggler's ball. Facts appear and disappear in his arguments like rabbits out of a hat." The text of the debate was subsequently printed by The Fatherland Corporation as a little booklet titled *Whether the Cause of Germany or That of the Allied Powers is Just?* An objective study of the two presentations by no means would favor the German side.

Viereck regularly attended meetings of the German propaganda cabinet, and he wrote that it was at one such conference, in late April 1915, that he recommended that the German government formally warn Americans not to book passage on British passenger steamers—for it was increasingly likely that a U-boat would sooner or later torpedo such a ship. Americans, Viereck pointed out, "cannot visualize one hundred thousand or a million children starving by slow degrees as a result of the British food blockage, but they can visualize the pitiful face of a little child drowning amid the wreckage caused by a torpedo of a German submarine." As Viereck later recalled, he shouted to the group, "You should issue a warning that will reach every passenger who risks his life by traveling in Allied bottoms." Among those present, William Bayard Hale demurred, according to Viereck, saying he preferred "a more indirect method. ...I still prefer the Florentine dagger to the sledge hammer of the Teutonic War God."[111]

Put to a vote, the measure was adopted unanimously, wrote Viereck. It was agreed that an advertisement would be the best and fastest way to get the message across. It was also agreed that Viereck and Hale would together write the advertisement and it would be inserted without delay, for the next large British passenger ship scheduled to depart for England, the *Lusitania*, would leave New York shortly.[112] The result was a small one-column, three-inch advertisement—without question, the most notorious small-space advertisement in U.S. history—scheduled to run on consecutive Saturday issues on the travel and resort pages of major East Coast newspapers.[113] While the date on the advertisement was April 22, the first insertion was not until May 1, coinciding with the departure of the *Lusitania* on her last voyage.

NOTICE!

TRAVELLERS intending to embark on the Atlantic voyage are reminded that a state of war exists between Germany and her allies and Great Britain and her allies; that the zone of war includes the waters adjacent to the British Isles; that, in accordance with formal notice given by the Imperial German Government, vessels flying the flag of Great Britain, or of any of her allies, are liable to destruction in those waters and that travellers sailing in the war zone on ships of Great Britain or her allies do so at their own risk.—IMPE-RIAL GERMAN EMBASSY, WASHINGTON, D.C., APRIL 22, 1915

The travel and resort pages also carried small advertisements announcing ship departures by the major lines, including Cunard's "Europe via Liverpool—LUSITANIA—Fastest and Largest Steamer now in Atlantic Service." The German Embassy's advertisement appeared next to, above, or very close to the Cunard advertisement, in the various newspapers in which it ran. This was actually a last-minute decision of the page-layout person on each newspaper, but was interpreted later by nearly everyone as proof that the conspiratorial Germans had planned to sink the *Lusitania*.

The May 1 issue of the *New York Times* carried a news story about the highly irregular advertisement, for it was extraordinary that a foreign embassy would address a message directly to the citizens of a nation to which it was accredited. The news story carried a prescient subheadline, "Building Up a Defense?" and quoted Cunard agent Charles B. Summer, who was asked about precautions taken concerning Cunard ships: "The danger zone does not begin until we reach the British Channel and the Irish Sea. Then one may say there is a general system of convoying British ships. The British Navy is responsible for all British ships, and especially for Cunarders." The Associated Press picked up the story of the warning and transmitted it nationwide.

The advertisement, which was front-page news in the New York newspapers, caused no passenger cancellations. The *Lusitania* did sail two and one-half hours late, however, taking aboard at the last minute the 163 passengers from the Anchor liner *Cameronia*, which was reported to have been commandeered by the British Admiralty just before that ship was due to depart for Glasgow.

What astounded the German propagandists in New York and Washington—and astonished much of the rest of the world, for few would believe the sinking had not been directly tied to the warning—was that the second insertion of the advertisement appeared on May 8, in the same editions that carried the sensational news of the sinking of the ship. On May 12, the German Embassy formally announced, lamely, that it had decided not to continue to run the advertisement because it had already "had the desired effect."

In late 1914, William Bayard Hale signed on as a publicity adviser and political writer for the German propaganda cabinet. His main duty was to be editorial director of the daily news bulletin published by the German Information Service, but the many-faceted Hale doubled as pamphleteer of anti-British literature, idea man, organizer of pacifist groups, public-opinion analyst, and a diplomat of sorts. He was retained at an extravagant salary of $15,000 per year. This was perhaps as much for his supposedly warm ties with Woodrow Wilson—which by that time had cooled noticeably—as for his writing skills and publicity contacts. There is no evidence, however, that Hale's principal reason for formally joining the German effort in the United States was pecuniary. His wife was German, he spoke German, he was widely traveled in Germany, and he had cultivated high-level political contacts in Germany. His motivation for embracing Germany's cause almost certainly arose out of his outrage at the avalanche of pro–Entente propaganda, for his extensive writings show that he deeply understood recent European history and geopolitics.

Hale was originally educated for the ministry at Boston and Harvard universities. As a clergyman, he had written radical political articles and had become a popular speaker and lecturer for liberal causes. In 1900, he stumped the West for William Jennings Bryan's presidential campaign. He then turned to magazine and newspaper journalism, moving frequently from one publication to another. He wrote for *Cosmopolitan, Current Literature, The World's Work,* the *New York World,* the *Philadelphia Public Ledger,* and the *New York Times.*

For the *Times,* Hale spent a week in the White House in 1908 observing President Roosevelt at work. Hale's article, "With the President at the Nation's Business," which ran in the Sunday magazine section in April and was published as a book the same year, *A Week in the White House with Theodore Roosevelt: A Study of the President at the Nation's Business,* established its author as a top political journalist. In August of that year, Hale conducted a sensational two-hour interview with Kaiser Wilhelm II on his yacht in a Norwegian fjord.[114]

In 1911, Hale, then on the staff of *The World's Work,* which was edited by Woodrow Wilson's close friend Walter Hines Page, was brought aboard the presidential campaign for the aspiring New Jersey governor. Hale wrote a series of articles for his magazine based on interviews with Wilson, turning them into a little book a year later. Hale said the purpose of his biography was to trace the background of New Jersey's governor and provides reasons that uniquely equipped him for higher office. In the book, which became the campaign's official biography, he liberally spread the usual political encomiums:

> People seemed suddenly to become aware that there was a man named Wilson who looked more like a great man than any who had been seen of late days. ...Governor Wilson is a man of positive opinion, relieved by an eager sense of humor. ...He is chock-full of energy; he likes action, hugely ... is an indefatigable worker. ...Be the weather cold or not, any one can walk, without touching a door-knob, from the street into the Governor's inner room.[115]

Governor Wilson sent a letter of thanks to Hale for his work on the book. His salutation and closing were quite formal, despite the hours the two men had spent together:

> April 30, 1912
>
> My dear Mr. Hale:
>
> ... It certainly has been got up very nicely indeed, and I want to again express my warm appreciation of the spirit and generosity with which you wrote from a scant material, an admirable sketch.
>
> Cordially and sincerely yours,[116]

One year later, although by this time knowing Hale well enough to ask him to become a personal secret agent, President Wilson still addressed him coldly:

April 19, 1913

My dear Mr. Hale:

I think that the situation of affairs in Central and South America is very much more difficult to get the threads of than the situation in California, and with the full acquiescence of Mr. Bryan I am writing to ask if you would be willing to undertake a tour of the Central and South American states, ostensibly on your own hook, in order that unofficially and through the eyes of an independent observer we might find out just what is going on down there.

Will you not be kind enough to regard this inquiry as strictly confidential?

Cordially and sincerely yours,[117]

Hale was obviously flattered by the sub-rosa assignment for the president and through the remainder of the year and into 1914 he traveled in Mexico and Nicaragua, meeting with high government officials in both countries.

Woodrow Wilson finally let his barriers down before Hale as far as his stern character would permit. This almost-affectionate note represented the high point of the relationship between the two men, as far as Wilson was concerned:

January 15, 1914

My dear Hale:

It distresses me very deeply to know that you have been temporarily knocked out.

It must be due to your present condition that you should think that you have "done little or nothing." You have in my opinion done a great deal and been of very great service to us and I shall be at a loss where to turn for similar service in the time immediately ahead of us. ... My warmest sympathy and most earnest good wishes will go with you wherever you go....

With warmest regard and sympathy,

Cordially and faithfully yours,[118]

Following his fact-finding assignments, Hale prepared another brief book for the new president, a compilation and reorganization of Wilson's unexceptional stump speeches; this carried Wilson's name as the author. In the preface by Wilson, the president unaccountably claimed that he "did not write this book at all. It is the result of the editorial literary skill of Mr. William Bayard Hale."[119]

At the end of 1914, Wilson refused a request by Hale that the president meet with Bernhard Dernburg. Although Wilson still maintained a friendly veneer, it was this incident that apparently pushed Hale onto the German payroll. Hale, who knew well that the president studiously avoided being confronted by ideas that ran contrary to his, had gotten an unmistakable signal from Wilson's note rejecting his request. He realized that the president's refusal to listen to the persuasive Dernburg meant he had already abandoned American neutrality.

Almost immediately afterward on December 31, the *New York Times* published a long letter from Hale that took up nearly half the editorial page. It was headlined "Great Britain and American Ships," and was Hale's detailed interpretation of international law concerning naval warfare—a field in which he would become expert—and its applicability to the U.S. note of December 28 protesting British interference with American commerce.

Hale continued stubbornly to court the president, particularly regarding a munitions embargo that would be enforced against all the belligerents. Wilson's responses, reverting to a formal salutation, also showed a perceptible change in tone, almost as if a stern college instructor were upbraiding an inattentive student:

March 31, 1915

My dear Mr. Hale:

I have your letter of March twenty-ninth with the accompanying sketch of an Act of Congress. ... The proposal you make is a very serious one indeed.

You will recall it is practically along the lines of some of our old embargoes which historians are agreed were much more hurtful to us than to the countries against which they were aimed.

This is a side of it which ought to be thought of very carefully.

Cordially and sincerely yours,[120]

April 5, 1915

My dear Mr. Hale:

The argument contained in your letter of April second is a strong one and contains certain persuasive features, but the suggestion is in effect a suggestion of reprisal and I should be very loath to see this nation ... adopt a policy which would seem to be in imitation or retaliation of anything proposed on the other side of the water. I really think we should cultivate a different spirit in the matter.

Cordially and sincerely yours,[121]

There is no record of further correspondence between the two men.

During 1915 and early 1916, Hale was busy on other fronts, frequently writing under pseudonyms. His major published effort was the compilation of *American Rights and British Pretensions on the Seas*, a 172-page oversize book designed to give the appearance of an official government document. It included all the important communications exchanged between the United States and Great Britain dealing with the contentious freedom-of-the-seas issue. The book was a powerful indictment of Great Britain's actions on the seas, and Hale vigorously covered every aspect. He claimed that armed merchant ships were relics of the distant past, when pirates existed, and that the advent of submarines had created a new situation. He made much of the orders by the British admiralty directing merchantmen to fire on U-boats before they had been fired on, and to ram them. As a result, Hale argued, it was entirely proper for U-boats to sink armed merchantmen on sight. He detailed how England had applied and extended the definition of contraband to suit its own purposes and had interfered with American ships and cargoes, including American mail.

Hale organized and directed the two nationwide embargo movements, that were funded by Germany, the American Embargo Conference and the American Organization of American Women for Strict Neutrality. The women's group appealed to the sensitivities of mothers who might have to send their sons into battle for a vague cause. Under its auspices, he published a booklet entitled *Thou Shalt Not Kill—The Exportation of Arms and Munitions of War: Should the United States Government Allow It or Forbid It?* It contained articles by Hale and other well-known native American pro—Germans describing and denouncing both the manufacture and the export of munitions. The pamphlet also argued that the Allies were getting most of the benefit from Great Britain's control of the seas, and that the United States was thus their silent partner. On behalf of the same organization, Hale published a pamphlet that summarized speeches made in the Congress in early 1916 on the question of submarine warfare. He pointed out that the overwhelming majority of opinion among the lawmakers was in favor of warning Americans not to take passage on armed belligerent ships; the anti-British parts of the speeches were printed in bold type. Hale's wife also got involved, writing a booklet opposing the export of horses on humanitarian grounds.

In May 1916, apparently convinced he could be of more help to the cause of American neutrality as a journalist in Europe, Hale joined the Hearst organization and went to Germany as a special correspondent for the *New York American* and the International News Service. He was at the front with the German armies on the Somme River during the summer, and in early September spent a week at the headquarters of the German crown prince. His almost-daily dispatches were widely published in Hearst's papers in the United States and in the German press.

Using his high-level political contacts in Berlin, Hale also worked quietly to promote U.S.-German amity as a private diplomat. Gottlieb von Jagow, former German foreign secretary, recalled in a letter to von Bernstorff after the war that it had been Hale who had invited him and U.S. ambassador James Gerard to dinner, just before Gerard went on leave, when "I begged him to induce Wilson to take some step in the direction of peace."[122]

Hale made sure he was at the press conference in the *Wilhelmstrasse* in Berlin on March 3, 1917, following the disclosure of Alfred Zimmermann's secret communication to Germany's ambassador to Mexico proposing an alliance if the United States came into the war. Hale was promptly recognized and he carefully phrased a leading question to Zimmermann to give the foreign minister a diplomatic opportunity to refute the damaging allegation. Hale did not ask if the dispatch was authentic. Instead, Hale began, "Of course, Your Excellency will deny this story." Zimmermann interrupted: "I cannot deny it. It is true."[123]

When America entered the war, Hale returned to the United States. In July 1918, he was questioned by a U.S. attorney general about his role as a paid German propagandist. Hale acknowledged that he had worked with the German propagandists, but what drew the most attention was the charge that it was Hale who had written Dernburg's press handout in Cleveland the day following the sinking of the *Lusitania*—more than three years earlier. Hale admitted to having made some minor editorial comments.

Like Viereck, who had been expelled from the Authors' League and the Poetry Society of America, Hale, too, suffered ostracism for his pro–German views. He was forced to resign from his clubs, magazines turned down his articles, publishers rejected his book manuscripts, and his name was expunged from biographical works. He went into seclusion and never completed the major biography he had planned on Woodrow Wilson. Instead, Hale's final book, published in 1920, was a vengeful, petty denunciation of Wilson's intellect and literary ability. In *Woodrow Wilson: The Story of a Style*, he tried to shatter what had become almost a tenet among Americans—a mystique, coincidentally, to which Hale had contributed mightily—that Woodrow Wilson was a master of English writing style. He seemed to have forgotten what he had written about the president eight years before, that "Mr. Wilson has long been known as an exquisite master of English prose. He speaks as he writes— with a trained and skillful handling of the resources of the language, a sureness, an accuracy, a power, and a delicacy surpassing anything ever before heard on the political platform in America."[124] To the contrary, Hale bitterly concluded in 1920, "it must be said frankly and with conscientious seriousness, that a study of Mr. Wilson's writings and speeches does not permit the conclusion that his is a high grade of mentality.... It is impossible to ignore the fact that his writings are marked conspicuously and obstinately by some of the signs most often associated with sub-normal intelligence. It is equally impossible to discern in them any evidence of compensating genius, as often accompanies idiosyncrasy. The conclusion enforced is that among writers he ranks as one of inferior mental power."[125]

Back in Germany after being driven out of the United States in mid–1915, Bernhard Dernburg was as good as his final words to American reporters: he was keeping up the pressure for a negotiated settlement. He was then Germany's most sought-after expert on the United States, and he continually warned—as von Bernstorff was also vainly doing—against underestimating the industrial and financial power of America. In September 1915, Dernburg was elected president of the German Economic Association for

South and Central America, an organization seeking expanded trade in Latin America. In his acceptance speech, Dernburg was candid, as always, in his appraisal that Germany then had only a few friends in the world, and that this was the fault of his countrymen, who had to learn to understand other people.

In November, Dernburg published a conciliatory article that covered the entire front page of the prestigious *Berliner Tageblatt*. It praised Woodrow Wilson's recent "neutral" note to England on the freedom-of-the-seas issue, and suggested that the president was defending the fundamentals of international law. In the summer of 1918, along with 80 other prominent Germans, Dernburg signed a broadly publicized petition that advanced the idea of self-determination and condemned the forced annexation of politically autonomous states.

In the postwar years, Dernburg emerged as finance minister and a leader of the Democratic Party in Philip Scheidemann's cabinet. When Hitler came to power in 1933, Dernburg, a Jew, then a bank president and a director of the Hamburg-Amerika Line, was forced to sever all his business interests and go into seclusion. He died in 1937.

When Count von Bernstorff returned to Germany in early 1917, he was proposed as von Bethmann-Hollweg's successor as chancellor by both Bethmann and the Reichstag. The Kaiser declared himself prepared to appoint von Bernstorff, but the generals were opposed because of his peace initiatives while he had been in the United States. Instead, von Bernstorff was named ambassador to Turkey, his last diplomatic post, where he remained until nearly the end of the war. When Prince Max of Baden was appointed chancellor in the last weeks of the war, von Bernstorff was ordered back to Berlin for final discussions prior to the Armistice.

After the war, he defended his country's wartime efforts to sway American public opinion, writing in his 1920 retrospective that

> the German propaganda in America in no way deserves the abuse with which it has been covered, in part, too, at home. If it had really been so clumsy or ineffective as the enemy Press afterwards claimed, the Entente and their American partisans would not have set in motion such gigantic machinery to combat it. ... As regards our justification for openly championing the German cause before the people of the United States by written and spoken word, this is self-evident in a country which recognizes the principles of freedom of the Press and free speech.[126]

Von Bernstorff was elected to the Reichstag in 1921, remaining there for seven years. During that period, he became a crusader for the League of Nations and other peace- and disarmament-related organizations, was an active president of the German League of Nations, and oversaw Germany's entry into the League in 1926. When the Nazis rose to power, he liquidated his properties in Germany and took up permanent residence in Geneva,

Switzerland. He lived in exile there, an outspoken anti–Nazi, until his death in 1939.

George Sylvester Viereck came out of World War I determined to set the record straight according to his own light and help restore Germany's good name. The best way to do this, he reasoned, was through the ex–Kaiser, who was in exile in Doorn, Holland. In 1922, he met Wilhelm II for the first time, and by the end of the following year he had been a guest of the former emperor three times. He continued to make annual pilgrimages to Wilhelm's estate throughout the 1920s and early 1930s, writing complimentary articles about the man and his times and, in effect, becoming his exclusive press agent. Viereck, with a political reporter's instinct for politicians on the rise, sought out an interview with Adolf Hitler in 1923. In his *American Monthly*, Viereck suggested that Hitler "looked more like a poet than a politician," predicting, "If he lives, Hitler for better or for worse, is sure to make history."[127]

Viereck was also busy mending fences in the United States. In 1930, he took advantage of his insider's knowledge of German propaganda work in America to publish *Spreading Germs of Hate*, a book based on a series of articles he had anonymously written for the *Saturday Evening Post* the previous year. Edward M. House, who had liked the articles, sought out the author and the two men subsequently formed a warm friendship. In 1932, Viereck published *The Strangest Friendship in History: Woodrow Wilson and Colonel House*, and in 1937, *The Kaiser on Trial*. This latter book was a dramatic, fictionalized biography that raked over the coals of the propaganda of World War I from Germany's perspective.

Chapter 4

AMERICA'S
NON-NEUTRALITY

The United States must be neutral in fact as well as in name during these days that try men's souls. We must be impartial in thought as well as in action, must put a curb upon our sentiments as well as upon every transaction that might be construed as a preference of one part to the struggle before another.

Woodrow Wilson, August 18, 1914

If Germany won, it would change the course of our civilization and make the United States a military nation.

Woodrow Wilson to Edward Mandell House, August 30, 1914

A comfortable myth that Americans continue to embrace is that their government was neutral during the months from August 1914 to April 1917, and only when an aggressive Germany became a threat to the nation's security did a reluctant America take up arms in defense. Precisely as all the earlier combatants had done, the United States declared that belligerency had been thrust upon a supposedly peace-loving nation. Woodrow Wilson, in asking the Congress for a declaration of war, went even further, and declared that the recent course of the Imperial Germany Government to be "in fact nothing less than war against the Government and people of the United States."[1]

In reality, America, as manifest in the views and actions, overt and covert, of its political leaders, diplomats, bankers, manufacturers, clergy, and press—the dominant powers that drove the nation and molded its public opinion—was distinctly non-neutral in spirit.[2] From the first weeks of the war, these forces were nearly universally pro–Ally, and as the flood of British propaganda enveloped them their attitudes solidified. In May 1915, the *Lusitania* sinking drove many of the dwindling numbers of influential moderates into the arms of the most rabid anti–German factions. By this time, too, America had well-organized pro–Entente, prowar propaganda forces of its own, parading under the euphemistic banner of "preparedness"—and generously funded by the nation's big businessmen. These private agencies and their spokesmen overwhelmed those opposed to America's military involvement by invoking one of the most fearsome words in the American lexicon, "unpatriotic."

Profoundly pro–Entente himself, Woodrow Wilson nevertheless sought to act as peacemaker, but was unwilling to accept that America's non-neutral actions precluded the role of mediator he sought. He finally brought America into the war when he was convinced that his nation was behind him, that public opinion was so incensed by Germany's sinking of ships without warning and by German plotting in Mexico that it demanded war with Germany— despite having won the 1916 election with the slogan "With honor, he kept us out of war."[3]

While most Americans were oblivious of their nation's non-neutral stance, it became clear to German-Americans and pacifist groups in the United States exactly where America stood. Far more important was how Germans in Germany reacted to the practical aspects of America's non-neutrality. America was seen as unwilling to hold England accountable for its violations of American neutrality while at the same time demanding from Germany strict adherence to international law. But it was the enormous private loans and the steadily rising shipments of munitions and food to the Allies that grated most harshly. As early as January 1915, James W. Gerard, the American ambassador to Germany, cabled the president about the bitterness growing in Berlin over what was perceived as grossly anti–German conduct by America: "I do not think that the people in America realize how excited the Germans have become on the question of selling munitions of war by Americans to the Allies. A veritable campaign of hate has been commenced against America and Americans."[4]

In April 1915, Wilson's chief foreign-policy advisor, Colonel House, indicated this hostile attitude of Germans in a politely worded cable from Paris: "My visit in Berlin was exceedingly trying and disagreeable in many ways. I met there no one of either high or low degree who did not immediately corner me, and begin to discuss our shipment of munitions to the Allies, and sometimes their manner was almost offensive."[5]

The next month, Gerard could react to a concrete example of America's non-neutrality: the famous incident of the "poison-shell" advertisement. The Cleveland Automatic Machine Company, a U.S. machine-tool manufacturer, had run an advertisement for a new lathe in a widely read American trade magazine. The copy candidly described the kind of artillery shell that the lathe was designed to machine efficiently:

> The material is high in tensile strength and Very Special and has a tendency to fracture into small pieces upon the explosion of the shell. The timing of the fuse for this shell is similar to the shrapnel shell, but it differs in that two explosive acids are used to explode the shell in the large cavity. The combination of these two acids causes a terrific explosion, having more power than anything of its kind yet used. Fragments become coated with these

acids in exploding and wounds caused by them mean death in terrible agony within four hours if not attended to immediately.

From what we are able to learn of conditions in the trenches, it is not possible to get medical assistance to anyone in time to prevent fatal results. It is necessary immediately to cauterize the wound if in the body or head, or to amputate if in the limbs, as there seems to be no antidote that will counteract the poison.

It can be seen from this that this shell is more effective than the regular shrapnel, since the wounds caused by shrapnel balls and fragments in the muscles are not as dangerous, as they have no poisonous element making prompt attention necessary.[6]

The advertisement for an American product designed to manufacture munitions to kill soldiers horribly—German soldiers, in particular—caused a sensation in Germany. Gerard reacted angrily when he learned that copies of "that infernal advertisement" had been "laid on the desk of every member of the Reichstag." He suggested to the State Department that perhaps it was "the work of German propagandists in the United States and if so, prompt exposure would be helpful."[7]

A June 23 news story in the *New York Times* from Bavarian army headquarters, based on visits to field hospitals, pointed out that German surgeons "had a very special grievance, alleging that the French were using poisonous American shells and that in many cases even slight wounds resulted in terrible infection, causing quick death." According to the story, all the surgeons had "read the sensational advertisement of alleged poisonous shells by the Cleveland Automatic Machine Company." The newspaper account also reflected what the reporter indicated was "the intense feeling among officers over the supplying of American ammunition to the Allies, resulting in powerful backing for the Admiralty in its determination to carry on the submarine war against England."

Germany's formally announced submarine blockade of the British Isles in early 1915, proclaimed as retaliation against the Royal Navy's surface-ship blockade of Germany, was its first attempt to cut off the flow of munitions from the United States. Following the *Lusitania* sinking, American threats of entering the war forced Germany to temper its U-boat tactics. When Germany announced resumption of unrestricted submarine warfare in February 1917, in a last-ditch effort to bring the stalemated conflict to a victorious conclusion, its government had decided that the hot war with America that would almost certainly result would scarcely be different from the phantom war the United States had been waging for nearly three years. America's "non-neutrality" had thus forced Germany's hand.[8]

Edward Mandell House first met Woodrow Wilson in New York City on November 24, 1911. From that date until sometime in March 1919, in Paris during the peace negotiations, when Wilson apparently had concluded that

House was usurping his negotiating responsibilities and henceforth was no longer to be trusted, House was Wilson's most valued political confidant and a warm personal friend—and unquestionably the second most powerful man in the United States. In a postwar appraisal, he was described thus:

> His hobby was practical politics; his avocation the study of history and government. ... Disqualified by physical delicacy from entering the political arena himself and consistently refusing office, he had for years controlled the political stage in his own state; in 1912, exercising strong influence in the national party organization, he had done much to crystalize sentiment in favor of Wilson as presidential candidate. ... [He was] slight in stature, quiet in manner and voice, disliking personal publicity, with an almost uncanny instinct for divining the motives that actuate men. ...Courteous and engaging, Colonel House was an unexcelled negotiator; he had a genius for compromise, as perfect a control of his emotions as of his facial expression, and a pacific magnetism that soothed into reasonableness the most heated interlocutor.[9]

House had been left financially independent by a wealthy English father, enabling him to follow his star, politics, as a behind-the-scenes planner, organizer, and manipulator. House understood the value of publicity and how to use it to advantage, but studiously avoided the limelight himself. When he was cornered by reporters, which was rarely, he gave them little and well-sifted information and even less encouragement. House had managed three successful Democratic gubernatorial campaigns in his home state of Texas starting in 1892. The honorary title of "Colonel" was acquired from the last of his appreciative benefactors.[10] But by the turn of the century, House had outgrown state politics and considered himself ready for king making on a grander scale. "During all these years," he bluntly wrote later in his diary, "I had never for a moment overlooked the national situation, and it was there that my real interest lay. In 1896 I was ready to take part in national affairs. My power in Texas was sufficient to have given me the place I desired in the national councils of the party."[11]

House, Diogenes-like, then went looking for his champion—a Democratic presidential contender who measured up to his exacting standards. William Jennings Bryan did not fit House's specifications and he never threw his weight behind Bryan's three losing candidacies, in 1896, 1900, and 1908; in fact, House was always quietly contemptuous of Bryan's views and activities. But the pragmatic House recognized the party power wielded by the Great Commoner and assiduously cultivated a close, if hypocritical, personal relationship with Bryan. (In the 1912 Democratic convention, it would be Bryan who finally swung the party behind House's chosen candidate, Woodrow Wilson.)

House patiently perservered. His candidate should preferably be from the

Woodrow Wilson (right) with his close friend, political confidant, and chief of for-eign policy, Colonel Edward Mandell House. Their nearly identical attires and sim-ilar stance reflect their consonance in more weighty matters. September 1917. *Edward M. House Papers, Manuscripts and Archives, Yale University Library.*

East and a liberal who could get votes from the West—someone he considered electable, and, by all means, someone who would listen to advice. In 1911, House's wait was over. In a letter to his brother-in-law two weeks after his first meeting with Wilson, House enthused about his "delightful visit ... and I would rather play with him than any prospective candidate I have seen. ... Never before have I found both the man and the opportunity."[12] Five years later he recalled:

> I have been in as close touch with Woodrow Wilson as with any man I have ever known. The first hour we spent together proved to each of us that there was a sound basis for a fast friendship. ...We soon learned to know what each was thinking without either having expressed himself. ...A few weeks after we met and after we had exchanged confidences which men usually do not exchange except after years of friendship, I asked him if he realized that we had only known one another for so short a time. He replied, "My dear friend, we have known one another always."[13]

In fact, Wilson, the neophyte politician, had as much to gain from the new relationship as House. Wilson's immediate problem was to secure his party's nomination. The road was through Bryan, the party leader, and House was needed to pave the way. Wilson could not do the job alone, for he had too often expressed publicly and privately his antipathy for Bryan.[14]

As important as House's skillful guidance and party management was his sensitive stroking of Wilson's ego. Early in their relationship House had discovered Wilson's deep psychological needs—for affection, praise, approval, and, above all, loyalty. Wilson also felt a quiet drive to achieve greatness. To maintain his newfound place in history, House catered diligently to all these yearnings of his friend. In his diary, House confided that when Wilson asked for suggestions dealing with drafts of his speeches, he nearly always praised at first to strengthen the president's confidence in himself, "which, strangely enough, is often lacking."[15]

His letters to the president were filled with syrupy phrases and affected terms of endearment, almost abnormally so. And Wilson responded in kind. For example, just before he left for Europe in January 1915, House recorded that he spent an extra day in Washington just so he could bid the president a personal goodbye: "I told him how much he had been to me; how I had tried all my life to find some one with whom I could work out the things I had so deeply at heart, and I had begun to despair, believing my life would be more or less a failure, when he came into it, giving me the opportunity for which I had been longing."[16] According to House, Wilson, who insisted on going to Washington's Union Station with House and walking to the train, had moist eyes when he said goodbye: "'Your unselfish and intelligent friendship has meant much to me,' he said, and he expressed his gratitude again and again, calling me his 'most trusted friend.' He declared I was the only one in the world to whom he could open his entire mind."[17]

The next day, unable to suppress his enthusiasm, House again wrote to Wilson: "My! How I hated to leave you last night. Around you is centered most of the interest I have left in life and my greatest joy is to serve you. Your words of affection at parting touched me so deeply that I could not tell you then and perhaps never can tell you, just how I feel." Finally, House gushed these words in yet another emotional outburst: "Goodbye, dear friend, and may God sustain you in all your noble undertakings. ... You are the bravest, wisest leader, the gentlest and most gallant gentleman and the truest friend in all the world."[18]

Once elected in 1912, Wilson, preoccupied with domestic political issues, happily turned over to House both the management and execution of the nation's foreign policy. It was House, not Secretary of State William Jennings Bryan nor his successor, Robert Lansing, who journeyed to Europe as America's principal foreign emissary. It was House who conducted the most confidential communications with the principal foreign emissaries in the United States. It would also be House who became the controlling behind-the-scenes negotiator for the Americans in Paris in 1919.

By 1913, House apparently had recognized what was obvious to most European diplomats—that the continent was a powder keg. He had also correctly divined the principal reason for the potential conflict: the growing friction between England and Germany. If Europe went to war, House reasoned, America might certainly become involved and, therefore, it was in the interests of the United States to try to avert the war. He would take the responsibility, with the president's blessing, somehow to mediate the differences—and gain for his client everlasting glory as a global peacemaker. Perhaps, in turn, the quietly ambitious House could insinuate himself into the presidency.

House prepared thoroughly. He cultivated the key diplomats who fit into the matrix—in Washington, German ambassador von Bernstorff, British ambassador Spring-Rice, French ambassador Jusserand, and Austro-Hungarian ambassador Dumba; and in London, U.S. ambassador Page, Foreign Minister Sir Edward Grey, and other British political figures. He probed the character of Europe's most dominating political figure, the Kaiser, by interrogating men who knew him. At the end of 1913, Sir William Tyrell, Grey's secretary, came to the United States and assured House "that England was ready to cooperate with Germany, and had been ready to do so for a long while." He also told House that he saw "no cause for difference between them." With England, United States, France, and Germany agreed, both men thought "the balance of the world would follow in line and a great change would come about." Tyrell primed House for his coming meeting with the German emperor; he said that Wilhelm was "a spectacular individual and partook more of French qualities than he did of German" and "likened him to Roosevelt."[19]

By this time, House had formulated a plan. He would go to three

European capitals—Berlin, Paris, and London—and talk to the most influential officials in each. He would spend as much time as necessary, for he was a patient man. He would act as an objective broker, or so he deluded himself into thinking. Perhaps the most telling flaw in House's vision was his disregard of Russia as a major player in European power politics. The colossus of the East was the biggest land-grabber of all, obsessed with gaining the straits—the Dardanelles and the Bosporous—with access to the Mediterranean, at Turkey's expense, and with domination of the Balkans, at Austria-Hungary's. Apparently House never considered adding St. Petersburg to his itinerary.

In May 1914, House left for Europe on his mission, which he romantically called his "great adventure." To his principal biographer, Charles Seymour, he was "a private American citizen whose only relevant title was 'personal friend of the President,' a single individual hoping to pull the lever of common sense that might divert the nations of the Old World from the track of war to that of peace."[20] House returned to Europe early in 1915 and again in the winter of 1915-16 to try to arrange peace. By the end of his second tour, however, House had moved comfortably into the Allied camp. His personal definition of peace in Europe had changed drastically. He came to think that peace could come only through the defeat of Germany, and from then on worked persuasively and unswervingly to this end.

In Berlin, the first stop on his 1914 visit, House's honorary title of colonel was misinterpreted by his hosts, who had no conception of Texas-made military officers. As soon as he arrived in the German capital, House was whisked to the local airfield for a demonstration of Germany's aerial might. The Foreign Office also thought that he would be more at home debating armaments with a conservative admiral, Alfred von Tirpitz, than discussing European politics with a scholarly chancellor, Dr. Theobold von Bethmann-Hollweg, and talking economics with a modern-thinking German businessman like Walter Rathenau. From these superficial preliminary contacts and impressions, House cabled Wilson on May 29 several odd and slanted interpretations that reflect the faint gleams of his newfound anti–German bias: "The situation is extraordinary. It is militarism run stark mad. ... Whenever England consents, France and Russia will close in on Germany and Austria. England does not want Germany wholly crushed, for she would then have to reckon alone with her ancient enemy, Russia; but if Germany insists upon an ever-increasing navy, then England will have no choice."

House concluded his message by pandering to his reader's thirst for fame: "It is an absorbing problem, and one of tremendous consequence. I wish it might be solved, to the everlasting glory of your Administration and our American civilization."[21]

Two days later, House had an audience with the Kaiser, and recorded in his diary his initial reaction to his first, and last, meeting with Wilhelm II:

I found that he had all the versatility of Roosevelt with something more of charm, something less of force. He had what to me is a disagreeable habit of bringing his face very close to one when he talks most earnestly. His English is clear and well chosen and, though he talks vehemently, yet he is too much the gentleman to monopolize conversation. It was give-and-take all the way through. He knew what he wanted to say, so did I; and since we both talk rapidly, the half-hour was quite sufficient.[22]

House obviously had been charmed by the persuasive and eloquent emperor, if only momentarily. He recorded that he was "much less prejudiced and much less belligerent than von Tirpitz" and that he wanted peace because it was in Germany's interest. The reason why Germany had such a powerful army, the Kaiser told him, was because his country was menaced on every side, and the reason for Germany's growing navy was to protect Germany's commerce "in an adequate way, and one commensurate with her growing power and importance." House told the Kaiser that he and the president "thought perhaps an American might be able to better compose the difficulties" in Europe and promote peace better than "any European, because of their distrust and dislike for one another." The Kaiser agreed. After House explained that he expected "to feel his way cautiously and see what could be accomplished," the Kaiser concluded the meeting by asking that House keep him informed.[23]

After a brief visit to Paris, where his only diplomatic discussion was with U.S. ambassador Myron T. Herrick, House went on to London, his final stop. There, farsighted English knights and lords exquisitely dined and thoroughly brainwashed their receptive guest. House showed again his newfound leanings, as Grey later recorded: "House left me in no doubt from the first that he held German militarism responsible for the war, and that he regarded the struggle as one between democracy and something that was undemocratic and antipathetic to American ideals. ... I felt sure that he did not differ much from Page in his view of the merits of the war."[24] His naiveté of the political realities in Europe, insofar as France was concerned, was revealed in a summary cable to Wilson from London on June 17: "Here they have their thoughts on Ascot, garden parties. ... In Germany their one thought is to advance industrially and to glorify war. In France I did not find the war spirit dominant. Their statesmen dream no longer of revenge and the recovery of Alsace and Lorraine. ... France, I am sure, will welcome our efforts for peace."[25]

While House was still in London, waiting for Grey to respond to his conciliatory initiatives, the Austro-Hungarian archduke Franz Ferdinand and his wife were shot dead in Sarajevo. The powder train had been ignited. In less than six weeks, the Great War would begin.

Over and over House strove persistently, but ever so gently, to swing the president to his way of thinking. His cables from London during the spring of 1915 were particularly insistent, surrounded as he was by the Anglophile U.S. ambassador, Walter Hines Page, and a nation desperately fighting for its empire. Following the sinking of the *Lusitania*, on May 9 House cabled Wilson that the United States must demand assurances from Germany that this would not occur again. "If she fails to give such assurance," House sternly advised, "I should inform her that our Government expected to take such measures as were necessary to ensure the safety of American citizens." It was almost as if House were dictating the principal lines of a vigorous diplomatic note of protest to the German government. House salved his warlike stance by suggesting, preposterously, that America's intervention would "save rather than increase, the loss of life." He closed poetically, training his guns on a reader whose every emotion he had by then learned intimately:

> America has come to the parting of the ways, when she must determine whether she stands for civilized or uncivilized warfare. We can no longer remain neutral spectators. Our action in this crisis will determine the part we will play when peace is made, and how far we may influence a settlement for the lasting good of humanity. We are being weighed in the balance, and our position amongst nations is being assessed by mankind.[26]

House nearly won over the president this early in the war, for Wilson was so enamored of House's views—and perhaps of his eloquent phraseology, as well—that he read the cable to his cabinet during the meeting in which he reviewed his first protest note to Germany over the sinking.

Perhaps as much as any other single action House took to bring America into the war on his own initiative was his Machiavellian plan that came to be known as the "House-Grey memorandum" of October 17, 1915. House called his encoded letter to Grey, transmitted as a "split message" intended to confuse German cryptoanalysts, "one of the most important letters I ever wrote."[27] One observer used a different adjective, calling it "certainly ... one of the most extraordinary letters in the history of diplomacy."[28]

House wrote: "It has occurred to me that the time may soon come when this Government should intervene between the belligerents and demand that peace parleys begin upon the broad basis of the elimination of militarism and navalism. ... In my opinion, it would be a world-wide calamity if the war should continue to a point where the Allies could not, with the aid of the United States, bring about a peace along the lines you [Grey] and I have so often discussed."[29]

House then laid out the details of his scheme to Grey, explaining that it was his intent to try to mislead Germany into thinking that the Allies would reject the proposed mediation. "This might induce Berlin to accept the proposal," he confessed, "but, if they did not do so, it would nevertheless be the purpose to intervene [diplomatically]. If the Central Powers were still obdurate, it would be necessary for us to join the Allies and force the issue." While imprecise in its intent, the letter was nevertheless unambiguous on the most important point: if Germany refused to participate in America's mediation initiative, America would go to war against Germany. House showed his letter to Wilson, who approved it immediately, but made a small but important insertion: "...it would *probably* be necessary...."[30]

Like practically every presidential cabinet, Woodrow Wilson's, instead of being filled with the party's brightest, was a collection of undistinguished political cronies rewarded for loyalty. House had selected most of them, and Wilson knew few personally.

The chief cabinet post, secretary of state, went to William Jennings Bryan. While Wilson continued to look upon Bryan as impractical and belittled his judgments, it would not have been possible to create a new Democratic administration without including the man who, as much as House, had put Wilson in the White House. Bryan had not only helped direct Wilson's nomination at the convention, he had also stumped indefatigably for candidate Wilson, averaging some ten speeches a day for nearly two months just prior to the election.

House and Wilson first considered an ambassadorship as repayment, then agreed that it was safer for Bryan to be in Washington, a visible part of the administration, not outside it and possibly a disruptive critic. Only the chief cabinet post would do for Bryan; besides, in 1913, nearly everyone foresaw that domestic rather than foreign policy making would be the focus of the new administration. Furthermore, Bryan's role would be carefully circumscribed by Wilson, who had planned to act as his own foreign secretary.[31]

If the president was usurping the secretary of state's prerogatives, the thick-skinned Bryan showed no apparent concern. He focused his considerable energies on a project that was close to his heart: a series of peace treaties among the nations of the world.[32] Bryan, a teetotaling Christian fundamentalist, was inspired by a belief that, with sufficient time for deliberation, any dispute could be settled peacefully, for alone among Wilson's cabinet officers and the president's entire coterie of would-be advisors, Bryan was a dyed-in-the-wool pacifist. From the outbreak of the war until he resigned ten months later, Bryan did the best he could to maintain a strict American neutrality. He tried to stop loans to the belligerents. When America's greatest banking house, J. P. Morgan & Co., asked if it might float a loan to France, Bryan responded, on August 14, 1914: "There is no reason why loans should not be made to governments by neutral nations, but in the judgment of this government, loans by American bankers to any foreign nation which is at war are inconsistent with the spirit of true neutrality." He said he considered that money, "being able to purchase all other contraband materials, was in effect the worst of contraband."[33]

He proposed that the warring nations adhere to the 1909 Declaration of London[34] and insisted that England, like Germany, be held equally accountable for offenses against American neutrality. Bryan pointed to Britain's interference with the U.S. mails, her flying of the U.S. flag on her merchantmen, her detaining of American ships and holding them in port so long that cargo owners were forced to sell their goods to the British at firesale prices. He took the moral position that while Americans were free to go where they pleased, they were obligated not to travel on belligerent ships and thus endanger their country's fragile neutrality. On April 23, 1915, following the sinking of the *Arabic*, which resulted in the first death of a U.S. citizen from a U-boat attack, President Wilson drafted a strongly worded note to Germany, to which Bryan wrote a logically considered objection:

> The note which you propose will, I fear, very much inflame the already hostile feeling against us in Germany, not entirely because of our protest against Germany's action in this case, but in part because of its contrast with our attitude toward the Allies. If we oppose the use of the submarine against merchantmen we will lay down a law for ourselves as well as for Germany. If we admit the right of the submarine to attack merchantmen but condemn their particular act or class of acts as inhuman we will be embarrased by the fact that we have not protested against Great Britain's defense of the right to prevent foods reaching non-combatant enemies.[35]

But Bryan could scarcely restrain the rapidly growing pro–Entente forces within the administration and without, and he was overruled again and again. Behind his back, House in the United States and ambassador Page in England were doing everything they could to undermine his prestige and his faltering peace initiatives.

The day following the sinking of the *Lusitania*, Bryan's note to Wilson asking for a moderate reaction to the disaster contained a simple yet sensible metaphor: "Germany has a right to prevent contraband going to the Allies, and a ship carrying contraband should not rely on passengers to protect her from attack—it would be like putting women and children in front of an army."[36]

Wilson's first *Lusitania* note, on May 13, protesting Germany's action was even more one-sided than Bryan had anticipated. The key passage that convinced Bryan of its brazen non-neutrality read:

> This Government has already taken occasion to inform the Imperial German Government that it cannot admit the adoption of such methods [unrestricted submarine warfare] or such a warning of danger [advising Americans not to travel on Allied vessels] to operate as in any degree an abbreviation of the rights of American shipmasters or of American citizens bound on lawful errands as passengers on merchant ships of belligerent nationality; and that it must hold the Imperial German Government to a strict accountability for any infringement of those rights, intentional or incidental.[37]

Bryan signed it, reluctantly, knowing that the term "strict accountability" carried the seeds of war between the United States and Germany.

It was Wilson's second *Lusitania* note, a demand that Germany virtually abandon submarine warfare, that pushed Byran beyond the point of no return. During discussion of the note in the cabinet on June 1, Bryan wanted to know what the country was going to do about England. Why was the United States always ready to press Germany hard and so reluctant to call Great Britain to account for its aggressive actions against the United States? Bryan also protested that some cabinet officers in the room were blatantly pro–Ally, but the president cut him off short. Courageously, Bryan refused to sign the note, and on June 7 concluded he could not remain secretary of state under conditions which would make him a responsible party to America's going to war. The next day, at a cabinet meeting, Wilson formally announced Bryan's resignation, to take effect when the note to Germany was sent. At a luncheon farewell that same day with several cabinet members, the high-principled Bryan said: "I must act according to my conscience. I go out into the dark."[38]

After serving for two weeks as interim secretary of state, Counselor Robert Lansing was sworn in as executive head of the State Department on June 24. He had worked for Bryan for a little over a year. Wilson considered Lansing by no means the ideal replacement, but the president intended no important role for his new appointee, and he told House that he planned to continue to be his own foreign secretary. In sharp contrast to Bryan's pacifism, Lansing was an out-and-out war hawk. Historian Arthur S. Link has described him further as "a professional at the practice of international law. A person of enormous reserve, he gave the superficial impression of a dignified law clerk; but the fire of strong conviction burned hot within him, even though his official statements rarely betrayed his secret thoughts. He often disagreed with the President's foreign policies but loyally strove to implement them, or to change them, if he could, by indirection."[39]

Two weeks later, in a private memorandum he titled "Consideration and Outline of Policies," Lansing recorded his interpretations of the war and his plans for conduct of America's foreign policy. They clearly show where his sympathies lay: "I have come to the conclusion that the German Government is utterly hostile to all nations with democratic institutions because those who compose it see in democracy a menace to absolutism and the defeat of the German ambition for world domination. ... A triumph for German imperialism must not be. ... Germany must not be permitted to win this war or even break even."[40]

Months before he became secretary of state, Lansing, in his role as the State Department's expert on international law, had skillfully implemented these pro–Entente views. In November 1914, he had ruled on the legality of shipping disassembled U.S.-manufactured submarines destined for England. Lansing asserted that such a deception by American shipbuilders was perfectly legal, despite a clause in America's neutrality proclamation against "fitting out

Robert Lansing, secretary of state following William Jennings Bryan's resignation over a stern U.S. note to Germany following the sinking of the *Lusitania*, was a war-hawk. In July 1915, two weeks after taking office, he recorded in a private memorandum that "Germany must not be permitted to win this war or even break even." *National Archives.*

and arming ... any ship or vessel ... in the service of either of the said belligerents." One historian has suggested that Lansing's interpretation of the government ban on the export of submarine parts "was an unnecessarily burdensome interpretation of neutral duties."[41] When he learned that both Wilson and Bryan disagreed, Lansing submitted the case to the State Department's neutrality board. Their opinion supported Lansing's broad interpretation. Even after Lansing sent Wilson this second legal opinion, the president resolutely held firm, writing to Lansing that it was "really our duty (in the spirit, at any rate, of the *Alabama* decision)[42] to prevent submarines being shipped from this country even in parts, and I hope that you will find a way of checking and preventing this if it is contemplated."[43] Yet the shipments of submarines were made on schedule. Some observers called them "Schwab's submarines," after one of the munitions makers who were in the forefront of America's headlong rush into non-neutrality.

Charles Michael Schwab was the very epitome of the self-made man and of America as the land of opportunity at the turn of the century. Schwab had begun his meteoric rise to power and wealth as a young engineer's helper, working for $1 a day at one of Andrew Carnegie's steel works. Ambitious, aggressive, and, above all, a great salesman, he became plant superintendent at 27. Eight years later, he was appointed president of the Carnegie Steel Company and earned $1 million a year. In 1901, he helped negotiate the formation of the largest of all American steel companies, U.S. Steel Corporation, and at 39 was named its first president. Impatient to run a company entirely his own way, he resigned to form his own company, the Bethlehem Steel Corporation. There he was president, board chairman, and largest stockholder. At the center of the corporation was the Bethlehem Steel Company, the nation's largest manufacturer of arms, warships in particular.

Schwab was his firm's top salesman, and whenever and wherever there was a revolution brewing or a war in progress—Asia, Europe, the Americas—Schwab could be found on site, competing with Europe's best arms manufacturers: Krupp of Germany, Vickers of England, Schneider of France. In 1914, when the U.S. steel industry as a whole was in the doldrums following the virtual completion of the bridges, trackage, and other structures for the nation's railroads, Bethlehem's main Fore River shipyards outside Boston launched a battleship for Argentina and were busily completing the U.S. dreadnought *Nevada*, nine submarines, two large merchantmen, two torpedo boats, and a submarine tender.[44]

At the outbreak of the war, orders started to come in to Bethlehem for cannons and artillery shells. While the machine gun became the preeminent infantry-killing weapon, World War I was fundamentally an artillery war, and America's principal arms orders from France and England were for shells, by the hundreds of thousands. In October, supersalesman Schwab was in London for a meeting with Admiral Fisher. The First Sea Lord wanted submarines, fast; Schwab said he could build and deliver, fast. The two shook hands to seal the agreement.

Had not Schwab committed his company to an obviously illegal activity? There was, first of all, a 120-year-old U.S. law, passed in response to the fitting out of French privateers in American waters to fight the British, that forbade delivery of warships to belligerents from neutral American territory. Then there was the more recent Civil War matter of the British-made Confederate raider *Alabama*. The United States was also a signatory of an 1871 treaty requiring neutral nations to exercise "due diligence" to prevent the departure of warships purchased by belligerents. Schwab knew all of these restrictions, but he planned to deliver the submarines in pieces, ready for reassembly. He reasoned that his company would be doing nothing different from selling ordinary tools of war. In fact, he had precedent on his side, for U.S. shipbuilders had furnished submarines to both belligerents in the Russo-Japanese War of 1904–5 using the same subterfuge.

At the end of February 1915, a news story from Washington, D.C., reported that U.S. Navy inspectors on duty at Bethlehem shipyards had told their superiors that submarines were being built for the Royal Navy. The news account said further,

> It was asserted in responsible quarters tonight that the Navy Department had definite assurances that these submarines were not to be delivered to any belligerent during the war and that none of their parts had been shipped. ... President Wilson is firm in his determination not to permit any submarines to be shipped out of this country to any belligerent during the war. He will not even allow the component parts of such submarines to be shipped, and Mr. Schwab is aware of this fact. The Administration has accepted Mr. Schwab's word. ...If any attempt is made to ship the submarines the

shipments will be stopped and the Department of Justice will be ordered to begin prosecutions for alleged violations of the neutrality laws.[45]

In late June 1915, ten 500-ton submarines, with Royal Navy ensigns snapping, sailed from Quebec in convoy for England. The news story that announced the event originated in Canada. It pointed out that the vessels had been designed in the United States and that "some of the parts" had also been made in America. There was no mention of Schwab, Bethlehem Steel, or its affiliate, Fore River Shipbuilding Company, where the submarines had been manufactured, disassembled, and shipped north. The Canadians, at war with Germany, were content to gain some small propaganda advantage from the announcement and had no reason to divulge more details. Obviously, Schwab had broken his "pledge" to the administration, in whatever form it supposedly had been given. Furthermore, there is no record of the Department of Justice initiating any "prosecutions for alleged violations of the neutrality laws" against Bethlehem. Lansing had quietly greased the way for Schwab, despite Woodrow Wilson's feeble wish that Lansing should prevent export of submarines in sections. In 1916 Bethlehem would earn more than $61 million, more than the total gross sales of the previous eight years under its leader's dynamic management.

Yet Lansing was punctilious when the occasion demanded. On December 9, 1914, in response to a complaint of pro–Ally bias by Harvard's Hugo Muensterberg, he wrote to Wilson, citing precedent in U.S. trade in munitions of war and echoing his earlier recommendations to Bryan: "It has never been the policy of this government to prevent the shipment of arms or ammunition into belligerent territory, except in the case of neighboring American republics, and then only when civil strife prevailed."[46] In another note to the president the same day, Lansing meticulously plugged any holes that might have remained in his airtight case for American sales of munitions to the Allies. He wrote: "If one belligerent has by good fortune a superiority in the matter of geographical or of military or naval power, the rules of neutral conduct cannot be varied so as to favor the less fortunate combatant. To change such rules because of the relative strength of the belligerents and in order to equalize their opportunities would be in itself an unneutral act, of which the stronger might justly complain."[47] He also left his reader in little doubt about whom he considered to be the "less fortunate combatant."

The Germans were unwilling to accept what they considered America's irrational interpretation of neutrality. Ambassador Von Bernstorff accurately summarized his nation's viewpoint in a rational note to the State Department on April 4, 1915, which went unheeded:

> In the present war all nations having a war material industry worth mentioning are either involved in the war themselves or are engaged in perfecting their own armaments, and have therefore laid an embargo against the exportation of war material. The United States are accordingly the only neutral country in a position to furnish war materials. The concept of

neutrality is thereby given a new purport, independent of the formal question of hitherto existing law. In contradiction thereto, the United States are
building upon a powerful arms industry in the broadest sense. ...This industry is actually delivering goods only to the enemies of Germany. The theo-
retical willingness to supply Germany also, if shipments thither were possible, does not alter the case. If it is the will of the American people that there
shall be a true neutrality, the United States will find means of preventing
this one-way supply of arms or at least of utilizing it to protect legitimate
trade with Germany, especially that in foodstuffs.[48]

What von Bernstorff was vainly seeking for his country was the "equal treatment" that both the Congress and the president had accorded warring factions
in Mexico in 1912. In March of that year Wilson had been given the authority to embargo American munitions going into Mexico. A year later, with the
war continuing, Wilson had told Congress, "I deem it my duty ... to see to it
that neither side to this struggle now going on in Mexico receive [sic] any assistance from this side of the border. I shall follow the best practice of nations in
the matter of neutrality by forbidding the export of arms or munitions of war
of any kind from the United States to any part of the Republic of Mexico."[49]

The State Department's initial policy concerning loans to belligerents—
the policy enunciated by Bryan—did not sit well with the aggressively pro-
Ally House of Morgan. It itched to take advantage, like the arms makers, of
the most stupendous profit-making opportunities in its history. As soon as
the war broke out, France immediately appointed Morgan as its financial
agent in the United States. In December 1914, the farsighted banking firm
negotiated directly with England's Prime Minister Asquith to create a Morgan purchasing agency for the British; the following spring, a similar central
agency was set up with the French. By the end of the war, the purchases of
American goods controlled by the Morgan bank "came to an astonishing $3
billion—almost half of all American supplies sold to the Allies during the
war." As for Morgan's profits, "skimming off a 1-percent commission, the
House of Morgan booked an astounding $30 million in fees."[50]

If Lansing represented a segment of anti–German-Americans who might
have been called moderates, the head of the bank underwriting the loans
would certainly have been called an extremist. Its chairman was "Jack" Pier-
pont Morgan, son of the founder. A more dedicated Anglophile was scarcely
to be found in the United States. In 1898, at 31, Jack had been assigned by
his father to the firm's affiliate in London, both to acquire the requisite social
and business contacts among England's rich and powerful and to acquire an
appreciation of the British gentleman's way of life. The young, rich Morgan
was an apt pupil and came to relish English life; its class structure befit his
own status as a merchant prince. He bought a grouse-shooting lodge in Scotland with 17,000 acres and he mingled smoothly with Great Britain's elite,
regularly spending months every year in England.

In July 1915, he was nearly killed by an intruder who forced his way into his house on a small island in Long Island Sound, a man who had sought to influence Morgan to embargo munitions sales. This incident further reinforced his anti–German views: "Jack told friends that the shooting had made him more fervently anti–German and more eager to see the United States enter the war on the Allied side. He reviled the Germans as 'Huns' and 'Teuton savages' ... and exhibited a latent bias against Germany that he had inherited from his father."[51]

In late August 1915, coincident with the drop in the value of Great Britain's pound sterling, the Morgan bank made its move to finance the Allied war effort on a scale commensurate with what it understood to be the need. It recruited two key administration officials to its cause and obtained Wilson's approval of the largest loan in the history of Wall Street. (Without this loan, most informed economists later agreed, the Allies would not have been able to continue the war and would have been forced to promptly conclude a negotiated peace with the Central Powers. Many other such private loans followed, and by April 1917, American bankers had lent the Allies over $2.1 billion.)

First came an optimistic note to the president from Treasury Secretary William Gibbs McAdoo. It focused on "prosperity":

> Great Britain is and always has been our best customer. ...The high prices for food products have brought great prosperity to the farmers, while the purchasers of war munitions have stimulated industry and have set factories going to full capacity. ...Great prosperity is coming. It is, in large measure, already here. It will be tremendously increased if we can extend reasonable credits to our customers. ...To maintain our prosperity we must finance it.[52]

Finance it to the tune of half a billion dollars, wrote McAdoo—but there was the unfortunate State Department ban on foreign loans. Wilson straddled the fence in a follow-on letter to Secretary of State Robert Lansing: "My opinion is that we should say that 'parties would take no action either for or against such a transaction,' but that this should be orally conveyed, and not put in writing."[53]

Lansing almost certainly prompted and well rehearsed by Morgan specialists in the intricacies of banking and international finance, expanded on McAdoo's arguments, at the same time painting for Wilson a dire picture of an America in depression:

> If the European countries cannot find the means to pay for the excess of goods sold them over those purchased from them, they will have to stop buying and our present export trade will shrink proportionately. The result would be restriction of output, industrial depression, idle capital, idle labor, numerous failures, financial demoralization, and general unrest and suffering among the laboring classes. ...Can we afford to let a declaration as to our conception of the "true spirit of neutrality," made in the early days of the war, stand in the way of our national interests which seem to be seriously threatened?[54]

Lansing had much data to support his gloomy scenario. As 1915 had begun, the nation's businessmen were anything but optimistic. Steel production was only 50 percent of capacity; cotton was selling at the lowest price in 15 years, far below the cost of production; European exports were running about half their normal rate; new railroad construction had dropped to the lowest mileage in half a century; bank drafts during the first quarter were the smallest in more than five years. As late as April 1915, the U.S. Bureau of Labor estimated that 398,000 workers in New York City alone were unemployed, over 16 percent of the working population; in other major cities, it was estimated that unemployment averaged 11 percent. By June, lawmakers in Washington were making plans for relief for those out of work.[55] Lansing's arguments apparently were irresistible, for two days later, on September 8, Wilson, to whom the implications of a German victory were more and more intolerable, responded that the issue had been resolved.

On September 25, J.P. Morgan & Co. signed the pivotal $500 million contract with a visiting commission headed by Lord Reading. Thereafter, the Allies felt free "to call without restraint upon an American market which, by that very fact, became dependent upon the Entente demand. The two economies were for the purposes of the war made one; each was now entangled irrevocably in the fate of the other."[56]

The British, gracious as always, were appreciative of this extraordinary service to the empire. In 1917, Prime Minister David Lloyd George wrote to Morgan Grenfell, Morgan's London affiliate, to say that Great Britain had been "fortunate enough to secure the assistance of a firm which have throughout done everything in its power to protect the interests of the British Government." Lord Northcliffe commented, upon visiting J.P. Morgan's Street headquarters after the war, "The war was won within these walls." Lord Moulton, wartime head of England's Munitions Board, spread the credit to American munitions makers as well, saying that "DuPont, Bethlehem Steel, and J.P. Morgan and Company had rescued the French and British armies in 1915."[57]

In the mid–1930s, with war brewing again in Europe, loud voices began to call for an investigation of the American bankers and munitions makers who, they claimed, had gotten the country into the war in 1917. A factual, widely read book, *Merchants of Death: A Study of the International Armament Industry*, shed light on the behind-the-scenes activities of J.P. Morgan & Co., National City Bank, DuPont, Bethlehem Steel and others, and of their enormous wartime profits. The book also contributed to the demand for Congressional hearings. Had these rich and powerful companies, separately or conspiratorially, subverted America's decision makers—Woodrow Wilson, in particular—in their greed? What other agencies had they influenced to help draw America into the conflict? Senator Gerald P. Nye, who headed what was called the Senate Munitions Investigating Committee during 1935 and 1936, fervently believed they had and was convinced furthermore that their clandestine influences had been widespread.

J.P. Morgan and his principal partners were the star witnesses during the Nye hearings, as much because of their prospective wartime influence as because of the bank's traditional reclusiveness. The well-rehearsed Morgan team vigorously denied conspiracy and no evidence was turned up that the company or any of its partners as individuals had exerted overt or covert pressures on U.S. government officials.[58] Overall, Nye was able to establish little support for his earlier contentions.

But had Nye and his main interrogator, Senator Bennett C. Clark, dug deeply enough? Had they been somehow overmatched by the bright, thoroughly prepared Wall Streeters? Was the impressive, formally dressed Morgan himself a deterrent to more incisive probing? In fact, there were vital questions that should have been asked during the Nye hearings, but never were. For example, did J.P. Morgan & Co. or any of its partners prior to April 1917 own, control, or hold major blocks of stock in any newspapers or magazines?[59] If so, did these media reflect in their editorial conduct the avowed anti–German policies of Morgan? Did J.P. Morgan & Co. otherwise try covertly to mold public opinion to its international views?

Likely answers to such questions can be found in a single four-page memorandum titled "Publicity Matters" written from one Morgan partner to another in June 1912,[60] just prior to the hearings of the House Banking and Currency Committee known as the Money Trust Hearings. The Morgan bank was one of the committee's chief targets and the company had made thorough preparations to take the sting out of its inquisitors. Not only was J.P. Morgan coached for the hearings by his young partners, Henry P. Davison and Thomas W. Lamont, but the bank hired its first publicist. Lamont laid out a secret plan, approved by Morgan, that would govern the banking firm's public relations for a generation. Aggressive and thorough—and discreet, of course—the Morgan company's 1912 plan was a model of effective public relations: guide the Washington press corps through one of its leaders; distribute literature and editorial material to key Washington papers; influence congressmen directly; invest in and control a national newspaper syndicate and its respected newsletter; perhaps buy a newspaper press association and a Washington newspaper. Two years later, when the stakes, both financial and philosophical, were immeasurably higher, it is almost inconceivable that J.P. Morgan & Co. did not adapt its earlier and successful publicity program to new demands.[61]

A second group of principal advisors to the president were America's ambassadors in the principal European capitals. These men, like the cabinet officers, were given their posts as rewards for party fealty and financial support. Not one was a career diplomat, and not one had a fundamental understanding of the country to which he had been posted or how it fitted into Europe's diplomatic jigsaw puzzle. If their postwar memoirs and retrospectives are accurate depictions of their wartime views, they were universally pro–Entente. To a man, they recorded for posterity that they had, of course, been keenly on the side of righteousness from the first days of the war.

In September 1914, America was represented by no fewer than three ambassadors to France: Myron T. Herrick, a Taft-appointee and the outgoing minister; Robert Bacon, Herrick's predecessor, who was in France to study the situation in his private capacity as an officer of the Morgan bank; and William Graves Sharp, Wilson's new appointee. The troika appeared together in Bordeaux in September, then the seat of the French government, and

> declared that at that time only 50,000 Americans desired to enter the War, but that the day was not far distant when a hundred million would be converted to that desire. This revelation was no surprise to those well acquainted with American affairs. The three Ambassadors ... were always well known as partisans of the Entente. And they bent themselves to bring about that "conversion" of American public opinion which they then predicted.[62]

Henry van Dyke was ambassador to the Netherlands and Luxembourg. On September 10, 1914, he summarized his views of the war in a letter to Wilson, saying that while he was strictly following the president's declaration of neutrality, he was impelled to give his impressions to his "friend and Chief": "The beginning of the war belongs to Austria and Germany. ... This is really a clash of systems: militarism against democracy." The most important part of his letter was his slanted perspective on what he claimed he knew of Germany's plans and how they conflicted with America's vital interests: "She does not wish to visit Paris again," van Dyke wrote. "She wants to go to London this time. The next station beyond London is on the shores of the new world. ... The domination of Europe by the sword of Germany would be a menace to the United States." Van Dyke concluded his analysis with a statement that begged for corroboration, for he was in The Hague, not America, and the war was only five weeks old: "The German propaganda in the United States is immense and subtle."[63]

Brand Whitlock, ambassador to Belgium, watched the German army passing through Brussels in late August 1914. His polemical description of the scene is a clear reflection of his anti–German stance:

> We stopped, and sat there in the motor, and gazed. Heavy guns, their vicious mouths of steel lowered, drawn by superb horses, were lumbering by, the officers erect, either very thin, of the Prussian type, with hard and cruel faces, scarred by duelling, or the heavier type, with rolls of fat at the back of their necks, and with red, heavy, brutal faces—smoking cigarettes, looked about over the heads of the silent, awed, saddened crowds, with arrogant, insolent contemptuous glances. ... It became monstrous, oppressive,

unendurable; monstrous, somehow, those black guns on grey carriages and grey caissons; and those grey uniforms, the insolent faces of those supercilious young officers—scarred in their silly duels—wearing monocles; those dull plodding soldiers—such backs, such thews and sinews, the heels of their stout, heavy boots beating on the pavement—all the attention to detail that distinguishes a circus in America. ... Then, suddenly, far down the boulevard, the crack of the music of a military band, high, shrill with the high, shrill, fierce notes, the horrid clang of mammoth brass cymbals, music calculated like that of savages to strike terror. A great band passed by, and then officers and again the grey hordes, pouring down over the peaceful earth, bringing ruin and destruction.[64]

Such professions of non-neutrality were scarcely in keeping with America's official declaration of neutrality as enunciated by the president. It should be remembered that two weeks after the outbreak of war, Wilson had urged all Americans—including the nation's chief diplomatic representatives—to be "impartial in thought as well as action."

James W. Gerard in Germany and Henry Morgenthau in Turkey bided their time until they were back in the United States to publicly proclaim their patriotism. The former feverishly wrote two books and oversaw the adaptation of the first book into a popular anti–German movie, all before war's end. To the latter, who also published a book of his overseas experiences, must be credited one of World War I's greatest hoaxes. As will be seen, Morgenthau's bold lie in his book was the source of the enduring legend of "sole German war guilt" that formed the most pernicious article in the vindictive Versailles peace treaty.

Among all of American diplomats, it was Walter Hines Page in London, who called most persistently for American intervention on the side of the Allies. The work he did in England undermined the generally feeble attempts made from Washington to demand British respect for America's neutrality. For his extreme pro–British efforts, Page earned the everlasting gratitude of England—and uniform condemnation from impartial American historians.

In 1913, Page had been a sensible choice by House and Wilson as ambassador to the Court of St. James, the plum of overseas posts. The former editor of the *Atlantic Monthly* and *The World's Work* had for years been outspokenly pro–British, and his views were certain to make him a darling of English society. If war had not intervened, Page undoubtedly would have gone down in history as a splendid emissary of goodwill. In a Europe at war, however, Page's role was no longer fundamentally ornamental. His essential duty was to defend his nation's interests. In England, these interests were constantly in conflict with those of his host country. That Page did not do so—that he followed his own narrow interpretations of American security—contributed to America's final intervention in the war on the Allied side.

Page's hagiographic biographer, Burton T. Hendrick, reported that a "great British statesman" once told him that

Mr. Page had one fine qualification for his post. From the beginning he saw that there was a right and a wrong to the matter. He did not believe that Great Britain and Germany were equally to blame. He believed that Great Britain was right and that Germany was wrong. I regard it as one of the greatest blessings of modern times that the United States had an ambassador in London in August, 1914, who had grasped this overwhelming fact. It seems almost like a dispensation of Providence.[65]

Page devoured every crumb of British propaganda. In his insistent letters to both House and Wilson in the early months of the war, and never letting up, he pounded away at what he considered German perfidy: sole guilt for starting the war; proven German atrocities ("they have perpetrated some of the most barbarous deeds in history"[66]); the certainty of Germany invading the United States if the Allies lost; the manifest evils of Prussian militarism and autocracy. He upheld Great Britain's fundamental right to its broadening blockade of Germany and insisted that there must be no peace talks and no mediation. In Page's dramatic view, "the Hohenzollern idea must perish—be utterly strangled in the making of peace. ... This is not a war in the sense in which we have hitherto used that word. It is a world-clash of systems of government, a struggle for the extermination of English civilization or of Prussian autocracy. Precedents have gone to the scrap heap. ... It is a matter of life and death for English-speaking civilization."[67]

Always, Page brought his subject to life, as in his November 12, 1915, letter to House: "I have a great respect for the British Navy. ...But for this fleet, by the way, London would be in ruins, all its treasure looted; every French seacoast city and the Italian peninsula would be as Belgium and Poland are; and thousands of English women would be violated—just as dead as French girls are found in many German trenches that have been taken in France."[68]

His devotion to England was so great that Page often took Great Britain's side rather than America's and sometimes even advised the British government how best to respond to America's infrequent stern notes. Grey, in his memoir, wrote that

> Page's advice and suggestion were of the greatest value in warning us when to be careful or encouraging us when we could safely be firm. One incident in particular remains in my memory. Page came to see me at the Foreign Office one day and produced a long despatch from Washington contesting our claim to act as we were doing in stopping contraband going to neutral ports. "I am instructed," he said, "to read this despatch to you." He read, and I listened. He then said: "I have now read the despatch to you, but I do not agree with it; let us consider how it should be answered."[69]

Ambassador Page's most flagrant act of non-neutrality came on January 23, 1915, when the merchantman *Dacia*, loaded with cotton, sailed from Texas for Germany. Formerly a German ship, she had been bought by an American citizen, had been registered in the United States, was crewed by

Americans, and flew the Stars and Stripes. The transfer took place after the State Department rendered an opinion that the transaction was legal. Before the ship sailed, the British formally notified the State Department that, despite her official U.S. registry, the *Dacia* was subject to capture by the Royal Navy as "enemy property" once she left port.

Could the United States allow Great Britain to carry out such a blatant high-seas challenge to American rights? Did Great Britain dare back down, setting a precedent for U.S. registry by German-Americans of all the German and Austrian ships then interned in American harbors, and, in effect, breaking the blockade of German ports? Page's biographer relates what came next:

> When matters had reached this pass Page one day dropped into the Foreign Office. "Have you ever heard of the British fleet, Sir Edward?" he asked. Grey admitted he had, though the questions obviously puzzled him. "Yes," Page went on musingly. "We've all heard of the British fleet. Perhaps we have heard too much about it. Don't you think it's had too much advertising?" The Foreign Secretary looked at Page with an expression that implied a lack of confidence in his sanity. "But have you ever heard of the French fleet?" the American went on. "France has a fleet too, I believe." Sir Edward granted that. "Don't you think that the French fleet ought to have a little advertising?" "What on earth are you talking about?" "Well," said Page, "there's the *Dacia*. Why not let the French fleet seize it and get some advertising?" A gleam of understanding immediately shot across Grey's face.[70]

The *Dacia* was subsequently captured by a French cruiser, taken into a French port, condemned as "enemy property" by a prize court, and sold to Frenchmen. As it turned out, and entirely as anticipated by both Page and Grey, there was little outcry in the United States over the high-handed seizure by the French. America had gone to war in 1812 with England, not France, over the freedom-of-the-seas issue.

Page did not confine his vigorous pro–British and anti–German views to quiet diplomatic channels. Apparently at every opportunity, to any Englishman who would listen, he verbalized his personal interpretation of America's neutrality as a gross mistake. His justification was that while a government might be neutral, no individual could be. As early as December 1914, Page's non-neutral outspokenness got back to the White House, and House was ordered to send a cease-and-desist order. House wrote: "The President wishes me to ask you to please be more careful not to express any unneutral feeling, either by word of mouth, or by letter and not even to the State Department. ...He feels very strongly about this, and I am sending the same message to Gerard."[71]

The sinking of the *Lusitania* brought Page to a fever pitch, from which he never retreated. In a private letter to his son Arthur, in early June 1915, he attacked Wilson and his policy of neutrality with obvious relish. The younger Page was then the editor of *The World's Work*, a broad-circulation monthly magazine whose editorial policies paralleled the views of the senior Page. The latter wrote, "We're in danger of being feminized and fad-ridden—...pensions, Christian Science; peace-cranks; ...petty coats where breeches ought to be & breeches where petty coats ought to be; ...white livers and soft heads and milk-and-water;—I don't want war. ...But to get rid of hyphenated degenerates perhaps it's worth while, and to free us from 'isms and soft folk & pious liars."[72]

In a letter to House on July 21, 1915, discussing, in his view, Wilson's too-pallid reaction to the sinking of the *Lusitania* by "the damnedest pirates that ever blew up a ship," Page concluded by saying, "It's a curious thing to say, but the only solution that I see is another *Lusitania* outrage, which would force war."[73]

Then, just weeks before Wilson decided for war, Page gloomily assessed the economic situation in a cable to the President:

> The financial enquiries made here reveal an international condition most alarming to the American financial and industrial outlook. England ... cannot continue her present large purchases in the United States without shipments of gold to pay for them. ... The almost immediate danger, therefore, is that the Franco-American and Anglo-American exchange will be so disturbed that orders by all the allied governments will be reduced to the minimum, and there will be almost a cessation of trans–Atlantic trade. This will, of course, cause a panic in the United States. ... Perhaps our going to war is the only way in which our prominent trade position can be maintained and a panic averted.[74]

Did Page's harping correspondence specifically affect Woodrow Wilson's foreign-policy decisions? How much was House influenced by Page's jingo views? Were Page's conniving relations with Grey vital to Great Britain's calculated defiance of America's rights on the seas?

There are no clear-cut answers to these questions. Early in the war, when Page's letters were mostly about English life under the stresses of war, Wilson was entertained by the vivid writing. At that time, Wilson remarked to the ambassador's secretary that he "could never resist him—I get more from his letters than from any other single source. Tell him to keep it up."[75] The president also would sometimes read the best of Page's letters to his cabinet. After the sinking of the *Lusitania*, however, when his letters became increasingly shrill, Wilson became irritated and turned away from Page, as he had so often before from associates whose views diverged from his.

At the start of the war, House enjoyed a close relationship with Page and when in London spent much time with the ambassador. House was already in consonance with Page's views, and House needed little prodding from Page to continue his behind-the-scenes work to strengthen Britain's war effort. Later on, House solidified his own ties with Britain's major diplomats and found he no longer needed Page as an intermediary. By 1918 the two men maintained only formal contacts.

There is much evidence that the British were sensitive as to how far they could go in violating America's rights on the seas, always pushing to the limit of what they could get away with. As Page helped define a line which England dare not cross, he contributed to the success of this policy at the expense of the United States.

Why did Wilson not recall Page, whom he sometimes disdainfully referred to as "more British than the British?" And why did he not accept Page's convenient offer of resignation, which was tendered after the November 1916 election in the form of a long letter reiterating his dogma that the war was simply a struggle between good and evil? There are also no certain answers to these questions. Wilson's official biographer suggested that it was

> the inevitable pattern of his character. He dreaded argument or controversy with friends whom he trusted or admired or loved; he feared the emotional strain, shrank from the break that might follow. Making new human relationships had, from his youth upward, been difficult for him; he preferred to continue to work with men whom he knew, however unsatisfactory they might be, rather than to choose new ones.[76]

Wilson was also not anxious to face what would have been adverse press reaction in the United States.

Perhaps another factor was that, despite Wilson's supposed antagonism toward the increasingly disagreeable information he was receiving from Page, he had come, perversely, to depend on Page's comments. Biographer Hendrick wrote of Page's letters to Wilson that "there are evidences," which he did not disclose, "that they influenced the solitary statesman in the White House, and they had much to do in finally forcing Mr. Wilson into the war."[77]

A month before the war's end, after Page had resigned for reasons of ill health, Lord Bryce sent a private note to Wilson to express his glowing admiration for the former ambassador. "No one could have been more tactful, more judicious, more kindly, better combining candour with prudence, better qualified to inspire confidence by his transparent sincerity and loyalty," wrote the dean of Britain's propagandists.[78]

In 1923, Great Britain commemorated Page's exceptional wartime service to the British Empire with a regal memorial service in Westminster Abbey. Grey eulogized Page, who had died five years before, and unveiled a small white marble tablet affixed to a wall in the Abbey's chapel that called Page "the friend of Britain in her sorest need." England's debt of gratitude to Page endured well beyond his enshrinement in Westminster Abbey. As late as 1965, British historian John Terraine opened his celebration of his native land's force-of-arms during World War I with a statement he attributed to Page in August 1914: "The German militarism, which is *the* crime of the last fifty years, had been working for this for twenty-five years. It is the logical result of their spirit and enterprise and doctrine. It *had* to come." Terraine then chauvinistically reflected that "this considered verdict of the United States Ambassador to London ... has stood the test of time."[79]

At the same time that Woodrow Wilson's chief advisors were quietly counseling pro–British and anti–German policies, a small group of ardent Americans were loudly espousing the same cause and molding American public opinion to the same end. They communicated, as individuals and through their well-financed agencies, a concept called "preparedness"—a term alluringly pacific but clearly martial. In fact, preparedness was an obfuscation cloaking the call for a militarily dominant, aggressive America, a nation ready and willing to fight Germany.

As has already been shown, British propaganda was fueling the American preparedness movement, spreading the conviction that if Germany won in Europe, her next move would be an attack on the United States. Preparedness was thus an irresistible issue for most Americans. The nation's jingoes greedily clasped the concept to their bosoms.

Of the nation's preparedness advocates, no one was more influential—and thunderous—than ex-president Theodore Roosevelt. No one relished war more. Roosevelt's wild, shoot-from-the-hip ultrapatriotism started well before he entered public life and continued to his last days.

> In 1886, elated by headlines predicting trouble with Mexico, he had offered to organize his Medora ranch hands into a cavalry battalion. ... In 1892, he watched with eager interest the friction with Chile and approved the American demands that an indemnity be paid for injuries to sailors in Valparaiso. ... By October, 1894, Roosevelt was demanding the annexation of the Hawaiian Islands and the construction of an oceanic canal through Nicaragua. ...As for war [in 1895, during the Venezuelan boundary dispute with England], let it come: "American cities may possibly be bombarded, but no ransom will be paid for them. It is infinitely better to see the cities leveled than to see a dollar paid to any foe to buy their safety. ... A great many of our friends ... seem to forget we will settle the Venezuela question ... in Canada. ...Canada would surely be conquered, and once wrested from England it would never be returned." ... "This country needs a war," he informed [Senator Henry Cabot] Lodge on December 27, 1895.[80]

As assistant secretary of the navy in 1898, Roosevelt operated behind the back of Secretary John D. Long, and cabled Admiral George Dewey in Hong Kong to ready his fleet for steaming to Manila Bay to fight the Spanish. As a newly commissioned lieutenant colonel in the Rough Riders, he gloried in the triumph of his troopers at San Juan Hill. As president, he orchestrated the revolution in Panama and its secession from Colombia—"I took the Canal Zone," he exulted. The canal was to provide mobility for the huge navy he believed befitted the world's newest imperial power. In May 1910, accepting the Nobel Peace Prize for his mediation efforts ending the Russo-Japanese war, Roosevelt reminded his audience that while he supported the idea of an

Theodore Roosevelt "on the stump." Wherever he went, he spoke persuasively and drew enthusiastic crowds. From his early years to his last embittered ones, he was an unwavering jingo. *All-World Photos.*

international police force, nations must be wary of reducing their armies and navies.

At the outbreak of war in 1914, Roosevelt joyfully assumed the mantle of leadership of the nation's superpatriots. He had relinquished the presidency six years before and had found private life unrewarding. He was restless and disenchanted with the leadership of William Howard Taft, whom he had put into the White House. Roosevelt again sought the presidency in 1912. Unable to gain the nomination from the Republican party, Roosevelt formed his own—the Progressive (Bull Moose) Party—which split the Republican vote and swung the election to Woodrow Wilson. Roosevelt remained an enormously popular figure. Wherever and whenever he spoke—and he spoke often and convincingly—enthusiastic crowds cheered his every word. Newspapers gave him front-page coverage and magazines vied for his frequent articles and published his steady flow of letters.

During the early weeks of the war, Roosevelt had mildly approved America's neutrality and even suggested that Wilson's policy was a sensible one. In a statement that appeared in the *Outlook* on August 22, he said he was "not now taking sides one way or the other." Concerning Germany's invasion of Belgium, Roosevelt was reluctant to pass judgment: "When giants are engaged in a death wrestle, as they reel to and fro they are certain to trample on whoever [sic] gets in the way of either of the huge straining combatants."[81] The following month, prompted by the visit of the Belgian Commission protesting alleged German atrocities and perhaps thinking that the claims were exaggerated, Roosevelt wrote in the same magazine that Germany had been justified in moving into Belgium because "disaster would surely have attended her [Germany's] arms had she not followed the course she actually did follow as regards her opponents on her Western frontier." He concluded that there could be "nothing but … praise and admiration due a stern, virile and masterful people, a people entitled to hearty respect for their patriotism and far-seeing self-devotion."[82]

These public words of praise for Germany would be the last of their kind to come from Roosevelt. By the end of 1914, he had dramatically changed his tune: Germany was a scourge and, therefore, America must do everything in its power to defeat that nation. Henceforth, he would be the most powerful American propagandist for the Allied cause until America went into the war. Then, until the Armistice, he became an insistent voice for the vigorous prosecution of the war.

Roosevelt left behind few clues establishing his reasons for what must be considered a perplexing reversal, especially by a man known for his steadfastness. As part of a purposeful attempt by his supporters to conceal what they considered an embarrassing period in his career, important letters of 1914 were suppressed.[83] Certainly, his views reflected the change in the nation's public opinion as British propaganda began to take hold. Another reason was Roosevelt's growing detestation of Woodrow Wilson. Roosevelt biographer Henry F. Pringle has suggested that rage against the president became the consuming passion of Roosevelt's last years. "No opinion that Roosevelt held, no action which he took, can be considered apart from that hatred," Pringle wrote.[84] Pringle traced the beginnings of Roosevelt's loathing for the president to Bryan's proposed treaty with Colombia in 1914, which would have included an apology and an indemnity of $25 million for Colombia's loss of Panama. Roosevelt was furious over what he considered the Wilson administration's public condemnation of the iniquity of his imperialistic action in Panama. Another observer, comparing the two men, suggested a deeper reason: "Roosevelt, with an insatiable passion for living, sailed boisterously the windy vastness of the seven seas; Wilson bent over the smooth waters of a forest pool, hynotized by what he saw. Wilson scorned Roosevelt, possibly because Roosevelt made him feel unimportant; Roosevelt despised Wilson before he ever heard of him, despising the type."[85]

Fundamental to Roosevelt's bitterness was jealousy of Wilson as chief executive during a time of great trial for the nation. Above all, the passionate Roosevelt yearned to be in the seat of power, to go down in history as a heroic wartime president, like George Washington or Abraham Lincoln, both of whom he regularly mentioned in his speeches as examples of the kind of leader who had made America great. Roosevelt also saw Wilson as stealing his progressive ideas in the administration's "New Freedom." Wilson was to him "the demagogue, adroit, tricky, false, without one spark of loftiness in him, without a touch of the heroic in his cold, selfish and timid soul."[86]

As he could not immediately shunt aside Wilson, at least he would do his vitriolic best to attack every statement and every action of the president, slashing at Wilson personally at every opportunity. Ever the consumate politician, Roosevelt also used the preparedness issue to discredit the hated "Princeton schoolmaster" and his "craven" neutralism to win back the White House for himself and the Congress for his Republican Party.

At first, Roosevelt kept to the high road, busying himself with a series of moderate position papers on U.S. foreign policy, which the *New York Times* published prominently in Sunday installments starting on September 27, 1914, and which were subsequently collected and published in book form under the title *America and the World War*. The articles carried such titles as "What America Should Learn from the War," "On the Danger of Making Unwise Peace Treaties," and "On Helping the Cause of World Peace." Their contents were sensible, middle-of-the-road interpretations of international politics and drew on the former president's intimate knowledge of the subject. After the November elections, Roosevelt accelerated his tempo and talked more heatedly about what had become his favorite topic: America's military unpreparedness. On November 15, the *Times* carried "Preparedness without Militarism" and, a week later, "Our Navy as a Peacemaker."

In the foreword to his widely read *America and the World War*, Roosevelt focused on preparedness as "the vital need" for the nation: "Preparedness against war does not always avert war or disaster in war, any more than the existence of a fire department ... always averts fire. But it is the only insurance against war, and overwhelming disgrace and disaster in war." As for the fellow travelers of the "unprepared," Roosevelt pointed out that in 1814 the nation had paid for its folly in having for 14 years refused to prepare for defense against possible foreign foes. "It behooves us now," he wrote, "in the presence of a world war, even vaster and more terrible than the world war of the early nineteenth century, to beware of taking the advice of the equally foolish pacifists of our own day."[87]

In December, in his State-of-the-Union message to the Congress, Wilson quashed the agitation for increased military expenditures initiated by Congressman Augustus Peabody Gardner of Massachusetts. Gardner was the son-in-law of Senator Henry Cabot Lodge, an equally ardent champion of a big army and navy. Roosevelt and Lodge were also close friends. As might be imagined, Wilson's proclaimed opposition to Roosevelt's beloved "preparedness" was the equivalent of throwing the ferocious Roosevelt a slab of raw meat to chew on.

By mid–1915, Roosevelt was in full cry. Acting as if he were on the stump—and, indeed, he was—he took every opportunity to lecture his fellow citizens. He lauded his followers and flayed his enemies on a broad range of topics. As always, he was unambiguous. On June 14, at a preparedness mass meeting in New York's Carnegie Hall, the full spectrum of Roosevelt's extreme jingo views were on display. Unable to attend, Roosevelt instead wrote a detailed letter to one of the principal speakers, Hudson Maxim, inventor of the machine gun and author of *Defenseless America*, who read it to the enthusiastic audience. Concerning "professional pacifists, the peace-at-any-price men," they were, according to Roosevelt, "probably the most undesirable citizens this country contains. ... For the nation as for the individual, the most contemptible of all sins is the sin of cowardice." As for peace, Roosevelt said that "an ignoble peace may be the worst crime against humanity, and righteous war may represent the greatest service a nation can render to itself and to mankind." Regarding the sale of arms to belligerents, he had a simple answer, one certain to bring an appreciative nod from gun-lobbyist Maxim: "Of course, the same moral law applies here between nations as between individuals within a nation. There is not the slightest difference between selling ammunition in time of war and in time of peace." ... Our legal right to sell ammunition to the Allies is perfect. It is also our moral duty to do so, precisely as it is a moral duty to sell arms to policemen for use against 'gunmen.'" Big-game hunter Roosevelt concluded by warning it was "absolutely essential that we should have stores where citizens can buy arms and ammunition."[88]

Roosevelt plumbed the depths of his personal vendetta against Wilson in his final campaign speech for Republican presidential candidate Charles Evans Hughes, in New York City on November 3, 1916. Near the end of his prepared talk, Roosevelt pushed aside his notes, raised the pitch of his shrill voice, and, noting that the president was then at Shadow Lawn in New Jersey, the summer White House, declared:

> There should be shadows now at Shadow Lawn; the shadows of the men, women and children who have risen from the ooze of the ocean bottom and from graves in foreign lands; the shadows of the helpless whom Mr. Wilson did not dare protect lest he might have to face danger; the shadows of babies gasping pitifully as they sank under the waves; the shadows of women outraged and slain by bandits. ...Those are the shadows proper for Shadow Lawn; the shadows of deeds that were never done; the shadows of lofty words that were followed by no action; the shadows of the tortured dead.[89]

When America was finally into the war, Roosevelt moved far to the political right in his incessant and crude denunciations of those people and forces he opposed and which he fervently believed were enemies of the United States—including Woodrow Wilson, of course. In the process, he became a demagogue of extreme proportions. These xenophobic views of the ex-president are revealed almost day by day in the 112 editorials he wrote that were published in the *Kansas City Star* from September 17, 1917, through January 13, 1919.[90] Viewed objectively many years later, these hate- and hokum-filled pronouncements in his last, bitter months of life, as reflected in the following excerpts, add little gloss to the memory of one of America's most popular presidents. But they contributed mightily to the image of a bloodthirsty foreign enemy who must be given no quarter, to the crushing of domestic dissent, and to the spy mania that was sweeping the country and eroding the constitutional rights of its citizens.

> The women who do not raise their boys to be soldiers when the country needs them are unfit to live in this republic.
>
> The Stones and La Follettes, the Hearsts and Hillquits are out of place in America. It is sincerely to be regretted that they cannot be put where they belong—under the Hohenzollerns.
>
> With deliberate purpose the German Government has carried on a war of horror, a war of obscene cruelty, of wholesale slaughter, of foul treachery and bestiality, a war in which civilians, including women, children, nurses, doctors, and priests, as well as wounded soldiers, have been murdered wholesale.
>
> Teaching German in the public schools should be prohibited. German language newspapers should have a time limit act, after which it should not be lawful to publish them save in English.
>
> To talk peace means to puzzle the ignorant and to weaken the will of even the stout-hearted. It is hailed with evil joy by all the men in this country who have opposed war and wish us to submit tamely to German brutality.
>
> Thank Heaven that our sons and brothers are now to stand at Armageddon. Thank Heaven that American soldiers are now to fight in the great battle against the bestial foe of America and of mankind.
>
> As for spies, preachers of sedition, men who practice sabotage, and all other such persons, the Government already has much power, but should be given any additional power to proceed against them, and this power should be used in drastic fashion, if necessary under martial law, and after a summary trial the guilty men should be shot.

Germany has habitually and as a matter of policy practiced the torture of men, the rape of women, and the killing of children.

Let us never forget that no promise Germany makes can be trusted. The *Kultur* developed under the Hohenzollerns rests upon shameless treachery and duplicity no less than upon ruthless violence and barbarity.

As for the spies, there is no question as to the treatment needed. They should be shot or hung. ...It was these German spies, agents, and propagandists who, in 1917, disintegrated and destroyed Russia, and inflicted a crushing disaster on Italy, and conducted the most dangerous intrigue in France, and aided and abetted the British pacifists. In this country, Senator Overman has estimated their number at four hundred thousand, and Mr. Flynn, the recently resigned chief of the secret service, has put them at over a quarter of a million.

Woodrow Wilson finally got the opportunity to respond to his tormenter. Early in the war Roosevelt had entertained the idea of leading a mounted troop of hand-picked volunteers in Europe, and as American intervention finally loomed, he was prepared to prostrate himself before the administration he scorned. On February 2, 1917, he wrote to Secretary of War Newton D. Baker: "I have already on file ... my application to be permitted to raise a Division of Infantry ... in the event of war (possibly with the permission to make one or two of the brigades of infantry, mounted infantry). ... If you believe that there will be war, and a call for volunteers to go to war immediately, I respectfully and earnestly request that you notify me at once."[91]

Baker talked with Roosevelt and raised technical difficulties. Finally, Roosevelt gained an audience on April 10 with the ultimate decision maker and the man who had so frequently been the target of his venomous personal attacks. Joseph P. Tumulty, Wilson's secretary, sat a few feet away from the two men during their meeting, and later wrote that "nothing could have been pleasanter or more agreeable than this meeting. ...The object of the Colonel's call was discussed without heat or bitterness."[92] Wilson was, of course, noncommittal, invoking the hostile attitude of the general staff toward a volunteer system.

Roosevelt's version of the meeting differed from Tumulty: "We had an hour's talk. I complimented him on his war message and told him it would rank with the world's greatest state papers if it were made good and I told him I wanted a chance to help him make it good. I found that ... there was a confusion in his mind as to what I wanted to do. I explained everything to him. He seemed to take it well, but—remember—I was talking to Mr. Wilson."[93]

Following the meeting, Tumulty asked the president for a press statement. Wilson wrote to Tumulty, "I really think the best way to treat Mr. Roosevelt is to take no notice of him. That breaks his heart and is the best punishment that can be administered."[94] Wilson saw to it that the old Rough Rider never got his fervent wish. He publicly defended his decision on the basis of Roosevelt's lack of military leadership experience. There were two other reasons: personally, Wilson almost certainly took quiet pleasure in finally being able to frustrate his loudmouthed antagonist; and politically, a second moment of military glory for Roosevelt could give him and the Republican Party irresistible power in the 1920 presidential campaign. As it turned out, Wilson need not have been concerned, for the rancorous old warrior died on January 6, 1919.

At Roosevelt's side spiritually was his military buddy of Spanish War days past, Leonard Wood. By 1914 , Wood was a major general, the senior general officer of the United States, and acknowledged as the nation's most distinguished soldier. His dossier was as impressive as his military bearing: military surgeon, Indian fighter, Rough Rider, governor of Santiago, military governor of Cuba, governor of the Phillippines' Moro Province, and commanding general of the Philippines Department. The ambitious, outspoken Wood, then completing his tour of duty as Chief of Staff, was looking for ways and means to become commander in chief. His best shot at the presidency would come later, once America was into the war, but meanwhile he stayed in the public's eye as the country's ramrod-straight principal advocate of preparedness. He lectured, gave press interviews, wrote, and otherwise energetically promoted his cause. He foresaw an America that would combine its powerful industrial base with aggressive nationalism. The basis of the effort was the new demand of American industrialism for armament orders at home, for the opportunities of foreign markets and foreign adventure, for the disciplines of military patriotism to preserve the social structure against its developing strains and stiffen it to support the world competitive struggle.[95]

Wood's vision was, in fact, the first glimmerings of what would later become the "military-industrial complex" against which President Dwight D. Eisenhower warned the nation in 1960. Wood had also conceived a scheme through which he would implement his views of a future America always prepared for war: voluntary summer camps to train reserve army officers. In 1913, Wood opened his first two camps, one in Gettsyburg, Pennsylvania, at the site of the Civil War's most famous battle, and one in Monterey, California. These inaugural camps had only 222 recruits, most of them college undergraduates. The following summer there were four camps, and Wood had tripled the enrollment of his fledgling officers. In 1915, Wood expanded his program with a large facility in Plattsburg, New York, training some 1,500 patriotic young businessmen and professionals as well as college students. They were taught how to march in step, take orders, shoot a rifle, and other rudiments of soldiering. In September, Wood even held a special "businessmen's" camp; more than 1,200 came, including several "preparedness" luminaries: Robert Bacon, the former French ambassador; John P. Mitchel, mayor of New York City; and Arthur Woods, New York City police commissioner. By the summer of 1916, attendance had grown to over 16,000 in 12 camps. There was even a special camp for boys ages 15 to 18.

Wood saw far beyond the limited military value of his training camps. He acknowledged, "We do not expect ... to accomplish much in the way of detailed military instruction ... but we do believe a great deal can be done in the implanting of a sound military policy."[96] For what Wood had thoughtfully created were not practical training grounds for war, but rather seminaries for missionaries of preparedness. Back in school or their offices in the fall, trim, tanned, and well indoctrinated cadres would sell their friends and families on the new doctrine.

The war in Europe, as might be expected, considerably brightened Wood's outlook. In 1916 he published a slim book summarizing his platform, *Our Military History: Its Facts and Fallacies*, to alert his fellow citizens on the urgency

Colonel Leonard Wood (left) and Lt. Colonel Theodore Roosevelt in 1898 in Florida, at the start of the Spanish War. In 1915 and 1916, Wood, as the nation's first soldier, and Roosevelt, as a popular ex-president, joined forces to promote "preparedness" and America's entry into the Great War. *National Archives.*

of preparation for the nation's defense. A friendly review in the May 21 issue of the *New York Times* stated that "the book is straightforward talk. It does not criticize anybody in power. It was written only after repeated requests. It is not an argument for a huge army or for the biggest navy in the world, but a common-sense argument for adequate national preparedness." In the book, Wood drew on every worn-out cliche he could dig up to support his thesis.

He argued that preparing for war meant promoting peace: "We must remember the world-old slogan, than which truer words were never uttered, 'In time of peace prepare for war.' We might vary it by saying, 'In time of peace make such preparation against war as will make it improbable' but, however, we state it, it means preparation—careful, thorough, and well thought out."[97]

How his followers could then support such a concept with a straight face, in light of the obvious lessons just being learned from Europe's arms race, defies logic.

As for the kind of military the nation should have, Wood cautioned that volunteerism was a system fraught with "uncertainties, unpreparedness, and lack of equality."[98] Universal military training was the only way to go, he insisted. Wood's most telling remark invoked one of the nation's military heroes. During the Revolutionary War, General "Light Horse" Henry Lee, when facing a detachment of raw recruits, was alleged to have said, "A government is the murderer of its citizens which sends them to the field uninformed and untaught, where they are to meet men of the same age and strength, mechanized by education and disciplined for battle."[99] Wood— and every partisan for preparedness in the United States—would purposefully tug on the heartstrings of the nation's mothers with this provocative message.

Wood, like Roosevelt, had antagonized President Wilson by public outbursts of anti-administration rhetoric and behind-the-scenes political conduct unbecoming to a high-ranking military officer. With America into the war, again remarkably like Roosevelt, Wood also came to the White House, hat in hand, to plead in vain for a field command in Europe. A close observer and strong ally of the president at that time summarized Wilson's feelings toward General Wood:

> At all times, the President was explicit with regard to Wood. His sense of justice had been outraged by the political elevation of a doctor over the heads of soldiers who had given laborious years to the study and practice of their profession, and his sense of taste was offended by the spectacle of a soldier in uniform plying the trade of a politician. He felt that this allowance of special privilege, this grant of immunity to insult and insubordination, struck a blow at the discipline of the army.[100]

Wood was publicly shunted aside to stateside training posts, never going to Europe as head of a combat corps, as he considered his due by rank and experience. He sought the Republican nomination for the presidency in 1920, seeing himself as Roosevelt's successor, but was unsuccessful in that attempt as well. He quickly faded from public view.

After the war, Walter Lippmann reflected the rapid decline in Wood's political fortunes in his scathing denunciation of the general's unsuitability for the office of U.S. president, in an article in the *New Republic*. Among other reasons for the general's lack of qualifications, Lippmann wrote that "the whole of Leonard Wood's claim to be President among the American people rests not on deeds but on words. Words about his relations to Roosevelt, speeches about preparedness, magazine articles about Americanism, talks to audiences in various parts of the country. There are no facts available about his deeds as an American statesman." Lippmann suggested that there had been a war party, and its inner sect "was Wood and Roosevelt, and that sect is Wood today." Everything about this sect was inimical to American principles, as Lippmann saw it: its unconcern about law, its radical jingoism, its exaltation of the federal government as supreme, its attacks on civil liberties. Mocking Wood's "statesmanlike contribution to the problem of how best to deal with the revolutionary immigrant," Lippmann quoted a recent statement of Wood's before a farmers' convention: "My motto for the Reds is S.O.S.—ship or shoot. I believe we should place them all on a ship of stone, with sails of lead and that their first stopping place should be Hell."[101]

There were some men with more pecuniary reasons for promoting the nation's military strength. One such person was Solomon Stanwood Menken, a wealthy, influential big-business attorney with clients in lumber, sugar, and railroads. Menken had been on a business trip to Europe when war broke out and was temporarily stranded in England. He occupied some of his spare time in the visitors' gallery in the House of Commons, soaking up the parliamentry discussions about how the British Empire should manage its latest war. Concerned that the United States was unprepared to fight a similar war—and fervently believing that Germany, should she defeat the Allies, would promptly send a fleet across the Atlantic to attack America—he returned to the United States convinced he must arouse the nation to the imminent threat. In December, after talking with such like-minded men as Roosevelt, Wood, Henry L. Stimson (Roosevelt's former war secretary), and Anglophile publisher George Haven Putnam, he founded the National Security League (NSL).

Among other prominent Americans happy to lend their names to this new jingo organization were Alton B. Parker, the Democratic candidate for president in 1908; John Grier Hibben, the president of Princeton University; former ambassadors Robert Bacon and Myron T. Herrick, both just back from France; and Elihu Root, former secretary of state (and, anachronistically, recipient of the Nobel Peace Prize in 1912). Principal contributors were rich eastern businessmen with a financial stake in a big U.S. military establishment. They included J.P. Morgan, John D. Rockefeller, Henry C. Frick, and T. Coleman Du Pont.

What the NSL stood for was straightforward: America must build the largest navy in the world, expand the regular army to half a million men, and institute compulsory military training and thus create a powerful reserve army. At an early meeting, Menken called for a detailed investigation of the nation's defense and adoption of a preparedness program that would not be influenced by sectionalism, politics, or personalities.

Peace advocates were not permitted to stand in the way of the preparedness crusade as enunciated by the League. In its jargon, the "pro–German" was the same as the "pacifist," the "neutralist," or the "socialist." Anyone who did not strongly support the Allied cause was unpatriotic. Even if an individual had no German forebears, if he supported American neutrality, he was labeled a hyphenate—or a spy or a traitor. Roosevelt chimed in that "pacifism and pro–Germanism are Siamese twins."[102]

In February 1916, announcing that "we have seen our propaganda go forward with amazing success," the National Security League opened a campaign for one million members nationwide, on the theory, as stated by Menken, that Germany's Navy League had been able to get one million members and Americans should be equally patriotic.[103] The National Security League never came close to Menken's ambitious membership goal; it is generally accepted that the total never reached 100,000. But despite what may have been a disappointing enrollment to its founders, the NSL nevertheless was the most powerful lobby in the United States for preparedness and its own narrow vision of patriotism. Until America was into the war and its massive campaign of preparedness became obsolete, NSL speakers traveled the country, frightening audiences with the imminence of an Allied collapse and the subsequent certainty of a German invasion of America. The League fervently supported the Plattsburg program, organized preparedness parades, attacked neutralist politicians, and flooded the country with its pamphlets on patriotism.

Once America was into the war, the organization found fertile new fields in loyalty crusades and education in the schools. As far as the NSL was concerned, using the German language in the United States was treasonous and the teaching of German in public schools was even worse. German-language newspapers were labeled subversive and the League put pressure on advertisers to discontinue their programs in those papers and newspaper distributors to stop handling them. In August 1917, editors of some 450 German-American newspapers were asked to subscribe to what the NSL called a "Confession of Faith":

1. I believe that the objects of America in this war are noble, unselfish, and that they square with the highest aims of morality and religion.
2. I believe that the aims of Germany in this war are sordid, selfish, and opposed to the principles of human liberty.
3. I believe that the statement of the German monarch and of his Prime Ministers as to German aims and purposes in the war have been false and hypocritical.

4. I believe that the methods sanctioned by the German Government and rulers in this war are brutal, barbarous and revolting to civilized thought.
5. I believe that the preservation of human liberties and the ideals of civilization and morality depend upon our victory in this war.
6. I believe that we cannot win this war alone, and that our own future and all that we strive for is inseparably bound up with the success of our allies.
7. I believe that the peace of the world cannot rest on any contract made with perjurers; and that our own preservation and the accomplishment of our objects in the war requires the permanent effacement of the present German dynasty and radical changes in the present system of German Government.
8. I believe that the war must continue until this result is achieved by military victory for ourselves and allies or by revolution within the German nation.
9. I believe that there can be no qualified allegiance to the United States and the principles for which it is struggling; those who do not support the war whole-heartedly cannot claim to be wholly loyal.[104]

This demand, which fell on deaf ears, followed an earlier one by the League to German-American organizations, in particular, the National German-American Alliance—"to stand up and be counted as opposed to the German Government." According to the *New York Times*, that NSL solicitation "met a brick wall in the determination of the German-Americans that they will do no such thing."[105]

The NSL retained the services of a busy group of Germanophobic historians from prominent universities to lecture and write slanted articles, pamphlets, and books. The two best known were Albert Bushnell Hart of Harvard and Robert M. McElroy of Princeton. The League paid its staffers well.

The hallmark of much of NSL's extremist propaganda was its perversion of truth. According to one observer, its printed material

> departed from the canons of thorough research, objectivity, and dispassionate presentation. The worst of … NSL pamphlets contained classic examples of selective research, distorted meanings, misquotations, national prejudices, ethnic stereotypes, and impassioned writing. Much of the propaganda attempted to emulate scholarly work and made its charade even more glaring; the professional earmarks of footnotes and bibliographies were frequently as misleading as the texts they supplemented.[106]

As the war wound down, the NSL shifted to new targets of opportunity to fulfill its reactionary mission, for the first time transparently grinding a political axe. In the fall of 1918, it struck out at those congressional candidates up for reelection whom the League considered "disloyal" based on their votes and speeches in the Congress. Most of those on its broadly circulated list of legislators not to be returned to office proved to be Democrats.

In December, a House Judiciary Committee of angry lame ducks opened hearings concerning contributions to the NSL and its efforts to influence elections. During testimony, founder Menken said he stood opposed to U.S. membership in the League of Nations and favored monopoly control of important industries. The committee stated in its final report, in March 1919, that the League had violated the Corrupt Practices Act, but took no further action. The reaction of the *New York Times* to the committees's gentle slap on NSL's wrist was predictable. In an editorial on March 8, it defended the League as "a human and fallible institution" that was guilty of making mistakes "in its methods." As for the NSL's critics, most were those "who either did not care whether we won the war or not, or who were zealous that we should not win it."

During the 1920s, the League dug in to fight those it considered to be the nation's latest threats to America's way of life, socialists and communists. Aligned with the NSL in this new crusade to promote public fear and hatred of radicalism and enforcement of "100 percent Americanism" were other militant patriotic organizations. Chief among these were the American Defense Society, founded in 1915 to promote war preparedness and proud of Theodore Roosevelt as its former honorary president; the National Civic Federation, created in 1901 to foster cooperation between management and labor, but since the war rigorously anti–Red; and the American Legion, founded in 1919 by World War I veterans and by year-end the largest organization promoting strict "Americanism," with nearly one million members. The extremist Ku Klux Klan, while not a "patriotic" organization in a general sense, employed the specter of radicalism in its drive against noncomformity in race, religion, and serial customs.

Warnings of the wolf-at-the-door, invariably in the guise of a uniformed soldier with a vertical spike on the top of his helmet and in German field gray, were trumpeted in the other media, notably books and motion pictures.

America Fallen! The Sequel to the European War was a popular little 1915 novel depicting Germany's successful invasion and takeover of the United States following a "Treaty of Geneva" in March 1916 which ended the European war. Germany had been defeated and England demanded transfer of the German fleet to the victorious Allies. Germany stubbornly refused, accepting instead a $15 billion indemnity. Germany's planned takeover of America thus had a single objective: to obtain the $15 billion as "ransom." The author suggested in his preface that his tale had a serious purpose: to emphasize the unpreparedness of America's naval and military forces to resist attack by a major power."

By every count, however, the most widely publicized and most broadly distributed text on the urgent need for America to be militarily strong was

Hudson Maxim's *Defenseless America*. Maxim had gained international fame and considerable fortune as the inventor of smokeless powder. Even more well known was his brother, Sir Hiram Stevens Maxim, who had created the first high-speed machine gun, which bore his name. (Sir Hiram's son, Hiram Percy, kept up the family tradition; he invented yet another famous killing device, the "Maxim Silencer.") On the title page of his book, the younger Maxim humbly credited the elder, at the same time setting his reader on the right track: "The quick-firing gun is the greatest life-saving instrument ever invented."

"The main object of this book," Maxim proclaimed in his opening sentence, "is to present a phalanx of facts upon the subject of the defenseless condition of this country, and to show what must be done, and done quickly, in order to avert the most dire calamity that can fall upon a people—that of merciless invasion by a foreign foe, with the horrors of which no pestilence can be compared."[107]

While, in fact, *Defenseless America* skirted the issue of "the most dire calamity," the book covered all other bases with remarkable clarity and effectiveness, damning pacifists, lauding jingoes, detailing needs of the army and navy, eloquently describing current military equipment, defending arms makers, outlining military strategies, echoing and reechoing the certainty of war. One chapter began with an obviously canned letter from Leonard Wood that concluded with General Lee's admonition that played so well among America's mothers. Anyone tilting toward preparedness was almost certain to be made an advocate by reading Maxim's convincing arguments.

J. Stuart Blackton's brazenly pro-war movie *The Battle Cry of Peace* was based on Maxim's book, and enlisted even more supporters to the cause of American preparedness. Blackton was English-born and a stout Germanophobe. He "counted Theodore Roosevelt, his neighbor at Oyster Bay, among his friends and 'blind pacifism' among his enemies."[108]

Blackton shrewdly dedicated the movie to America's mothers, "with respect, reverence and admiration, and with the earnest prayer that their eyes may be opened to the peril which menaces, and will continue to menace them, their children, and their loved ones, until the present state of 'unpreparedness' has been remedied."[109] The story line was simple: an enemy spy urges on an advocate of disarmament, the enemy lands in an unprepared America, then general disaster. The film starts out with the bushy-bearded Maxim himself standing on a podium with maps behind him, artillery shells all around, and, at his side, a machine gun, which he pats affectionately as he warns his audience, with extensive subtitles, against the scourge of unpreparedness. Then the drama gets underway in earnest. "The Invasion" shows soldiers of an unnamed country (but garbed in field gray with spiked helmets) coming ashore in New York City. "In the Hands of the Enemy" shows the bombardment and capture of the city. America finally counterattacks in "The

Price." The film ends with a mother dramatically shooting her two daughters rather than allow them to fall into the hands of drunken, rapacious enemy soldiers. Throughout, pacifists are depicted as sniveling, yellow-bellied cowards.

Parading through the film, stout preparedness advocates were luminaries from America's political, military, and ecclesiastical ranks, attesting to Blackton's close ties to the nation's power elite: former president Taft, Secretary of State Lansing, Secretary of War Garrison, Admiral Dewey, Reverend Lyman Abbott, among others.[110]

All the preparedness groups heartily endorsed the film for its great educational value and recommended it for Americans of all ages. Roosevelt declared that "every good American should be grateful to Mr. Blackton for having produced 'The Battle Cry of Peace.' Every uninformed but well-meaning American should attend the exhibition and profit by it. The men who oppose it ... are thoroughly bad Americans and are engaged in an action hostile to the vital interests of the United States."[111]

Most of the early wartime films did not depict the Germans quite so brutally as Blackton did. In fact, during the first few months of the war, Americans who went to the movies were encouraged to be neutral. Patrons were requested not to demonstrate, by clapping or hissing, as the case might be, in favor of one belligerent or the other, in line with the president's call for even-handedness. At the start, films were mostly documentaries—parades of goose-stepping German soldiers in smart uniforms and Royal Navy dreadnoughts belching smoke from their cannons—because directors were not yet sure how to produce fictional war stories.

In one of the earliest movie war dramas, titled *Kultur*, the war begins, Hollywood-style, as a quarrel over the affections of a girl, with Archduke Franz Ferdinand a party to the spat. A second maiden, jealous of the attention given her competitor, hires an assassin to kill the archduke. Presto, World War I. There were several intentionally neutral films, such as *Be Neutral* and *Neutrality*, and one that purported to be pacifist in nature, *Civilization*. Woodrow Wilson, who saw the latter movie, agreed to appear in a special introduction to it. However, *Civilization* featured a world war, the sinking of the *Lusitania*, and an aggressive monarch who was depicted as driving his people into war for conquest and personal ambition.

Well before *Civilization* was completed in mid–1916, pacifist films were no longer being produced in the United States. While American moviegoers had to wait for the nation's entry into the war for the most exciting depictions of German bestiality, there was much for the Germanophobe to relish before then. Films like *Bullets and Brown Eyes* creatively illustrated the savagery of the Huns in fictitious wars, while *The Belgian*, *Who Goes There?*, and *The Heart of Humanity* focused on the wanton despoliation of "poor little Belgium."

On May 13, 1916, in what was billed by an exultant *New York Times* as "the greatest civilian marching demonstration in the history of the world," the Citizens' Preparedness Parade got under way in Manhattan. Starting on lower Broadway at 9:35 A.M., orderly files of 20 abreast marched up Park Row, Centre Street, Lafayette Street, Fourth Street, into fabled Fifth Avenue and on to the foot of Central Park. All day long and into the night the paraders rolled north, 135,683 "by actual count of *Times* reporters," accompanied by more than 200 blaring military bands and 50 booming drum corps. For 12 hours without stop the marchers passed the official reviewing stand seating 9,000. The parade's chief dignitary was General Wood, who stayed for 11 hours in the reviewing stand, standing most of the time and coming to attention smartly and saluting every national ensign that was carried past.

The New York City parade immediately triggered others in different cities and tens of thousands of Americans were soon tramping in some semblance of cadence to a new chant: Prepare! Prepare! Those individuals and organizations preaching preparedness for America—Roosevelt, Wood, Maxim, Blackton, the National Security League, the American Defense Society, and others—had obviously won their battle, if not their war.

Not all defenders of the allied cause in America focused their energies on preparedness. There remained the important question of which nation had started the war, and there were plenty of war-guilt pundits to step forward. Of all the perspicacious analysts, the Hon. James M. Beck, a former assistant attorney general of the United States, stood at the top. He got his jump on the pack because the *New York Times* had selected him immediately after the outbreak of the war to sift the evidence from the belligerents' apologias and render supposedly dispassionate judgment. On October 25, 1914, the paper splashed the headline for his long-winded analysis across the first two pages of the magazine section: IN THE SUPREME COURT OF CIVILIZATION, the case of The Double Alliance vs. The Triple Entente. Under the headline was a large pen-and-ink portrait of the judge-turned-propagandist, looking appropriately serious.

After presenting the salient "facts," Beck allowed that an impartial court would not hesitate to pass the following judgment:

1. That Germany and Austria in a time of profound peace secretly concerted together to impose their will upon Europe....
2. That Germany had at all times the power to compel Austria to preserve a reasonable and conciliatory course, but at no time effectively exerted that influence. On the contrary, she certainly abetted and possibly instigated Austria in her unreasonable course.
3. That England, France, Italy, and Russia at all times sincerely worked for peace....
4. That after Austria had mobilized its army, Russia was reasonably justified

in mobilizing its forces. Such act of mobilization was the right of any sovereign State....

5. That Germany, in abruptly declaring war against Russia for failure to demobilize when the other Powers had offered to make any reasonable concession and peace parleys were still in progress, precipitated the war.

Beck concluded by cautioning his readers that "in visiting its condemnation, the Supreme Court of Civilization should ... distinguish between the military caste, headed by the Kaiser and the Crown Prince, which precipitated this great calamity, and the German people." This charitable interpretation was later embraced as an effective propaganda ploy by Wilson once America was into the war.

Beck promptly expanded his material into a book he called *The Evidence in the Case.* To the five items he had used to conclude his original "judgment," Beck added more:

6. That the invasion of Belgium by Germany was without any provocation and in violation of Belgium's inherent rights as a sovereign State. The sanctity of its territory did not depend exclusively upon the Treaty of 1839 or the Hague Convention, but upon fundamental and axiomatic principles of international law....

7. England was justified in its declaration of war upon Germany, not only because of its direct interests in the neutrality of Belgium, but also because of the ethical duty of the strong nations to protect the weak. ...England was, under the treaty of 1839, under an especial obligation to defend the neutrality of Belgium, and had it failed to respect that obligation it would have broken its solemn covenant.[112]

As can be imagined, the British adored Beck. In a show of appreciation for his good works, he was invited as an honored guest to both England and France and given carefully orchestrated tours of the British fleet and the battlefronts in France. Just before he returned to the United States, after his first visit, during the summer of 1915, Beck assured a *London Daily Telegraph* reporter that he had "absolute confidence in the ultimate and not distant triumph of the Allies," of which he had seen "so many striking evidences."[113]

Sir Gilbert Parker, of Wellington House, later singled out Beck for special thanks in his March 1918 article in *Harper's.* Parker wrote: "It should also be remembered that it was the Pilgrim's Society which took charge of the Hon. James Beck when he visited England in 1916, and gave him so good a chance to do great work for the cause of unity between the two nations. I am glad and proud that I had something to do with these arrangements."[114]

Some American-authored treatises were much more subtle pro–Ally propaganda. Perhaps the most popular work of this genre during 1915 and 1916 was Owen Wister's little book *The Pentacost of Calamity.* Wister, a well-known author of books on the American West, meticulously crafted a seductive portrait of Germany for his readers. The first half of the book was almost a celebration of Germans and Germany. Wister, who had spent two months in Germany in 1914, recorded, at the end of June,

> a clean, beautiful, orderly Germany, peopled with friendly, efficient Germans. The trains ran punctually, the conductors were courteous. Frankfurt-am-Main is a name to me compact with memories—memories of clean streets; of streets full of by-passers who could direct you when you asked your way; of streets empty of beggars, empty of all signs of desolate, drunken or idle poverty ... of excellent shops; the streets full of prosperous movement and bustle; an absence of rags, a presence of good stout clothes; a people of contented faces....
>
> Such was the splendor of this empire as it unrolled before me through May and June 1914, that by contrast the state of its two great neighbors, France and England, seemed distressing and unenviable. Paris was shabby and incoherent, London full of unrest. ...Suppose a soul, arrived on earth from another world, ...were given its choice after a survey of the nations, which it should be born in and belong to? In May, June, and July, 1914, my choice would have been, not France, not England, not America, but Germany.[115]

Carefully, almost imperceptibly, Wister led his readers on. Suddenly: "The world is in agony. We witness the most terrible catastrophe known to mankind—most terrible, not from its huge size, but because it is a moral catastrophe." Wister probed "some diplomatic and philosophic precepts laid down by Machiavelli, Neitzsche and Trietschke." Then, almost too suddenly: "The case of Germany is a hospital case ... this diseased mental state. ...We have heard the wild incoherent ring in many German voices besides the Kaiser's." Wister concluded, "Nothing in the whole story of mankind is more strange than the case of Germany—how Germany through generations had been carefully trained for this wild spring at the throat of Europe. ...The Serbian assassination had nothing to do with it; save that it accidentally struck the hour. Months and years before that, Germany was crouching for her spring."[116]

Another medium—the pulpit—was perhaps more persuasive than newspapers, movies, and books, for it carried with it the prospective threat of eternal hellfire for transgressors. While most of the country's clergy waited for America to enter the war before exhorting their flocks to take up arms in a holy crusade, some were quicker to react to the trumpets of Armageddon from Belgium and France.

One of the first out of the lists and galloping fast was the Rev. Dr. Charles Henry Parkhurst, pastor of Manhattan's snobby Madison Square Church. Parkhurst had made a name for himself 24 years earlier when he had begun lecturing his congregation on Tammany Hall and sin, focusing on "the official and administrative criminality that is filthifying our municipal life, making New York a very hotbed of knavery, debauchery and bestiality.[117] "In the intervening years, Parkhurst insinuated himself into local politics, becoming a power broker in his own right. In a letter to the *New York Times*, published on August 23, 1914, and presumably based on one of his most recent sermons, Parkhurst laid out his personal interpretation of the war in Europe and of European history in general, employing the vivid metaphors of his calling. Credit his recommendations for being farsighted, for they would soon be echoed by clergymen and laymen alike:

> When a mad dog runs amuck, the policeman shoots him on the spot— not by way of revenge, but as a humanitarian contribution to the security of the public. Now has a more rabid creature than Emperor William ever run amuck through the peaceful and prosperous domain of Europe? The policeman makes no argument with the dog and enters into no compromise with him, but deals with him in exclusive regard to the requirements of society, and simply blots him out as a public menace; deals with him exactly as Germany dealt with Poland at the time of partition; deals with him as Germany meant to deal with France in the war of '70 when she intended to impose a war indemnity so heavy, and so to cripple her military means of offense and defense as to crush her as a military power and render Germany invulnerable from the side of France.
>
> Now the same kind of medicine is exactly the kind that should be administered to her. It may not be necessary to strangle her, but her claws should be clipped and her teeth filed, and enough of her fortifications dismantled to render her harmless, and as heavy a war indemnity imposed as will not drive her to absolute penury. This policy should be adopted in no spirit of revenge, but in pursuance of a policy essential to universal security, comfort, and well-being. Anything less than this will necessitate the eventual repetition of the present tragedy.

Across the East River, in Brooklyn, the Rev. Dr. Newell Dwight Hillis, minister to the Plymouth Congregational Church, became the most famous of all American clergymen to call upon the Almighty to hurl the Germans into an eternity of fire and brimstone. Before the war, Hillis had traveled extensively in Europe, using his firsthand experiences as the basis for popular lectures in the United States. His favorite topic had been Germans and Germany—"The New Germany"—and he drew on the orderliness, cleanliness, industriousness, and proclaimed arrow-straight character of Wilhelmine society, all eminently Christian traits, as parables for his audiences. He was also a busy author of religious tracts with such ecumenical-sounding titles as *Faith and Character* and *Right Living as a Fine Art.*

It took Hillis only a short time after the outbreak of the war to see the obsolescence of his earlier views. In his sermons in the fall of 1914 and in a little book he published based on these talks, *Studies of the Great War*, Hillis said that friends of his who had left Belgium in late August brought stories of German frightfulness that filled their listeners with horror. Refusing, Hillis said, to accept their testimony without proof, he began what he called a careful program of research—studying letters, published evidence, eyewitness testimony, photographs, and reports of the various commissions in Europe, particularly the Bryce Report.

After April 1917, like most clergyman of nearly every denomination in the United States, Hillis enthusiastically threw himself behind the war effort. In May, he was a prominent salesman for the First Liberty Loan drive, touring 18 states and making up to five addresses each day. He called this first series of lectures "What the United States and Her Allies Are Fighting For," a theme soon to be wellworn. Hillis's interpretation of America's reason for going to war against Germany was simplistic: "Either Germany must conquer England, France and the United States, and impose autocracy upon them, and enthrone the Kaiser as the world emperor, or else the Allies must conquer Germany, and overthrow autocracy and militarism."[118]

According to his contorted understanding of history, the United States also had an obligation to England—to repay "our immeasurable debt to the motherland" and to "pay our debt to France," because France once had "helped Washington expel thousands of German invaders from America."[119] As for the Kaiser, "already the hemp is grown to twist into the noose for the royal neck."[120] Hillis closed these early talks on a topic he would soon hone to a razor's edge—German atrocities: "Let all our people say to the Kaiser and his War Staff, 'You shall not skewer babes upon your bayonets; you shall not crucify officers upon the trees; you shall not nail young nuns to the doors of the schoolhouses; you shall not violate the sanctities of infancy and old age; you shall not mutilate the bodies of little girls and noble women.'"[121]

In July and August 1917, Hillis toured the European battlefields as a special guest of the British and French governments, who by then had recognized the fiery preacher's value to their cause. When he returned to the U.S. lecture circuit in the fall, Hillis was well stocked with "authenticated" atrocity stories, including photographs.

In October, for the Second Liberty Loan, Hillis integrated his latest material into a new lecture and barnstormed across the country, covering 30 cities with his savage gospel of German inhumanity. He began the talks promising to tell the truth about the war but also to present firsthand information about German atrocities, "to tell about the crimes of these men, fiendish devils they are, who drink human blood out of their enemies' skulls, who commit murder and rape as pastimes, with crimes upon women their specialty."[122] He told of "little children too innocent to invent what they are old enough to describe," and showed pictures of massacred dead, of men "who had defended the honor of their wives" and had been "hacked into shreds" and mutilated "in ways that can only be mentioned by men to men and in whispered tones."[123] Hillis also shared with his intent audiences a remarkable scientific discovery he had made while in Europe:

> When the Hun joins the army, he must pass his medical examination. A few drops of blood are taken from the left arm, and the Wassermann blood culture is developed. If free from disease, the soldier receives a card giving

him access to the camp women, who are kept in the rear for the convenience of the German soldier. If, however, the Wassermann test shows that the German has syphilis, the soldier bids him report to the commanding officer. The captain tells him plainly that he must stay away from the camp women upon peril of his life, and that if he uses one of the girls he will be shot like a dog. Having syphilis himself, the German will hand it on to the camp girl, and she in turn will contaminate all the other soldiers, and that means that the Kaiser would soon have no army. Therefore, the soldier that has this foul disease must stay away from the camp women on peril of his life. Under this restriction the syphilitic soldier has but one chance, namely, to capture a Belgian or French girl; but using this girl means contaminating her, and she in turn will contaminate the next German using her. To save his own life, therefore, when the syphilitic German has used a French or Belgian girl, he cuts off her breast as a warning to the next German soldier.[124]

Hillis also developed a talk on another theme, "The Pan-German Empire Scheme, for Which Germany Lost Her Soul." This presentation was much milder in content and was used among women's groups. It was a deceiving interpretation of recent European events, emphasizing the evils of "Prussianism," the "crimes" of the Kaiser, the "scrap of paper," and the more frightening exposure of Germany's supposed plans to invade America. There was little he had not borrowed from Frenchman André Cheradame, a proponent of the evils of pan–Germanism more virulent than its chief scourge in the United States, Roland G. Usher. But Hillis made his images come alive:

> At last the woven web was spread all over the world through spies. Could any man have been lifted up above Berlin, and had full power to survey the whole world, he would have seen a spider's web, with its center in Berlin, with the Kaiser as the big black spider, sending out along the sinuous thread into every capital of every country and of every continent his evil plans and plots. ...The only difference between Judas and the average German spy is that the modern spy in the United States would not only have betrayed Jesus for thirty pieces of silver, but would have given ten per cent off for cash.[125]

Hillis's final wartime book, *The Blot on the Kaiser's 'Scutcheon*, based on yet another summer tour of Europe's battlefields, featured an astonishing if ingenious proposal to rid the world of "the Hun":

> Statesmen, generals, diplomats, editors are now talking about the duty of simply exterminating the German people. There will shortly be held a meeting of surgeons in this country. ...These surgeons are preparing to advocate the calling of a world conference to consider the sterilization of the ten million German soldiers and the segregation of the women, that when this generation of German goes, civilized cities, states and races may be rid of this awful cancer that must be cut clean out of the body of society.[126]

Other pastors chose to join in the patriotic search for enemy agents. One of the most enthusiastic of the clergyman spy-hunters was the Rev. Dr. Charles Aubrey Eaton, of the Madison Avenue Baptist Church in Manhattan. His job as chairman of the National Service Section of the Emergency

Fleet Corporation was to visit shipyards nationwide and deliver motivational messages. During one stopover, Eaton advised his listeners that "when he [the spy] comes sneaking around with a bomb, don't say, 'Let us pray,' but take him out there on the marsh and tie him down and place the bomb on his chest. Light it and stand off and watch him blown to his Kaiser—to hell! Be regular he-men."[127]

Eaton also had compiled a homily appropriate for a gathering of East Coast shipyard workers:

> Out on the Pacific Coast the men have what they call the Rail Committee. This is formed of workmen and is charged with seeing that every hand in the yard is 100% American and on the job eight hours a day, six days a week. In the yard at Seattle the Rail Committee has an iron pipe which is called the Liberty Rail. It is kept near the blacksmith's forge. When a workman utters a disloyal sentiment, fails to buy bonds or war-savings stamps, or in other ways proves that he is lukewarm, the Liberty Rail is heated on the forge and the disloyal workman is ridden about the yards on the hot rail. At one time, I was told, there were twelve men in a Seattle hospital recovering from Liberty Rail rides.[128]

Like so many other Americans who had accepted as truth the wartime lies of propaganda, the preachers reacted with dismay and then disillusionment after the Armistice. The list of prominent clerical penitents was a distinguished one. Five years after the Armistice, the most acclaimed war time chaplain, Father Francis Duffy, confessed, "War is something so opposed to God! It is so full of the Satanic. ... Most men have seen in war-experience nothing but evil in its nakedness. ... Forever stand these words over war which Dante placed over the entrance to Hell—'All hope abandon, ye who enter here.'"[129] The prominent theologian Harry Emerson Fosdick wrote,

> When the Great War broke, the churches were unprepared to take a well-considered Christian attitude. We, too, had been hypnotized by nationalism, had taken patriotism at its current values and had understood it in its ordinary meanings. We, too, had regarded as a sacred duty the loyal support of the country's army and navy in almost any task to which the government might put them. We, too, vaguely looking forward to a warless world, sometime, somewhere, nevertheless had looked on war as an easily imaginable, highly probable necessity of national action. ... For my part, I never will be caught that way again. ...Today we must make unmistakably clear our position against war, against competitive preparation for war, against reliance on war. ... We can tell the diplomats who lead us to it that we will not follow them.[130]

Reinhold Neibuhr pledged similarly: "Every soldier, fighting for his country in simplicity of heart without asking any questions, was superior to those of us who served no better purpose than to increase or perpetuate the moral obfuscations of nations. ... I am done with this business."[131]

In 1931, a leading Christian magazine, *The World Tomorrow*, published the results of a questionnaire mailed to 53,000 Protestant clergymen to poll their views on war. Of the nearly 20,000 replies, 54 percent stated that it was their "present purpose not to sanction any future war or participate as an armed combatant."[132]

Celebrating his twenty-fifth anniversary as religious leader of New York City's Free Synagogue in 1932, America's most distinguished rabbi, Stephen S. Wise, asked forgiveness from the congregation for his wartime pronouncements. He said that he viewed his actions with "everlasting regret" and vowed "without reservation or equivocation" never again to bless "any war whatsoever."[133]

In the United States as in most of the world, the dominant communications medium of the war period—and the most powerful propaganda tool— was the newspaper. In 1914, according to the listings and classifications of the most respected directory of the period, there were 19,416 newspapers and 3,561 magazines published in America, an astonishing number by any yardstick and a measure of the nation's high literacy. Included were some 2500 dailies, of which 175 were published in cities with populations of 100,000 or more.[134] These big-city newspapers were also profitable big businesses. The largest American newspaper, the *New York World*, had an annual payroll of more than $2 million and 1,300 full-time staffers. It was estimated to be worth some $10 million, with profits of about $1 million annually.[135]

In the late summer of 1914, where did the sympathies of these powerful molders of public opinion lie? *The Literary Digest*, a well-respected journal of opinion, sought the answer in a questionnaire it mailed to editors of leading newspapers and magazines. The results were tabulated in the November 14 issue. In the 367 returns, 105 editors indicated that they favored the Allies, 20 sided with Germany, and 242 said they were neutral. Among the pro–Ally respondents, 34 were from publications in the East, 47 from the South, 13 from the Midwest, and 11 from the western United States. Only one pro–German editor was from an eastern state, while ten were from the Midwest, five from the South, and four from the West. Among neutral editors, 112 were from the Midwest, 51 from the South, 43 from the East, and 36 from the West.[136]

How did the Allies achieve this five-to-one ratio in their favor so early in the war? Was the main reason that the editors had begun to believe the German "atrocity" propaganda they were printing? Or was an even more important reason an existing anti–German bias? Indeed, the generally pro-Ally stance of America's news media during World War I was deep-seated. It owed its origins to England years before the war and was due in no small part to Lord Northcliffe and his newspaper empire. For, to an astonishing degree, international news in American newspapers reflected the war-loving character of the world's most influential newspaper publisher and, at the turn of the century, his nation's militant imperialism and especially its focused Germanophobia.

From before the turn of the century until the outbreak of war in 1914, Northcliffe kept up his propaganda barrage on the dangers of a new power in middle Europe that had become England's newest economic and military rival. He commissioned one prominent British journalist after another to journey to Germany and to report through the pages of his papers—in particular, his wide-circulation tabloid, the London *Daily Mail*—a nation girding its loins to spring at the throat of a peace-loving England. In 1909, for example, Northcliffe contracted with a noted British socialist for a series of blatantly anti–German articles titled "Germany and England." The author began his series in the *Mail*'s inflammatory style: "I write these articles because I believe that Germany is deliberately preparing to destroy the British Empire; and because I know that we are not able or ready to defend ourselves against a sudden and formidable attack."[137]

There were important reasons why Northcliffe's anti–German propaganda inevitably found its way into America's newspapers. London was not only the cultural and social capital for many of America's wealthiest, most influential individuals but was a convenient location from which reporters could quickly cover all of Europe. United States newspapers and their press associations naturally headquartered there. News stories destined for the United States were thus fleshed out with background information extracted from British newspaper and magazine sources. The common language and common blood also made it convenient for American news organizations to employ British reporters as staffers or freelancers. Whether consciously or not, these English journalists infused their own patriotic attitudes into their U.S. dispatches.

The *New York Times*' London bureau chief, Ernest Marshall, was himself British. The paper's correspondent in Berlin, Frederick W. Wile (who also worked for the *Chicago Tribune* and the *Daily Mail*), was notoriously anti–German. The London correspondent for the *New York World* was Irish and had never worked in America. Edward Price Bell, of the *Chicago Daily News*, acknowledged as the dean of American newspaper correspondents in London, had gone there right after college and stayed in England the rest of his career. It was natural that other American newspapermen, immersed in the stimulating London environment, came to reflect Great Britain's interests.

American newsmen in Europe during the war were similar to their country's "pack journalists" of 50 years later. Every four years, these modern newswriters accompany the presidential candidates around the country. They fly when "their" candidate flies (in his plane, if specially anointed, or in the "zoo" plane, which is informal and apparently much more fun) and follow the motorcades in buses to cover speeches. They often eat the same rubber chicken as the candidate and share his trials, humorous moments, and dulling routine. Pack journalists quickly develop a vested interest in the success of "their" candidate. If he starts out in the primaries and wins his party's nomination, the amenities for the covering press will improve. The media will also treat the filed stories from their correspondents with greater respect. Newspapers will be more apt to run the stories and feature them more prominently; journalists are, after all, writers—and all writers want to see their material published. Irrevocably, each pack identifies with its candidate, leading to an incestuous relationship and biased reporting.

There were also publishing arrangements between major newspapers in the United States and England. In 1900, an agreement between the *New York Times* and Northcliffe's influential London *Times*, giving each paper rights to publish the other's material, had been "seriously discussed, and fairly complete plans for it were made." However, contrary to a widespread wartime view in the United States that Northcliffe owned or controlled the New York paper of the same name, there were no official ties between the two. Actually, when war came in 1914, Adolph Ochs, publisher of the *New York Times*, and Northcliffe were not on good terms. During "negotiations for an exchange of news service—and their relationship never got beyond that in the fifteen years they knew each other—there was a bitter split, just before World War I."[138]

The *New York Times* did set up a wartime exchange with the London *Chronicle* that gave it exclusive use of the superlative dispatches of Philip Gibbs from the British battlefront. Gibbs, very much a patriotic Englishman (he would be knighted for his services to the empire), was also a vivid writer, perhaps the best Allied reporter in the war. His stories, invariably filled with the wondrous exploits (if not clear-cut victories) of his always-heroic side, nevertheless managed to strike a sensible wartime balance between propaganda and exciting fact-telling; he conceded that enemy soldiers were also courageous. Gibbs wrote little that was superficial, as this example shows:

> Special Cable to The New York Times. With the British Armies in France, Nov. 5 [1918]—...The Fourth British Corps ... was in the centre of this attack, with the 37th and New Zealand Division on this side of Glussignies and Le Quesnoy. The last-named place is a mediaeval town, defended by high ramparts and inner and outer bastions, strengthened by Vauban, the famous Engineer of Military Works under Louis XIV, and it was garrisoned by over 1,000 Germans, with orders to defend it at all costs. They were brave men, and determined to obey this command.
>
> The New Zealanders, however, were equally determined. ...They stormed the outer ramparts of Le Quesnoy in old-fashioned style with scaling ladders, and made breaches in the walls, as in the old days of Henry's men-at-arms....[139]

The *New York World* had ties to London's *Morning Post* and *Daily News*. William Randolph Hearst's large-circulation *New York American* received reports from the London *Times* and *Telegraph*, and each, in turn, was linked to Hearst's International News Service (INS).

The *New York Times* and the *New York World*—the latter the editorial mouthpiece for the Wilson administration—were the two most influential newspapers in the United States during the wartime period, and both were staunchly anti–German. They were also the most important sources of news reports sold by metropolitan dailies to other papers across the country. Other large-circulation New York City newspapers included the *Tribune*, thoroughly pro–Ally; the *Sun*, less biased toward the Allies; and the *Evening Post*, even more impartial in the tone of its editorial comments.[140] The biases of these papers were reflected not only on their editorial pages, but in the selection of stories, placement within the paper, sizes of headlines, use of illustrations, even the day of the week in which the stories were run.

All of these newspapers, nevertheless, published articles, letters, and interviews from both sides. Early in the war, according to one critic, Ochs

> wanted the *Times* to publish with objectivity both the British and German sides of the news. But some of his editors were emotionally incapable of this complete objectivity in 1915, and ... the treatment of the news was subtly slanted in Britain's favor. "The *Times* prints a very great deal of pro–German stuff and yet, the cumulative typographical effect of the paper is extremely anti–German," Garet Garrett wrote in his journal on June 29, 1915. "You can't prove it on any one day. It is the continuing effect that comes from having day after day unconciously accepted the *Times* appraisal of news values...." One evening Garrett visited the newsroom and asked [*Times* editor-in-chief] Van Anda's assistant, Frederick T. Birchall, a British citizen, if he realized what editorial power lay in the control of news display. "Yes, I know," Birchall said. "Let me control the headlines and I shall not care who controls the editorials."[141]

The *Providence Journal*, as will be seen, was perhaps the nation's most flagrantly anti–German newspaper. Hearst's newspapers and his INS, by contrast, were so stridently anti–British during the wartime period as to have been considered by many as pro–German. In October 1915, the British government denied to the INS the right to use the cables or the mails to transmit dispatches from London and expelled INS correspondents. The British said their act of retaliation was in response to Hearst's publication of "damaging and untrue" news stories. The French, Japanese, and Portugese governments reacted promptly with similar restrictions, and Canada went one better, barring all Hearst papers from the country.

As important for the gathering and distribution of news were America's cooperative news organizations, or "wire services" as they came to be known because transmission was by telegraph—the Associated Press, the United Press, and the INS. The oldest was the Associated Press (AP), founded by six New York City newspapers in 1848. Until 1902, the AP obtained its international news almost exclusively from sources in London, and the organization's general manager maintained that British public opinion was American public opinion. In that year, the AP opened its own bureaus in Europe's main capitals, with full-time staffers in London, Paris, Berlin, and St. Petersburg. By 1914, the AP had grown to 895 member newspapers, with overseas offices and staffers in principal cities. The power of the wire services was spelled out in a magazine article shortly before war broke out:

> About nine hundred daily newspapers in the United States, comprising the great majority of the journals of influence and circulation, receive and print the news dispatches of the Associated Press. This means that concerning any event of importance an identical dispatch is printed about fifteen million times and may be read by thirty million persons. According to the construction and wording of that dispatch, so will be the impression these thirty million persons will receive, and the opinion they will form and pass along to others. Here is the most tremendous engine for Power that ever existed in this world.[142]

The United Press (UP) was formed in 1907 as a strictly commercial organization. Stimulated by the E. W. Scripps interests, it offered its service to any paper which chose to pay its price. It started out with 247 client newspapers, catering only to afternoon papers; when the war began, a morning service affiliate, the United News, was inaugurated. By 1914, UP had 515 clients. The INS was established in 1911 and had far fewer clients and overseas staffers than either the AP or the UP.

These American press services also tied in with their European equivalents: Great Britain's Reuters, which covered Great Britain and her dominions, China, Japan, and Egypt; France's Havas, encompassing the Latin countries of Europe and South America; and Germany's Wolff, covering the Teutonic, Slavic, and Scandinavian countries.

Contributing to the nation's spirit of anti–Germanism—indeed, one of the articles of faith that helped propel America into the war in 1917—was a belief that German agents were under nearly everyone's bed, stealing U.S. secrets, forging documents, dynamiting munitions plants, blowing up bridges, firebombing ships, fomenting strikes. This myth of widespread German spy activity was a creation of America's non-neutral press, for not only was there a newfound plethora of "adventure, villainy, melodrama" for their readers, as phrased by one chronicler, which sold newspapers, but there was also the opportunity to paint Germans as criminals.

Almost daily there were front-page stories with big headlines about factory and shipboard explosions, nearly every one of "suspicious origin." Rust-bucket tramp steamers pressed into service that caught fire and leaky barges that sank at their docks all did so "mysteriously." Fires, large and small, were attributed to "arson." The probability is that nearly every one of these occurrences was due to the inexperience and carelessness that were part and parcel of America's fast-expanding munitions business and the nation's shortage of bottoms. This explanation was purposefully overlooked by most patriotic reporters and their editors. When there were no arms-plant explosions on the front pages, there were stories and pictures about the "omnipresent" German spies and agents; even when their alleged crimes were not in violation of any law, as most were not, the perpetrators were vaguely labeled conspirators. Words like "sabotage," "espionage," "sedition," "conspiracy"—unheard of if not unpronounceable by most Americans before the war—came into the nation's lexicon.

Woodrow Wilson, too, was convinced there were German spies and saboteurs everywhere. In his speeches he invoked the German spy mania that would become the "Red Scare" in 1919 and the legitimate start of the "Cold War" between the United States and the Soviet Union. When he asked for war against Germany, Wilson had declared, "One of the things that have served to convince us that the Prussian autocracy was not and could not be our friend is that from the very outset of the present war it has filled our unsuspecting communities and even our offices of Government with spies and set criminal intrigues everywhere afoot against our national unity of council, our peace within and without, our industries and our commerce." Wilson added, naively—for nearly every nation spies on nearly every other nation, during peace and war—"It is now evident that its spies were here even before the war began."

In his Flag-Day speech two months later, defending his decision to take America into the war, the president's German spies had turned "vicious":

> It is plain enough how we were forced into the war. ... The military masters of Germany denied us the right to be neutral. They filled our unsuspecting communities with vicious spies and conspirators and sought to corrupt the opinion of our people in their own behalf. When they found that they could not do that, their agents diligently spread sedition among us and sought to draw our own citizens from their allegiance. ...They sought by violence to destroy our own industries and arrest our commerce.[143]

Earlier, the president had expressed to House his belief in a preposterous rumor making the rounds of Washington. According to the hearsay, the Germans had quietly built and disguised concrete pads in strategic locations in France and Belgium before the war, intended to serve as heavy-gun platforms once the war was underway. He told House "there was reason to suspect" the Germans had constructed similar foundations for their big cannons throughout the United States. According to House, "He almost feared to express this knowledge out loud, for, if the rumor got abroad, it would inflame our people to such an extent that he would be afraid of the consequences."[144]

A popular book on the subject of German sabotage in America during World War I was published in 1937. It meticulously listed, chronologically, from January 1, 1915, through January 11, 1917, incidents at 43 American factories and freight yards where "arson or explosions caused either partial or complete destruction" and on 47 ships on which "bombs or other incendiary devices were found while en route to Allied countries." Its author concluded: "A few of the disasters can be written down to accidents or carelessness due to the sudden increase in the manufacture of munitions, but German sabotage agents were undoubtedly responsible for the bulk of them. ... At least $150 million damage was done in the United States by sabotage agents during the World War."[145] Another investigator more than 50 years later casually recorded that the Germans had "committed nearly 200 acts of sabotage prior to the U.S. entry into the war in 1917."[146]

Such undocumented generalities about the supposed extent of German sabotage—that there was a giant undercover organization for spying and destruction set up before the war that operated at full efficiency while America was still at peace with Germany—are typical of the prejudiced views that prevailed after the war, views that were reinforced by similar fables of Nazi "fifth columnists" undermining the United States during the 1930s. They continue even today as part of the overall myth of German sedition in the United States during World War I.

While certainly not on the exaggerated scale attributed to them, German and Austro-Hungarian nationals in the United States nevertheless were involved in planning, executing, and financing sabotage and other less violent actions, some clearly lawless, others made to appear to be. Freelancers sent over from Europe and unemployed German army reservists with time on their hands performed what they considered patriotic service for the fatherland. To enable their reservists to pass through the British blockade and return to their units in Germany—and also to slip spies into Allied countries—the Germans forged passports. To provision German cruisers raiding in the Atlantic, the Hamburg-Amerika Line organized a fleet of small ships and issued to U.S. customs officials false cargo manifests and misleading information concerning ownership of the vessels and their destinations. During the trial of the resulting "Hamburg-Amerika Case," the presiding judge ruled that the defendants had not violated any law by sending out ships to supply German warships, but that attempts to "defraud" the U.S. government were illegal.

German consular officials in San Francisco made plans to ship arms to India for a Hindu insurrection, which misfired because of inadequate logistics. There was a scheme to foment strikes among Austrians and Hungarians working in munitions plants, which was exposed before it could be implemented. There were the shadowy machinations of Franz von Rintelen, a German naval officer who had come to America from Germany in April 1915 with plenty of money to try to slow the movement of munitions for the Allies. His case led to convictions for conspiring to violate the Sherman Antitrust Act. Attempts were made to smuggle rubber and nickel to Germany and there was an unsuccessful plan to destroy horses intended for the Allies with bacterial injections.

More violent were the plots hatched to blow up transportation facilities inside Canada, with whom Germany was at war, in order to stall shipments of war materials and troops to Europe. Plans were made, but never carried out, to dynamite grain elevators at Fort William and locks and railroad bridges at Sault Ste. Marie. There were two abortive attempts on the Welland Canal that linked Lake Ontario to Lake Erie; one was by Horst von der Goltz, a German citizen who came to the United States from Mexico, and the other by Paul Koenig, head of security of the Hamburg-Amerika Line. There was a plan, also never implemented, to blow up the tunnels through which the Canadian Pacific Railway passed under the Selkirk Mountains in British Columbia.

Measured by the newspaper publicity he received, the most famous of all German saboteurs was Reserve Captain Werner von Horn. He tried to dynamite the Canadian Pacific railroad bridge over the St. Croix River at Vanceboro, Maine. The bridge constituted the international boundary between eastern Maine and the Canadian province of New Brunswick, and was a link in the through-route from upper and western Canada to important ports on the east coast. Horn's explosion partially damaged one span of the bridge on the Canadian side. He was arrested the same day in the United States and later indicted on the charge of violating the laws regulating interstate transportation of explosives.

There is evidence that there was a German bomb factory of sorts in one of the interned German ships in New York harbor that turned out ingenious time bombs that were to be placed in the holds of eastbound Allied cargo ships. A similar bomb-making operation in a garage on the Hudson River waterfront manufactured bombs designed to be attached to a ship's rudder. The chief bombmaker, Lieutenant Robert Fay, was a former German officer who had come to America in April 1915. He and five accomplices were later tried and convicted.

Another noteworthy German "spy," whose activities captured newspaper headlines for many days running, was no spy at all. He was former Harvard professor Erich Muenter, alias Frank Holt, who decided on his own initiative to strike a mighty blow for his native Germany. On the morning of July 3, 1915, he forced his way into J.P. Morgan's summer home on an island in Long Island Sound brandishing two guns and announcing he intended to hold the family hostage until the financier agreed to help stop the shipment of munitions to the Allies. In a scuffle, Muenter slightly wounded Morgan, and the intruder was taken into police custody. He admitted he was the person who had exploded a bomb in the Capitol in Washington, D.C., the day before. A letter was then discovered that said he had planted bombs on two New York-to-Liverpool liners. Both liners were searched at sea and no bombs were found. Muenter, who was reported to have committed suicide while in custody, would never learn that his aborted hostage taking had backfired; his actions had served only to intensify Morgan's already robust anti–German views.

Three high-level diplomats from the Central Powers figured prominently in the spy hysteria: Dr. Constantin Theodor Dumba, the Austro-Hungarian ambassador; Captain Franz von Papen, the German military attaché; and Captain Karl Boy-Ed, the German naval attaché. Their illegal activities were first hinted at in testimony at several of the spy trials and in the *New York World*'s sensational exposure of Dr. Albert's papers, but incriminating proof awaited the disclosures resulting from yet another example of Austro-German diplomatic stupidity. Again, it was captured documents. This time, instead of being in a briefcase carelessly left on a New York City elevated train, as in the case of Albert, they were aboard a ship in Falmouth harbor, England, in the cabin of James F. J. Archibald. His cabin and belongings were supposedly secure from search, for Archibald was a U.S. citizen traveling with a valid passport. Archibald was a pro–German American newspaperman friendly with both von Bernstorff and Dumba, and was on his way back to Europe in the summer of 1915 when Dumba asked him to act as a courier to deliver documents to the Austrian Foreign Office in Vienna. Dumba was apparently pleased with his choice of communication methods, for in one of his documents he referred to "this rare, safe opportunity."

Acting on a tip from Allied agents in the United States, Royal Navy investigators went through Archibald's luggage and found what looked like incriminating papers. They whisked them away to London for translation, study, and interpretation. Found among Dumba's mostly innocuous documents was a handwritten letter dated August 20 to Baron von Burien of the Austrian Foreign Office. The key sentence was:

> I am under the impression that we could, if not entirely prevent the production of war material in Bethlehem and in the Middle West, at any rate strongly disorganize it and hold it up for months, which, according to the statement of the German Military Attaché, is of great importance, and which amply outweighs the relatively small sacrifice of money.[147]

Another letter from Dumba to his superior, while totally innocuous, contained two phrases that were critical of two of America's most important people. One was a response to Lansing's reply to von Burien, who had protested the deliveries of arms to the Allies: "The legal arguments are certainly very weak." On the front page of the September 22 issue of the *New York Times*, this phrase was twisted into unrecognizable shape as a sub-headline, "LANSING IS CALLED WEAK." The second phrase referred to "the self-willed temperament of the President." It was by no means an unusual observation, but people close to Wilson were offended, or feigned offense, by what they considered an inappropriate reference by a foreign diplomat. What apparently rankled them even more than Dumba's conspiracy were jocular comments in his letters that downplayed the significance of the recent newspaper exposé of Albert's papers—especially since the loud publicity about the earlier papers had been engineered by some of the same people reading Dumba's personal correspondence in Washington.

When confronted with the evidence, Dumba defended his proposals as entirely proper for an ambassador to transmit to his government. In fact, he pointed out that it was his duty to attempt to call out the workmen of his country from the munitions plants serving the Allies and, through an agency he and von Bernstorff had set up, the Liebau Labor Relief Bureau, to provide other employment for them. "This seems to me to be a legitimate and entirely satisfactory means of preventing the making and shipping of war materials to our enemies," was Dumba's response to reporters.[148]

On September 9, the U.S. government informed the Austro-Hungarian government that Dumba was "no longer acceptable." Dumba had "conspired to cripple legitimate industries of the people of the United States and to interrupt their legitimate trade" and was guilty of "a flagrant violation of diplomatic protocols" when he employed a U.S. citizen to deliver official documents.[149] On September 17, 1915, he was given his passports.

In 1913, Captain Franz von Papen was a young cavalry officer assigned to the German Embassy in Washington, a post then considered so unimportant that he was also attached to the German legation in Mexico City. He owed his first diplomatic appointment more to his wife's wealth and social status than to his own military accomplishments. He was tall, athletically built, and erect; his face was marked by a large nose, protruding ears, sharp eyes, and a well-trimmed mustache. According to a critic, prominent among von Papen's characteristics was his "intolerance, and arrogance, and bluntness in criticizing his associates. Coupled with all these was a capacity for cunning, intrigue, and hard work. He liked women and used them whenever he could."[150]

Von Papen's opposite number was the more experienced Captain Karl Boy-Ed, who had come to Washington in 1914 following postings as naval attaché in other countries. At the beginning of his naval career, he had been one of six young officers selected by the German Naval Command for special training for high executive positions within the government. He had been a member of Grand Admiral von Tirpitz's staff, and had headed a publicity campaign within Germany in 1909 to promote increased naval expenditures. In his mid-forties, he was considered to be one of the ablest of German naval officers. He spoke English fluently, "like all the members of his service, and, in order to 'Americanize' his appearance, shaved off the 'Prince Henry whiskers' which German naval officers traditionally affect when he took up his duties at Washington."[151]

Once the war was under way, the two military diplomats had the same orders: prevent the shipment of munitions and supplies to the Allies. Boy-Ed focused most of his energies on strictly legal, albeit hidden, business transactions. He purchased or arranged options to buy such important war materials as copper and rubber, thereby effectively denying their use to the Allies. He also played a behind-the-scenes role in the Hamburg-Amerika Lines affair.

Von Papen was the more brazen. Many years later, he acknowledged, euphemistically, that he had "engaged in two forms of enterprise which were in conflict with the letter of United States law." He was referring to his financing of von Horn's and von der Goltz's sabotage operations in Canada. He suggested that "neither activity endangered either American lives or security, although, in the strictly legal sense, it was improper to use neutral territory as the base of such operations." As for his own obviously inept management of the amateur saboteurs, von Papen admitted that his work had not been "particularly intelligent ... and must be put down to the confusion of those early days and my lack of experience in this particular field."[152]

Von Papen's undoing, and Boy-Ed's by association, was directly related to Dumba's downfall. Among the papers Archibald had been carrying was a letter from von Papen to his wife in which he had written, "I always say to these idiotic Yankees that they should shut their mouths." Von Papen, trying to explain away his reference to "idiotic Yankees," said the British had "pounced with avidity on the two words that have caused all this trouble" and that anyone reading the letter in its entirety would have understood he was referring to the publishers "of a New York newspaper[the *World*] which had been calling us conspirators and applying other objectionable epithets." Furthermore, the supposedly chivalrous von Papen said that to publish a man's letter to his wife was "deuced bad form."[153]

In a note to Wilson on November 21, 1915, pushing hard to aid the Allied cause, House asked, "Would it not be possible to let some of the obnoxious underlings of the offending Embassies go? ...[and] sever diplomatic relations with Austria because of the *Ancona* [sinking]?"[154] Seventeen days later, Secretary of State Lansing announced that he had asked for the recall of both von Papen and Boy-Ed. Lansing's reasons, given orally to von Bernstorff, were vague. They referred to "objectionable or improper activities" and the two men's association with persons "under suspicion or who had been brought before the courts."[155] When the German government asked for clarification, Lansing refused to comply, citing diplomatic precedent in not admitting the right of Germany's Foreign Office to inquire into the specific details.

Von Papen sailed on December 22. His press handout was generally courteous, thanking "all those who did not permit their friendly personal feelings to be poisoned by the hatred created by the war among the nations." He also said that the *New York World*, which certainly was not subject to the suspicion of harboring especially friendly feelings for his country, pointed out very fairly when discussing his recall that "certain newspapers had made reckless charges which could not be supported by evidence, but the United States Government never intimated that it believed these charges to be true." Von Papen's statement concluded, "After all, this war will not be won by the *Providence Journal*."[156] More than three decades later, in his memoirs, von Papen reflected,

> I am supposed to have organized a widespread net of saboteurs, to have instigated strikes in the docks and munitions factories, to have employed squads of dynamiters, and to have been the master spy at the head of a veritable army corps of secret agents. ... It should be realized that the reputation I acquired in those days was deliberately fostered by the well-organized Allied propaganda services as part of their campaign to arouse emotions in the United States to the point of active intervention in the war.[157]

Boy-Ed sailed a week later. In his farewell press handout, Boy-Ed also took a measured swipe at the hated *Providence Journal*: "This paper, with its British-born Mr. Rathom, has done its utmost to create an almost hysterical suspicion of spies throughout the country in order to prejudice public opinion against Germany." He closed his statement defending the Hamburg-Amerika incident on ground of recent precedent:

> While our enemies have been and are being supplied from this country with all the forms of death-dealing munitions of war, without which they would long since have been overcome, I have been denounced from one end of the country to the other for having been concerned at the outset of the war in chartering ships to provision our cruisers at sea with coal and food, as though it was a crime, instead of being as it is and has been considered to be by your courts, a strictly lawful act. The ships that brought coal, provisions, and supplies from Hongkong to Admiral Dewey's fleet during the Spanish-American war in 1898, were cleared for Macao and China, and not for the American warships at sea, and in their clearance papers it was stated that their cargo consisted of scrap iron.[158]

The next day, December 30, the *Providence Journal* lashed back at Boy-Ed, stating that his farewell statement was a "willful and deliberate falsehood" and that it was a "farewell insult to a Government and a press that have treated you with unexampled patience in the face of evidence which, had it not been for the protection given you by your official standing, would long ago have placed you behind prison bars."

On January 2, when von Papen's steamer dropped anchor at Falmouth, came the last of the monumental foul-ups that plagued Germany's propaganda efforts in the United States. It was the Archibald incident played all over again, for, incredibly, von Papen seemed to have learned nothing from his associate's recent gaffe. Among his personal belongings were many of his papers, which he assumed, incorrectly, were also covered by diplomatic safe conduct rules. The thorough British authorities searched his baggage and removed for further study what appeared to be useful to their war effort.

Two weeks later, the story broke in American newspapers. The most incriminating documents were, in fact, only supplements to what had already been throughly aired in the press. There were bank books and check stubs that appeared to cover payments made to von Papen's agents for their unlawful actions—to von der Goltz, to von Horn, and to the alleged bomb manufacturers. There was other material in the cache. The *New York Times* commented on January 16 that "four letters found among Captain von Papen's effects are thought the most interesting part of the correspondence turned over to the American Embassy." One, written by a former German consul in New Orleans to von Papen just after his recall, was reproduced in a two-column box on page one. It was headlined by an ominous phrase taken out of context from the letter: "May Here Also the Day of Reckoning Come." The second letter was from Albert, mostly about personal matters. The third was from von Bernhardi, dated September 1915, thanking von Papen for sending him tear sheets of his newspaper articles. The last was from a Dr. F.W. Meyer, congratulating von Papen on his work in America. The four bland letters scarcely embarrassed von Papen—but America's propaganda mills made them appear as somehow sinister.

Both Boy-Ed and von Papen were warmly greeted on reaching Germany. Boy-Ed was moved to a position of authority in the Admiralty and von Papen was made a major and transferred to the staff of General Liman von Sanders in Palestine, where soon some more of his private papers found their way into the hands of the British, and, in turn, on to the front pages of American newspapers.[159]

What was it about the *Providence Journal* that prompted two departing diplomats to target it in their farewell statements? Even von Bernstorff, in a note to Lansing in November 1915, had singled it out for disapprobation. He called it a "hypenated Anglo-American paper" that, "to borrow the phrase of the United States President, ... is obviously a greater friend of other countries than its own."[160] In fact, the *Journal*'s focus on sensational fables of Teutonic spies and their intrigues marked it as the nation's loudest, most venomous vilifier of Germans and Germany. Its editor, John Revelstoke Rathom, was a vocal and persistent Germanophobe with few peers. According to a close collaborator, the patriotic Rathom had "seen more clearly than most men the terrible dangers that beset this country." In particular, the danger was "Germany's conscienceless, subtle, relentless campaign, waged in the dark for twenty-five years, to hamstring democracy in America and ultimately to dominate the Western Hemisphere."[161]

Rathom was born in Australia of English parents and educated at Harrow in Britain. He had been a correspondent in Australia, Hong Kong, and China, and a reporter for newspapers on America's West Coast. He had worked his way east as a stringer for the *New York Herald* before joining the

Providence Journal as managing editor. He later become editor and general manager of the Rhode Island paper.

Through the pages of his daily newspaper and in frequent speeches, the arch spy-hunter Rathom boasted that he was guarding the nation's ramparts against the onslaughts of a treacherous and evil Germany. He was the man, he said, who had forced the recall of the "precious" von Papen and the "notorious" Boy-Ed. It was a *Journal* reporter, Rathom asserted, who had obtained the papers as a result of which Dumba was declared persona non grata. He claimed that it was he who had uncovered the machinations of Dr. Albert and "his $40,000,000 corruption fund" and that it was he who had "proved" that the famous German Embassy advertisement was a specific warning of the sinking of the *Lusitania* ordered from Berlin. After a fire broke out at the Canadian parliament building in Ottawa, Rathom said he had known all about the plot three weeks before and had warned the attorney general. He declared he employed 13 spies in the German Embassy in Washington and in German consulates in other cities.

In 1915 Rathom began a series of exposés of what he called the "German spy system" busy at work in the United States. These stories were contracted for by major newspapers across the country, including the *New York Times*. Each was previewed with a teaser beginning, "The Providence Journal will say this morning...." Innuendos, half-truths, embroidered facts, hyperbole, and downright lies were Rathom's stock-in-trade. Rathom sometimes took previously published information dealing with alleged German plots in the United States and added his own embellished interpretations. He was also fed stacks of British propaganda by his fellow Australian, Royal Navy Captain Guy Gaunt, the British naval attaché.

Rathom's self-appointed role as a private "big brother"—forerunner of the grotesque American Protective League once America was into the war—was an even more ominous threat to America's democratic principles. He professed that he maintained a card index of some 7,000 people in the United States, "hundreds of them American citizens, dozens of them honored leaders in professional and public life ... known to be working the Kaiser's will in every important city in the United States. These are traitors, many of them unsuspected by neighbors and friends who respect and trust them."[162] Rathom trumpeted that by shadowing the most dangerous of his thousands of "traitors," he was able to track their subversive activities and, in turn, pass on important "inside information" to authorities in Washington.

Once America was into the war, Rathom ratcheted up his campaign against the disloyal, admonishing readers of the *Journal* daily, in jumbo-size, boldface type at the head of its editorial columns, on precisely how to be a patriot:

> Every German or Austrian in the United States, unless known by years of association to be absolutely loyal, should be treated as a potential spy. Keep

your eyes and ears open. Whenever any suspicious act or disloyal word comes to your notice communicate at once with the Bureau of Investigation of the Department of Justice.

We are at war with the most merciless and inhuman nation in the world. Hundreds of thousands of its people in this country want to see America humiliated and beaten to her knees, and they are doing, and will do, everything in their power to bring this about.

Take nothing for granted. Energy and alertness in this direction may save the life of your son, or husband, or your brother.

By January 1918, Rathom was running out of viable spies and cast about for new targets. Like Senator Joseph McCarthy, some 35 years later, he turned his scrutiny on "traitors" within the administration in Washington. Unlike McCarthy, however, who would be destroyed as a result, Rathom would be only temporarily discredited; the loyal New England readers of his *Journal* looked upon its editor as a martyr to their cause of militant patriotism.

Rathom began his assault by telling a New York City audience that "German pacifists" were in posts of authority within the War Department. Not content to let his case rest there, he frontally attacked Secretary of War Newton D. Baker.

> Great Britain and France and other nations in this war have found it necessary to change their Cabinets ... and I do not see how we can hope to win this war with a pacifist, a professed pacifist, an out-and-out pacifist at the head of the War Department. ...He has appointed to important posts in the department under him a number of rabid Socialists, a majority of whom are rabid pacifists and some of whom are German pacifists....

Warming to his task, Rathom went further, indirectly heaping scorn on the attorney general, the Department of Justice, and even the Bureau of Investigation:

> A great many German spies who have been under arrest have been freed, nobody knows why. Some of them, it seems, have sick wives. ...We shall never make progress against German spies in this country until the present system, which is dead wrong, is changed. The practice is now, when evidence is found to indicate that a certain man is a German spy, to look into the law books and find out if there is not some clause in some law which makes it possible not to arrest him.[163]

Five weeks later, on February 27, the New York *World* gave its readers an exclusive story about Rathom on its front page. It focused on the "suppression" of a series of articles by him, called "Germany's Plots Exposed," that had been scheduled to appear in *The World's Work*. The first of the series had been run in the February issue, and in it its author loudly claimed that "German agents had been busily undermining America for nearly a generation." During this period, Rathom wrote,

> German influence on American school boards had been insidiously shaping public sentiment here through our school books and histories. Exchange

professors, liberally sprinkled with Imperial decorations, had maintained and increased a constant propaganda of reverence for Germany and German institutions through many of the educational centres of the United States. And the great German commercial houses which had secured a foothold in this country, and which were virtually outposts of the German Foreign Office, had gained strong positions in many vitally important elements in our commercial life.

From this firm base, according to Rathom, von Bernstorff and his associates "began their work of intensive cultivation of Prussianized doctrines ... to mold the United States to their will, to stultify our national ideals, and so drug our national conscience that, regardless of what might happen in Europe, we would stand by, a disinterested spectator, except for the growth of a keen desire to see Germany triumphant."

Rathom, the *World*'s story related, had been hailed before a federal grand jury in New York and invited by the Department of Justice "to submit facts concerning some of his statements" in the article. Rathom was said "to have disclaimed any intent to evade the provisions of the Espionage Law, which makes it a felony to make or publish false statements relating to the war." The *World* added candidly that "his reflections upon the Department of Justice and charges he boldly made against its inefficiency, made it necessary that something should be done to put a stop to his misrepresentations. From the very best information obtainable in Washington ... it is said to be the opinion of the Department of Justice that Rathom will no longer be a source of trouble." Random was not prosecuted because, the *World* explained, "While it has been realized in Washington ever since Rathom began his disclosures that a large majority of them had no basis in fact, nevertheless many felt it was good propaganda work, and that Rathom was intensely pro–Ally and would do everything in his power to embarrass the Kaiser's Government. ... The American Secret Service never regarded his efforts as worthy of more than a passing notice."

Rathom defended the integrity of his and his newspaper's patriotic work by declaring in a statement the following day that "not one of the hundreds of stories of German propaganda printed by the *Providence Journal* ... has ever been shown to be misleading or not founded on fact." The discontinuance of his articles in *The World's Work*, he pointed out obliquely, was based on "motives of patriotism and a desire to perform the largest possible service during the present War."

Rathom turned back to his reactionary newspaper and stepped up its patriotic outpouring. On March 17, 1918, in a front-page editorial titled "The Poison Gas of Propaganda," the *Journal* flailed out against "enemies" of every description, fostering fear and hatred, as its acid-penned writers did so expertly. It also transparently called for vigilante justice:

> Hidden in the mutterings of anarchy; in "mysterious" factory fires; in explosions, in the destruction of foodstuffs; in seditious speech; in sneers at

the efforts of those who are honestly trying to help; in the fomenting of labor strikes everywhere; in the financing of the propaganda of the I.W.W.; in the incomprehensible changing of plans for war construction work; in the whole crawling mass of so-called pacifism; in the attempt to divide the nation over the subject of universal military training; among the foul nests of Prussianized professors in our universities; in the distortion of history through the school books which shape the minds of our children; in the columns of every brazen Zeitung and Abendpost in the country;—concealed in all the pathways of America's life this one last hope and weapon of the enemy festers and thrives.

...For we at home stand face to face with a danger that may shed the life blood not of the body but of the soul, that may rend not the physical flesh but the spiritual temple which has been rendered, to the glory of God and the hope of the world, on foundation stones that the sons of freedom of every race and creed have laid with sublime faith through the labor of a thousand years.

Watch and pray. But let us watch unceasingly, and strike unerringly, whether the object of our just vengeance faces us in the trenches abroad or seeks to poison our morale at home.

A remarkable article, "Spies, Plotters, and Hysteria," appeared in the magazine section of the *New York Times* on February 17, 1918, at the very height of the war. Its author boldly suggested that many news stories that attributed fires, explosions, and labor disturbances to enemy agents were either unfounded rumors or exaggerations.

To the reporter's question, "Since the beginning of the European war, has there been any destruction of railway tracks, bridges, tunnels, switches, or signal systems that looked like the work of German plotters?" R.V. Wright, managing editor of *The Railway Age*, the leading magazine serving America's railroads, replied: "Of course, something may have happened in some part of the country, and I have no knowledge of it. But it is unlikely. ...With the exception of Horn's attempt, we know of nothing." As for canals, dams, reservoirs, and similar waterworks, also supposedly tempting targets for the dynamiter, "there has been no suspicious interference with any of these systems of water works in any part of the country since the beginning of the European war."

Concerning the large increase in strikes, especially since America's entry into the war: "Is there any evidence that German propaganda has or is playing any part in this widespread industrial trouble?" Fred W. Keough, editor of *American Industries*, official publication of the National Association of Manufacturers: "There were some rumors from Detroit that enemy influences were at work ... but they never got beyond the rumor stage. The evidence, as I see it, points to only one conclusion: it is a demand for more wages, based on present opportunity."

Question: "Since the outbreak of the European war, have there been any ships lost at sea for which the Germans might be held responsible other than by the use of the submarine?" Captain Thomas J. Tunney, commander of the Neutrality and Bomb Squad of New York City: "No complaint has been received at Police Headquarters of any ship leaving New York Harbor that has been destroyed by fire or explosive bomb. Before we went into the war, complaints were made to this office that fires broke out on certain vessels while they were at sea, and that bombs were found in the cargo of others on their arrival on the other side of the ocean. The total number of these ships was about thirty-five."

What about destruction by fires? An official connected with the National Board of Fire Underwriters said this to the *Times* reporter:

> There are now abnormal conditions in the manufacture, transportation, and storage of goods, and these in themselves cause an increased fire hazard. ...Many factories have suddenly been converted from the purposes for which they were constructed and hastily adapted to the manufacture of war supplies. ...Hasty construction is apt to be burnable. ...Many factories are running on semi-skilled labor. They are obliged to employ anyone they can get. ...Much of the manufacturing is concerning itself with explosives and other highly inflammable materials. ...The present fire hazard is further increased by the large quantities of goods in storage. ...There is another factor it is impossible to estimate. ...The army draft has drawn heavily on the Fire Departments, and it takes a couple of years to make an efficient fireman.

What about cases in which fires were positively established as having been of incendiary origin and where evidence pointed to the German arsonists? The head of the Committee on Arson of the National Board of Fire Underwriters stated,

> Now, as in all other times, there are many fires of unknown or "mysterious" origin. In ordinary times the public accepts the statement "cause unknown"; but in these times, if it happens to be war material that is destroyed, the public immediately jumps to the conclusion "enemy alien." Mind you, I do not say that the enemy alien is not responsible for some of these fires. All that I say is that we have no evidence to show that he is.

Asked whether, considering the great increase in manufacture, the rate of explosions in ammunitions plants was any greater that it had been before America entered the war, and had been at that time any greater than it was in ordinary times of peace, an unnamed explosives manufacturer said, "Taking it pound for pound, I do not believe that there are any more explosions now than there were when this country was neutral or during ordinary peace times."

The insistent proddings of House, Lansing, and Page; the greedy actions of the bankers and munitions makers and their conspiratorial ties with chauvinisitic organizations; the preparedness bellows of prestigious national leaders; the books with skewed messages; the frightening sermons from preachers intent on guiding their flocks into a holy war; and the bold headlines and exaggerated yarns of German plots in the press—all contributed to an over-whelming demand that President Wilson should lead America into the conflict.

Indeed, Woodrow Wilson adhered, as too few of his successors would, to Article I, Section 8, Paragraph 11 of the U.S. Constitution, which confers on the Congress, not on the president, the power to declare war. On April 2, 1917, when he asked the Congress to vote for war against Germany, his first words reflected this executive obeisance. He said there were "serious, very serious, choices of policy to be made, and made immediately, which it [is] nei-ther right nor constitutionally permissible that I should assume the respon-sibility of making." As for American neutrality, Wilson became a propagan-dist for a war he deemed to be both just and inevitable. He declared neurality "no longer feasible or desirable where peace of the world is involved and the freedom of its peoples." Only by the use of force, he concluded, could the United States survive and be able to work for a peaceable world order.

Supporters of the memory of Woodrow Wilson as a peacemaker claim that he was forced, as he said in his war message, to take up the sword by "the wanton and wholesale destruction of the lives of non-combatants, men, women and children engaged in pursuits, which have always, even in the darkest periods of modern history, been deemed innocent and legitimate." They cite a story—one accepted by most historians[164]—that in the very early morning hours of April 2 Wilson had a remarkable meeting with Frank I. Cobb of the *New York World*. According to Cobb's amiable biographer, two of his longtime associates on the paper, Maxwell Anderson and Laurence Stallings, claimed that "President Wilson had a way of summoning Cobb to Washington" and that "Cobb rarely spoke of these visits to the White House." Following Cobb's death, and then Wilson's, these friends, supposedly unbur-dened, alleged that Cobb had said to them, about the "most momentous" of all his clandestine visits,

> The night before he asked Congress for a declaration of war against Ger-many he sent for me. I was late getting the message somehow and didn't reach the White House till 1 o'clock in the morning. "The old man" was wait-ing for me, sitting in his study. ...I'd never seen him so worn down. He looked as if he hadn't slept, and he hadn't. He said he was probably going before Congress the next day to ask a declaration of war, and he'd never been so uncertain about anything in his life as about that decision. For nights, he said, he'd been lying awake going over the whole situation; over the provo-cation by Germany, over the probable feeling in the United States, over the consequences of the settlement and to the world at large if we entered the melee.
>
> ...He said he couldn't see any alternative, that he had tried every way he knew to avoid war. ...He said war would overturn the world we had known; that so long as we remained out there was a preponderance of neutrality, but that if we joined the Allies the world would go off the peace basis and onto a war basis.

...It would mean that a majority of people in his hemisphere would go war-mad, quit thinking and devote their energies to destruction. The President said a declaration of war would mean that Germany would be beaten and so badly that there would be a dictated peace, a victorious peace.

...“Once lead this people into war,” he said, “and they’ll forget there ever was such a thing as tolerance. To fight you must be brutal and ruthless, and the spirit of ruthless brutality will enter into the very fibre of our national life, infecting Congress, the courts, the policeman on the beat, the man in the street.”

...He thought that the Constitution would not survive it; that free speech and the right of assembly would go. He said a nation couldn’t put its strength into a war and keep its head level; it had never been done.

“If there is any alternative, for God’s sake, let’s take it,” he exclaimed. Well, I couldn’t see any, and I told him so.[165]

Chapter 5

AMERICA AT WAR

We are glad, now that we see the facts with no veil of false pretense about them, to fight thus for the ultimate peace of the world and for the liberation of its peoples, the German peoples included; for the rights of nations great and small and the privilege of men everywhere to choose their way of life and obedience. The world must be made safe for democracy.

...For the right of those who submit to authority to have a voice in their own governments, for the rights and liberties of small nations, for a universal dominion of right by such a concert of free peoples as shall bring peace and safety to all nations and make the world itself at last free. To such a task we dedicate our lives and our fortunes, everything that we are and everything that we have, with the pride of those who know that the day shall come when America is privileged to spend her blood and her might for the principles which gave her birth and happiness and the peace which she has treasured. God helping her, she can do no other.

Woodrow Wilson addressing the Congress,
April 2, 1917, asking for a declaration of war against Germany.

At 1:18 P.M. on April 6, 1917, in the chief usher's room in the lobby of the White House, Woodrow Wilson unceremoniously signed his name to a declaration of war against Germany, affirmed at 3:12 A.M. that day by the House of Representatives. Only his wife and his cousin, who were lunching with him when the war resolution arrived, his executive clerk, the chief usher, and his principal Secret Service agent were present as witnesses to this critical moment in American history.[1] Wilson was, above all, a private man.

Four days earlier he had asked a joint session of the Congress, which he had called back to Washington from recess, for the war declaration. It was a rainy night; while the president spoke, U.S. cavalry patrolled Pennsylvania Avenue from the White House to the Capitol in response to rumors of bombings. Instead of the national consensus Wilson sought, there was still ambivalence. While most Americans had finally been conditioned to support the Allied cause, many fewer wanted their country to go to war. Once the nation was at war, however, nearly every recalcitrant patriotically swung into line or was forcefully pressed into line—as was the case during every subsequent American war in the twentieth century.

Wilson—successively lawyer, college professor, American-history scholar, Ivy League college president, governor of New Jersey in 1910, and president of the United States in 1912—had delivered a memorable speech that kindled spontaneous cheering and applause from the packed House chamber. As a speaker, Wilson had neither the fire of Theodore Roosevelt nor the oratorical power of his former secretary of state, William Jennings Bryan. But Wilson had been a winning debater as a college student and later a popular lecturer. He had published history books that got favorable reviews, and he handled the language with skill. He needed no speech writers, nor did he have any.[2] The ringing, emotional phrases that punctuated his speech were Wilson's own. Referring to the noble journey on which he said America was then embarking, Wilson used a simple phrase: "to make the world safe for democracy." It proved to be a memorable and enduring slogan, precisely correct for the massive American-made communications onslaught that was about to be unleashed. In his fifth year in office, Wilson had become an accomplished propagandist.

The Congress was next to act. By tradition, the Senate was first to vote on the war resolution. Senator Henry Cabot Lodge, ranking Republican on the Foreign Relations Committee, had been for more than two years a powerful voice for preparedness. Undoubtedly gratified that the nation was following his lead, he reflected the views of nearly every one of his Senate colleagues in his speech of support:

> There are, in my opinion, some things worse for a nation than war. National degeneracy is worse; national cowardice is worse. ... Our future peace, our independence as a proud and high-spirited nation, our very security are at stake. ... We are fighting against a nation which in the fashion of centuries ago drags the inhabitants of conquested lands into slavery; which carries off women and girls for even worse purposes; which in its mad desire to conquer mankind and trample them under foot has stopped at no wrong.[3]

Only four Senators spoke up in opposition. James Kimble Vardamann; William J. Stone, the respected chairman of the Foreign Relations Committee and long opposed to American involvement in the war; Robert M. La Follette, the most steadfast pacifist in the Congress, who spoke for over four hours; and George W. Norris who pointed his finger at bankers, munitions makers, the press, and their propaganda as the reason for America's entry into the war:

> We have loaned many hundreds of millions of dollars to the allies in this controversy. While such action was legal and countenanced by international law, there is no doubt in my mind but that the enormous amount of money loaned to the allies in this country has been instrumental in bringing about a public sentiment in favor of our country taking a course that would make

every bond worth a hundred cents on the dollar and making the payment of every debt certain and sure. Through this instrumentality and also through the instrumentality of others who have not only made millions out of the war in the manufacture of munitions, etc., and who would expect to make millions more if our country can be drawn into the catastrophe, a large number of the great newspapers and news agencies of the country have been controlled and enlisted in the greatest propaganda that the world has ever known, to manufacture sentiment in favor of war.[4]

The final tally in the Senate was 82 to 6.

In the House, exactly 100 speeches were delivered. The *New York Times* of April 6 suggested that "debate" was not the word to apply to the prolonged discussion. It was, rather, "a speechmaking festival, member after member having his say, with few making the effort to answer any of the arguments that had been advanced for or against war with the German Government." Claude Kitchin, the powerful Democratic majority leader, surprised the assembly by stating that he would vote his convictions regardless of the consequences:

> By the passage of this resolution we enter the war, and the universe will become one vast drama of horrors and blood, one boundless stage upon which will play all the evil spirits of earth and hell. All the demons of inhumanity will be let loose for a rampage throughout the world. Whatever be the future, whatever be the rewards or penalties of this nation's step, I shall always believe that we could and ought to have kept out of this war. ... No invasion is threatened. No foot of our territory is in danger. No vital right is contested.[5]

The undoubted highlight of the House's deliberations was the dramatic vote by Miss Jeanette Rankin, the first woman in the nation's history to play a part in a declaration of war by the Congress. On the second roll call, obviously distressed, the first-term Congresswoman rose to her feet, saying hesitatingly, "I want to stand by my country—but I cannot vote for war."[6] The final House vote was 373 to 50 in favor of war. Twenty-four years later, on December 8, 1941, Rankin would cast the House's only vote against war with Japan.

Some observers at the time suggested that the votes in the Congress might not have been so lopsided had secret ballots been used, for powerful pro-war forces were closely watching the deliberations.

Following the vote for war against Germany, pacifists and the organizations that had worked to keep America out of the war had little to say. It was reported that the executive committee of the Emergency Peace Federation, for example, had decided that all its official statements henceforth would be reviewed by legal counsel. The purpose of the new policy, one federation official was quoted as saying, was "to be able to continue our work and keep out of jail."[7] The war juggernaut of conformity was trundling forward. On April 7, the avowed pacifist Andrew Carnegie, who had so passionately portrayed Germany's emperor as a princely peacemaker a few short years before, found a new champion. In a letter to Wilson, he wrote, "You have triumphed at last. God bless you. You will give the world peace and rank the greatest hero of all."[8]

On April 13, three members of the cabinet—Secretary of State Robert Lansing, Secretary of War Newton D. Baker, and Secretary of the Navy Josephus Daniels—addressed a letter to the president, on Lansing's stationery, calling for him to create, "without waiting for further legislation," what they called a Committee on Public Information, adding, "because of the importance of the task ... we trust that you will see fit to do so." It was the opinion of the signers that "the two functions—censorship and publicity—be joined in honesty and profit." They proposed that the chairman should be a civilian, "preferably some writer of proved courage, ability, and vision, able to gain the understanding of the press and at the same time rally the authors of the country to a work of service."[9]

Wilson responded to the letter the next day by meeting with George Creel to offer him the chairmanship, which Creel enthusiastically accepted. The president then signed Executive Order 2594, which established the Committee on Public Information (CPI) precisely as recommended.[10] Wilson predated his order April 13, for the supposedly modern-thinking president was a deeply superstitious man, and considered 13 (the number of letters in his name) his lucky number.

Several historians credit Daniels, former editor and publisher of the *Raleigh News and Observer*, as the likely writer of the letter.[11] But there is evidence that Creel was behind it and was sufficiently motivated to write a preliminary draft for Daniels, with a job specification tailored to his own background and personality. In correspondence with Wilson and in several magazine articles, Creel had earlier emphasized that to mold the nation's public opinion most effectively, "publicity" rather than "censorship" should be employed, and that the need was for "expression" and not "repression."

More important, Creel had been anything but bashful in expressing directly to the Navy secretary his interest in heading up such an agency. Three weeks before America entered the war, Creel had ended a letter to Daniels, "By the way, I am in the field for a job. If a censor is to be appointed, I want to be it."[12] He followed up with a detailed letter a week later that began, "This business of a censor is as imperative as it is important. Something ought to be done and done at once." What he called a "Bureau of Publicity" should "issue the big, ringing statements that will arouse the patriotism of the nation." He pushed Daniels hard at the same time he promoted his own candidacy. He wrote, "I think that you should take this up with the President at once. Show him this letter. I am willing to take the post and I know that I could fill it better than anybody else. I know the newspaper game, I can write, I have executive ability, and I think I have the vision. ... I don't want to leave home and family if I can help it, and God knows I can't afford it, but this looks like the chance for service that I can give, and if you want me, I'll come."[13]

George Creel was 41 when he was named CPI chairman. While certainly "not recognized as a leading journalist by the great body of newspapermen in the country," according to Melville E. Stone, general manager of the Associated Press,[14] Creel nevertheless had excellent credentials as a journalist and public-relations man. He had owned and edited a small-circulation weekly newspaper in the Midwest, the *Kansas City Independent*, from 1899 to 1909, whose editorial policy was "crusading for civic honesty, for the clean-up of government, for justice ... for the recall, the initiative and the referendum, for workmen's compensation and child labor laws, for woman suffrage."[15] He subsequently was an editorial writer for the *Denver Post* and the *Rocky Mountain News*, and wrote many bylined articles for the leading magazines of the period—*Collier's*, *Cosmopolitan*, *Harper's Weekly*, *McClure's*, and others. These articles typically were vigorous attacks on what he considered to be corruption, both political and social.

Many years later, Ray Stannard Baker, in researching for his biography of Wilson, met with Creel in New York City, and wrote discerningly, "Creel gave me, as he had many times in the past, an impression of vivid, even impatient life. He has the big chin of the fighter and the glowing eye of the enthusiast. He is warm-hearted and loyal, but impulsive and likely to be injudicious in his talk, going to extravagance and extremes."[16]

Creel, a self-taught writer with little formal education, had published three books on diverse subjects by 1917. He was one of the earlier supporters of Woodrow Wilson, helping form the first Woodrow Wilson Club in Colorado in 1912 when he wrote for the *Rocky Mountain News*. In 1916, he was one of the leaders of the Non-Partisan League, which worked for Wilson's election. His *Wilson and the Issues*, published just before the 1916 elections, when Creel was publicity director of the Democratic National Committee, was shallow, like all his books, but was nevertheless a useful image builder for the incumbent president.

His writing overall had earned Creel at least peripheral membership in the then-elite group of "muckraking" writers of the Progressive era in American history. Historian David M. Kennedy too enthusiastically credits him as being prominent among such "passionate muckrakers as Ida Tarbell, Ernest Poole, Will Irwin, and Ray Stannard Baker" with whom Creel surrounded himself."[17] (Poole, Irwin, and Baker, incidentally, became CPI staffers later under Creel.) Creel had also served as public-relations counsel to the Federal Commission on Industrial Relations that investigated the Colorado Coal Strike of 1913–14. As a former police commissioner of Denver, Creel could add administrative experience to his eclectic dossier.

According to Daniels, "The President had an affection for Creel, who had won his heart, while his brilliancy compelled his admiration. Wilson

George Creel was chairman of the Committee on Publication Information and America's chief propagandist during World War I. Indefatigable, brash, unprincipled, and hypocritical, he was precisely the right man for the job. *National Archives.*

loved good writing. He was himself a master of style, and Creel's ability to write with elegance and vigor intrigued him. Their common devotion to real liberalism cemented the regard."[18]

While Creel later unabashedly would declare that the Committee on Public Information was all his idea, others within the administration and without, particularly Edward Mandell House and Walter Lippmann, had also begun to talk about a government propaganda organization. Lippmann, who was then a principal writer for the newly founded *New Republic*, and his editor, George Croly, had made a practice of meeting once a week with House, "to get information in order to write intelligently," according to an entry in House's diary.[19] The young Lippmann already had impressive credentials as a journalist and political analyst.

On April 9, Lippmann wrote to House, offering his services "for government publicity work, especially toward any organization designed to wake up the country to its international responsibilities."[20] Two days later, Lippmann met with House alone. House's diary entry of April 11 includes the following: "I discussed with Walter Lippmann the subject of a publicity bureau. I advised that he get in touch with Professor Canby of Yale and work out a plan with him and I would help them put it through."[21] There is no record of Lippmann taking House's advice. In fact, correspondence shows clearly that Lippmann had other plans—and other individuals more influential than an English professor to whom he would urgently press his case. There is strong evidence that Lippmann himself wanted to head America's propaganda agency.

Following his meeting with House, Lippmann wrote to Secretary of the Interior Franklin K. Lane, "I was talking this morning with Col. House and the need for a government press bureau. He asked me to do what I could to draw up a plan for such a bureau and to consult with you. The nucleus of a publicity organization already exists in a syndicate which was about to be formed in Washington and the number of men who are ready to volunteer for work is very large."[22] A letter dated April 11 from House to Lippmann as a follow-up to their meeting indicates that House had had further discussions that day with others; he wrote that he would be "very glad to place your name beside other patriotic men who have offered their services to the government."[23]

On April 12, Lippmann wrote to House outlining his views of a press bureau, to "give an outline of the progress of the work which you asked me to do yesterday."[24] The letter was poorly typed, with strikeovers and corrections; House's initials had even been transposed. It was also not persuasively written—a hallmark of Lippmann's style. The impression is unmistakable: Lippmann was apparently working feverishly, perhaps already learning that Creel was the front-runner because of his close ties to both Wilson and Daniels. A man of Brobdingnagian ego, Lippmann almost certainly saw himself as the optimal choice to be the nation's chief propagandist, despite his suggestion to House in the letter that Vance McCormick was "the ideal man for the chief of this bureau."

A further incentive may well have been to deny the powerful post to someone Lippmann considered "reckless and incompetent." Two years before,

Lippmann had responded vigorously to an article by Creel in *Pearson's Magazine* about the Rockefeller Foundation and the violent Colorado coal strike. Creel had suggested that the nation's millionaires had contributed to philanthropic organizations principally "to chloroform public opinion." In his no-holds-barred rejoinder in the February 20, 1915, issue of the *New Republic*, Lippmann, in an unsigned editorial, had attacked Creel with seeming relish, calling the article "one of the worst cases of brutal stupidity that muckraking has produced. ... There is no excuse for Mr. Creel but to state the plain fact that he is a reckless and incompetent person who has at last revealed the quality of his mind. He has shown himself incapable of judging evidence, and determined to make a noise no matter what canons of truthfulness he violates."[25] Lippmann was closer to revealing the "real" Creel than he perhaps knew. For Creel was only superficially a liberal. Most of all, he was a narrow-thinking opportunist, always willing to compromise his diminishing bag of marketable ideals for expediency's sake, as a careful study of his political record over the years reveals.[26]

Lippmann's letter to House on April 12 was prescient, if not particularly original, since he had the successful British propaganda model to emulate. He suggested that the propaganda organization should "consist of a very small council, one member of which would be the executive head of the organization. Under him would be the state, military, and naval censors; a staff of reporters; a staff of men from the trade journals who can popularize technical news; and a group of copy readers and a corps of special writers who would volunteer their services."[27]

Lippmann's later actions appear to support the view that he never forgot having lost out to Creel. When he was in Europe in 1918 as a captain in U.S. Army Intelligence, he sent sniping letters to House about the supposed ineffectiveness of the CPI.[28] Later, when he returned to the *New Republic*, he wrote a bitter postwar denunciation of the committee's European operations.

According to Josephus Daniels, "No other name was suggested as the executive head of that committee except that of Mr. Creel."[29] If this was so, Daniels himself must have kept the slate clean, for he owed Creel a significant political debt. The journalist had helped restore the tarnished image of the Secretary of the Navy , who had made himself unpopular with U.S. business interests and with the navy's conservative officer corps.[30] Creel had written an impressive feature article about Daniels in the March 26, 1916, issue of the *New York World*, then an overly enthusiastic chapter, "The Case of Josephus Daniels," in his book *Wilson and the Issues*. Employing the flamboyant, hyperbolic style that was his trademark, Creel called Daniels "at once the most maligned and most misunderstood man in the United States today. To wade through the lies that have been told about him, to discover the truths that have been hidden or distorted, is to come to a new loathing of the greed that poisons when thwarted and to an added contempt for the public that takes no larger interest in a public servant than to swallow every slander circulated about him.[31]

The president's Republican opponents in Congress grudgingly accepted Creel's appointment as political cronyism. They viewed him principally as the president's personal public-relations counsel on the government's payroll. The nation's newspapers, on the other hand, were immediately antagonistic. Creel's bureau was seen chiefly as a press censor, and Creel himself as not quite a bona fide member of the establishment. A biting, sarcastic *New York Times* editorial of April 16, mirroring the fear of censorship, set the tone:

> We are unable to discover in his turbulent career ... any evidence of the ability, the experience, or the judicial temperament required to "gain the understanding and cooperation of the press," as the three Cabinet officers put it. That he is qualified for any position of authority over the press is made further doubtful by his publicly expressed hostility toward certain newspapers.
>
> As to "rallying the authors of the country," ...those estimable and gifted ladies and gentlemen can doubtless be made useful in various ways, but essential to the information of the public during the war will not be pleasing fictions prepared by imaginative writers without facts, even painful facts, accurately described by conscientious and competent reporters.

In 1919, a retrospective correctly summarized the general attitudes of the press toward the CPI's chairman:

> From the very moment of his appointment Creel became the object of severe attack. This was nothing new to George Creel. In all his public career, neutrality toward him has been the one impossible attitude. To some he was a fearless crusader, untamed, untamable. To others he was the obnoxious muckraker, with a record of spectacular conflicts in print and in public office. Creel is a man who always attracts bitter enmities and wins ardent support. But in the gigantic new task, as far as the public could discern, his enemies far exceeded his friends. ... But the war went on—and so did George Creel.[32]

Wilson, nevertheless, had sound reasons for his decision, and never backed down in his support of the frequently contentious propaganda czar. Their political views were in consonance, the two having worked together successfully during the presidential campaigns of 1912 and 1916. Creel had showed his loyalty to both man and party—and Wilson highly valued loyalty. The reclusive Wilson also saw in Creel the easygoing and cheerful associate who would stand by his side in the trying months ahead. Creel could tell jokes that made the dour president laugh and he was acknowledged as one of the best storytellers in Washington. He claimed that years before, as a young man in New York City without a regular job, he had supported himself "by selling jokes at the standard of a dollar apiece."[33]

George Creel was able to sustain his close relations with Woodrow Wilson up to Wilson's last days. As one close observer put it, "Few, if any, public men thrown into intimate association with Wilson made the whole political distance with him [George] Harvey, [Henry] Watterson, [James] Smith, [James] Nugent, [William] McCombs, [Lindley] Garrison, Bryan, House, Lansing, all fell by the wayside."[34]

Ostensibly operating as a committee of four, as outlined in the executive order, the CPI was run dictatorially by Creel himself, almost from the day he took office. Lansing's comments in his memoir not only verified Creel's one-man rule but also accurately corroborated the close working relationship between Creel and Wilson. He wrote that Creel's autocratic governance of the agency was "not distasteful" to Wilson, for he had great confidence in Creel's ability. As for Creel himself, the arch-conservative Lansing saw the head of the CPI as politically too far to the left to please him. Lansing wrote,

> Creel's socialistic tendencies ... were well known and ... were evidenced by some of the persons whom he employed. ... Though this radicalism caused distrust and apprehension among many officials of the Administration, I do not believe it disturbed Mr. Wilson, who viewed with toleration, if not with a degree of approval, certain socialistic ideas which he termed "progressive," although they were utterly hostile to the fundamental principles of his party. ... Creel was hostile to me personally ... and sought in various ways to discredit me as Secretary of State.[35]

While one-man rule worked satisfactorily in the domestic sphere, Creel's management prerogatives in the foreign sector ran counter to those of the State Department under Lansing. The result was a well-known feud between the two men, until Lansing became opposed to the very concept of the CPI. If Lansing bore a grudge for the CPI's director, the feeling was mutual. The depth of Creel's dislike for Lansing is reflected in a note, dated June 29, 1917, attached to a memorandum titled "Excerpt from the President's letter to Mr. Lansing: "Mr. Lansing, a dull, small man, bitterly resented my chairmanship of the Committee, and made himself so unpleasant at the first meeting that I never called another. As a consequence, he refused to work with the Committee, and did everything that he could, in his mean, cheap way to hinder and embarrass."[36] Daniels put the conflict between the two men in a different light: "He [Lansing] approved the British policy of strict censorship, which amounted to suppression" and wanted to "shut off all the news."[37] In fact, neither Daniels nor Secretary of War Baker, both of whom were on good terms with Creel, played any advisory role on the Committee either.[38] Nevertheless, it was in the national interest that the CPI be understood by the public to be a democratic committee of four rather than an autocracy of one. And that is exactly the message that was communicated. For example, the lead story on the front page of the July 6, 1917, issue of the *New York Times*, dealing with press censorship by the War Department, was headed "COMMITTEE HELD MEETING." It began, "Mr. Creel presided this afternoon over a meeting of the Committee on Public Information, at which Secretary Lansing, Secretary Baker, and Secretary Daniels were present."

Creel answered to Woodrow Wilson and no one else, and their extensive correspondence, starting in April 1917 and concluding nine months before Wilson died in February 1924, establishes the close personal relationship that developed between the two. Wilson's collected papers include more than 100 letters to Creel, all short, some typed personally by Wilson on his famous portable.[39] Several were handwritten, but most were dictated to his stenographer. Typically, the letters acknowledged receipt of information from Creel, but some were cover notes with modest suggestions. Wilson's correspondence also shows that he had an easygoing and respectful relationship with his public-relations counsel.

It was just a few minutes' walk to the White House from Creel's headquarters at 10 Jackson Place, and he met regularly with Wilson during the wartime period.[40] Sensitive to Wilson's busy schedule, he generally asked in his memos requesting an appointment for "only 5 minutes of your time ... to review an important matter." Most of the one-on-one meetings, however, lasted longer, generally a half hour.[41]

If the mark of an effective public-relations practitioner is to perform on behalf of clients while remaining in the background, then Creel fell far short. He was anything but inconspicuous, and purposefully so. The CPI's stationery had his name and title emblazoned at the top—above the titles of the three cabinet officers, who were unnamed. It was as if Creel wanted his correspondents to understand that, while he was a permanent fixture, his associates were subject to removal. Creel's name and title appeared on nearly every printed piece that originated from within the CPI. Correspondence, newspaper stories, and magazine articles of the wartime period routinely referred to the "Creel Committee"; books published a generation later did the same. Indeed, George Creel succeeded to a remarkable degree in making U.S. propaganda during World War I a reflection of his own vigorous personality and strong will—and of his narrow interpretation of patriotism.

While Creel thoroughly understood all the methodologies of state-of-the-art publicity, his organization, of necessity, was hastily assembled and its structure was continually being improvised, reflecting the frenetic environment of wartime Washington, D.C. Divisions and subdivisions sprang up, were integrated into the overall organization, and then were decommissioned overnight. There was also a constant turnover of CPI staffers, freelancers, and volunteers.[42]

Funding for the CPI during the first year came from the president's "discretionary" war chest. Congress was able to gain some measure of fiscal control over Creel's organization in mid–1918, showing its collective displeasure with CPI's independence by cutting its budget to nearly half of what had been requested by Creel. Overall, $6.85 million were allotted to the CPI: $5.6 million from Wilson's National Security and Defense Fund and $1.25

million from Congress plus an additional $2.8 million from CPI's direct earnings.[43]

For its domestic program (there was also a foreign section that eventually had offices in over 30 countries), the CPI took advantage of every existing communications link between Washington's wartime policies and every identifiable segment of the American people—and forged new ones. The CPI prepared press releases and news stories by the bushelful and enlisted scholars to write propaganda pamphlets, much as Oxford University's professors had done and were doing so expertly for England. It then printed and distributed them by the tens of millions. The CPI organized and coordinated a nationwide network of tens of thousands of speakers; prepared and placed advertisements in hundreds of newspapers and magazines; designed, printed, and distributed untold numbers of posters, which were pasted up all over the country; produced its own film documentaries and rigidly controlled the content of Hollywood-made motion pictures; published a daily newspaper; ran war expositions and scheduled lecturers; prepared collateral publicity and advertising material such as photographs, slides, cartoons, and postcards. Behind the scenes, CPI ghost writers quietly wrote newspaper stories, magazine articles, and books for government figures to put their names on.

Creel saw CPI's function simplistically: to convince a lukewarm population that the nation was engaged in a life-and-death struggle against the forces of darkness. He told a congressional appropriations committee in 1918 that the CPI worked "to bring home the truths of this great war to every man, woman, and child in the United States, so that they may understand that this is a just war, a holy war, and a war in self-defense."[44] The vehicle for "the truths," as Creel interpreted them, was his super public-relations and advertising agency. For the first time in United States history, a government organization not only "conditioned" all important news originating in Washington, but totally controlled it.

At the end of May 1917, Creel announced, through a 20-page "Preliminary Statement to the Press of the United States," "just what it is that the committee proposes and desires, so that there may be the least possible impairment of public confidence in the printed information presented to it." On the cover of the booklet was a message from the president, already sensitive to charges that "his" Committee on Public Information being used for partisan purposes: "I can imagine no greater disservice to the country than to establish a system of censorship that would deny to the people of a free Republic like our own their indisputable right to criticize their own public officials. While exercising the great powers of the office I hold, I would regret in a crisis like the one through which we are now passing to lose the benefit of patriotic and intelligent criticism." More ominous was a section titled "The Responsibility of Editors," which suggested that "the vicious and abusive be avoided in opinion" and that criticism be constructive:

Reckless journalism, regrettable enough in time of peace, is a positive menace when the Nation is at war. Victory rests upon unity and confidence, and those who imperil national solidarity by attack upon men and measures should be at infinite pains to establish their facts and to test their motives. In this day of high emotionalism and mental confusion, the printed word has immeasurable power, and the term traitor is not too harsh in application to the publisher, editor, or writer who wields this power without full and even solemn recognition of responsibilities.[45]

Through the harshest federal legislation restricting speech and press freedoms in the country's history, beginning with the Espionage Act passed the following month, Creel had the "teeth"—supported by the most reactionary of all administration officials, Postmaster General Albert Sydney Burleson—to threaten those who might "imperil national solidarity." He used this power willfully and arrogantly to dominate the news media and play the role of press censor, despite his almost continuous—and hypocritical—statements to the contrary.

One of numerous examples of Creel's heavy-handed censorship of material concerned the publication of a multi-volume set of books titled *The Story of the Great War*. Creel wrote that while "a thorough examination of all six volumes had not yet been completed, enough had been found already to warrant almost any charge against the honesty and loyalty of the books." His correspondence with the publisher was filled with arrogant statements: "I ask, therefore, for an instant reply to your attitude. ... Above all, I wish to know the name of the man responsible for the preparation of the material that is so peculiarly German in its very essence. ... I must insist that the changes be made that were suggested by me in my former letter."[46]

Creel also maintained an ongoing correspondence with Ernest J. Chambers, Canada's chief press censor. On October 23, 1918, for example, Chambers asked Creel for the list of books which U.S. soldiers were forbidden to have in their possession or to read. Creel responded with a list of 15, including books by Edward Lyell Fox, Bernhard Dernburg, Hugo Meunsterberg, and Max Eastman, editor of *The Masses*.[47]

Creel was not hesitant to move beyond his purview as chief propagandist into the political arena, reflecting the beginnings of a powerful anti-Soviet bias that would intensify over the years, as his correspondence with State Department ounselor Frank L. Polk shows. In a January 1918 memorandum, Creel wrote, "In one of your cables to Ambassador Francis, will you ask him as to the activities of John Reed? You gave this man a passport, and I consider him a very dangerous person to have loose."[48] The next day, Creel asked Polk, "What do you think about directing your representatives in Cuba to ask President Menocal for a statement showing the Cuban attitude to the U.S.? One of the things we are running up against in Russia is the lie that we took Cuba by force of arms and have held it in slavery ever since."[49] In August 1918, he involved Polk in another passport case. "I hear," he wrote, "that Louis

Edgar Brown of the Chicago Daily News is asking for a passport to return to Russia. I want to go on record as strongly as I can against the issuance of this passport. While in Petrograd, Brown sent open cables to the Bolsheviki censorship that betrayed our plans and exposed our representatives to danger. Since returning to this country, he has played the Lenin-Trotsky game from start to finish. Another thing, he is within the draft age and ought to be in the army."[50]

Creel had three associate chairmen, all men he knew well, all experienced journalists and writers: Edgar Sisson, former reporter and city editor of the *Chicago Tribune*, managing editor of *Collier's*, and editor of *Cosmopolitan*; Harvey J. O'Higgins, author and playright; and Carl Byoir, previously circulation manager of *Cosmopolitan*. Sisson, as will be discussed, would personally bear the scars from the tainted diplomatic correspondence he brought back from the Soviet Union in the spring of 1918. Byoir, on the other hand, built a renowned public-relations firm that in 1930 bore his name. Another CPI staffer, Edward L. Bernays, who was in charge of news for Latin America, found even more postwar fame and fortune in public relations.

Guy Stanton Ford was director of the CPI's Division of Civic and Educational Cooperation. A well-respected scholar, Ford had done graduate work in Berlin, and had been a professor of European history at the University of Minnesota, chairman of its History Department, and dean of its graduate school. After the war he served as president of that university and president of the American Historical Association. Ford apparently never had any reservations about the level of the superpatriotic "scholarship" that was under his direction for the CPI. He told fellow historians after the war with a straight face that he had "carefully avoided stirring up hatred for the German people, forbidding the use of the word Hun" in any of the CPI's booklets and that he had maintained high standards by insisting that the quality of the work performed by those to whom he assigned projects "be the kind of work they would not be ashamed of 20 years later."[51]

Salaries for CPI principal staff members were modest: Creel, $8,000 per year; Sisson and O'Higgins, $6,000; Byoir, $5,200. Lesser staffers and special freelancers were generally compensated at market rates, some taking pay cuts in exchange for what they saw as opportunities to make important career contacts, and others looking to avoid the draft. On June 27, 1917, Creel wrote a personal letter to Carl Byoir's Brooklyn draft board asking for a deferment for his assistant, calling him "absolutely indispensable."[52]

CPI's Division of News was the first to be set up and put into operation. Creel, with characteristic overstatement, described the division as "official machinery for the preparation and release of all news bearing upon America's war effort—not opinion nor conjecture, but *facts*—a running record of each day's progress in order that the fathers and mothers of the United States might gain a certain sense of partnership. ... Our job, therefore, was to present the facts without the slightest trace of color or bias, either the selection of news or the manner in which it was presented."[53]

The staple of the CPI's output was the short press release or news release, today still universally used for mass distribution of "news" to the media. It was a story in newspaper style and format suitable for instant use by editors. These generally one- or two-page stories were made available to Washington-based correspondents and representatives of the wire services and were mailed to the nation's newspapers and magazines. With its news offices open 24 hours a day, seven days a week, the CPI wrote, mimeographed, and distributed an avalanche of releases—some 6,000 different ones during the wartime months, an average of ten a day. The CPI had a monopoly on the sources of the most important news, such as decrees from the White House, overseas communiqués from the American Expeditionary Force of General John J. Pershing, and the daily press briefings from Secretary of War Baker. Numerous other government agencies also sent out their own news announcements, but the CPI usually "scooped" them.

Nearly all of these press releases were mundane announcements from a government at war to its citizens, and they dealt with a broad spectrum of topics, for example, personnel appointments, agency formations, and exhortations of support for every kind of cause, from food conservation to bond drives. Some releases were targeted at farmers or manufacturers, suggesting how both could produce more efficiently. Later during the war, as material scarcities developed, the press announcements admonished citizens and businesses to make do with less of everything. A July 24, 1917, release was titled "Why Sign the Food Pledge"; a September 26, 1918, release announced "preferential treatment in the matter of priorities" for the typewriter industry; a October 9, 1918, release covered a new conservation program directed at the manufacturers of oil stoves, announcing that nickel was to be eliminated and brass "confined to the burner parts."

Review by the author of a tiny portion of the CPI's news releases revealed their objective, straightforward presentation of facts—the "who, what, when, why, where, and how" of basic journalism. According to Creel in his postwar retrospective, all of the releases "ran the gauntlet of incessant and hostile scrutiny, yet only *three* were ever subjected to direct attack on the score of inaccuracy. In two of these cases the Committee was justified by investigation, while the fault in the third instance was that of a high official whose word could not be questioned."[54] At the time, the CPI's extravagantly enthusiastic chairman wrote that "no news organization in the world equals, or even approaches this record of painstaking accuracy established by a war organization hastily assembled and driven at all times under tremendous pressure."[55]

Creel estimated some 20,000 columns per week were published by the press from the CPI's prodigious output, yet one wonders if the CPI's news-release barrage was not, in fact, counter productive. A busy newspaper editor, confronted with the day's stack of releases from a familiar source, might well throw them all out rather than take the time to select the most significant. A letter from Wilson to Creel on December 31, 1917, indicated that the problem of over production of "news" was recognized at the highest levels in the government. "The other day," wrote the president, "you called my attention to the immense amount of government publicity matter being unloaded on the newspapers ... and I brought the matter up in Cabinet where we discussed it rather fully, and my net conclusion from the discussion is this, that the matter with which the newspapers are burdened goes out, not directly from the departments themselves, but from the Congressmen and Senators who have mailing lists and who send to the newspapers within their constituencies practically everything that the Government publishes, with many duplications of course and without any attempt at winnowing the wheat from the chaff, and I must say I despair of suggesting a solution for that difficulty."[56]

An extension of the CPI's efforts to dominate and thus control news information was its publication of the *Official Bulletin*, the first government daily (except Sundays and holidays) in the nation's history. The *Bulletin's* first issue was May 10, 1917. The 9-by-11-inch minitabloid was as well designed and clearly written as most privately published newspapers. Early issues generally ran to eight pages, but by the fall of 1918, 36-pagers were common. Offered at the then-high subscription price of $5 a year to soothe concerns from newspapers that the government was trying to take business from them, the *Bulletin* went free to newspapers, government officials and agencies, military camps, and the over 50,000 post offices in the country, where it was pinned on bulletin boards. Its circulation ultimately reached a peak of about 115,000.

While part of its contents was "best of the day" information already disseminated by the CPI, the *Official Bulletin* had a far broader charter. Among its many functions, it listed army and navy casualties and the names of men taken prisoner and those cited for bravery; it printed important military communiqués and papers, proclamations, and addresses by the president and the heads of the major governments departments; and it printed major contract awards, texts of important laws, proceedings of the U.S. Supreme Court, and noteworthy actions of the Congress.

The concept of such a propaganda outlet was Wilson's, although it carried Creel's name and title atop the front page of every issue. Indeed, Wilson finally had his own propaganda sheet, a medium through which he could present information precisely in the form he wished, without the press interposing its editorial interpretations.[57] In a July 1917 memo to his secretary Joseph P. Tumulty , the president exulted, "The Bulletin is extremely useful, is an immense success, and is doing the greatest service, very much to the astonishment of Creel, who did not at first believe in it."[58]

There is evidence that Creel probably *never* believed in it. As an ex-newspaperman, it was natural that he would be defensive about the *Bulletin*, especially when he talked to journalists, for they understandably looked upon it as a government-financed competitor. The last two paragraphs in the CPI's comprehensive "Preliminary Statement to the Press of the United States" appear to have been Creel's attempt to smooth ruffled feathers:

> Many misunderstandings have arisen with regard to the Official Bulletin. This is *not* a newspaper in the accepted sense of the word. Its single purpose is to assure the *full* and *legal* printing of the official announcements of Government heads in connection with governmental business.
>
> Exclusive publication is not its thought or ambition. It will not interfere with the legitimate functions of the press in any manner, nor will official news be delayed or withheld in order to give the Bulletin any special news significance.

Far more important to the domestic propaganda effort than the bundles of news releases parceled out to the nation's newspapers and magazines and to the daily *Bulletin* were the over 100 booklets and leaflets produced by CPI's Division of Civic and Educational Cooperation (later more properly called the Division of Civic and Educational Publications). This propaganda literature emphasized two main themes. The first was that militaristic Germany was a threat to the United States. The second was that America was justified to go to war, not only because Germany threatened U.S. security but for the unselfish, noble principles enunciated by Woodrow Wilson. To a lesser degree, there was an attempt to "educate" the public on the meaning of American democracy at a turning point in its history. Also stressed were the supposed common interests of America, Great Britain, and France and the nations' close cultural and political kinship.

The CPI printed the booklets in enormous quantities; two of them had printing runs of over five million each. According to Creel's bookkeeping, a total of more than 60 million copies for American consumption came off the presses. Nearly all were free to anyone "writing plainly ... typewriter preferred" to the CPI's headquarters in Washington, D.C. Postage-free reply cards were inserted in the booklets to simplify ordering by individuals. Creel wrote that distribution of the pamphlets "at no time was haphazard." He claimed that no less than three quarters of the booklets were sent out only upon request "as a safeguard against waste."[59] To distribute the remaining 25 percent, a host of government departments and public and private organizations, was enlisted, such as the Departments of State and Agriculture, the American Federation of Labor, the U.S. Chamber of Commerce, the Y.M.C.A., and the American Library Association. Big-city daily newspapers reprinted many of the pamphlets in total or summarized their contents, and state defense organizations also made reprints for local distribution, adding enormously to their readership.

While Creel vividly defended his organization's literature in his postwar book on the CPI as the "most sober and terrific indictment ever drawn by one government of the political and military system of another government,"[60] an objective review establishes the fact that most of the pamphlets were anything but sober. While designed to appear as honest scholarship, generally they were raw and obvious propaganda, calculated to instill in their readers intolerance, fear, and hatred of Germans, things German, and Germany itself. Two CPI booklets specifically pandered to the popular interest in German brutality and bloodlust, although there never was an American equivalent of Britain's atrocity-filled Bryce Report.[61]

Drawing on Wellington House's notable experience as producers of deceitful propaganda booklets much of the literature relied on quotations from German authorities, taken out of context, and selected "evidence" from questionable sources. As might be imagined, every warlike statement made by a German in the recent past that could be dredged up as an example of the "true German nature" was employed. Copious footnotes and long, incestuous bibliographies, including CPI pamphlets and books and articles by Great Britain's and America's loudest Germanophobes and jingoes, served as a patina for the creative blends of fiction and fact. The patriotic university professors who put their names and academic affiliations on the covers lent artificial credibility to their work. Especially to those who had never picked up a serious book since elementary or high school days, the CPI's booklets projected the desired aura of authenticity.

Viewed three-quarters of a century later, the booklets generally merit high marks as propaganda, if grotesque failures as history. The best were easy to read, with simple sentence structure and grammar, man-in-the-street vocabulary, short paragraphs, plenty of boldface headings and type faces for emphasis, and white space to draw the reader along. Others were scarcely comprehensible, written by would-be historiographers for their learned peers and crying out for an editor's sharp pencil. Some were just too long to hold a casual reader's attention. In his summary report to the president, Creel audaciously concluded "that the directors of English, French, and Italian propaganda were a unit in agreeing that our literature was remarkable above all others for its brilliant and concentrated effectiveness."[62]

The books ranged in scope from four-page "Loyalty Leaflets" ("designed for the busy man or woman who wants the important facts of the war and our participation in it put SIMPLY, BRIEFLY, and FORCIBLY") to the 320-page *War Cyclopedia: A Handbook for Ready Reference on the Great War* ("Over 1000 articles ... Suitable for speakers, editors ... THE BEST SINGLE VOLUME ON THE WAR"). The most widely distributed were the 21 booklets in the "War Information Series" and the ten in the "Red, White, and Blue Series." These series were issued concurrently and, except for a tricolor band on the top left of the front cover identifying the latter series, were similar in format and style.

There were also seven brief "Loyalty Leaflets" aimed at the nation's poorest readers.[63]

Three of the booklets in these series relied heavily for their contents on speeches by the president. *The War Message and Facts Behind It*, CPI's first booklet, included 40 intricate footnotes, some nearly a full page in length, responding to Wilson's main points in his speech to the Congress on April 2. If the litany of Germany's perfidy as detailed in the footnotes—breaker of treaties, torpedoer of hospital ships, drowner of American women and children, violator of American sovereignty, precipitator of war, and saboteur extraordinaire—was not sufficiently memorable, the reader could use a "Compact Summary of the Grievances of the United States and the Necessity of War":

> As a reward for our neutrality what have we received at the hands of William II?
> He has set the torch of the incendiary to our factories, our workshops, our ships, and our wharves.
> He has laid the bomb of the assassin in our munitions plants and in the holds of our ships.
> He has sought to corrupt our manhood with a selfish dream of peace when there is no peace.
> He has willfully butchered our citizens on the high seas.
> He has destroyed our commerce.
> He seeks to terrorize us with his devilish policy of frightfulness.
> He has violated every canon of international decency and set at naught every solemn treaty and every precept of international law.
> He has plunged the world into the maddest orgy of blood, rapine, and murder which history records.
> He has intrigued against our peace at home and abroad.
> He seeks to destroy our civilization. Patience is no longer a virtue, further endurance is cowardice, submission to Prussian demands is slavery.

A second Wilson speech that promptly became a booklet was *The President's Flag Day Address, with Evidence of Germany's Plans*. Its academic annotators dug deep into past and current German history to buttress with fatiguing footnotes assertions by the president, for example, that "we are fighting their [the German people's] cause, as they will some day see it, as well as our own" and that "extraordinary insults and aggressions of the Imperial German Government" left America "no self-respecting choice but to take up arms in defense of our rights as a free people and of our honor as a sovereign Government." According to Wilson, not only was America imperiled by Germany's aggression, but smaller countries were also in jeopardy; Germany's diabolical plans for world domination included expansion to the east, "into the heart of Asia, and a broad belt of German military power and political control across the very center of Europe."

How the War Came to America, fleshed out with three of Wilson's addresses, was a straightforward exposition of America's case against Germany.

It began with a review of this nation's traditions, based on a belief in settling international disputes peacefully, and moved to a current chronology of German-American relations, particularly regarding submarine warfare. Purported evidence of German "bad faith" toward the United States was emphasized, including reference to the hallowed Monroe Doctrine:

> While expressing a cordial friendship for the people of the United States, the Government of Germany had its agents at work both in Latin America and Japan. They bought or subsidized papers and supported speakers there to rouse feelings of bitterness and distrust against us in those friendly nations, in order to embroil us in war. ... Everywhere in South America they were abroad sowing the seeds of dissension, trying to stir up one nation against another and all against the United States. In their sum these various operations amounted to direct assault against the Monroe Doctrine.

The booklet lamely attempted to justify Great Britain's rejection of the Declaration of London by declaring that Britain could not be expected to accept a limit on its naval powers when its neighbors [i.e., Germany and Austria-Hungary] were unwilling to limit their land forces.

The German War Code, Contrasted with the War Manuals of the United States, Great Britain, and France set out to convince its readers that the German army was uniquely brutal and "cold-bloodedly programmed" by the German government to be so. Its authors relied on excerpts from and interpretations of a 1902 manual of military instructions for the German armed forces, *Kriegsbrauch im Landskriege (War Customs in Land War)*, to drive home their theme. Reaching back to the Declaration of St. Petersburg of 1868, which declared that war was a contest between armies rather than peoples, the authors of the booklet said that the German manual proclaimed that the purpose of war was, rather, "to destroy the spiritual and material power of the enemy country." Furthermore, wrote the CPI propagandists, since the manual declared that "the laws and customs of war must yield to the law of military necessity,"—it was therefore, "permissible to destroy private property, to devastate systematically evacuated regions, to terrorize the civil population of invaded districts, to deport them for compulsory service in the enemy country, thereby releasing its own men for the army, to compel them to aid the enemy in the construction of fortifications, to dig trenches, to serve as guides, and even to furnish information regarding their own army." The German ordinances also violated current "Hague rules," to which Germany was a signatory.

Before turning to the war manuals of the United States, Great Britain, and France—"a refreshing contrast"—the authors concluded that German army officers were "warned against being misled by the excessive humanitarianism of the present age," which, the manual stated, often degenerated into "sentimentality and flabby emotion." In sharp contrast were the "enlightened and humane" armies of the Allies, as reflected in their war manuals. The first

American war manual, for example, laid down the rule that only such measures may be adopted against the enemy as "are lawful according to the modern laws and customs of war." The same was true, of course, for the British and French military, both of whose soldiers were bound by international agreements and by the dictates of "religion, civilization, and chivalry."

An article originally appearing in the July 1, 1917, issue of the *New York Times*, "Germany, Last Stronghold of Autocratic Monarchy," and reissued by the CIP under the title *The Government of Germany*, was a polemical overview of the undemocratic and unrepresentative nature of the German government. The author selected quotations that fit his thesis. Rudolph Gneist ("once considered a great authority on public law") was quoted as describing Germany as "absolutism under constitutional forms." Prince von Bulow ("the ablest chancellor since Bismarck") was quoted as stating, "Prussia attained her greatness as a country of soldiers and officials. ... To this day she is still, in all essentials, a State of soldiers and officials." The author suggested that readers should "not be hoodwinked by Easter messages from William II, or by cloudy and ambiguous utterances of Bethmann Hollweg, as presaging forthcoming liberalization of Germany. Prussian Kings have shown that not only are treaties scraps of paper, but that constitutions are also scraps of paper when their provisions annoy the monarch."

Furthermore, Americans should not forget the debt of gratitude they owed to America's new ally. The author wrote that "one has only to recall the great chapters in English history which tell of the struggle for liberty to know that it has been obtained solely by the recognition of the supremacy of Parliament over royal prerogative and over military power."

The Study of the Great War: A Topical Outline with Extensive Quotations and Reading References was a 96-page mini-textbook with ten chapters, starting with the conflict's "fundamental causes" and concluding with "proposals for peace." Originally published in *History Teacher's Magazine*, it was not intended to be read at one sitting, nor could it be. Rather, the fat little booklet was an in-depth reference source for discussion in America's high schools and colleges. As much as any other CPI booklet, *The Study of the Great War* masqueraded as honest history, with its "extensive quotations and reading references." It hoodwinked a whole generation of American teachers and their students.

An even thicker book was the 160-page *Conquest and Kultur: Aims of the Germans in Their Own Words*, a tiring collection of hundreds of selected "testimonials," edited, organized, and indexed, that intended to establish once and for all the fundamental warlike nature of the German people. The usually conservative Professor Ford was so delighted with the results achieved that he wrote in the booklet's introduction that "the pied pipers of Prussianism who have led the German people to conquest and to ignominy and to infamy are here given their unending day before the court of public opinion. It is a motley

throng who are here heard in praise of war and international suspicion and conquest and intrigue and devastation."

The quotations filled chapters with such inflammatory titles as "World
Power or Downfall," "The Worship of Power," "War as the Sole Arbiter,"
"Dispossessing the Conquered," "Pan-Germanism and America," and "The
Coming War." One caustic critic later discounted the booklet this way:

> The serried ranks of quotations presented a swaggering display of incrimi-
> nation and the editors provided additional testimony with vignettes of the
> most frequently quoted sources. Kaiser Wilhelm II appeared at least twelve
> times with such utterances as "I shall stand no nonsense from America after
> the war." Henrich von Treitschke ... appeared nine times with "blood and
> iron" adages; Frederick the Great espoused militarism six times; Nietzsche
> expounded his philosophical worship of war; and Friedrich von Bernhardi, the
> soldier-scholar, advocated Germany's "place in the sun" sixteen times.[64]

*The Kaiserite in America: One Hundred and One German Lies, Published
Especially for the Commercial Travelers of America* sought to counter the dangerous falsehoods and rumors said to be "circulated by enemy propagandists and
their dupes" by listing "one hundred and one lies" that alert Americans should
be prepared to refute. Among the more ludicrous examples:

> Lie No. 2.—That a sweater knit in St. Louis for the soldiers in France was
> sold by Red Cross workers and identified by the woman who knew it by a
> piece of currency sewed into the fabric. *(Heads of the Red Cross Society in St.
> Louis have branded this as a bald fabrication.)*
> Lie No. 12.—That all the money invested in Liberty bonds by men and
> women and children throughout the United States will be lost. *(Liberty
> bonds are backed by all the finances of the United States. Whenever the money so
> invested is "lost," the United States will have collapsed.)*
> Lie No. 70.—That two transports, bearing 11,000 men, and the superdread-
> naught Texas, had been sunk, and that the American Government was sup-
> pressing the news. *(The Government at Washington announced that the source
> of this lie, termed propaganda, had been unearthed in Guadalajara, Mexico,
> where it was printed in a Spanish newspaper, and said to have been a cablegram
> received from Spain. The Government announces this is more German propa-
> ganda and that there is no word of truth in it.)*
> Lie No. 90.—J. Richard Garstang, an attorney of Chamois, Mo., reports that
> a retail merchant of that place is circulating the tale that, in Gasconnade
> County, relatives received the bodies of two soldiers, sent back from camp
> for burial, with the casket marked "Contagious, Do Not Open." It was fur-
> ther averred that when the two parents opened the caskets, the soldiers were
> found to have two bullet holes each in their heads. *(This faint attempt to jam
> the machinery of the National Army furnishes denial in itself. The War
> Department has announced repeatedly that official publication of all deaths in the
> National Army will be made, regardless of the nature of such deaths. If soldiers
> are to be shot, notification of their death penalty will be spread broadcast as a
> warning to others. Just another morsel for the unintelligent to chew on is this
> obviously pro–German lie.)*

German Plots and Intrigues in the United States during the Period of Our Neutrality was a compilation of the well-worn and thoroughly publicized tales of the exaggerated machinations of German diplomats in the United States prior to America's entry into the war. Von Bernstorff had been the alleged ring-leader, assisted by underlings Dumba, von Papen, Boy-Ed and others in trying to prevent the export of war materials, provoking strikes, destroying ships and cargoes, aiding Indian nationalists in their efforts to overthrow British rule, and helping Irish revolutionaries. German money had been behind pacifist prop-aganda favoring Congressional actions to prohibit Americans from traveling on ships of belligerents, to embargo munitions, and to cut off loans to the Allies.

A pair of booklets, *German War Practices: Treatment of Civilians* and *German War Practices: German Treatment of Conquered Territory*, while promis-ing the substantiation of Belgian, British, and French reports of atrocities by Germans, actually came out as lukewarm versions of the originals. Limited by wartime restrictions to material in American files and secondary sources, their authors nevertheless did their best to verify German brutality.

The first pamphlet covered German treatment of conquered civilians in Belgium, France, and Poland, and focused on Germany's organized and calcu-lated program of *Schrecklichkeit*, or frightfulness, to cow the local populace. There were incriminating extracts from Ambassador Gerard's 1917 book *My Four Years in Germany* and accusing testimony from Americans who had been in Belgium, including Ambassador Whitlock. There were diaries supposedly taken from the dead or captured, filled with "verified" atrocities; juicy items picked up from the Bryce Report; even the Kaiser's famous *bon voyage* speech in 1900 wishing his troops "good hunting" in China and suggesting they act like Attila the Hun. Readers were told that German soldiers shot husbands dead in front of their wives, used civilians as shields in combat, and raped women, all as part of their daily routines.

The second booklet dealt with the German army's supposed systematic pillage and uncaring destruction of captured territory. This was to be consid-ered even worse than the exploitation and murder of civilians, because as a result of such wanton actions the very young, the old, and the sick were certain to starve. Even more sinister, the Germans purposefully crippled Belgian man-ufacturing, readers were told, to restrict future industrial competition. This policy was based on what was called the "Rathenau Plan," the master plot that would allow Germany to capture overseas markets after the war from the weak-ened economies of Belgium and other countries. Lists of products Germany had supposedly requisitioned from Belgium were included as proof of such a policy. There was more damning testimony from Americans with first-hand experience and the usual excerpts from German soldiers' diaries.

Perhaps the least useful booklet was *American and Allied Ideals: An Appeal To Those Who Are Neither Hot nor Cold*, a tedious, befuddling 20-page essay written by an English professor who lost his way—and, mercifully, nearly all his readers—early in his presentation. It was originally prepared as an address before the author's peers; its erudition was out of place in the new pamphlet. The author quoted Goethe, Micah, Confucius, Cicero, and Milton as supporting the ideals of the Allies, and further garbled his presentation with disjointed references to Tennyson, Simon Bolivar, "18th century deists—men like Paine, Franklin, and Jefferson," Washington, and Lincoln. The following passage typifies the arcane style: "Contemporary German thought is prehistoric, reversionary, paradoxical. It seeks to fly against the great winds of time, to row against the deep current of human purposes. ... The Allies are seeking to cooperate with the power not ourselves which has been struggling for righteousness through the entire history of man; and their cause will be borne forward by the confluent moral energies of all times and peoples."

Another booklet that almost certainly was unread—neither good history nor useful propaganda—was *The Great War: From Spectator to Participant*, also originally an article written by a scholarly author for his peers and clearly showing its origins. It consisted of page-long paragraphs, complex sentences, and vague generalities. According to the author, the main reason America went to war with Germany was because of German espionage: "Democracy can not survive in an atmosphere of indecent intrigue; the Government at Washington was forced to conclude that we can not act in friendliness or cooperate with a government whose ways are devious, ungenerous, purely selfish, and unreliable." The musty historiographer concluded his learned essay in laughable fashion: "So far we have given only a meager outline of the story and told it ineffectively, for not even in many words can one sketch the growing uneasiness and distrust, the sense of despair, or the conflict between despair and hope. Was the world falling?"

Amazingly, CPI printed over 200,000 copies of *American and Allied Ideals* and one and a half million copies of *The Great War*—indicative, perhaps, of the paucity of well-written propaganda works by "scholars" that were the CPI's stock-in-trade.

Probably the best propaganda booklet produced by the CPI to drive home the point that it was Germany's atrocious acts that forced a peace-loving America into the war was *Why America Fights Germany*. It was only 12 pages long, easy to read, simply organized, aimed right at most Americans: "Suppose your neighbor X dislikes your neighbor A. Suppose he announces that if he sees you on the steps of A's house, or even walking on the public sidewalk near it, he will kill you, and proves his seriousness by shooting you through the arm with a revolver. Will you go home and say indulgently, that `it is no affair of yours, that you are a lover of peace, and will leave them to settle their own quarrels?'" It was the author's creative version of the compelling necessity of America fighting Germany in Europe so that she would not have to fight her in America, however, that distinguished *Why America*

Fights Germany. The booklet presented a graphic narrative of "what a sudden invasion of the United States by these Germans would mean; sudden, because their settled way is always to attack suddenly." The author pointed out that he was telling "not just a snappy story ... not fancy. ... The general plan of campaign against America has been announced repeatedly by German military men." He went on:

> First they set themselves to capture New York City. While their fleet blockades the harbor and shells the city and the forts from far at sea, their troops land somewhere near and advance toward the city in order to cut its rail communications, starve it into surrender, and then plunder it. One body of from 50,000 to 100,000 men lands, let us suppose, at Barnegat Bay, N.J., and advances without meeting resistance, for the brave but small American army is scattered elsewhere. They pass through Lakewood, a station on the Central Railroad of New Jersey. They first demand wine for the officers and beer for the men. Angered to find that an American town does not contain large quantities of either, they pillage and burn the post-office and most of the hotels and stores. Then they demand $1,000,000 from the residents. One feeble old woman tries to conceal twenty dollars which she has been hoarding in her desk drawer; she is taken out and hanged (to save a cartridge). Some of the teachers in two district schools meet a fate which makes them envy her. The Catholic priest and Methodist minister are thrown into a pig-sty, while the German soldiers look on and laugh. Some of the officers quarter themselves in a handsome house on the edge of the town, insult the ladies of the family, and destroy and defile the contents of the house. By this time some of the soldiers have managed to get drunk; one of them discharges his gun accidentally, the cry goes up that the residents are firing on the troops, and then hell breaks loose. Robbery, murder and outrage run riot. Fifty leading citizens are lined up against the First National Bank Building, and shot. Most of the town and the beautiful pine-woods are burned, and then the troops move on to treat New Brunswick in the same way—if they get there.

In conclusion, the author wrote, America was fighting Germany for six reasons:

1. The German Government has drowned our citizens, sunk our ships, destroyed our property, insulted our flag, contrary to all law and all humanity. Every such act was an act of war against us.
2. By its cruel and treacherous treatment of Belgium, and by its manner of waging war, it has excited the horror of all decent people. Mercy and justice through all the world are at stake.
3. Its constant love and desire for war proves it the greatest menace on earth to the peace and happiness of free peoples.
4. On our side are the democracies of the world, great and small; on the German side are the autocracies of the world, warring against the principles on which our democracy and all others are founded.
5. Germany plans to dominate the Old World from its center, and to-day has largely accomplished the plan. In a few years it will be too late to stop her.
6. Germany's ambitions for expansion in the New World have shown that we

should have to fight Germany later, if not now; and without help, instead of with the help of all other great free peoples.

One propaganda booklet of the CPI, however, must be analyzed in greater depth, for it uniquely reflected the CPI's bold contributions to patriotic hysteria in the United States during the war and for decades afterward. This booklet tars the integrity of Woodrow Wilson, highlights the hypocrisy of George Creel, and seriously diminishes the credibility of two leading American historians.

The German-Bolshevik Conspiracy was based on 68 documents smuggled out of the new Soviet Union early in 1918 by CPI associate chairman Edgar Sisson, who had been sent into Russia in the fall of 1917 to supervise American propaganda efforts in that country. The documents, which became known as the Sisson Papers, purported to prove not only that Germany had materially assisted the Bolsheviks in their October Revolution but that the top Bolshevik leaders, Lenin and Trotsky included, were paid agents of the German General Staff.

In fact, the supposedly incriminating documents which Sisson triumphantly brought back to the United States in May 1918 had already been published in Europe and were recognized in England and in the U.S. State Department as forgeries intended to discredit the fledgling Bolshevik government. Yet the president of the United States gave CPI's chairman the go-ahead to publish and broadcast them as if they were fresh discoveries and genuine. Creel, too, must be pilloried for his devious attempt to later paper over the existence of the controversial CPI booklet. In his formal document listing all publications of his committee, *Complete Report of the Chairman of the Committee on Public Information*, published in 1920, there is no mention of *The German-Bolshevik Conspiracy*, and in his patently self-serving book, *How We Advertised America*, published a year later, Creel devoted only a single sentence to it, merely crediting Sisson with authorship. It was as if Creel had become embarrassed by the booklet and wished away the whole sordid business.[65]

To understand Wilson's motivation in allowing Creel to publish the questionable documents, it is necessary to look at the president's posture in the weeks following the Bolshevik takeover in November 1917. Lenin had promptly called for a halt to the war, suggesting clearly that the Soviet government was planning to pull out of the fighting unilaterally. It was this fear of the Soviets leaving the war—thus releasing huge German armies to bulwark the western front, which could turn the tide of battle in Germany's favor—that first drove Wilson's decision making. At all costs, Wilson reasoned, the Soviet Union must be kept in the war. The administration was also concerned about the designs in the Far East of an aggressive Japan capable of taking advantage of the military weakness of the fledgling Communist regime.

But Wilson, who had hoped for the success of a constitutional government in Russia under Alexander Kerensky, a fellow professor, was being fed a straight diet of vitriolic anti–Communism from his advisors in St. Petersburg, including Sisson. One historian has written that it was the president's "personal hostility" toward the Bolsheviks that led quickly to concrete actions to subvert the Soviet government. Wilson actively aided counter-revolutionaries, maintained an economic embargo, helped Poland to acquire territories in the Ukraine, and "in the last hours of his administration approved a plan calculated to maneuver Lenin out of power."[66]

Sisson had arrived in the Soviet capital in late November 1917, just days after Lenin's coup, and spent three months in the country. Sisson's critical correspondence shows him almost overnight becoming a zealous anti–Communist. After a January 11, 1918, meeting with Lenin, Sisson's views hardened. He became convinced that the Soviet government's policies represented a threat to America's security, and decided to brand Lenin as a German spy.

Uncertain about the diplomatic fallout, Wilson withheld public disclosure of the Sisson documents for four months. House recorded in his diary that he told the president that publication of the documents meant "a virtual declaration of war upon the Bolshevik Government" and that Wilson acknowledged he understood their foreign-policy import.[67] But by the end of the summer, Wilson's antagonistic views toward the Soviet government had hardened, and he gave in to the entreaties of Creel, who released them to the press for publication in seven installments, starting on September 15. Creel was also readying the material for production as a formal CPI propaganda booklet, *The German–Bolshevik Conspiracy*.

The only major English-language newspaper to express its skepticism about the integrity of the documents was the *New York Evening Post*. It declared editorially on September 16 that there was "plenty of ground for doubt. ... The plain fact is some of the most important charges in the documents brought forward by Mr. Sisson were published in Paris months ago, and have, on the whole, been discredited." Subsequent issues of the *Evening Post* cast further doubt on the CPI revelations.

Creel was furious at what he read in the *Evening Post*. The *Evening Post*, which had earlier drawn the ire of the administration as one of the very few American newspapers to publish the texts of the Allies' "secret treaties," was upsetting CPI's printing schedule, and Creel lashed out in a long, threatening letter to the newspaper's editor. It was filled with typical Creel hyperbole:

> I say to you flatly that the New York Evening Post cannot escape the charge of having given aid and comfort to the enemies of the United States in an hour of national crisis. These documents were published with the full authority of the Government behind them. They were not given out until there was every conviction that they were absolutely genuine.... I do not make the charge that the New York Evening Post is German or that it has taken German money,

but I do say that the service it has rendered to the enemies of the United States would have been purchased gladly by those enemies, and in terms of unrest and industrial stability this supposedly American paper has struck a blow at America more powerful that could possibly have been dealt by German hands.[68]

London *Times* reporter Arthur Willert, while something of a disinterested observer to the goings-ons, nevertheless expressed patriotic self-satisfaction in a letter of October 3, 1918, to his editor:

I cannot remember if I told you of the denouement of the Bolshevik documents business. It was that both Creel and the State Department were most irritated, not by the perfectly reasonable excuse of the safety of our consuls but because the first reason from all they heard was doubt about authenticity. "Now," they proclaim, "nothing that the US puts about will be believed. We are crucified as fakirs." I told the State Department, but not Creel, that the whole thing might have been avoided had they consulted us before publishing.[69]

But Creel could not ignore the *Evening Post*'s jibes. On October 18 he sent a letter to the vice-chairman of the National Board for Historical Service, a wartime group of college history professors organized to serve the nation, asking him to convene a small, authoritative committee, to pass judgment on the validity of the *Evening Post*'s criticisms. Creel said that time was critically important. He sent along page proofs of *The German-Bolshevik Conspiracy* with Sisson's "interpretative notes," together with second- and third-generation photostatic copies of the documents, some in German and some in Russian.

A committee of two with supposedly impeccable credentials was appointed the next day. One was J. Franklin Jameson, head of the Department of Historical Research at the Carnegie Institution in Washington and managing editor of the prestigious *American Historical Review*. The other was Samuel N. Harper, professor of Russian language and history at the University of Chicago. The men spent one week examining the material and concluded in a formal report to Creel that, as far as they could tell, most of the documents were authentic. In the report, Jameson and Harper stated that they understood that they were not expected to comment "upon Mr. Sisson's inferences." Furthermore, to protect their supposed integrity as scholars, they said they did not "desire to express, or to be influenced by, any opinions respecting the conduct of Bolshevik leaders or German officials."[70]

Remarkably, one month earlier Creel had received a letter from Philip Patchen of the State Department. Patchen sent along a telegram from Ambassador Page, at the direction of Secretary Lansing, that pointed out that "the War Office, the Foreign Office, the Postal Censor and the Admiralty" had studied the documents carefully and concluded that those "which appeared to be genuine were old and not of any particular value, and those which had propaganda value were of a doubtful character." Page's telegram also stated that a British military intelligence officer had told Sisson in London, when he was on his way back to the United States with the documents, that many were forgeries and he had "urged Sisson to go slow with them."[71] Creel the same day wrote to Patchen saying that Sisson denied that anyone in British intelligence had told him anything of the sort, and that he, Creel, rejected the British view of the worth of the papers as propaganda, and concluding that he would be the judge of that. This response reveals Creel's headlong drive to publish the material despite growing evidence of its false nature.

Subsequent analyses in less frenzied circumstances have long since established conclusively that the papers were forgeries, and clumsy ones at that. As early as the January 21, 1920, issue of the *New Republic*, a book review of E.H. Wilcox's *Russia's Ruin* summarized Wilcox's "proof of the suspicious character of Mr. Creel's 'discovery'":

> The pamphlet includes some fifteen or sixteen facsimiles by way of corroboration. One of the facsimiles purports to be a circular sent out on November 28, 1914, by the "General Staff" of the German High Sea Fleet. Now such a body as a "General Staff" does not exist in the German Navy. ... The circular itself consists of eighteen lines. In these eighteen lines are two mistakes in grammar, seven mistakes in spelling and seven mistakes in phrasing. ... The documents in question say nothing, because they produce an uneasy impression of forgery. ... They leave a comic impression that the German General Staff was very anxious to divulge, in very trivial order, the most important state secrets.[72]

In 1928, Frederick L. Schuman, in *American Policy toward Russia since 1917*, wrote that the documents "were pronounced forgeries by Soviet representatives soon after their appearance and have been regarded as such since, even in many anti–Bolshevist circles. ... While perhaps not entirely spurious, they show many evidences of crude fabrication and their genuineness is most questionable."[73]

In 1931, Sisson finally published his version of the events surrounding the controversial papers that bore his name, his government's first official anti-Soviet polemic for American consumption, in what he called "A Personal Chronicle of the Bolshevik Revolution." He wrote that he had waited twelve years to assure himself that "time would develop two conclusions reached through observations of the Bolshevik Revolution in Russia in 1917 and 1918." The first, he wrote, was that "there could be no peace in the world while the masters of one nation warred upon all other nations. ..." The second "was that the leaders of the Soviet adventure were doomed to die by violence—unless overthrown from within by revolt in consequence of famine or of reckless oppression."[74]

In 1956, George F. Kennan, then the nation's most well-respected expert on the Soviet Union, was unambiguous in his criticism of the integrity of the documents—and of the two American historians, Jameson and Harper, who had patriotically put their stamp of approval on them. Harper presumably had been able to read the documents in their original Russian and to pass on the accuracy of the English translations. But he could scarcely have been considered an objective reviewer, since, as a member of the anti–Soviet Russian Information Bureau in New York, he was a known opponent of the new Bolshevik government. "Jameson," according to Kennan, "knew no Russian and hence could not read the documents." Kennan concluded his analysis:

> The state of affairs suggested in the main body of the documents is of such extreme historical implausibility that the question might well be asked whether the documents could not be declared generally fraudulent on this ground alone.... The authenticity of the documents is open to question in a large number of technical aspects.... [including] The letterhead of the alleged divisions of the German General Staff was obviously false.... The letters from the German offices are written in excellent Russian. This would be most unusual, particularly in Russia.... In the winter of 1917-18 the Soviet government was in a state of transition from the old Julian to the western Gregorian calendar. Not one of the documents bears a double date or any indication whether the dates were in the old calendar or the new.... A close examination of the typing reveals quite plainly that five different machines were used in the preparation of these documents.[75]

Early in the twentieth century American adults had been conditioned by oratory, and in 1917 were pliant and attentive listeners. It would be four years before regular voice broadcasting by radio made its American debut, and years more before the newfangled radios became commonplace. The CPI bridged this communication gap with an innovative and forceful propaganda medium almost the equivalent of radio: the Four Minute Men.[76]

The CPI's volunteer speakers got their name from the duration of the speeches they delivered. The speeches were given mostly in movie theaters and their duration was based on the approximately four minutes it took for projectionists to change film reels. Needless to say, the name was also intended to evoke a glorious episode early in the nation's history, when Massachusetts militiamen held themselves in readiness to take up arms against the common foe. That this foe was not Germany but England was never mentioned.

The concept of a band of speakers stirring the emotions of the passive millions of Americans who nightly went to the approximately 12,000 motion-picture theaters across the country originated in Chicago in March 1917 among a group of patriotic businessmen. Its chief spokesman went to Washington immediately after America declared war against Germany to discuss with government officials how his communications concept might serve the nation. Creel colorfully described the opening minutes with his visitor: "In the very first hours of the Committee, when we were still penned in the navy library, fighting for breath, a handsome, rosy-cheeked youth burst through the crowd and caught my lapel in a death-grip ... and the plan he presented was the organization of volunteer speakers for the purpose of making patriotic talks in motion-picture theaters."[77]

Creel wrote that he might have rejected the proposition if he had had the time to weigh it more carefully "for it was delicate and dangerous business to turn loose on the country an army of speakers impossible of exact control and yet vested in large degree with the authority of the government."[78] However, CPI's chairman decided in ten minutes, he claimed, in favor of a national organization called the Four Minute Men, and appointed the "rosy-cheeked" Donald M. Ryerson its director.

Once it was formed into a full-fledged CPI division, the Four Minute Men grew fast. By May 1917, there were 1,500 speakers; by July, 2,500; by November, 15,000; by March 1918, 25,000; by September 1918, 40,000. On December 31, 1918, when the organization was formally disbanded, there were 74,500 speakers organized into chapters in all 48 states, plus Alaska, the Canal Zone, Hawaii, Puerto Rico, Guam, the Philippines, and Samoa.[79] The division's vigorous contribution to CPI's domestic propaganda efforts was a result of thoroughgoing direction from Washington; frequent and effective communication, both informative and motivational, from headquarters to the speakers in the field; and CPI's unrelenting insistence on high standards for speakers.

Starting in May 1917 and running until six weeks after the Armistice, 38 different "campaigns," or speakers' themes, were developed, most running for two weeks, but some lasting only one day and several running for a full month.[80] The campaigns tied in closely with those of other government departments. For example, whenever the Treasury Department kicked off a major bond drive, the Four Minute Men delivered appropriate speeches in support. When food shortages loomed in Europe among the Allies, the Food Administration asked the Four Minute Men to commend food conservation to their listeners. There was an income tax campaign to sell the nation's workers on the purpose of the federal government's new assessment on their wages; "Eyes for the Navy" sought donations of quality binoculars, formerly a chief export of Germany; one talk thanked theater managers for their support. Some talks complemented themes in newly published CPI literature. When popular war campaigns such as "Why We Are Fighting," "What Our Enemy Really Is," and "Unmasking German Propaganda" were deemed opportune, and whenever supplementary historical information was needed for any Four Minute Men campaign, Guy Stanton Ford's creative historiographers came to the forefront.

These themes, plenty of background details, and sample speeches as guides for neophytes were communicated to speakers through the biweekly *Four Minute Men Bulletin*. Speakers were admonished constantly to stick to the topics given to them. "Extraneous comments" and personal viewpoints were to be avoided. Over and over again, the bulletins emphasized the four-minute time limit, for to exceed it meant jeopardizing the hospitality of the theater owner. Local chairmen were directed to check up on their speakers' deliveries and their messages, but particularly on their observance of the time limit. If a speaker should be interrupted by a question from the audience, he was advised to either ignore it or point out that he could not take the time then to answer questions. Speakers who exceeded their allotted time were to be struck from the rolls. An early issue of the *Bulletin* spelled out "What the Government Expects of the Four Minute Men":

> The Four Minute Men is a volunteer organization and is not conducted under military discipline. Nevertheless when anyone enrolls in this organization he assumes an obligation for the period of the war, and promises his Government the following service:
>
> 1. That he will read this bulletin on the purpose and plan of the Four Minute Men and all other communications from the national headquarters, and endeavor in so far as in him lies, to adopt the suggestions therein contained.
> 2. That he will read each *Four Minute Men Bulletin* as it is delivered to him, and immediately prepare a speech which in his opinion covers it in the most convincing way, adaptable to the audience to which he is assigned.
> 3. That whenever he is assigned as a Four Minute Man, and introduced by the Government slide, he will confine his remarks to Four Minutes only.
> 4. When speaking at schools, churches, and other general public gatherings, he will also maintain the Four Minute limit, unless specifically requested to speak longer.
> 5. That if local classes in the study of Four Minute speeches are established, he will cheerfully submit his efforts to criticism, and will willingly give of his experience for the benefit of others.
> 6. That he will accept whatever assignments his local chairman may give him.
> 7. That in case of sickness or inability to fill an assignment, he will immediately notify his local chairman that a substitute may be provided. He will in no case select his own substitute except with the permission and consent of the local chairman.
> 8. That he will attend all meetings of the local Four Minute Men and endeavor in every way possible within his power to increase his own personal efficiency as a spokesman for the United States Government.[81]

Bulletins not only told speakers what to say but helped them deliver their messages effectively. Punchy writing was used to illustrate the kind of pithy, no-nonsense speechmaking expected from their readers. As *Bulletin No. 11*, July 22, 1917, declared, "You should prepare at once for these speeches. Master thoroughly the above pamphlets. Go over carefully the material below. Select, compress, and drive home the things that your people need. Try to cover vigorously and effectively a few points, even one point. Don't try to cover all."[82]

The CPI also published the *Four Minute Men News*, similar in format to the *Bulletin*, and distributed it to the field force for motivation. Issues contained human-interest stories, photographs of speaker groups, and unusual activities of the far-flung member organizations. Six editions were published, starting in November 1917 and ending with an issue of 82 pages on

December 24, 1918. These two broadly distributed publications unquestion-ably helped build and maintain an esprit de corps among the dedicated volun-teers. The CPI files record that print runs were 110,000 copies each in the fall of 1918.

In the beginning, nearly all those who considered themselves brave enough to stand up in front of an audience were welcomed as Four Minute Men. It soon became apparent, however, that higher standards had to be imposed, and local chairmen were urged to screen applicants for their speaking skills, not merely their willingness to serve. One bulletin stated, "We cannot emphasize too strongly the necessity of enrolling good speakers only; a poor speaker is worse than none and lowers the standard of your organization." No attempt was made to strive for a representative cross section of the adult population as speakers; rather, the strategy was to enroll community leaders and men with above-average formal education, such as attorneys, physicians, and educators.

Big-city organizations could afford to be selective, and were. The secre-tary of a Chicago Four Minute Men organization reported in August 1917 that "things began to take a decided change. The Admissions Committee announced ... no one would be admitted to membership in the organization who did not have previous experience in public speaking ... and all new mem-bers would be required to appear before the Committee and demonstrate their ability to hold and interest an audience in a Four Minute Talk."[83]

The patriotic messages delivered by these well-organized speakers were a nightly feature in virtually every movie house across the nation throughout the war. Daily movie advertising often included not only the film attraction but also the name of that evening's speaker and his topic. Each speaker was gener-ally introduced by a standard slide, which he had given to the projectionist on his arrival at the theater; it carried his name (and, typically, George Creel's, as chairman of the CPI) and sometimes the subject of the speech. At an agreed-upon time, usually during a reel changeover, the slide would be shown on the screen, the houselights would be switched on, and the Four Minute Man would stride purposefully down a side aisle and on to the stage to deliver his perora-tion.

The confines of a theater, with its a captive audience, was the best pos-sible environment for a speaker delivering a brief talk. Furthermore, the lis-teners were often particularly receptive to a "live" patriotic message, having just rousingly cheered a celluloid American hero and hissed a celluloid Ger-man villain. Nearly all speakers were from the locale, and spoke with famil-iar accents and idioms, contributing to further rapport with their listeners. According to the CPI, the speaker had a right to assume that his audience was eagerly awaiting his message, and "as loyal Americans" were ready to respond to the needs of the nation so far as they were able. "He will never take the attitude that he is intruding upon an evening's pleasure at the theater and must beg their indulgence. He has a supreme right to be there and should feel this to the utmost."[84]

The Four Minute Men also spoke in churches and synagogues, schools, granges, concert halls, even on "soap boxes" at busy street corners. They spoke at town meetings, at picnics, and on trains. To reach labor groups, speakers went into factories, mills, mines, and logging camps. Four Minute Men gave speeches from "the running boards of Model T's" and in a tiny North Dakota town where the one church could not be used, "arrangements were made for a talk each week in the village pool hall."[85]

There were contests for Junior Four Minute Men, supporting Liberty Loans and the Red Cross. Secretary of the Treasury McAdoo exhorted on the front page of one leaflet for schoolchildren, "Let every girl do her part; let every boy do his part; and let every mother and father do their part; and the military despotism for which the Kaiser stands will be swept away by universal liberty and triumphant democracy!"[86] There was a Women's Division, whose speakers worked women's clubs and theater matinees, and a Junior Division targeted at elementary schools and high schools. Late in the war, the Four Minute Men were sent special slides from Washington for patriotic sing-alongs as complements to their regular speeches.

Wayne Alfred Nicholas's 1951 Ph.D. dissertation, "Crossroads Oratory: A Study of the Four Minute Men of World War I," is far and away the most thorough and well-written analysis of the subject. For part of it, Nicholas mailed a questionnaire to 400 former Four Minute Men. One of the questions asked recipients whether "it would be accurate to say that the Four Minute speeches were used for the purposes of propaganda?" So many years later, the respondees still recoiled from the pejorative word; it had been an article of faith that Americans never engaged in propaganda, only their enemies. Nicholas reported that

> most participants would not be ready to agree that the work of the Four Minute Men came under the heading of "propaganda." The speakers were not happy with the word. On one questionnaire it was crossed out and the word "truth" written in instead. Another speaker was willing to accept "proper propaganda" as a possible description. Another could in no wise tailor the term to make it fit; the program in which he had taken part was "absolutely not" propaganda—it was "pure patriotism by the interested and upright citizen."[87]

George Creel, in his "Complete Report," wrote that 755,190 speeches were given, with a total audience of 314,454,514. Then, backing away from such scientific precision, CPI's chairman added that "a very reasonable allowance for the considerable number of communities from which incomplete or no reports were received justifies an estimate of a final total of a million speeches heard by four hundred million individuals during the 18-month life of the organization."[88]

Newspaper and magazine advertising was another element of CPI's mul-
timedia communications program, and a separate Advertising Division was set
up in New York City, then, as today, America's advertising headquarters. The
principal "client" of this division was the Liberty Loans drives, but advertisements were also prepared for other agencies, such as the Red Cross, the U.S.
Shipping Board, the Fuel Administration, the Department of Agriculture, the
War Department, and the Y.M.C.A. Most of the advertisements were nonpolemical calls for action to a nation at war, such as "WANTED 3,000 Red-
Blooded Men" (for the Y.M.C.A.); "He *Must Not* Overstay His Leave! Save
trouble for him by keeping your eye on the clock" (aimed at wives and sweet-
hearts of servicemen); "Women of America—You, too, are Called to the
Colors" (U.S. Student Nurse Reserve); "The Greatest Mother in the World ...
holds a sacred place of honor within our homes and in our hearts" (Red Cross
Christmas Roll Call); "Write him cheerful letters. ... The *more hopefully* you
write, the *easier* for him—and the quicker he comes back"; "Our Casualty Lists:
Let's not get used to them—Let's STOP them—quickly!" (Fourth Liberty
Loan); "The Right Men in the Right Jobs Will Win The War" (U.S.
Employment Service); "More Shells—Fewer Casualties ... To learn to operate
your furnace efficiently, get from your local fuel administrator a leaflet entitled
'Save Coal in the Home.'" (United States Fuel Administration); "KILL EVERY
RAT" (U.S. Department of Agriculture).

By the fall of 1918, such moderate service-oriented advertisements had
given way to advertisements featuring German atrocities. Four advertisements,
in particular, used large, hideous illustrations of "rape and pillage" by German
soldiers, leaving little to the imagination. One, aimed at college students, had
the headline "Bachelor of Atrocities." It depicted Louvain burning in the background, a German soldier bayoneting someone on the ground, and a monacled,
grinning German officer dragging off a woman. Grimly looking out at the
reader was a likeness of General von Hindenburg, with mortarboard headgear
rather than his spiked *Pickelhaube*. If the illustration was grotesque, the copy
was worse:

> In the vicious guttural language of Kultur, the degree A.B. means Bachelor
> of Atrocities. Are you going to let the Prussian Python strike at your Alma
> Mater, as it struck at the University of Louvain? The Hohenzollern fang
> strikes at every element of decency and culture and taste that your college
> stands for. It leaves a track so terrible that only whispered fragments may be
> recounted. It has ripped all the world-old romance out of war, and reduced it
> to the dead, black depths of muck, and hate, and bitterness....

Someone should have known that pythons kill by crushing rather than with poisonous fangs, and who says war ever had "world-old romance"?

Far better as effective atrocity propaganda was "Remember Belgium,"
with its stark scene of Germany debauchery. Standing tall at half-page height,
with a rifle and bloodied bayonet in his left hand, was an ox-faced Uhlan,

holding tightly with his right hand a captive maiden in a flimsy white dress, her head bent over and her hair tousled. Everyone knew what was about to happen to her! In the background, other German soldiers were leaning forward, driving their bayonets into prostrate civilians.

Another vicious advertisement was "This is Kultur," with a somber-toned illustration focusing on a bare-breasted woman being wrestled to the ground by a German officer. Closely observing the action was another officer, with a bloody sword, and standing at attention on the right were rows of soldiers. In the foreground was an already-ravished maiden lying on the ground and in the background were two more young women being gruesomely manhandled.

> There is no sharper contrast between German Kultur and the civilization that our forefathers died for, than the difference in the attitude of the two civilizations toward women and children. Kultur in Belgium, and other devastated countries, is a tale so terrible that never yet has one dared more than whisper fragments of it. Yet the wrongs of Belgium, as a state outraged, pale besides the wrongs inflicted in savage, bestial revenge upon its defenseless women and children.

"That Monstrous Thing Called Kultur" was the most depraved and monstrous advertisement created by the CPI's Division of Advertising. Its half-page illustration showed two men already crucified on doors and a third being fastened down by gleeful German soldiers while an officer looked on approvingly. The hate-filled copy was in keeping with the demeanor of the illustration:

> You haven't believed. Because your mind is clean, because you have been surrounded from childhood by an atmosphere of uprightness, and decency, and kindliness, because you hate to see even a dumb brute suffer—you haven't believed.
>
> You have listened, with a doubting shrug, to the tales of German atrocities—doubting because these tales were so bestial, so revolting that to you they were unthinkable. But you, but we, must believe, because they are the truth.
>
> The official documents of England, of France and of Belgium confirm them—absolutely. More—the half, the worst half has never been told in this clean land of ours, has never been told because unprintable.
>
> There's a fester spot on this fair world—a spot that has spread from Berlin until it has poisoned all of Germany. And there's just one cure—the knife. The poison cannot be dammed up, it must be cut out else this monstrous thing called Kultur will fasten its hideous self on all the world....

Whether through indirect pressure or patriotic fervor, both advertisers and media donated considerable space to the CPI. At the end of the war, Creel compiled a list of so-called free advertising. It included 1,500 insertions in general magazines, 1,400 insertions in farm publications, 4,400 insertions in trade magazines, 650 insertions in newspapers, and 830 pages in house organs.[89]

Poster art also was a principal propaganda medium in the United States, as it was in all the belligerent countries. Through the CPI's Division of Pictorial Publicity, illustrators and painters made dramatic use of emotion-laden symbols—the American flag, Uncle Sam, the Statue of Liberty, the bald eagle (*American*, not German!), and glorious womanhood in virginal white—to market the war to the nation.

The poster designers echoed in their themes the same urgent calls to patriotism and loyalty used in other media: enlist in the U.S. Army, Navy, Marines, and Air Service; build more ships, mine more coal ("Consider the possible consequences if you are careless in your work"); buy Liberty Bonds and War Savings Stamps; support the Red Cross; give to the Y.M.C.A.; don't waste food ("Eat more fish—they feed themselves. Eat less wheat, meat, sugar and fats," "Can Vegetables, Fruit and the Kaiser too"); save light, save coal.

James Montgomery Flagg's stern Uncle Sam pointing his finger—"I WANT YOU"—was called "the most famous image to come out of World War I" in an exhibit of posters in the National Archives in February 1987. In fact, Flagg's creative effort in 1917 was a "Chinese copy" of British illustrator Alfred Leete's 1914 poster featuring Lord Kitchener's heavily mustachioed visage, index finger straight out, with the legend "YOUR COUNTRY NEEDS YOU."

America's artists also employed their talents to graphically depict Germans as subhuman, as rapers and pillagers, as wallowers in blood. Among the most vicious of these hate-filled posters was one titled "Destroy This Mad Brute," created by H.R. Hopps in 1916 (see frontispiece). The brute in question was a horrible caricature of a long-fanged, open-mouthed primate, replete with *Pickelhaube*, striding onto America's shores. Cradled in his left arm was a bare-breasted maiden; held in his bloody right hand was a club labeled KULTUR. Some versions of this poster included a subsidiary message overprinted in small type: "If this War is not fought to a finish in Europe, it will be on the soil of the United States."

"Rape and pillage" by the enemy, the two perpetual staples of the propagandist, were graphically depicted in "Remember Belgium" (Ellsworth Young, 1918). Silhouetted against orange flames of his own army's making, a thick German soldier was shown determinedly dragging behind him a young girl, to (the viewer was led to understand) a rendezvous far worse than death. "Beat Back the Hun" (Fred Strothman, 1918) used the colors available to the poster designer to good advantage. A green-eyed German soldier was depicted peering out cruelly, right hand grasping the barrel of his rifle, red blood dripping off its bayonet and from the fingers of both hands. Germans also strode in ankle-deep red blood, if the bloodied officer's boots illustrated in "Keep These Off the U.S.A." (John Norton, 1918) were believable representations.[90]

With America into the war, there was a burst of returnees from Europe. Whether they were U.S. diplomats or private citizens, nearly all were "eye-

witnesses" to German perfidy. They were welcomed at the docks not only by
their families, but, it is safe to assume, by patriotic and greedy book publishers
and ghostwriters, both freelancers and government employees.

The hottest property, unquestionably, was James W. Gerard, former
ambassador to Germany. He had been in Berlin since 1913 and had so much to
relate that it took two books to tell it all. He and his publisher hurried out *My
Four Years in Germany*, written, said its author, "because I believe that our people should be informed." Gerard awkwardly suggested that he was, "of course,
compelled to exercise a great discretion, to keep silent on many things of which
I would speak, to suspend many judgments and to hold for future disclosure
many things, the relation of which now would perhaps only serve to increase
bitterness or to cause internal dissension in our own land."[91]

Despite Gerard's professed reticence, the origin of the war was, nevertheless, clear to him: "It is because in the dark, cold Northern plains of Germany
there exists an autocracy, deceiving a great people, poisoning their minds from
one generation to another and preaching the virtue and necessity of war; and
until that autocracy is either wiped out or made powerless, there can be no
peace on earth."[92] As for a negotiated settlement of the conflict, Gerard was
unequivocal: "There must be no German peace. The old regime, left in control
of Germany, of Bulgaria, of Turkey, would seek only a favorable moment to
renew the war, to strive again for the mastery of the world."[93]

According to a news report in the *New York Times* on August 30, 1917,
Germany's chancellor, Theobold von Bethmann-Hollweg, had read the book
and claimed Gerard had misquoted him. He said that "when diplomats undertake to exploit their official career for journalistic purpose, they are very apt to
be misled into putting into the mouth of foreign statesmen utterances which
either are the creation of an ample imagination or are based on faulty memory.
Discussion of political opinions is bound to be transitory and fleeting." He also
compared America's "impetuous" diplomats with old-world Europe's more discreet ministers:

> You do not seem to permit even your retiring diplomats to observe the tra-
> ditional silences nor have you the patience to abide the post-mortem publica-
> tion of their memoirs. Sir Edward Goschen [former British ambassador to
> Germany] or Jules Cambon [former French ambassador to Germany] proba-
> bly could excel Mr. Gerard in revelations of entertaining history and gossip.
> Count von Bernstorff, ... too, I imagine might startle us with a diary of his
> Washington experiences. In Europe, publication of such matters was best
> postponed by common consent to a later period, when judgments are both
> calm and more mature. Mr. Gerard, however, may hold the special license
> conferred by "shirtsleeve" diplomacy ... and I shall not dispute his preroga-
> tives. But he must not give his imagination the free rein.

Despite containing a handful of ridiculously chauvinistic statements—
Gerard claimed that the heavy eating and drinking habits of Germans "had

made the people more aggressive and irritable and consequently readier for war"
and that German workers were "undoubtedly the most exploited in the
world"[94]—the former diplomat's first book was more an informative travelogue
than a useful piece of anti–German propaganda. Gerard—and his CPI advisors—did not make the same mistake twice. In the next book he put his name
on, *Face to Face with Kaiserism*, the mild and mannerly Dr. Jekyll became the
predatory Mr. Hyde. The book was as savage and sustained an indictment of
Germans and Germany as any made by a high American official during the
war. In such provocatively titled chapters as "When the Kaiser Thought We
Were Bluffing," "Germany's Plan to Attack America," "Home Life and
'Brutality' of the People," and "Kaiserism in America," the former ambassador
and his team of ghostwriters spewed forth streams of lies, nonsense, and exaggerations at their readers. Reflecting the frenzied efforts to put it together
quickly, the book ended with a hodgepodge of so-called diary entries, anecdo-
tal polemics, and warped history.

Who was responsible for the sinking of the *Lusitania?* Gerard answered:

> All evidence points to the Emperor himself as the responsible head who ...
> ordered or permitted this form of murder. ... When I saw the Kaiser in
> October, 1915, he said that he would not have sunk the *Lusitania*, that no gen-
> tleman would have killed so many women and children. Yet he never disap-
> proved the order. ... I have heard that in parts of Germany school children
> were given a holiday to celebrate the sinking of the *Lusitania*.[95]

Gerard said of course he did not believe all the atrocity stories, but noted
that while he was in Berlin "one of our servants ... came back from the East
front recently and said the orders were to kill all Cossacks. Our washerwoman
reports that her son was ordered to shoot a woman in Belgium and I myself
have heard an officer calmly describe the shooting of a seven-year-old Belgian
girl child."[96]

Gerard's historians dug back 300 years and more into European history to
establish a supposedly congenital German love for war and conquest. *Face to
Face with Kaiserism* observed:

> After the Thirty Years' War (1615 to 1645), German peasants were fre-
> quently bartered as slaves to the war-god, as the Hessians were sold by their
> ruler to the British in our War of the Revolution. The Germans were then the
> mercenaries of Europe, savages skilled in war, without mercy towards the
> towns unfortunate enough to be given to pillage. There is no more horrible
> event in all history than that of the sack of Rome by the German mercenaries
> in the year of 1527. ... The most awful outrages were perpetuated. Prelates
> were tortured. ... Altars were defiled, sacred images broken. ... In fact condi-
> tions in Belgium today had their counterparts centuries ago in the treatment
> of Roman Catholic Priests and the people of Rome.[97]

Incredibly, Gerard maintained that in Germany "military training is
always in view and the use of the knapsack on walking tours is universal, even

school children carry their books to school in knapsacks and so become accustomed, at an early age, to carry this part of the soldier's burden."⁹⁸

Hollywood converted *My Four Years in Germany* into a popular thriller of the same name, whose emphasis on alleged German brutality was closer to Gerard's second book. Scenes of German prison-camp atrocities in the movie, claimed by the producers to have come from captured German footage, actually had been staged by the director in New Jersey. The "chief merit" of the movie, according to a contemporary account in an industry journal, "is its authenticity. It reveals the German emperor and his advisors in their true light—a lot of ruthless savages, whose lust for conquest has made them lower than the beasts."⁹⁹ Gerard was a high-profile guest at the movie's New York premiere, promoting the movie as factually representing what he had observed first-hand.

In 1951, in *My First Eighty-Three Years in America*, Gerard appeared to have forgotten nothing—nor learned anything. His views of European history were still skewed by an earlier war's exigencies: "War is inbred in the German people. ... In 1913 everything in Germany was subordinated to preparation for war."¹⁰⁰ As for which nation started the war, Gerard still harbored no doubt. He recalled a conversation in the summer of 1914 with the kaiser, who had expressed his anger at the Social Democrats in the Reichstag for slighting him and confided to Gerard, "Pretty soon something will start that will fix those fellows." "Of course he meant the war, but I thought that he merely had in mind more repressive measures against the Social Democrats."¹⁰¹ Gerard also fondly remembered the motion-picture based on his first book as having been "a great success."¹⁰²

Another foreign diplomat who made a prompt literary contribution to America's wartime propaganda efforts was the former ambassador to Turkey, Henry Morgenthau. He put his name on a single book—not two, like Gerard, and had no accompanying motion picture. Like Gerard, Morgenthau protested that it had taken a herd of oxen, figuratively, to draw the true story from his discreet lips:

> By this time [October 1918] the American people have probably become convinced that the Germans deliberately planned the conquest of the world. Yet they hesitate to convict on circumstantial evidence and for this reason all eye witnesses to this, the greatest crime in modern history, should volunteer their testimony. I have therefore laid aside any scruples I had as to the propriety of disclosing to my fellow countrymen the facts which I learned while representing them in Turkey. I acquired this knowledge as the servant of the American people, and it is their property as much as it is mine.¹⁰³

Morgenthau's tale featured one of World War I's most carefully crafted lies, a lurid hoax whose political fallout far exceeded the wildest expectations of its author and its ghostwriter, Burton J. Hendrick, who was one of America's foremost Germanophobic journalists. Their joint creative effort was the famous legend of the Potsdam Crown Conference of July 5, 1914, a happening and a date that American and Allied propagandists would fix as the ultimate proof that Germany started World War I. The consequences were momentous. This war-planning conference that never took place was cited by the Commission on Reparations at the Paris peace conference, chaired by U.S. Commissioner Robert Lansing, as one justification for the infamous "sole war guilt" Article 231 of the treaty, which would prove to be among the most fecund seeds of World War II.

Morgenthau's career, as reflected in his 1922 autobiography, was a fast-track American success story. He was born in Germany, came to the United States in 1865 as a young boy, put himself through Columbia University Law School, and was admitted to the bar at the age of 21. He founded his own law firm in New York City and through shrewd real estate operations was wealthy by the turn of the century. In 1912, he was attracted to politics and, with his eye on the Treasury Department, decided to support Woodrow Wilson's candidacy for president. He pledged $20,000 to help launch the campaign, became chairman of the Democratic Finance Committee, and gave another $10,000, becoming one of the largest individual contributors. His reward when Wilson won the presidency was not the cabinet seat he sought, but rather the "Jewish" diplomatic post, a minor ambassadorship in faraway Turkey.

Morgenthau claimed that when Wilson offered him the post in Constantinople, he rejected it, as he had at first turned down the finance committee chairmanship. He said he told the president that "the Jews of this country have become very sensitive over the impression which had been created by successive Jewish appointments to Turkey, that that is the only diplomatic post to which a Jew can aspire."[104] Under pressure from Rabbi Stephen W. Wise, a leader of American Jewry, who pointed out that as Turkish ambassador, Morgenthau could be of great service to Jews in Palestine, Morgenthau finally accepted.

He arrived in the Turkish capital in November 1913 and left it in early 1916, "for a leave of absence," he recorded, "so that I might pay a visit to the United States, which I had not seen for more than two years. I had begun to feel the effects of the nervous strain of my labors to avert the terrible fate of the Armenians and Jews."[105] Perhaps Morgenthau yearned for New York City's lights, but more likely he still coveted the post of secretary of the treasury and saw an opportunity to enhance his chances by working for Wilson's reelection. He resigned his ambassadorship in April 1916 to devote himself more fully to the presidential campaign and, indirectly, to his personal quest.

Morgenthau wrote that the origins of his wartime book, *Ambassador Morganthau's Story*, were based on his contact with voters during the 1916 congressional elections, which convinced him that many citizens were still pacifists. Since he had inside information about Germany's premeditation of war, patriotically he was bound to "testify"—despite his hesitancy to disclose private information. He recorded that he then consulted the president. At the end of November 1917, Wilson responded that he thought Morgenthau's plan for a full disclosure of some of the principal lines of German propaganda was an excellent idea.

Morgenthau's "testimony" was based entirely on what he called his "private conversations" with Germany's ambassador to Turkey, Baron Hans von Wangenheim. In a chapter unambiguously titled "Wangenheim Tells the American Ambassador How the Kaiser Started the War," Morgenthau and Hendrick wove an intricate fable.

It was because Wangenheim "was sometimes led into indiscretions," especially when the German Army scored military successes in the summer of 1914, that Morgenthau learned certain facts which he thought would "always have great historical value." The German ambassador disclosed precisely how and when Germany had precipitated the war. According to Morgenthau's account, Wangenheim left for Germany shortly after the Sarajevo assassinations. The reason: the Kaiser had summoned his Turkish ambassador for an imperial conference on July 5. The Kaiser himself had presided at the high-level meeting and "nearly all the important ambassadors" were present.

"In telling me who attended this conference Wangenheim used no names," Morgenthau wrote, "though he specially said that among them were— the facts are so important that I quote his exact words in the German which he used—'die Haupter des Generalstabs und der Marine' (the heads of the general staff and of the navy)—by which I assumed that he meant Von Moltke and Von Tirpitz. The great bankers, railroad directors, and the captains of German industry, all of whom were as necessary to Germany's war preparations as the army itself, were there."[106] According to Wangenheim, the Kaiser had solemnly asked each man in turn,

> Are you ready for war? All replied "yes" except the financiers. They said that they must have two weeks to sell their foreign securities and make loans. At that time few people had looked upon the Sarajevo tragedy as something that would inevitably lead to war. This conference ... took all precautions that no such suspicion would be aroused. It decided to give the bankers time to re-adjust their finances for the coming war, and then the several members went quietly back to their work or started on vacations.[107]

Those skeptical of his account, said Morgenthau, should examine quotations on the New York Stock Exchange for the period July 5 to July 22. One would find, he said, "astonishing slumps in prices," especially those securities traded internationally. For example, Union Pacific dropped from 155½ per share to 127½, Baltimore and Ohio from 91½ to 81, and U.S. Steel down from 61 to 50½. Morgenthau said that financial analysts at the time had blamed the Simmons-Underwood tariff or the new Federal Reserve Act for the declines—but "how little the Wall Street brokers and the financial experts realized that an imperial conference ... was the real force that was then depressing the market!"[108]

Morgenthau, the attorney, and Hendrick, the journalist, concluded their intricate story of German war guilt in a homespun way:

> This indiscretion certainly had the effect of showing me who were really the guilty party in this monstrous crime. ... For my conclusions as to the responsibility are not based on suspicious belief or the study of circumstantial data. I do not have to reason or argue about the matter. I know. The conspiracy that has caused this greatest of human tragedies was hatched by the Kaiser and his imperial crew. ... One of the chief participants, flushed with his triumph at the apparent success of the plot, told me the details with his own mouth. Whenever I hear people arguing about the responsibility for this war or read the clumsy and lying excuses put forth by Germany, I simply recall the burly figure of Wangenheim puffing away at a huge black cigar, giving me his account of this historic meeting. Why waste any time discussing the matter after that?[109]

Why, indeed?—except that Wangenheim was never able to provide a rebuttal; he had died in August 1915. And, as Sidney Bradshaw Fay, the Harvard revisionist historian, wrote in 1930, in the second volume of his *Origins of the World War*, "the contemporary documents now available prove conclusively that there is hardly a word of truth in this whole narrative either as to (1) the persons present, (2) the Kaiser's attitude toward delay, and (3) the real reason for delay, or, finally, (4) the alleged selling of securities in anticipation of war."[110]

Morgenthau's list of officials attending the supposed meeting included "nearly all the important ambassadors," but, according to Fay's evidence, the following could not have attended: Lichnowsky, ambassador at London; Tschirschky, ambassador at Vienna; Schoen, ambassador at Paris; and Pourtales, ambassador at St. Petersburg. Military and business leaders who should have been, but were not, present included General von Moltke, chief of staff; General Waldersee, acting chief of staff; Grand Admiral von Tirpitz, head of the navy; Gustav Krupp von Bohlen-Halbach, head of the Krupp munitions works; and Albert Ballin, head of the Hamburg-Amerika Line. In fact, Wangenheim himself never saw the kaiser; he reported only to the Foreign Office.

As for the story that the Kaiser and his council had decided to delay the start of the war for two weeks, Fay pointed to the reputable Kautsky Documents as proof that the Kaiser "wished that, whatever action Austria took against Serbia, she should not delay. She should take it as quickly as possible, while the sentiment of Europe, shocked by the horrible crime at Sarajevo, was still in sympathy with the Hapsburgs and indignant at regicide Serbs."[111] Fay also demolished as "equally without foundation" the claim that Austria's two-week delay in sending her ultimatum to Serbia was because the financiers needed the time to sell their foreign securities and to make loans. Fay pointed out that the "real reasons for the delay came wholly from Vienna and not at all from Berlin" and were "repeatedly referred to in the German and Austrian documents which were published in 1919."[112]

Furthermore, an examination of the quotations of the New York stock market for the weeks in question did not show "much evidence, either in the price of stocks or the volume of sales, that large blocks of German holdings were being secretly unloaded and thereby depressing the New York market during those two weeks." As for the stocks mentioned by Morgenthau, Fay argued that they "declined only slightly or not at all; such declines as did take place were only such as were to be naturally expected from the general trend downward which had been taking place since January, or are quite satisfactorily explained by local American 'bearish' influences, like the publication of a very depressing report by the Interstate Commerce Commission."[113]

Fay summed up his findings thus:

> It is clear that the "Potsdam Council" was a myth. It is an interesting example of the way a legend will grow up, flourish, and receive the widest currency in an atmosphere of war propaganda and readiness to believe anything about an enemy....
>
> Is it not extraordinary that Baron Wangenheim should have given to Mr. Morgenthau so many picturesque details which are in flat contradiction with the facts? How could he have dared to make such an important revelation so prejudicial to the interests of his Government? Germany at this time, in the early weeks of the war, was trying hard to win the good-will of the United States and make the world believe she was fighting for self-defense in a war forced upon her. A statement such as Wangenheim's would have done Germany infinite damage.
>
> And is it not difficult to understand why the American Ambassador did not report to Washington what was perhaps the most important thing he ever heard at Constantinople? Yet a careful search through the files of the State Department at Washington shows that there is no dispatch or telegram recounting this interesting conversation with Baron Wangenheim; nor does Mr. Morgenthau in his book say anything about having made a report on the subject to Washington.[114]

Another returnee from overseas, an eyewitness of purportedly peerless credibility, was America's most experienced observer of U-boat warfare, Wesley Frost. From the lecture platform and through a popular book, "he exposed" the inhumanity of German U-boat commanders and their crews. What gave his harrowing presentations particularly dramatic impact was their close-up perspective, as if Frost himself were in a U-boat conning tower. More often, however, he playacted as if he were a survivor of a torpedoed Allied merchantman, tossing on a cold, unforgiving sea in a leaky lifeboat.

At the outbreak of war, Frost had been the American consul at Queenstown, County Cork in Ireland. This large port was close to the best U-boat hunting grounds—the Atlantic Ocean between Fastnet Rock lighthouse and the Scilly Islands, an area crowded with Allied shipping. As a result, the city became a clearinghouse for survivors of submarine attacks. Frost became a first-hand observer, interviewer, and collector of information from American survivors, both crew and passengers.

Once America was into the war, Frost was obviously more valuable as a propagandist back in the United States, where he was promptly requisitioned by the CPI. According to Frost, one of his first addresses, called "The Tragedy of the *Lusitania*," "became somewhat of an international classic on the subject and has since done wide service." An excerpt from this talk illustrates how Frost unfolded his creative tales to breathless audiences:

> It was quite black out there on the Atlantic, and in the blackness the life-boats alternately rose on the crests of the waves and sank back into the black valley between. The boats carried women and children whose hair hung in icicles over their shoulders and their half-frozen bodies yielded to the rolling and pitching of the frail boats. Now and then a half-dead passenger uttered a shriek of pain or anguish as she realized that a friend or relative had died in her arms. Meanwhile, in the dark hull of the German submarine, the captain watching through the periscope finally turned his head away. Even this man, agent of Prussian cruelty, had witnessed a scene upon which he did not care to gaze.[115]

Of more lasting propaganda worth than his talks was Frost's book, *German Submarine Warfare: A Study of Its Methods and Spirit*, which lent powerful credence to the myth of German cruelty on the high seas. His first chapter was devoted to the "gathering of evidence," creating the impression that its author was objective, even scientific in his compilation and reduction of data:

> The American passengers showed every shade of responsibility and irresponsibility. I take the liberty of dwelling upon this feature in order that the reader may be assured that proper discounting was made as to the reliability of each piece of testimony.
> The lady passengers, we found, made either very good or very poor witnesses.
> The newspaper men ... made the very best witnesses we had. ... The next class in responsibility was that of the business men. ... On the whole we were rather disappointed in the statements elicited from the professional men.
> The seamen, horse-tenders, and firemen who had some smattering of education or sophistication were eager and responsible; but their observations did not appear to be quite so trustworthy as those of the men who had always earned their livelihoods by stern physical labor.
> Especially did we learn to distrust the city boys....
> It is no disparagement of the negro race to say that negro seamen often seemed anxious principally to give whatever answers they thought might please us best.[116]

He wrote that early in the war, "to be quite fair," most submarines came to the surface and warned their "intended prey" with two or three purposely wide cannon shots. Later on, warning shots were more accurately aimed and

U-boat commanders began to set short time limits for abandoning ships. By 1917, according to Frost, "U-boat men were plunging deeper and deeper into inhumanity. Their so-called warnings had degenerated in the main into unremitting and vicious bombardments without cause or pity." Passenger ships were never simply torpedoed, they were cruelly "bushwhacked without forewarning."[117] He was at his best when "documenting" high-seas atrocities such as the raking of lifeboats by submarine gunfire and attacks on unarmed fishing boats.

Preposterously, Frost criticized the Germans for not having developed a method of warning their targets before they fired torpedoes:

> Devices for giving warning without exposing the submarine to counter-attack must be easily within the inventive capacity of the men who have perfected the modern German *Unterseeboot*. ... Smoke bombs could be used without emerging; or blank torpedoes, to strike with noise but not force. ... No stories have ever come out from Germany of inventors laboring to introduce humanizing devices for the submarine, either to give warning or otherwise. Would this have been true if America had been using submarines for three years?[118]

Concerning the conduct of U-boat officers and crew toward their victims, Frost wrote that their "demeanor ranges all the way from a maudlin and teary sympathy, through a shoddy brand of 'Made-in-Germany' courtesy, to bluster and bullying, and finally to cruelties which would seem to be silly and puerile phantasmagoria were they not so revolting and so fatal."[119]

Frost devoted a chapter to the desertion of lifeboats at sea, with further ludicrous suggestions for U-boat commanders. He wrote that "it would be manifestly easy for commanders of U-boats, without fracturing their duty, to keep slow steamers under surveillance for several hours during violent weather, so as to postpone the attack until the sea could give the victims at least a decent chance to get their boats away favorably. In many cases, too, when such a ship is sighted far out from the land the Germans might follow her for a day or two until she attained some proximity to the shore."[120]

Frost concluded his dutiful literary effort with a chapter devoted exclusively to the *Lusitania*. Drowned mothers and infants played a starring role in his patently exaggerated account: "Drowned bodies of women and children were numerous, and many had been mangled or disfigured in the surge and grinding of the wreckage so as to stain the ocean with blood. ... I saw five or six drowned women with drowned babies in their arms; and the corpse of one mother who had a dead infant clasped to each of the cold breasts which had so recently been their warm nestling-places."[121]

In fact, nearly everything Frost and his team of CPI writers wrote about U-boat atrocities was poppycock, if the statements of Rear Admiral William Sowden Sims, commander of U.S. naval forces in the European theater during World War I are to be believed. In 1923, Sims wrote that nearly all of the accounts of atrocities popularly attributed to German U-boat commanders were untrue. "Barring the case of the hospital ship Llandovery Castle," he declared, "I did not know of any case where a German submarine comman- der deliberately fired upon the boats of a torpedoed vessel; the commanding officer and two other officers of the submarine that torpedoed that vessel were tried in Germany after the war and punished; the submarine commanders gen- erally acted in a humane manner in carrying out the orders of their Government, in some instances giving the boats of torpedoed merchant vessels food and water and a tow toward land, and sending out wireless signals giving their position."[122]

Sims also wrote that of the thousands of merchant ships sunk by hundreds of U-boat commanders during the war, he understood that only 57 cases of alleged atrocities against 18 commanders were reported for trial by the Allies. He pointed out that "a number of these were acquitted." Sims summed up his argument by stating that "if the Allies could report but fifty-seven cases, this alone would appear to be conclusive evidence that there is no justification for the absurd belief, so universally held in America, that practically all the German submarine commanders were just devils in human form, capable of firing on defenseless men in open boats. As a matter of fact, this evidence shows that the vast majority were decent seamen."[123]

Five years before, few Americans had dared question the legitimacy of German atrocities, on land or on the sea. One exception was General John J. Pershing, who, in July 1918, firmly denied, based on his experiences, "that the Germans give poisoned candy to the children to eat and hand grenades for them to play with; that they show glee at the children's dying writhings and laugh aloud when the grenades explode; that they feed American prisoners tuberculosis germs."[124]

The CPI had its own division of films. It was initially set up to create short documentaries that would not compete with Hollywood's productions, but gradually these gave way to feature-length dramas mixing fact with fiction to take advantage of the propaganda opportunities inherent in movies.

The highlight of CPI's in-house film propaganda efforts was *Pershing's Crusaders*—"far and away the best compilation of war pictures exhibited here since the beginning of the European struggle," according to an ecstatic review in the *New York Times* on May 22, 1918. The film opened "before an audience which, in social and military distinction, surpassed any that ever assembled for moving pictures," and featured an intermission address by former ambas- sador Gerard and a concert by a 70-voice choir of "Four Minute Song Men" during reel changes. The picture began with a representation of "Germany's aggression"—a mailed fist rising from a map of Germany—and the cargo sub- marine *Deutschland* in Baltimore to show "the length of the German arm." The nation's preparedness was detailed, and then scenes of American doughboys in "front-line trenches" were shown, causing, according to the review, "one of the most pronounced thrills felt by the spectators." Finally, the theater audience "united in loud hissing when a pre-war picture of the Kaiser reviewing his troops was shown."

The CPI's output, nevertheless, was only a fraction of Hollywood's, and it was the private movie industry that must be credited with the most excessive movie wartime propaganda. With America finally into the war, Hollywood's directors and scriptwriters were no longer under pretexts of neutrality. Anything and everything German became fair game. If the newspapers carried shocking fables of German cruelty and depravity, the movies brought them to silent life, gaudily decking them out in coarse melodrama. The films were typically absurd fiction: sneaky German spies in closets and behind hedges, sadistic German soldiers coming ashore in America and attacking defenseless young women (who were then rescued by brave young American males).

Watered-down atrocity scenes were woven into many pictures. While baby-bayoneting was avoided, older children were fair game for rapacious German soldiers. In *For Liberty*, a German officer ruthlessly murdered an American boy. *Till I Come Back to You* showed Belgian children being herded across the Rhine to become slave laborers in German munitions factories.

There was also a splendid new villain for audiences to hiss at—the dastardly German emperor himself, a more popular blackguard than any yet discovered by Hollywood's talent scouts. His withered arm and lecherous countenance, exaggerated by makeup artists and actors alike, made him the perfect menace to the fairer sex. As a movie subtitle described one action, "we all knew his weakness for soft white hands and we shuddered."[125] Michael T. Isenberg, in his 1981 study *War on Film*, observed,

> Most of the films of the war period endorsed the axiom that the wearer of the German uniform was invariably a drunk, a looter, or a rapist, following the cue of his emperor. ... The most scurrilous films about Germans depicted them as lusty barbarians issuing from the depths of the primeval forest. If looting, killing, and mindless destruction was their business, rape was their sport. ... With their emperor leading the way, the German army spent as much time molesting women as it did in razing Europe.[126]

Hollywood took full advantage of their biggest wartime box-office attraction with one "Kaiser" movie after another. *To Hell with the Kaiser* told of the experiences of an American flyer, carrying America's war plans, who somehow arrived in Berlin and was captured by the enemy. The movie hero was forced to turn over his secret packet, and when the Kaiser opened it, instead of a treasure trove of military secrets, a big American flag popped out. Intrepid American aviators then captured the Kaiser, took him behind American lines, and forced him to salute General Pershing. Also featured was the caricatured German crown prince, always depicted with a shrunken chin, who tried to put his hands on a young American woman; she righteously shot him dead. At the end, the audience cheered lustily as the Kaiser was driven into a smoky, flaming hell.

The most brutal of all the Kaiser movies was *The Kaiser, the Beast of Berlin*, depicting a life-and-death struggle between the forces of good and evil and filled with as many of the atrocities claimed in the Bryce Report as were acceptable on the screen. At the end, while the Allies were noisily celebrating final victory, the defeated Kaiser was remanded to the custody of King Albert of Belgium. While a reviewer in the July 1, 1918, *New York Times* suggested that the film "seems a travesty of war and America's serious purpose in it," *Moving Picture World* clucked, "The scenes are said to be historically accurate and picture a strong, dramatic series of events in a commendable way."[127]

Having thus indelibly marked the Kaiser as both war fomenter and archvillain, Hollywood moved on to justice—and punishment. *The Kaiser's Finish* told the tale of an illegitimate son of the Kaiser who had been brought up as an upstanding American. The youth then returned to Germany as an American spy and killed both his father and half-brother. The scriptwriters for *America Must Conquer* showed more compassion, if not more sense: all the German leaders were given a choice between execution and sterilization.

As far as the moviemakers were concerned, no one in the country with a German name was to be trusted, and one movie after another "exposed" the traitorous conduct of the German-American turned enemy agent. There was a 20-episode pseudo-real serial, *The Eagle's Eye*, written by no less an authority than former Secret Service chief William J. Flynn, who had traded his low-paying government job for a fat Hollywood contract. It detailed every evil act conceivably performed by Germans and their government. The movie featured grotesque likenesses of all the important German "spies"—Johann von Bernstorff, Heinrich F. Albert, Franz von Papen, and Karl Boy-Ed, among others—and suggested that the Kaiser was personally involved in every nefarious activity of every double-dealing agent.

Me und Gott told the story of a former Prussian army officer who had emigrated to America and ended up as the owner of a delicatessen in Hoboken, New Jersey. He insisted that his son help him blow up munitions plants. But the young man, a pacifist turned patriot, fought off his father, and all ended well for the son and the United States. The plot of son-versus-father was popular; *The Hun Within* reversed the roles, the son becoming the German spy.

Why America Will Win was an early example of the fictional "docudrama," blending hokum with fact. It told the story of General Pershing's life, preposterously relating that the fire in California in 1915 that actually took the lives of his family had been set by German spies. After winning the war, Pershing was shown entering Berlin in triumph under lines of crossed swords held by U.S. troops. Pershing then lectured the Kaiser, with long subtitles, about how to make the world safe for democracy. In the film's final sequences, Berlin was destroyed, the Kaiser killed by a bolt of lightning, and the crown prince shot to death.

By 1917, beauteous womanhood had become a staple of Hollywood, and Mary Pickford, the brightest star of all, did her best to win the war all by herself in two famous movies, *The Little American* and *Johanna Enlists*. The first gave a broad panorama of the war—the sinking of the *Lusitania*, the German invasion of America, and "Huns" lusting after Red Cross nurses. The hero was a noble German officer who renounced his country and the Kaiser for the heroine's love. The second was more in the Hollywood tradition, with a regiment of American soldiers encamped behind the heroine's farm. According to the formula, all of the soldiers fell sweetly in love with the farmer's daughter.

When one of the handsome officers became ill, heroine Pickford nursed him back to health.

Western-movie heroes Bill Hart and Tom Mix also did their bit. Hart directed and played the lead role in *The Border Wireless*, fighting German spies where few would expect them to be. After plenty of galloping over hills and across fields, and close-ups of determined faces to satisfy aficionados of Westerns, the hero captured a pro–German and forced him to kiss the flag—certain to draw huzzahs from audiences. At the fade-out, Hart, in a U.S. Army uniform, was off to Berlin. In *Mr. Logan, U.S.A.*, cowboy Mix exchanged his chaps for ordinary pants and became a U.S. Secret Service Agent who discovered an enemy plot to blow up an important mine needed for the war effort.

Some of Hollywood's contributions to America's war effort nevertheless covered positive themes for a nation at war. *The Road to France* focused on two young ne'er-do-wells brought to manhood by hard work in a shipyard (the patriotic phrase of the day being "a bridge of ships is the road to France"). There were movies on food conservation (*Little Miss Hoover*), and on the Y.M.C.A. and the fine times U.S. doughboys were having "over there" (*Too Fat to Fight*). Warnings to draft dodgers were found in *Claws of the Hun, Her Boy, The Slacker*, and *Draft 258*."[120]

The only wartime film that critics considered had any claim to artistic or dramatic merit was D.W. Griffith's *Hearts of the World*. With the release of his famous *The Birth of a Nation* in 1914 and his epic *Intolerance* in 1916, Griffith was acknowledged worldwide as the cinema's leading director. In 1916, the British War Office Cinematograph Committee enlisted Griffith's services, suggesting he was the only director able adequately to present the Great War on the screen. What the British wanted from Griffith was a propaganda film that would help draw America into the war. According to a pre-opening review, the film was

18 months in the making and many of the scenes were taken on the actual battlefields of France by Griffith, with the official aid and assistance of the British and French Governments. Griffith however, desires to remove any apprehensions that Hearts of the World is primarily a war picture. It is, he announces, primarily a love story ... and for more than 40 minutes during the exposition of the story, there is not a cannon shot, not a suggestion of war's alarm. ... The battle-scenes shown were taken in the trenches during the death struggles of the French and the Germans. ... One sees life in the trenches; charges of the French soldiers; thrilling hand-to-hand conflicts and the thrusts of the bayonets; the great guns in action; the tanks; the attack by liquid fire; the charges and the retreats; the German pill-boxes; flight of the villagers; ruthless destruction of property; the treatment of young girls who fall into the hands of the Germans; the whole culminating in the arrival of the American troops, victory and a hint of future happiness.[129]

While a huge success both creatively and financially, *Hearts of the World* was released just before the Armistice, making it superfluous as war propaganda. After the war, Lillian Gish, the movie's leading lady, said, "I do not believe that Mr. Griffith ever forgave himself for making *Hearts of the World*. 'War is the villain,' he repeated, 'not any particular people.'"[130]

Another movie that stood out, but for a far different reason, was *The Spirit of '76*. Its producer, Robert Goldstein, had been a well-known associate of Griffith's during the filming of *The Birth of a Nation*. Goldstein was indicted and tried under the Espionage Act for a single scene from his film that showed British soldiers bayoneting women and children and dragging off girls. Goldstein, government prosecutors contended, had presented a film that was intended to arouse hatred and distrust between the American people, in particular their armed forces, and the British, at a time when the two countries were allies. The motion picture was seized, the production company thrown into bankruptcy, and Goldstein sentenced to ten years in a federal penitentiary (the sentence was commuted after the war to three years).

Even in Hollywood, the war was rarely a subject of mirth. But the medium's master comedian, Charlie Chaplin, managed not only to find humor in the subject but to transcend the mediocrity of the vast majority of war movies.

Of all this mess of absurdity, nationalistic hatred and bad acting, but a single picture seems destined to be remembered, Charlie Chaplin's comedy *Shoulder Arms*. In outline *Shoulder Arms* was pretty much like all the other war films. In a dream Charlie "captured the Kaiser" according to the formula of the day, and marched him behind American lines, but the whole thing was magnificently comic. His villains were too absurd and his own adventures too fantastic to mean much as propaganda[131]

Far more malevolent a censor than Creel was Postmaster General Albert Sydney Burleson. One historian has described Burleson as "narrow, intolerant, so self-consciously pompous that Wilson called him 'the Cardinal.' A

Texan, a follower of William Jennings Bryan, a protector of small business-men and farmers, Burleson hated, as only a certain species of white Southern Populists could, all of his fellow citizens who did not fall into one of those categories."[132]

On June 15, 1917, the Congress gave Burleson the weapon he needed in his vendetta against those he perceived to be radicals, pacifists, and "hyphenates"—troublemakers in America's virtuous quest to build a new world order—the Espionage Act (40 Stat. 451). Under the new law,

> Whoever, when the United States is at war, shall willfully make or convey false reports or false statements with intent to interfere with the operation or success of the military or naval forces of the United States or to promote the success of its enemies and whoever, when the United States is at war, shall willfully cause or attempt to cause insubordination, disloyalty, mutiny, or refusal of duty, in the military or naval forces of the United States, or shall willfully obstruct the recruiting or enlistment service of the United States, shall be punished by a fine of not more than $10,000 or imprisonment for not more than twenty years, or both.[133]

Only once before in the nation's history had the Congress dared enact such a restrictive law. That law was the 1798 Alien and Sedition Act, which gave the president the power to deport aliens he considered dangerous to the nation's "peace and safety" or who were suspected of committing "treasonable activities" against the government. "False, scandalous, and malicious writings" directed at the chief executive or the Congress were also subject to punishment under that act. Opponents had bitterly attacked the law as contrary to constitutional guar-antees of freedom of the press, and Thomas Jefferson questioned its constitu-tionality. When Jefferson took office as president in 1801, he pardoned all those imprisoned by the act and the Congress eventually repaid all fines. The 1917 law, reflecting a growing national phobia against "enemies from within," was far harsher, yet a unanimous decision of the Supreme Court in 1919 upheld the Espionage Act as constitutional.

On the day after the Congress passed the Espionage Act, Burleson sent a secret note to all postmasters, instructing them to maintain a "close watch on unsealed matter, newspapers, etc. containing matter which is calculated ... to cause insubordination, disloyalty, mutiny, or refusal of duty in the military or naval service ... or otherwise to embarrass or hamper the Government in conducting the war." He ordered that such material be forwarded to his office.[134]

Increasingly restrictive federal legislation followed. On October 6, 1917, the Congress passed the Trading-with-the-Enemy Act, which authorized censorship of messages between the United States and foreign countries. A section of this act gave the federal government a whip hand to control all of the foreign-language press in the country. No foreign-language newspaper or magazine containing any material "respecting the government of the United

States or of any nation engaged in the present war, its policies, the state or conduct of the war, or any matter relating thereto" could be mailed unless a sworn translation had been filed with the postmaster.

Using as a subterfuge several gruesome examples of mob violence against agitators and the nonpatriotic, the Senate Judiciary Committee on May 16, 1918, amended the Espionage Act by adding nine new offenses. It became known as the Sedition Act, and prohibited

> disloyal, profane, scurrilous, or abusive language about the form of govern-
> ment of the United States, or the Constitution of the United States, or the
> military or naval forces of the United States, or the uniform of the army or
> navy of the United States, or any language intended to bring the form of gov-
> ernment of the United States, or the Constitution of the United States, or the
> flag of the United States, or the uniform of the army or navy of the United
> States into contempt, scorn, contumely, or disrepute.

These amendments also gave the postmaster general extraordinary powers of censorship, allowing him, upon "satisfactory evidence," to return mail to those he personally deemed violators of the law. Publications which were nonmail-able were effectively put out of business. Burleson's cup of vitriol and intoler-ance had run over.

Burleson wielded his power of censorship capriciously and ruthlessly. He cracked down on radical publications, although he "didn't know socialism from rheumatism," according to the prominent socialist Norman Thomas.[135] He cut off mailing privileges from a single issue of *The Masses* because it con-tained what he considered to be antigovernment cartoons and editorial mate-rial, and then refused to reinstate the publication's second-class mailing per-mit because it had missed an issue and was thus not a bona fide periodical. A generation later, historian Zechariah Chafee, Jr., ridiculed the Burleson cen-sorship thus:

> Let us see now what Mr. Burleson has considered to violate the Espionage
> Act. By no means did he limit himself to pro–German and pacifist articles
> and books. ... He suppressed an issue of the *Public* for urging that more
> money be raised by taxes and less by loans. He suppressed Lenine's *Soviets
> at Work*, a purely economic pamphlet, although we were not at war with
> Russia. He censored any adverse comments on the affairs of the British
> Empire ... the *Freeman's Journal and Catholic Register* for reprinting Jeffer-
> son's opinion that Ireland should be a republic ... the *Irish World* for express-
> ing the expectation that Palestine would not be a Jewish kingdom, but on
> the same footing as Egypt. ... And finally, Thorstein Veblen's *Imperial Ger-
> many and the Industrial Revolution*, which was published in 1915, was rec-
> ommended by Mr. Creel's Committee on Public Information as containing
> damaging data about Germany, and then excluded by Mr. Burleson from the
> mails.[136]

Woodrow Wilson let his postmaster general operate with a free rein. In the fall of 1917, the president meekly asked Burleson if he did not agree "that we must act with the utmost caution and liberality in all our censorship."[137] A week later, Wilson prefaced an inquiry about suppression of the socialist *Milwaukee Leader* by writing, "I am afraid you will be shocked, but I must say that I do not find this hearing very convincing."[138] When Wilson received angry protests concerning Burleson's brazen action against *The Masses* and suggested moderation, the postmaster general threatened to resign. Only in one instance, late in the war, did Wilson overrule a Burleson decision. That was when the postmaster general had cut off mailing privileges to the liberal *Nation* because of its criticism of the reactionary labor leader Samuel Gompers.

Burleson maintained his choke hold on the nation's press for two and a half years after the Armistice, although Wilson had formally ended censorship on November 27, 1918. Like most Americans, the postmaster general smoothly made the transition from hatred of Germans, the former enemy, to hatred of Bolsheviks, the new enemy. Socialist and radical newspapers which had been banned from the mails during the war petitioned him to have their mailing privileges restored, to no avail. Burleson won a final victory three days after the inauguration of Warren Harding on March 21, 1921, when the Supreme Court ruled in the case of the banned *Milwaukee Leader* that a publication losing its second-class mailing privileges for violating the law had no legal grounds for restoration of such privileges.

Years later George Creel tried to disassociate himself from the punitive actions of the Post Office Department under Burleson. In 1939, he lamely insisted that he had strongly opposed such policies. He claimed that he had been "disgusted" with Burleson's use of his censorship power "only against little radical papers," and once protested to the president "that Mr. Burleson's one and only purpose was to crush every liberal voice." Creel related that after Burleson learned of his views, the two men did not speak to each other for the rest of the war.[139]

Another cabinet officer who shared Burleson's reactionary views, and was in a position to implement them, was Attorney General Thomas W. Gregory, a former antitrust lawyer from Texas and a protégé of House's. Gregory had been appointed in 1915 to replace James C. McReynolds when he was elevated to the Supreme Court.

Gregory at first had been opposed to surveillance of German aliens, but had promptly come around to the popular view that large numbers of German-Americans, citizens and noncitizens alike, posed security risks to the nation. To watch over these dangerous minions of an evil foreign power, Gregory integrated into his department an organization of volunteer vigilantes unique in the nation's history, the American Protective League (APL).

The APL was organized in March 1917 by a Chicago advertising executive who had proposed the novel idea to A. Bruce Bielaski, head of the Justice Department's Bureau of Investigation. According to a principal apologist for the organization, right-wing journalist French Strother, the APL had two main functions: "to make prompt and reliable report of all disloyal or enemy activities and of all infractions or evasions of the war code of the United States" and "to make prompt and thorough investigation of all matters of similar nature referred to it by the Department of Justice." In so doing, the league, according to Strother, "far from running wild in its enthusiasm to corral all enemy agents, tried to give every alien it investigated an American square deal."[140]

The APL caught on fast. Strother wrote enthusiastically that by May 1917 "there were a thousand men engaged in the absorbing new game. Thousands of investigations taxed the young ardour and endurance of the League—suspected spy activities, seditious speeches, lying reports about the Red Cross, Y.M.C.A., and Knights of Columbus, pro–German propaganda, suspected treasonable conspiracies, sabotage cases and, later, organized and individual efforts to evade the draft."[141] And in August, Gregory reported that "he had several hundred thousand private citizens—some as individuals, most of them as members of patriotic bodies, engaged in ... assisting the heavily overworked Federal authorities in keeping an eye on disloyal individuals and making reports of disloyal utterances."[142]

In the view of many others, however, the American Protective League routinely violated the civil rights of tens of thousands of Americans, contemptuously mocking fundamental American democratic principles. Historian David M. Kennedy summarized the wartime activities of the League as constituting, in fact,

> a rambunctious, unruly *posse comtatus* on an unprecedented national scale. Its "agents" bugged, burglarized, slandered, and illegally arrested other Americans. They opened mail, intercepted telegrams, served as agents provocateurs, and were the chief commandos in a series of extralegal and often violent "slacker raids" against supposed draft evaders in 1918. They always operated behind a cloak of stealth and deception, frequently promoting reactionary social and economic views under the guise of patriotism. The League sometimes counseled its members to commit outright physical assault on dissenters.[143]

The APL's amateur sleuths swore their loyalty, were given certificates attesting to their membership, and went out "into the field" armed with badges proclaiming the official nature of their work. Organized in a hierarchy of inspectors, captains, lieutenants, and ordinary operatives, they were inspired in their patriotic efforts by official communications with all the trappings of authority: a handbook, law digests, regular bulletins, even special report forms.

Members of the APL spied on their coworkers and neighbors but focused their attention mainly on "suspicious" individuals, those with German or German-sounding names, especially "suspicious travelers." Such strangers to the community were carefully shadowed, in detective-story fashion, and notes were taken concerning whom they had met and talked with. "Only when in a private house or in a hotel room would they escape observation. ... A record would be made of every telephone call, every telegram, every letter received, with particular reference to the postmark, dates, and the return cards on the envelopes. Their baggage would be inventoried and described, even to its hotel labels, its character, and its probable price and origin."[144]

The civilian spy hunters never managed to catch a single genuine German spy, but nevertheless kept busy. When their lists of enemy aliens dwindled, they turned their scrutiny to those suspected of sedition and disloyalty. Alleged draft dodgers, "slackers," and military deserters were also prime targets. There were scarcely any prospective intrigues that escaped the APL, as the following categories from the organization's master file in Washington showed:

> Unfriendly neutrals, disloyal government employees, pro–German applicants for government positions, citizens or aliens living in luxury without visible sources of income, alien extortion cases, I.W.W. agitators, check of jury panels to keep out pro–Germans, incendiary fires in war material plants, wireless stations, seditious utterances, seditious publications, seditious meetings, organizations to resist draft, attempted draft evasions, desertion of wife to enlist in army, impersonation of officers, sale of liquor to soldiers and sailors, hoarding of food, character and loyalty of applicants for commissions.[145]

George Creel never again approached the pinnacle of power he had enjoyed for nearly two years as propaganda czar during World War I.[146] In fact, before he returned to postwar political writing and "consulting" to make a living, he signed on with two get-rich-quick schemes. The first was as president of a sleazy, Manhattan-based mail-order business, the Pelman Institute of America, which sold a proprietary self-improvement program called "Pelmanism." One company advertisement ballyhooed the home-study course as "neither an experiment nor a theory." It claimed it "teaches people how to think; how to use fully the powers of which they are conscious; how to discover and to train the power of which they have been unconscious." Rapid and large salary increases, "from 20 to 200 per cent," could be expected, according to the same advertisement.

The second of Creel's schemes was "to make a stack of money" in the oil business, as he lightheartedly testified in 1924 before a Senate panel investigating what came to be called the Teapot Dome oil scandal. Creel admitted that in November 1919 he had accepted a check for $5,000 to convince his old friend, Secretary of the Navy Josephus Daniels, to lease two government-owned oil fields to private oil interests. Creel said that the extent of his "influence" was to arrange a meeting for his client with Daniels, but Daniels refused to open up the Navy oil reserves to private development. The government had more prominent influence peddlers to investigate, and no further action was taken against Creel.

During the Franklin D. Roosevelt administration, Creel maintained close ties to the Democratic party and was rewarded from time to time with New Deal patronage for his loyalty. The high point of this stage in his career was his run for the Democratic candidacy for the governorship of California in 1934; he actively sought, but never got, Roosevelt's support. Ironically, he was defeated by the muckraking ex-socialist Upton Sinclair.

With America at war again in 1941, Creel went to Washington to offer his expertise to the nation's new propaganda agency, the Office of War Information (OWI). But Roosevelt apparently had passed the word along that he did not want any more of Creel's type of propaganda work, which he had apparently deplored as navy undersecretary during the past war, and Creel was shunted aside.

In an August 1942 letter to OWI's head, Elmer Davis, the avuncular-sounding Creel advised that "divided authority and unrestrained competition," such as existed in the organization that Davis had recently taken over, was a serious problem. "I am more sorry than I can say that your control over Army, Navy, and State is not real in any sense of the word," he wrote. The success of the CPI was "due to the fact that neither the Army or the Navy had the right to sit in arbitrary judgment on what should or should not be printed." When these agencies disputed his authority, Creel wrote, he won out because "Woodrow Wilson hammered them down. 'Coordination by conference' never worked and never will work." He concluded, "Just one last word, dear Elmer. In your letter I seemed to perceive a tendency to make the best of things as you have found them. Such a course is possible when things are fairly good, but when things are downright bad, nothing is more fatal than an amiable effort to make the best of them. ... All the luck in the world, old boy, but remember, amiability can be a vice."[147]

As late as 1944, Creel's views regarding Imperial Germany's guilt remained unchanged. In another of his trashy books, *War Criminals and Punishment*, Creel wrote,

> The United Nations, individually and collectively, have given repeated pledges that Axis terrorists will be made to answer for their crimes against the laws of God and man. Even so, it is well to remember that similar promises, declared by the Allies and Associated Governments when the Kaiser's hordes ravaged Europe, were dishonored and unkept ... the merciless brutes of that other day were shown mercy out of a preposterous assumption that demands for punishment necessarily proceeded from the baser emotions.[148]

Creel's extensive correspondence, magazine articles, and books of the period clearly show his fervent anti–Communist stance. He tried to create a coalition of right-wing elements of the both parties and, when unsuccessful, turned to the ultraconservative wing of the Republican Party. He was sought out as a quasi advisor by Richard Nixon and Joseph McCarthy, in the early 1950s, and reluctantly supported Dwight D. Eisenhower for president in 1952. He died in October 1953, active up to his last weeks in far-right political schemes.

The last chapter in the World War I propaganda war in the United States opened on November 19, 1918, in Washington, a week after the Armistice, when a U.S. Senate Judiciary Subcommittee heard its first testimony during hearings chaired by Senator Lee Slater Overman. What would be only the first phase of the hearings was called "Brewing and Liquor Interests and German Propaganda." A week later, one of the Senators said that he doubted that the investigations would result in "any considerable number of prosecutions" but that they were intended principally to "disclose to the public the identity of a large number of persons who, until a comparatively recent date, were active in this country in behalf of the Kaiser and his allies. In other words, we are going to disclose to the people a new 'Who's Who' in German propaganda."[149]

In fact, no prosecutions resulted from the investigations—but, as promised, there were plenty of names, many already infamous from prior sensational press coverage. There were the familiar German "conspirators"—von Bernstorff, Dernburg, von Papen, Boy-Ed, Albert, Fuehr—and their American "henchmen"—Viereck, Hale, Fox, Archibald, Burgess, Muensterberg, von Mach, O'Leary, Hearst. New names were dug out from private correspondence of the proven perpetrators; the process was "guilt by association" honed to a fine edge. In late January 1919, to publicize its successes in exposing dangerous Americans in high places, the committee released the names of 62 so-called pacifists and radicals, among whom were many prominent liberals. Paul U. Kellogg, editor of *The Survey*, wrote sarcastically,

> I find Socialists listed of the same point of view as those who have just overthrown the Kaiser. I find Quakers who represent the far extreme from Prussianism, and to confuse the two is like saying the equator runs through the north pole ... I find people who were actively for the war before we went into it, who have been unreservedly for it since, but in a struggle against Prussianism abroad kept faith with liberty at home and stood out for freedom of the press and speech. To class them as pacifists is like classing the torpedo boat destroyers with a Staten Island ferry. As a whole, the list is about as intelligent as it would be to take Brigham Young, Cardinal Gibbons, Robert G. Ingersoll and Billy Sunday and lump them together as advocates of religion. There is only one type of mind that could commit that blunder, and that is the mind of the extreme reactionary who divines that this was a war for democracy and is afraid that democracy will come out of it.[150]

The committee was mainly concerned with American brewers, nearly all of whom were of German origin. It attempted to establish how, through their wealth and influence, they had supported the seditious goals of German propagandists in the United States. Testimony from key officials of the United States Brewers' Association and the National Wholesale Liquor Dealers' Association confirmed that both organizations' main preoccupation had been to lobby against prohibition, and, in so doing, had funded the National German-American Alliance which had an anti-prohibition plank in its program. Naturally, like other trade groups, the brewers gave financial backing to politicians who supported their business goals. Too, the brewers and liquor makers were big advertisers and hence, like other large businesses, exerted a powerful, if discreet, influence over the editorial policies of the newspapers and magazines in which they advertised. From such skimpy evidence, the committee concluded that the brewers "furnished large sums of money for the purpose of secretly controlling newspapers and periodicals"; that they "frequently succeeded in controlling primaries, elections, and political organizations"; and that their contributions of "enormous sums of money to political campaigns" violated federal statutes.[151]

Much was made of German plans to buy American newspapers while the United States was still neutral, as if foreign control of newspapers was somehow an unclean practice. A witness who had worked with Bernhard Dernburg in his attempt to buy the *Washington Post* was asked by Senator Overman, "You knew he was an agent of the German Government, did you not?" The witness's reply put the matter in its proper perspective. "No, I did not know he was an agent," the witness said. "I knew that he was—this was in 1915—a man of considerable prominence, known all over the world; and he came over here and was received everywhere. ... At that time nobody had even the slightest suspicion that this country was going to get into any war at all. We were neutral, and, from what I know about continental newspapers and customs, I know that every country always has a media in which it expresses its own interests."[152]

The hearings inadvertently unearthed a dark side of American activities before America went into the war, clearly discomforting several of the investigators.

> MR. [GASTON B.] MEANS [a private detective formerly in the employ of the German propagandists]: Now, shall I tell you about the tapping of the telephones in New York City; how the telephones were tapped, etc., and by whom?
>
> SENATOR OVERMAN: By the Germans, you mean?
>
> MR. MEANS: No; I am not talking about the Germans. They were tapped by Mr. Bielaski, through the police commissioner, Arthur Woods, and his second deputy, Frank A. Lord.
>
> SENATOR OVERMAN: No; we do not care to know about that, unless Germans had something to do with it.
>
> MR. MEANS: They were tapping the German wires. We knew about that.

SENATOR [JOSIAH O.] WOLCOTT: I do not think we are interested in that—United States Government activities.

MR. MEANS: They tapped all the wires—

SENATOR WOLCOTT: Never mind; we do not care anything about what the United States Government did in the way of tapping wires.[153]

Inadvertently, too, the testimony punctured several of the myths of all-pervasive sedition and sabotage by German agents.

SENATOR [KNUTE] NELSON: Was there not an attempt to get up a strike among the longshoreman?

MR. [A. BRUCE] BIELASKI [chief of the Bureau of Investigation]: Yes, sir.

SENATOR NELSON: At Hoboken and New York Harbor?

MR. BIELASKI: Yes, sir, there was, but the proof as to the direction and financing of that by the Germans was never absolutely clear, although we have no doubt that morally they were responsible for it.[154]

SENATOR NELSON: Do you know anything about strikes or bomb plots in factories and munitions plants?

MR. BIELASKI: No; very little, if anything. During the period of our neutrality I do not think there were any cases developed for criminal prosecution.[155]

SENATOR OVERMAN: Was there any evidence of any efforts to injure our airplanes in the process of manufacture?

MR. BIELASKI: Of course, before the war I think our airplanes were rather scarce, Senator. There were some attempts to injure them after the war started, and there have been some indictments under the sabotage act; but it is not fair to charge those things up against the German Government, because there was no proof of anything of that kind, and it is much more likely they were the individual acts of either careless or ill-disposed workers.[156]

There was also "eyewitness" atrocity testimony two months after the end of the war. Grant Squires, an officer in U.S. Military Intelligence who had been a relief worker in Belgium, had been called in to counter Edmund von Mach's responses to the Senate panel concerning the truth of German atrocities. Von Mach, one of the leading German-American propagandists, had angered his inquisitors by suggesting that the treatment of Belgians by Germans had been no worse than General William Tecumseh Sherman's treatment of southern civilians in his march to the sea or by the U.S. Army's treatment of captives in the Philippines. When Squires was called before the panel, he testified, "I have seen cities destroyed—leveled to the ground. ... I have seen old men and women brained because they did not work fast enough to suit their new rulers in the baking of bread. I have seen places where babies were crucified on the doors of houses."[157]

When Overman asked him about ill treatment of women and whether German officers were present, Squires replied, "It was mostly the work of private soldiers. ... At the doors of houses I have heard the shrieks of women upstairs recovering from their treatment of the night before."[158] Senator Nelson asked about the crucification of children. Squires responded:

> I have had places pointed out to me by fathers who had been crazed by the sight of their children hanging on door bells the night before. One man took me up to a door and showed me the nail points in the door where his little baby had been nailed the night before because the baby got in the way of the German guard of four or five men and in some way hindered their passage; one of the men snatched up the baby and held it up against the door, probably in his drunkenness, nailed it up against the door, and it was dead in five minutes, I suppose.

Senator [William A.] King asked whether Squires had seen the child. Squires said, "No. The child was not permitted to remain there more than a minute or two after the soldiers went on. I know it is very difficult to believe these stories, gentlemen, and that is one reason why I hesitate to tell them ... but I have seen all that I have told you myself."[159]

At the conclusion of the "German propaganda" segment of the hearings, when some Congressmen were planning to introduce a bill outlawing propaganda by foreign governments, an influential private organization, the Council on Foreign Relations, announced its opposition to any such prohibition. Its letter to Overman on February 10, 1919, showed the depth of its ignorance of propaganda, mirroring the views undoubtedly held even by informed and educated Americans. Ridiculously, the Council drew a mythical line between "good" and "bad" propaganda, stating that its position was "in full accord with legislative action aimed to make impossible the sowing of secret and insidious propaganda in the United States. Nothing too stringent can be done to avert any repetition of the underground propaganda of Germany. ... "However," the letter continued, "any prohibition against the establishment in this country of recognized foreign bureaus of information tends to encourage and aid rather than suppress the evil propaganda. ... If foreign governments and foreign peoples maintain responsible bureaus of information whose reputations must be built upon the truth of their output. ... An outlet of honest and open expression of foreign nations will tend to make unnecessary and unwise the use of secret and surreptitious propaganda."[160]

EPILOGUE

By a campaign of publicity and advertising on a scale history had never witnessed before, by chicanery and lying, by exaggeration and misrepresentation, by persistent and long-continued appeals to the basest as well as to the noblest traits of man, by every imaginable and unprecedented manner and method, the great financial interests, eager for war and aided by the international Junkers, thrust humanity into the world war. ... Hatred, intolerance, persecution and suppression—the efficient "educational" factors in the preparedness and war campaign—are now permeating the very heart of this country and propagating its virulent poison into every phase of our social life.

But there is no more "Hun" to be hated and lynched. ...But the Frankenstein and intolerance and suppression cultivated by the war campaign is there, alive and vital, and must find some vent for his accumulated bitterness and misery.

Oh, there, the radical, the Bolsehvik! What better prey to be cast to the Frankenstein monster?

Alexander Berkman and Emma Goldman, *Deportation:
Its Meaning and Menace* (Ellis Island, New York, December 1919)

On January 23, 1919, Senator Lee Slater Overman summed up his judiciary subcommittee's performance to date. More important was his job of work yet to be done. "German propaganda has gone over the wheel," he said, "and now we are up against a worse propaganda than that."[1] What he was referring to was Bolshevik propaganda, and on February 4, the Senate unanimously passed a resolution to extend the committee's investigation to focus on the new menace to the nation. An expanded title was pinned on the hearings: "Brewing and Liquor Interests and German and Bolshevik Propaganda."

What triggered the Senate action was the sensational general strike called the day before in Seattle, Washington, and the perceived threat of a Communist revolution on the West Coast that could envelop the whole nation. Starting one week later, on the same day the Seattle strike collapsed, and running through March 10, the committee heard testimony from 26 witnesses. Most of those who testified were fervent anti–Communists who related astonishing fables to the appropriately stern-faced panel. There was near unanimity

277

that Lenin and Trotsky were German tools who from the start had been financed by Germany; that the Red Army consisted mostly of criminals; that the new Soviet government enthusiastically sponsored "free-love" clinics and fostered immoral behavior; and that those who opposed the new regime were summarily shot or hanged. Most sinister of all, the witnesses told the expectant Senate panel that Bolshevism was anti–Christ.

One witness blandly claimed that "more than half of the agitators in the so-called Bolshevik revolution were Yiddish" and most that of these "apostate Jews" had come from Manhattan's lower east side. Almost in the same breath, the witness stated that the revolution had been financed by Germany, drawing the response from Overman that "it would be a very remarkable thing if the Bolshevik movement started in this country, financed by Germans, would it not?" Senator King asked the same witness a loaded question, whether the Bolsheviks, "the males, rape and ravish and despoil women at will?" "They certainly do," was the prompted answer, and they "are the dirtiest dogs" he had ever seen in his life.[2] A Russian émigré soberly testified that in the first year of Soviet rule, the number of Russian men, women, and children killed by the Bolsheviks was twice that of the Russian soldiers had died on the war fronts from 1914 through 1917: "They shoot, for instance, thousands and thousands of them at once."[3]

The first adverserial witness was Louise Bryant, a Socialist activist like her husband John Reed, who also testified. She referred to herself as "the only witness so far, who wants to bring about amicable relations between Russia and America."[4] Bryant made her mark when, prior to her swearing in, she was asked if she believed "in a punishment hereafter and a reward for duty?" She put a provocative overall interpretation on the hearings by responding that "It seems to me as if I were being tried for witchcraft."[5]

Near the end of the hearings, on March 8, America's former ambassador to Russia, David R. Francis, made his appearance. There was no further need to probe the cruelties of the new Soviet regime. Rather, the senators, who had become full-fledged anti–Soviet propagandists, were intent on publicizing their purposefully skewed views of the origins of the Bolshevik revolution with testimony from their most prestigious witness. They were also seeking a rationale for America's aggressive new posture toward the Soviet Union. In the process, the panel almost convinced Francis to agree that America was justified, in the name of world peace, to overturn the dangerous new Soviet government.

> SENATOR KING: Mr. Ambassador, generally speaking, then, you would say that the Kerensky government stood for law and order and for the establishment of a democratic form of government something like our own?
>
> MR. FRANCIS: Exactly.
>
> SENATOR KING: ... and that that government, so long as it was in power,

attempted to do all that it could in the prosecution of the war and to stand
by the side of the allies in fighting the central powers?

MR. FRANCIS: I think so.

SENATOR KING: That while they were engaged in that laudable and proper
effort the Bolsheviks were attempting to undermine them, primarily for the
purpose of getting control and establishing a proletariat dictatorship and sec-
ondly for the purpose of betraying the cause of the allies and getting Russia out of the war?

MR. FRANCIS: Exactly.[6]

SENATOR KING: Mr. Ambassador, what would you say as to what was
being done, during that period when the Kerensky government was in power,
by the Bolsheviki?

MR. FRANCIS: Lenine was disbursing money freely. I said that I believed
Lenine was a German agent. Subsequent developments have confirmed me
in that belief.

SENATOR KING: You believe that Germany furnished him money for
debauching his own country and to aid in betraying the allied cause?

MR. FRANCIS: Exactly; I think she did.[7]

SENATOR NELSON: Do you not regard this Bolshevik government in Russia as a menace to the peace of Europe?

MR. FRANCIS: I regard it as a menace to the peace of Europe and to the
peace of the world.

SENATOR NELSON: A menace to the peace of the world; and there never
can be an effective peace until that Bolshevik government is eliminated?

MR. FRANCIS: I think not. That is my judgment, derived from two years
and eight months' residence in Russia.

SENATOR NELSON: Do you believe that our Government and the allies are
justified in helping the Russian people get rid of that Bolshevik government?

MR. FRANCIS: You are asking a question of policy now that I do not feel
like answering.[8]

The *New York Times* on June 15, 1919, celebrated the committee's eight
months of work by devoting a full page to its findings. The headline—SEN-
ATORS TELL WHAT BOLSHEVISM IN AMERICA MEANS—told its
readers of an immediate shift to be made in their priorities. A single sentence
in the second paragraph disposed of German propaganda, and the testimony
of dozens of witness, weeks of questioning, and hundreds of exhibits devoted
to uncovering the propaganda machinations of a former enemy by the Overman committee: "That part which deals with German propaganda is a resume
of the various activities directed by Boy-Ed, von Papen, and other plotters."

The *Times* story then swung into Bolshevism as interpreted in the sub-
committe's final report, suggesting that the subject was dealt with "from a new
angle. After telling what Bolsehvism is, it applies the system, theoretically, to
the United States and points out what would happen if the American Government were replaced by one patterned after the 'red terror' of Russia." The
newspaper reproduced from the report 29 "salient features which constitute
the program of Bolshevism as it exists to-day in Russia and is presented to

the rest of the world as a panacea for all ills." Among the most pernicious planks in the Soviet platform: "the confiscation of all factories, mills, mines, and industrial institutions and the delivery of the control and operation thereof to the employees therein"; "the absolute separation of churches and schools"; "the establishment, through marriage and divorce laws, of a method for the legalization of prostitution, when the same is engaged in by consent of the parties"; "the refusal to recognize the existence of God in its governmental and judicial proceedings"; and "the conferring of the rights of citizenship on aliens without regard to length of residence or intelligence."

Almost overnight, American patriots in and out of government had manufactured a new bogeyman to fit the nation's imperial destiny—the godless Soviet Bolshevik, out to subvert everything that this nation stood for (according to these chauvinists' narrow prescriptions). While other powerful antiradical forces were also at work, the well-publicized Overman committee played an important role in helping trigger the hysteria of America's first "Red Scare." It was time for America to embark on a new propaganda crusade.

Indeed, America would wage the new propaganda war in earnest for most of the remainder of the twentieth century. And in 1991 many Americans would toast final victory over a crumbled Soviet Union. Others would ask, At what cost? and suggest that America had plundered its national treasure en route to the supposed triumph over the "evil empire": witch-hunts, loyalty oaths, spy paranoia, bloody wars in Korea and Vietnam, covert support of one cruel dictator after another, and so many political intrigues and corruptions, all in the name of anti–Communism.

Some would say that America, principally as a result of its preoccupation with fighting Communism, is a nation in serious decline, unable to cope with myriad intractable domestic problems and unfit to compete in the global economy of the coming century. Some would even question whether America had won its nearly century-long propaganda war after all.

NOTES

Introduction

1. John C. Miller, *Sam Adams, Pioneer in Propaganda* (Stanford: Stanford University Press, 1936), 113.
2. Arthur M. Schlesinger, introduction to *School Histories at War: A Study of the Treatment of Our Wars in the Secondary School History Books of the United States and in Those of its Former Enemies*, by Arthur Walworth (Cambridge: Harvard University Press, 1938), xiii.

Chapter 1—Myths and Legends

1. George Sylvester Viereck's letter to his mother, December 19, 1916, following Viereck's return from Muensterberg's funeral: "He was ostracized socially and insulted publicly. Even his family had to feel the malice of New England. Thus, several ladies left the Chapel at Harvard when they saw that his two daughters were worshipping there." Elmer Gertz Papers, Manuscript Division, Library of Congress.
2. Protestant Germany's fecundity was of most interest to its neighbor and implacable foe, Catholic France, who saw herself falling farther behind every year in what was perceived as a critical race. A large population was considered not only an economic asset but a source of army reservists. England, on the other hand, was concerned with other statistics. It watched with dismay as Germany's industrial productivity soared, rushing past England's in one category after another that spelled national greatness. By 1913, Germany had the most powerful economy in Europe.
3. Carnegie had first attracted attention as a peace advocate in 1905, when he delivered a speech denouncing war at St. Andrews University in his native Scotland. At his own expense, the multimillionaire printed thousands of copies of his talk in various languages and distributed them worldwide. He followed up with numerous articles and pamphlets on the same antiwar theme, calling Britain's fear of Germany unfounded and playing up the pacifist nature of Germany's emperor. He even orchestrated the visit of Theodore Roosevelt to meet the Kaiser after the ex-president's African safari in 1910. The same year, Carnegie established the Carnegie Endowment for International Peace with a $10 million trust fund, "to hasten the abolition of war." Once the Great War began, however, the onetime leading American pacifist became convinced that the only way to achieve world peace was through the defeat of Germany. He wrote to Wilson in February 1917, "There is only one straight way of settlement. You should proclaim war against her, however reluctantly, and then settlement would come soon. Britain and France cooperating with us, would insure peace promptly beyond question, and at the next meeting at the Hague, we would abolish war forever." Joseph Frazier Wall, *Andrew Carnegie* (New York: Oxford University Press, 1970), 1033.
4. In 1917, when America went to war, Butler would see to it that no Columbia University faculty member would be allowed publicly to voice opposition to the nation's wartime role. Incongruously, he would share the Nobel Peace Prize in 1931 with Jane Addams.

5. Alice Roosevelt Longworth, *Crowded Hours* (New York: Charles Scribner's Sons, 1933), 121–122.

6. In 1908, during an extraordinary interview with the Kaiser aboard his yacht, *New York Times* reporter William Bayard Hale recorded that the loquacious Wilhelm told him he held President Roosevelt in highest esteem. When Roosevelt later read details of what the Kaiser had said about him, he allowed that he felt the same way about "Bill." Big-game hunter Roosevelt said, "They say that the Emperor and I are alike, and have a great admiration for each other on that account. I do admire him, very much as I do a grizzly bear." Oscar King Davis, *Released for Publication: Some Inside Political History of Theodore Roosevelt and His Times, 1898–1918* (Boston: Houghton Mifflin, 1925), 88.

7. As president, Taft had negotiated arbitration treaties with England and France that were models for the subsequent and inadequate Bryan Conciliation Treaties of 1914. After losing the presidency in 1912 to Wilson, Taft became an active promoter of the League to Enforce Peace.

8. Edward VII, had he been alive, would certainly not have permitted his name, nor that of his brother-in-law, to be associated positively with his nephew. The biographer of Lord Lansdowne, British foreign secretary from 1900 to 1905, wrote that Lansdowne was forced to admit that "the King talks and writes about his Royal Brother in terms which make one's flesh creep and official papers which go to him, whenever they refer to his Imperial Majesty, come back with all sorts of annotations of the most incendiary character." Lord Newton, *Lord Lansdowne, A Biography* (London: Macmillan, 1929), 330. There were plausible reasons for Edward's anti–German attitude, in addition to the royal philanderer's well-publicized predilections for shapely Parisian courtesans: Germany was increasingly a powerful industrial and commercial competitor and her fast-growing navy was perceived as a direct threat to England's vital naval preeminence. Germany had become the dominant power on the continent, and Great Britain could not tolerate such dominance by any nation. For 400 years, Britain had fought one war after another—against Philip II of Spain and Louis XIV and Napoleon Bonaparte of France—to maintain a power equilibrium among the continental nations. Diplomatic foes of England could suggest that historically England sought to have Europe arrayed into two hostile camps, as equally matched as possible. If an imbalance occurred, England would throw her might onto the weak side so as to restore the balance that best served her national interests at the time.

9. Kenneth Rose has described England's monarch as having the limited education of a typical nineteenth-century officer in the Royal Navy. He knew little and cared even less about his nation's politics and history, according to Rose. The king's one interest was bird shooting, and he indulged his passion in kingly fashion. "He shot with elegant ease ... an appreciative female audience improved his performance. ... One day he fired 1,700 cartridges and killed 1,000 pheasants. Behind the King and his loaders, a detective clicked up each addition to the bag on a pocket instrument that could record a four-figure total." *King George V* (New York: Alfred A. Knopf, 1984), 99, 100.

10. Cable, House to Wilson, March 1, 1915. In the cable, House reported other interpretations of George's views of Germany and Wilhelm: "I had hopes that he might want to talk concerning peace plans, but he evidently wanted to impress me with the fact that this was no time to talk peace. His idea seemed to be that the best way to obtain permanent peace was to knock all the fight out of the Germans. ...He spoke kindly of the Germans as a whole, but for his dear cousin and his military entourage, he denounced them in good sailor-like terms. He is the most pugnacious monarch that is loose in these parts." Charles Seymour, *The Intimate Papers of Colonel House* (Boston: Houghton Mifflin, 1926), 1:385.

11. Sarah Bradford, *The Reluctant King: The Life and Reign of George VI, 1895–1952* (New York: St. Martin's Press, 1989), 64.

12. The so-called secret treaties were wartime agreements among the Allied powers dealing with the division of the anticipated spoils of war. The principal agreement was the Treaty of London, in April 1915, between England, France, Russia, and Italy, to bring Italy into the war on the side of the Allies. Italy was promised the Austrian territories of Trentino, south Tyrol, and Istria, and part of Dalmatia, as well as the sovereignty of the Dodecanese islands, which Italy had already occupied, plus a "just share" of the Ottoman Empire in Asia in the event of its partition. The same protocol also promised Constantinople and the straits to Russia. Rumania was drawn into the war on the side of the Allies on the basis of an August 1916 treaty signed by Ruma-

nia, England, France, Italy, and Russia which committed large areas of Austria to the new ally. The tripartite Sykes-Picot agreement of October 1916 called for the partition of the Ottoman Empire by Britain, France, and Russia. A second tripartite agreement (St. Jean de Maurienne), in September 1917, covered further dismemberment of the Ottoman Empire by Britain, France, and Italy. The clandestine correspondence between England's Sir Henry McMahon and Arab leader Sherif Hussayn in October 1915, in which Great Britain agreed to help expel the Turks from Arab countries, is also considered one of the "secret treaties" of World War I. Finally, there were the wartime agreements between England and Japan concerning transfer of German colonies in the Pacific Ocean north of the equator already captured by Japan (German island colonies south of the equator were already in the hands of Australia and New Zealand) in exchange for Japanese naval coverage of the Pacific.

13. Franz Joseph, emperor of Austria and king of Hungary, was an old and tired man. He had experienced two personal tragedies: the suicide of his son and heir in 1889 and the assassination of his wife in 1897. He was considered about average, intellectually; reportedly, his only passion as a younger man had been "the chase." He died in 1916, spared overseeing the dissolution of the nation he had ruled paternalistically since 1848.

14. It was not until January 31, 1915, that Dr. Constantin Theodor Dumba, Austria-Hungary's U.S. ambassador, finally was represented in the *Times*, when the Sunday magazine section devoted a full page to Austria's views. Dumba concluded his interpretations of the conflict by insisting that it was "not a war waged by a Government for its own aggrandizement. It is a struggle for life, undertaken by a people whose temper has been long and sorely tried by the malicious machinations of neighbors."

15. Barbara Tuchman has described Russia's last czar as "a sovereign who had but one idea of government—to preserve intact the absolute monarchy bequeathed to him by his father—and who, lacking the intellect, energy, or training for his job, fell back on personal favorites, whim, simple mulishness, and other devices of the empty-headed autocrat. ...The impression of imperturbability he conveyed was in reality apathy—the indifference of a mind so shallow as to be all surface. When a telegram was brought to him announcing the annihilation of the Russian fleet at Tshushima, he read it, stuffed it in his pocket, and went on playing tennis." *The Guns of August* (New York: Macmillan, 1962), 59.

16. The territory of Alsace and Lorraine had been long disputed. It was nominally German from the time of Charlemagne in the ninth century, then conquered by the French in the seventeenth and eighteenth centuries, remaining French until the Franco-Prussian War of 1870–71. German chancellor Otto von Bismarck apparently had been hesitant to demand the territory as a spoil of war, but his military advisors insisted its annexation would secure German borders. France's wartime president, Raymond Poincaré, who had grown up in Lorraine, confessed after the war that during his school years his "spirit, oppressed by the defeat, unceasingly crossed the frontier which the Treaty of Frankfurt had imposed on us, and when I climbed down from my castles in the air, I saw no reason for existence for my generations but the hope of recovering the lost provinces." Harry Elmer Barnes, *The Genesis of the World War* (New York: Alfred A. Knopf, 1929), 77.

17. The *World's* editorial-page editor, Frank I. Cobb, would become one of reclusive President Wilson's very few newspaperman confidants. In 1918, Cobb was given consideration by Edward Mandell House as a replacement for Walter Hines Page, the ailing ambassador to England. Cobb was later tentatively selected by both Wilson and House for the sensitive post of U.S. publicity director at the Paris Peace Conference, but he was never actually appointed because of a supposed misunderstanding.

18. Harold D. Lasswell, *Propaganda Technique in the World War* (New York: Alfred A. Knopf, 1927), 31–32.

19. The statue remained on display until mid–April 1917, when it was removed as part of a general U.S. housecleaning of objects of German origin. According to a report in the *New York Times*, April 14, 1917, it was "laid away in seclusion in a cold, damp storeroom in the cellar" of the War College, the action "taken at the suggestion of President Wilson." Sauerkraut and hamburger were renamed "liberty cabbage" and "Salisbury steak," American cities of German origin were given new names, and many states and communities prohibited the teaching of German in the public schools and forbade the playing of music composed by Germans; some towns even passed ordinances making it a crime to speak German in public.

20. Quoted in Tuchman, *Guns of August*, 71.

21. Barnes, *Genesis of the World War*, 609–610.

22. Quincy Wright, *A Study of War* (Chicago: University of Chicago Press, 1942), 221.

23. Pitrim A. Sorokin, *Social and Cultural Dynamics* (New York: American Book, 1937), 3:351.

24. Russell Grenfell, *Unconditional Hatred: German War Guilt and the Future of Europe* (New York: Devin-Adair, 1953), 55.

25. Kirby Page, *War: Its Causes, Consequences, and Cure* (New York: George H. Doran, 1923), 11.

26. Edmund Dene Morel, *Truth and the War* (1916; repr., New York: Garland, 1972), 94.

27. "The Future of Anglo-German Rivalry," *Atlantic Monthly*, July 1915, 130. Russell included the following figures for the total area of colonies, which he suggested "are not without interest": Great Britain, 11,429,078 square miles; France, 4,512,543 square miles; Germany, 1,027,820 square miles. The increase in area of colonies since 1900: Great Britain, 324,500 square miles; Germany, 100,820 square miles; France, 92,180 square miles. Russell and Morel each spent six months in jail during the war for their "anti-government" activities. The British Empire's share of the post–World War I spoils would come to over a million square miles.

28. Count Alfred von Schlieffen, chief of the German general staff from 1891 to 1906, planned to divide his armies at the start of the anticipated two-front war; most of his forces were to fight France and the balance were to hold Germany's eastern frontier against the Russians. The German armies would first march against France by making a giant enveloping pivot on their right wing, crossing Belgium from Liège to Brussels; they would then sweep south to take advantage of the open countryside of Flanders and descend on Paris. Since surrounding the French armies was the key to success of the German battle plan, von Schlieffen expected his armies to swing as far west as possible: "When you march into France, let the last man on the right brush the Channel with his sleeve."

29. An independent, neutral Belgium was Great Britain's creation, for the Belgian coast lay directly across the narrow English Channel. In 1815, Napoleon's armies—the most serious threat to the British Isles since the Armada—had been defeated on the flat plains of Waterloo, Belgium. England was determined to prevent another such threat. Following the Congress of Vienna, the powers agreed to cede the territory to the Netherlands. The Belgians revolted in 1830. A scramble for hegemony between the Dutch and the French followed. England succeeded in 1839 in securing a treaty signed by Austria, England, France, Russia, and Prussia that guaranteed Belgium would be "perpetually neutral."

30. The Kaiser might perhaps have rued the day, July 27, 1900, when he used the word "Hun" to exhort German troops embarking from Bremerhaven en route to China as part of an international police force to put down the Boxer Rebellion: "When you meet the foe you will defeat him. No quarter will be given; no prisoners will be taken. Let all who fall into your hands be at your mercy. Just as the Huns a thousand years ago, under the leadership of Attila, gained a reputation in virtue of which they still live in historical tradition, so may the name of Germany become known." George T. Blakey, *Historians on the Homefront: American Propagandists for the Great War* (Lexington: University Press of Kentucky, 1970), 46. Etzel, or Attila, became king of the Huns in 433 and waged war with other central European barbarian tribes. For nearly 20 years, he ruled supreme from the Rhine river to the Caspian Sea. In his battles, he ruthlessly sacked and burned captured cities, killing and torturing captives. The French also used "Boche" (loosely, "hard-head" or "thick-skull") as a derogatory term for German soldiers. American doughboys in France happily embraced both terms of derision, "Hun" and "Boche."

31. Even with America safely on the side of the Allies in April 1917, and with German propaganda effectively muted, British pressure was not relaxed. An Office of Information was openly established in New York City, and the propaganda floodgates were opened full. Agile British propagandists expertly swung their emphasis to a new objective: to make sure that America thought only in terms of unconditional surrender and did not negotiate a premature peace contrary to England's interests. After the Armistice, too, the British worked clandestinely to limit publicity coverage of the Paris peace conference so as to mask British intents.

32. Charles A. Beard, *The Rise of American Civilization* (New York: Macmillan, 1935), 616–618.

33. Both collective and individual German "guilt" were emblazoned in the Treaty of Versailles, in the infamous Articles 231 and 237.

34. "As early as 1894 Theodore Roosevelt proclaimed that this nation had no need for German-Americans, but for Americans only. As he used the hyphen, it signified divided political loyalties, as though the pursuit of ethnic group goals was somehow un–American and based on a deep-seated political loyalty to the immigrants' native land." Frederick C. Luebke, *Bonds of Loyalty: German-Americans and World War I* (DeKalb: Northern Illinois University Press, 1974), 68.

35. James Duane Squires, *British Propaganda at Home and in the United States—from 1914 to 1917* (Cambridge: Harvard University Press, 1935), 67.

36. Secret Directive (declassified May 3, 1972) from U.S. Chief of Naval Operations to Commander-in-Chief Pacific Fleet and Commander-in-Chief Asian Fleet: DEC 07 [1941] 2252 GCT. OPNAV TO CINCPAC & NAVAL COASTAL FRONTIERS. EXECUTE UNRESTRICTED AIR AND SUBMARINE WARFARE AGAINST JAPAN. INFORM ARMY. CINCAF INFORM BRITISH AND DUTCH. U.S. Navy Historical Center.

Chapter 2 – The British

1. The Royal Navy apparently had second thoughts about leaving the severed cables on the sea bottom, where they might be retrieved, spliced, and put back into the service by the Germans—and the *Teleconia* went out again, this time to reel in the cables. One of the "captured" New York–bound cables was landed at Penzance, at the southwestern tip of England; the other was delivered to the French at Brest.

2. The British Empire in 1900 was over three times the size of the Roman Empire at its zenith, and encompassed about one-quarter of the globe's land area. This was more than 90 times that of the British Isles. "Nearly all of this vast empire was acquired by war, either upon England's European neighbors, or upon the native peoples, or upon both. The Portuguese and the Dutch were the first Europeans in India. England acquired India by war, first upon the Dutch, second upon the French, third upon the native peoples. The Dutch were first in South Africa. England took Cape Colony in war from Holland, abolished by force the republic of Natal, and completed the conquest in the twentieth century by cutting down those two small nations, the republics of the Transvaal and the Orange Free State. France colonized Canada. Holland colonized New York. Both fell to England as spoils of war. Later, France sold its Louisiana territory to the young republic of the United States to prevent it from being taken in war by Britain. The large island of Malta was taken from the French. Gibraltar, Spain, was taken and kept simply because the British liked its commanding position. Jamaica was wrested from Spain. Other British possessions in the western hemisphere were either taken, by conquest, from Spain or held in defiance of the claims of the American republics." John Kenneth Turner, *Shall It Be Again?* (New York: B. W. Huebsch, 1922), 217.

3. Paul Kennedy, *The Rise and Fall of British Naval Mastery* (New York: Charles Scribner's Sons, 1976), 206. Kennedy (like the French before him) considered the cable network so important to the security of the British Empire that he included the same map of "naval bases and submarine cables of the Empire, c. 1900" in this book and in his popular *Rise and Fall of the Great Powers* (New York: Random House, 1987).

4. On March 5, 1915, in a letter to his editor, Geoffrey Dawson, the Washington correspondent of the London *Times*, Arthur Willert, reported that the German government was trying to persuade the U.S. State Department to demand that a cable link between Germany and the United States be reestablished—that it was the desire of Americans "for more and better news from Germany." Nothing came of either the reported German "try" or the American "desire." Sir Arthur Willert Papers, Manuscripts and Archives, Yale University Library.

5. C. Hartley Grattan, *Why We Fought* (New York: Vanguard Press, 1929), 44.

6. Johann von Bernstorff, *My Three Years in America* (New York: Charles Scribner's Sons, 1920), 54.

7. The *New York Times* of August 5, one day after England entered the war, ran a long anti–German article by H.G. Wells. It also took less than a month for Foreign Secretary Grey to write to the influential ex-president and omnivorous reader Theodore Roosevelt that "J.M. Barrie and A.E.W. Mason, some of whose books you no doubt read, are going to the United

States. Their object is, as I understand, not to make speeches or give lectures, but to meet people, particularly those connected with Universities, and explain the British case as regards this war and our view of the issues involved." September 10, 1914, cited in C. Hartley Grattan, *Why We Fought* (New York: Bobbs-Merrill, 1969), 52.

8. See the letter from Asquith to King George V, August 31, 1914, cited in M. L. Sanders and Philip M. Taylor, *British Propaganda During the First World War, 1914–18* (London: Macmillan, 1982), 39–40. Earlier sources suggest it was Sir Edward Grey or Chancellor of the Exchequer David Lloyd George who made the appointment. George Sylvester Viereck wrote in *Spreading Germs of Hate* (New York: Horace Liveright, 1930) that, based on his discussion with Masterman himself, it was Grey (129). Masterman's widow, Lucy, in *C. F. B. Masterman: A Biography* (London: Frank Cass, 1939) had a sharply different recollection: "The earliest news that I personally had of a propaganda department was a conversation after a Sunday luncheon at Walton Heath Golf Club during August 1914, when Mr. T. P. O'Connor pressed on Mr. Lloyd George the necessity for countering the propaganda already begun by the Germans in the United States in the form of leaflets given away in the streets, and thrust into the hands of passengers arriving by steamer." According to Mrs. Masterman, it was Lloyd George who casually said to her husband, "Will you look into it, Charlie, and see what can be done" (272). This version is, however, open to question because it was Lloyd George, when he became prime minister in December 1916, who circumscribed Masterman's propaganda responsibilities, an unlikely decision had Lloyd George been Masterman's original supporter.

9. Ivor Nicholson, "An Aspect of British Official Wartime Propaganda," *Cornhill Magazine*, May 1931. Concerning the makeup of Wellington House, Nicholson wrote, "I could not afford, like a number of my colleagues, to give my services voluntarily, but the remuneration which we received was really in the nature of a subsistence allowance. We were either totally unfit for military service or in a sufficiently low category to justify the authorities in claiming we were more usefully employed as Government servants than soldiers" (603).

10. Ibid., 595.

11. Masterman, *C. F. B. Masterman*, 272.

12. Quoted in *The Dictionary of National Biography, 1931–1940* (London: Oxford University Press, 1949), 671. The same source quietly understated Parker's wartime role: "For two and a half years during the war of 1914–1918 he was in charge of publicity in America (672).

13. In 1895, a long-festering boundary dispute in South America between Venezuela and British Guiana nearly erupted in war between the United States and England. President Grover Cleveland sent a blunt message to the Congress, but directed at the British, stating that the nation must resist through every means in its power British aggression in Venezuela. The Congress unanimously appropriated $100,000 for an investigative commission and the public, driven by a frenzied press, clamored for war. Forces of moderation on both sides tamped down the potential conflagration, however, and a peaceful compromise was worked out four years later.

14. Squires, *British Propaganda*, reported only two instances of Parker publicly discussing his work. In April 1915, he gave a speech in London to the Pilgrim's Society in which he said: "I have watched American opinion; I have read scores of American newspapers steadily; I have received vast numbers of letters from prominent Americans of all professions and positions" (52). Several weeks later, in an article published in London, "What Is the Matter with England?" Parker repeated his theme that he had "watched closely the trend of opinion in the United States" (53). In a long article in the *New York Times* magazine section of August 15, 1915, "Is England Apathetic? No," Parker tried to summarize Great Britain's "progress" during the first year of the war. He castigated the enemy, defended his country's democracy, and rejected what American newspapers had written about drunkenness in Britain as "the most cruel libels upon the British workingman." He concluded the article with the mandatory sugar-coated flattering of America—but nary a word about propaganda. Parker also showed up in person in New York in late January 1917, telling reporters that he was not in America in an official capacity, nor "to lecture or act as publicity representative of the Allies." He did have the gall, however, to say that "neither England nor France will establish any press bureau in the United States." Parker also took the opportunity to regale his interrogators with his nation's interpretation of modern world history: "Remember that the people of England are like the people of the United States, a peace-loving people, who, with all their naval prowess, have never abused the right of the strong arm.

...It must be remembered that in this war England had nothing to gain either in indemnity or in territory or in increased security." *New York Times*, January 23, 1917.

15. In 1917, under the new Lloyd George government, hush-hush Wellington House was first exposed to the light when it was integrated into a Department of Information headed by fiction-writer John Buchan. A year later, a broader-based Ministry of Information was created under newspaperman Lord Beaverbrook.

16. Gilbert Parker, "The United States and the War," *Harper's Monthly Magazine*, March 1918, 522.

17. Reproduced in H.C. Peterson, *Propaganda for War* (1939; repr. N.Y.: Kennikat Press, Port Washington, 1968), 52–53.

18. World War I Documents Collection, Manuscripts and Archives, Yale University Library; and the author's collection. When Parker stepped down in early 1917, Dixon replaced him as head of Wellington House.

19. *The Germans: Their Empire, How They Have Made It; The Germans: What They Covet; India and the War; Russia: The Psychology of a Nation; Nietzsche and Treitschke: The Worship of Power in Modern Germany; Serbia and the Serbs; The War and the British Dominions; French Policy since 1871; and Just for a Scrap of Paper.*

20. *Is the British Empire the Result of Wholesale Robbery?; England's Mission; August, 1914: The Coming of the War; The Battle of the Marne and Aisne; The Germans in Africa; All for Germany: or, The World's Respect Well Lost; Germany, the Economic Problem; German Sea-Power; What Europe Owes to Belgium; Poland, Prussia, and Culture; Turkey in Europe and Asia; Greek Policy Since 1882; North Sleswick under Prussian Rule, 1864–1917; Thoughts on the War; The Leadership of the World; The Leading Ideas of British Policy; The War and its Economic Aspects; Food Supplies in War Time; Non-Combatants and the War; Troyon: An Engagement in the Battle of the Aisne; Scandinavia and the War; Asia and the War; German Philosophy and the War; Does International Law Still Exist?; Through German Eyes; The Action off Heligoland, August, 1914; The Southern Slavs; Christmas and the War; The Church and the War;* and *Outline of Prussian History to 1871.*

21. Squires, *British Propaganda*, 52.

22. Willert Papers. Dawson, like Willert, would continue to influence Great Britain's foreign and domestic policies in the years after World War I. Fired by *Times* owner Lord Northcliffe soon after the end of the war, he returned as editor-in-chief after Northcliffe's death in 1924 and he served in that capacity until his retirement in 1941.

23. Arthur Conan Doyle, *Great Britain and the Next War* (Boston: Small, Maynard, 1914), 5.

24. Ibid., 48.

25. Friedrich von Bernhardi, *Germany and the Next War* (1911; trans. by Allen H. Powles, New York: Chas. A. Eron, 1914), 7, 235.

26. Doyle, *Great Britain and the Next War*, 21. This event was the origin of the infinitive "to Copenhagen," two twentieth-century examples of which have been furnished by Japan, first in 1904 at the outset of the Russo-Japanese war, when, on the night of February 8, Japanese destroyers torpedoed the anchored Russian eastern fleet outside Port Arthur and then on the morning of December 7, 1941, when Japanese carrier-based aircraft bombed, torpedoed, and strafed the U.S. Pacific fleet and military installations in Pearl Harbor, Hawaii. Following the first surprise attack, the London *Times* crowed of the exploits of England's new ally: "The Japanese Navy has opened the war by an act of daring which is destined to take a place of honour in naval annals." Cited in James Leasor, *Singapore: The Battle That Changed the World* (Garden City, N.Y.: Doubleday, 1968), 63. The newspaper's tone would be markedly different 37 years later.

27. James Bryce, *Neutral Nations and the War* (New York: Macmillan, 1914), 12.

28. Gilbert Murray, *Faith, War, and Policy: Addresses and Essays on the European War* (New York: Houghton Mifflin, 1917), viii. The Trinity College (Connecticut) Library copy I examined was a gift to that institution from Gilbert Murray, signed but undated.

29. Ibid., 20.

30. H.G. Wells, *The War That Will End War* (New York: Duffield, 1914), 80, 88.

31. H.G. Wells, *Italy, France, and Britain at War* (New York: Macmillan., 1917), 9–10.

32. H.G. Wells, *Mr. Britling Sees It Through* (New York: Macmillan, 1917), 422–423.

33. H.G. Wells, *In the Fourth Year: Anticipations of a World Peace* (New York: Macmillan, 1918), v–vi.

34. *The Idea of a League of Nations* (Boston: Atlantic Monthly Press, 1919) was originally published as articles in the January and February 1919 issues of *Atlantic Monthly*. It was written by Wells in collaboration with Viscount Grey, Lionel Curtiss, William Archer, A.E. Zimmern, J.A. Spender, Viscount Bryce, and Gilbert Murray. The reasoned arguments presented followed two lines: first, because the interests of men and nations had become so closely drawn together, an international organization had become a natural step and second, such an organization had become the only alternative to further war. The book contained little residual anti–German polemics. In fact, the authors' view of the postwar world even saw a role for a chastened Germany.

35. H.G. Wells, *Experiment in Autobiography: Discoveries and Conclusions of a Very Ordinary Brain (Since 1866)* (New York: Macmillan, 1934), 571–572.

36. Lasswell, *Propaganda Technique*, 94

37. Alice Cholmondeley, *Christine* (New York: Macmillan, 1917), 240.

38. Lasswell, *Propaganda Technique*, 96.

39. Bernard Shaw, *What I Really Wrote about the War* (London: Constable, 1930), 2.

40. Ibid., 5.

41. *New York Times*, November 23, 1914.

42. Ibid., November 18, 1914, as translated by the *New York Times*.

43. Shaw, *What I Really Wrote*, 125.

44. Ibid., 117.

45. Ibid., 136.

46. Norman Angell, one of England's most well-known pacifists, also championed the cause of his country's approximately 2,000 imprisoned conscientious objectors: "If you suppress the right to private judgment you suppress the capacity for public judgment, and that is why I believe these conscientious objectors are doing their country and English tradition a very real service." *New York Times*, August 26, 1916.

47. Shaw, *What I Really Wrote*, 220. One of Shaw's main interests was practical phonetics, the application of which had enabled him to transform his native Irish brogue into standard English pronunciation. He never quite lost his Irish accent, and conciously never adopted the upper-crust's affected drawl. He later willed his substantial fortune to an organization promoting a strictly phonetic reform of English spelling.

48. George J. Hecht, *The War in Cartoons: A History of the War in 100 Cartoons by 27 of the Most Prominent American Cartoonists* (New York: E.P. Dutton, 1919), 3.

49. Louis Raemaekers, *Raemakers' Cartoons* (Garden City, N.Y.: Doubleday, Page, 1916), 5.

50. Alice Roosevelt Longworth in her memoirs, *Crowded Hours* (New York: Charles Scribner's Sons, 1933), mentions that she went to a Raemaekers exhibit and "bought a particularly savage one. It was done before we got into the war, at the same time Mr. Wilson said that aims of the belligerents were virtually the same. It represented Wilson warding off Europe—a woman with a raised sword—from Germany—a ruffian in a Pickelhaube, about to mutilate liberty, justice, and humanity. In our opinion it was a graphic and accurate representation of the President's position at the time it was drawn. How we did cherish and nourish our hatreds in those days!" (260).

51. Raemaekers, *Raemaekers' Cartoons*, 5.

52. Ibid., 6.

53. Ibid., 7.

54. Louis Raemaekers, *Kultur in Cartoons* (New York: Century, 1917).

55. Louis Raemaekers, *America in the War* (New York: Century, 1918).

56. As might be expected of America's chief public-relations executive, Creel had previously gone on record as the author of a glowing, exaggerated appraisal of Raemaekers as a "Dutch genius" in an article, "Raemaekers—Man and Artist," in *The Century Magazine* of June 1917. Creel trumpeted preposterously that the Dutch cartoonist "will go down into history. ...It is one of the great works of the world which he has done," 259. The article was accompanied by color reproductions of four of Raemaekers' more conservative cartoons, perhaps an intentional selection by the editors to balance Creel's hyperbole. In the February 1918 issue, *Century* published another article on the cartoonist, "Raemaekers, a Mainspring of Armed Force," by S. Stanwood Menken,

the founder of the jingoistic American Security League. This was a less hysterical analysis than Creel's, suggesting that the "portraiture of the national figure [Uncle Sam] ... prove[s] that Raemaekers, by grasping the highest spirit of American patriotism, has done much of the vital work of unifying America in its belief of the necessity of our entrance into the war," 559. Woodrow Wilson, too, was enamored of Raemaekers' art. In agreeing to meet with him at the request of Arthur Brisbane, editor of the *Washington Times*, the president stated he "greatly admired the cartoonist's work." Ray Stannard Baker, *Woodrow Wilson, Life and Letters* (Garden City, N.Y.: Doubleday, Doran, 1935), 7:242.

57. Quoted in Hecht, *The War in Cartoons*, 4.

58. Adolf Hitler, *Mein Kampf* (New York: Stackpole, 1939), 180.

59. American propagandists also used J.B. Pond Lyceum. Leon Debo, described as "The Distinguished American Painter" in a four-page Pond promotional brochure, was available to lecture on "The War As I Saw It." Debo had accompanied the Rev. Dr. Newell Dwight Hillis and his atrocity-seeking entourage to Europe as "official photographer." The brochure claimed that he "had seen things he dare not tell; things too hideous to believe." It added the patriotic disclaimer that "Leon Debo does not want to make money out of his lectures; neither does the J.B. Pond Lyceum Bureau. All personal ideas of gain have been set aside. Nominal fees to cover expenses will be charged, except when lecture is secured as an entertainment." George Creel Papers, Library of Congress, Manuscript Division.

60. "Not only did the [story of the] Belgian baby whose hands had been cut off by the Germans travel through the towns and villages of Great Britain, but it went through Western Europe and America, even into the Far West. No one paused to ask how long a baby would live were its hands cut off unless expert surgical aid were at hand to tie up the arteries (the answer being, a very few minutes). Everyone wanted to believe the story, and many went so far as to say they had seen the baby. ... Babies not only had their hands cut off, but they were impaled on bayonets, and in one case nailed to a door." Arthur Ponsonby, *Falsehood in War-Time* (New York: E.P. Dutton, 1928), 78–79.

61. Ibid., 128.

62. Barnes, *Genesis*, 557.

63. E.D. Morel, *Red Rubber: The Story of the Rubber Slave Trade Flourishing on the Congo in the Year of Grace 1906* (New York: Nassau Print, 1907). The Congo Free State, according to Morel, was not a state, nor an African protectorate nor a dependency, but an estate "claimed by one man—although he has never set foot in it—living in Europe, as his exclusive property, he having dispossessed the native inhabitants of their land, and the produce of the land which they alone can gather, and enslaved them in their hovels to collect the produce for himself and generally to work the property for him. ... Here is raid, massacre, mutilation, torture, incendiarism, and destruction visited upon a people" (136–137, 200).

64. *New York Times*, September 2, 1914.

65. Cobb related his experiences in *Paths of Glory: Impressions of War Written at and Near the Front* (New York: George H. Doran, 1915). After America entered the war, a second edition of the book was published with two new chapters. In these "patriotic" chapters, Cobb asserted that, while he still believed the atrocity stories had been exaggerated, he had personally observed numerous other crimes committed by the German army in Belgium.

66. *New Yorker Staats Zeitung*, January 2, 1915, as cited by James Morgan Read, *Atrocity Propaganda, 1914–1919* (New Haven: Yale University Press, 1941), 30.

67. Collection of World War I Propaganda Documents, BTZE p.v., New York Public Library.

68. Dawson, the London *Times'* editor, boasted to Arthur Willert, his Washington correspondent, how his staff had helped rewrite the French *Yellow Book*, that country's official report of alleged German atrocities in Belgium. Its emphasis was on the sexual crimes of the invaders. The January 8, 1915, issue of the *Times* of London, which published excerpts from the report, suggested that "The stories of rape are so horrible in detail that their publication would seem almost impossible were it not for the necessity of showing to the fullest extent the nature of the wild beasts fighting under the German Flag for German ideals and civilization." Sir Arthur Willert Papers, Yale University Library, Manuscripts and Archives.

69. Dumdum bullets were either hollow-point or flat-nosed bullets designed to mushroom on impact, creating huge, jagged wounds. Individual soldiers could also make their own dum-

dums by cutting slots into or filing down the points of ordinary military cartridges. Dumdums were expressly forbidden by the Hague treaties of 1899 and 1907. The name has its origins in the Indian city of Dum-Dum, where the British are accused of using the first such bullets, against Indian insurgents.

70. While there is no evidence that either France or Britain prompted the activities of the Belgian *francs-tireurs* in the Great War, during World War II in occupied Europe the situation was otherwise, according to Russell Grenfell: "The Germans, as we know, began with the endeavor to be the irreproachable conquerors. British newspapers in 1940 reported the excellence of their manners in France, German soldiers jumping up in trams and buses to offer their seats to women passengers and so on. But Mr. Churchill successfully sabotaged that endeavor by encouraging and arming the European resistance movements, largely composed of the Communist underworld, who by guerrilla terrorism provoked the Germans into reprisal measures against the civil populations of their occupied countries, and thus wrecked the chances of fraternisation." *Unconditional Hatred,* 101.

71. *New York Times,* September 17, 1914.

72. Lalla Vandervelde, *Monarchs and Millionaires* (New York: Adelphia, 1925), 53–54.

73. Ibid., 96.

74. *Report of the Committee on Alleged German Atrocities.* Collection of World War I Propaganda Documents, BTZE p.v., New York Public Library.

75. Ibid.

76. Stephen R. Graubard (editor of *Daedalus* and history professor at Brown University), in the *New York Times Book Review,* January 15, 1989.

77. Sir Arthur Willert, *Washington and Other Memories* (Boston: Houghton Mifflin, 1972), 45. However, according to Willert, Bryce was far less successful as a professional diplomat. Willert pointed out that, as ambassador, Bryce did not get along with President Roosevelt, who would have much preferred his old friend Cecil Spring-Rice. Bryce did not work well with the press, asking questions rather than answering them and becoming known as the "human question mark." He played little part in the Anglo-American negotiations concerning reciprocal tariff reductions between Canada and the United States and the more important Panama Canal tolls controversy during the Taft administration. Johann von Bernstorff, the German ambassador to the United States during part of Bryce's tenure, assigned Bryce far higher marks as a diplomat in his memoirs: "The most successful diplomacy in the world, that of England, almost always and everywhere represented by professional diplomats, was never so well served in Washington as by James Bryce. I was very often thankful in years 1914–1917 that he was no longer my opponent." (*Memoirs of Count Bernstorff,* New York: Random House, 1936), 279.

78. Trevor Wilson, "Lord Bryce's Investigation into Alleged German Atrocities in Belgium" *Journal of Contemporary History* 14 (1979), 371.

79. Read, *Atrocity Propaganda,* 203.

80. More than 70 years later, the use of titles in Great Britain continues to thrive. According to Robert Worcester, chairman of Market and Opinion Research International, a London polling firm, "There is an overwhelming public support for the honors system in Britain. It's the cheapest coin of the realm for the Government. It is enormously valuable in terms of generating good will and costs almost nothing." *New York Times,* December 31, 1987.

81. Wilson, "Lord Bryce's Investigation," 372. According to Wilson, "Concerning the use of poison gas against combatants, of torpedoes against passenger ships, of aircraft against cities, all that need be said is that the Germans did employ these measures, and that Britons did deem them atrocious. But the Bryce Report of May 1915 has a different sort of interest: as an example of the manner in which the pressures of the war could affect the standards of conduct of honorable, enlightened, fastidious Englishmen" (370).

82. H.A.L. Fisher, *James Bryce* (New York: Macmillan, 1927), 2:133–134.

83. The report was printed for the United States as a booklet of 60 pages. A separate 300-page volume included five appendixes: Appendix A, some 500 depositions and extracts from depositions; Appendix B, diaries in the original German with English translations, with photographs; Appendix C, German proclamations posted in Belgian and French towns; Appendix D, the rules of the Hague Conventions dealing with the conduct of war on land; Appendix E, a selection of statements collected in France by a Professor Morgan.

84. Another example of timely proclamation by the British was its treatment of the noto-

rious secret "Zimmermann Telegram" of January 17, 1917, which most historians agree was a key element in finally convincing Wilson that he must take America into the war. It had been intercepted and decoded by British cryptoanalysts almost immediately, yet it was not until February 23 that it was given to Ambassador Page for transmittal to Washington. Germany had announced resumption of unrestricted submarine warfare effective February 1. The author presumes the five-week delay was purposefully calculated to coincide with a sharp rise in allied ship sinkings, which occurred, and thus provide enhanced leverage for Britain's propaganda efforts. The telegram (from German Foreign Minister Arthur Zimmermann to Herr von Eckhardt, the German minister in Mexico) read: "We intend to begin unrestricted submarine warfare on the first of February. We shall endeavor in spite of this to keep the United States neutral. In the event of this not succeeding, we make Mexico a proposal of alliance on the following basis: make war together, make peace together, generous financial support, and an understanding on our part that Mexico is to reconquer the lost territories in Texas, New Mexico, and Arizona. The settlement in detail is left to you. You will inform the president [of Mexico] of the above most secretly as soon as the outbreak of war with the United States is certain and add the suggestion that he should, on his own initiative, invite Japan to immediate adherence and at the same time mediate between Japan and ourselves. Please call the president's attention to the fact that the unrestricted employment of our submarines now offers the prospect of compelling England to make peace within a few months. Acknowledge receipt." Barbara W. Tuchman, *The Zimmermann Telegram* (New York: The Viking Press, 1958), 146.

85. Read, *Atrocity Propaganda*, 206. The author also included this note: "Letter to Professor B.E. Schmitt from Sir Stephen Gaselee, librarian of the foreign office, of June 22, 1939, confirmed the loss" (207).

86. *Reports on the Violations of the Rights of Nations and of the Laws and Customs of War in Belgium*, as cited by Read, 90. Bitter German retaliation against those they labeled *franc-tireurs* was not limited to the Belgians. On July 29, 1916, British merchant captain Charles Fryatt was executed in Germany following a trial during which he was called a "*franc-tireur* of the sea." In March 1915, as master of the *Brussels*, Fryatt had unsuccessfully tried to ram the *U-33* after the submarine had surfaced and signaled the British steamer to show her flag and heave to. In June 1916, a German destroyer finally captured the *Brussels* along with its master and took him to Germany for a trial during which Fryatt admitted that he had acted under British admiralty orders. The Germans built their case against Fryatt on international law: if the submarine had attacked or Fryatt had judged that the U-boat was about to attack, he had the right to counterattack; if Fryatt had attacked first, as the Germans claimed, then the merchant captain had acted outside the law and was subject to summary execution upon capture. For British propagandists, such an issue was irrelevant; Fryatt's execution was yet another example of German atrocities on the high seas. A booklet, *The Murder of Captain Fryatt*, was promptly prepared and published in seven languages. After the Armistice in 1918, the second of the three charges preferred against the Kaiser by the British was "Offenses in the Category of the Execution of Captain Fryatt."

87. Fisher, *James Bryce*, 2:134.

88. *The German Army in Belgium: The White Book of May 1915*, trans. E. N. Bennett (New York: B. W. Huebsch, 1921), xiii–xiv.

89. Ibid., xviii.

90. *Germany's Violation of the Laws of War, 1914–15—Compiled Under the Auspices of the French Ministry of Foreign Affairs*, trans. J.O.P. Bland (New York: G. P. Putnam's Sons, 1915), v, xii. (The Trinity College [Connecticut] Library copy I examined was a gift to that institution from Sir Gilbert Parker, signed and dated February 14, 1916.)

91. William G. Shepherd, "The Free Lance and the Faker: An Inside Story of War Reporting," *Everybody's Magazine*, March 1917, 339–340.

92. Philip Gibbs, *Now It Can Be Told* (New York: Harper & Brothers, 1920), 521.

93. George Creel, *War Criminals and Punishment* (New York: National Travel Club, 1944), 139.

94. Creel to Deirdre Mason, a student leader of the National Student Federation of America, at the NSFA convention in 1929, as cited by Joseph E. Persico in *Edward R. Murrow: An American Original* (New York: McGraw-Hill, 1988), 57.

95. *Encyclopaedia Britannica*: 2:380.

96. William H. McNeill, *Arnold J. Toynbee: A Life* (New York: Oxford University Press, 1989). "Both pamphlets were prepared in haste, and printed in enormous editions, intended to strengthen public conviction of the righteousness of the Allied Cause. Their tendentiousness, especially in claiming that the Germans were responsible for Turkish atrocities, makes these pamphlets far better propaganda than the big book, and rather more deserving of the regret Toynbee later felt for his participation in the wartime distortion of truth," 74.

97. "Atrocities" committed against Christian Armenians, this time by Muslims in the republic of Azerbaijan in the Soviet Union, was front-page news again, in the *New York Times* of January 17, 1990. Refugees from Azerbaijan's capital city of Baku told of Armenians being "burned, stabbed, beaten to death, and thrown from windows."

98. The historian, H. Pirenne, recorded in 1928 that 5,246 Belgians civilians had been killed by the Germans in 1914. Read, *Atrocity Propaganda*, 83.

99. Fisher, the eccentric yet brilliant naval strategist, had promoted development of the all-big-gun battleship that ostensibly had revolutionized naval warfare; he also supervised the Royal Navy's switch from coal to oil. Fisher had first been appointed First Sea Lord in 1904, retired in 1910, was recalled to the Admiralty in October 1914, and resigned in May 1915 (along with Churchill) over the failed Dardanelles campaign. Fisher understood the realities of submarine warfare when he wrote, "The question arises as to what a submarine can do against a merchant ship when she has found her. She cannot capture the merchant ship; she has no spare hands to put a prize crew on board; little or nothing would be gained by disabling her engines or propellers; she cannot convoy her into harbour and, in fact, it is impossible for the submarine to deal with commerce in the light and provisions of international law. ...There is nothing else the submarine can do except sink her capture. ...One flag is very much like another seen through the light of a periscope ... and the fear is natural that the only thing the officer of the hostile submarine would make sure of would be that the flag seen was not that of his own country." Fisher concluded his analysis of submarine warfare: "The essence of war is violence, and moderation in war is imbecility." *Memories and Records* (New York: G H. Doran, 1920), 2:178–180.

100. Germany built 344 submarines during the war, added to the 28 with which her navy began the conflict. Only in the last half year of the war did the number sunk each month exceed the rate of replacement. In November 1918, 226 were under construction and 212 more were on the drawing boards. Dan van der Vat, *The Atlantic Campaign: World War II's Great Struggle at Sea* (New York: Harper & Row, 1988), 41.

101. R.H. Gibson and Maurice Prendergast, *The German Submarine War, 1914–1918* (New York: Constable: London, 1931), 351–382.

102. Colin Simpson, *The Lusitania* (Boston: Little, Brown, 1972), 74–75.

103. Winston S. Churchill, *World Crisis* (New York: Charles Scribner's Sons, 1923), 4:67–68.

104. Simpson, *The Lusitania*, 36–37.

105. Churchill, *World Crisis*, 426.

106. Admiral Reinhardt Scheer, *Germany's High Sea Fleet in the World War* (New York: Cassell, 1920), 227.

107. From the start of the war until April 6, 1917, 209 American citizens died as a result of German submarine attacks. More than half of that total died in the *Lusitania* sinking. Only 28 lost their lives on U.S. bottoms. In contrast, the Scandinavian nations, all of which remained neutral throughout the war, lost thousands of their citizens to German U-boats. Norway alone lost over 3,000 sailors and about half its merchant fleet. David A. Shannon, *Twentieth Century America* (Chicago: Rand McNally, 1963), 168.

108. Cunard Archives, National Maritime Museum, Greenwich, England, cited in Simpson, *The Lusitania*, 26. James Dugan in *The Great Iron Ship* (New York: Harper & Brothers, 1953) suggests that the monstrous *Great Eastern*, launched in 1858 (and which bankrupted its succession of backers over her 31-year life), was the financial model that drove British (and German) commercial ship owners to their government for subsidies by the turn of the century. According to Dugan, the first such liner designed to Royal Navy standards was the *Teutonic*, paraded by the Admiralty at a fleet review in 1889. A decade later, another giant White Star passenger ship was launched, also built to Royal Navy auxiliary-cruiser specifications. This was the *Oceanic*. More of a stimulant was the intensifying naval armaments race between England and Germany. In Great Britain, the Royal Navy agreed to share the escalating construction and operating costs of

new passenger liners that would bring prestige to England's maritime service in peacetime and, perhaps more important, operate as armed cruisers in the event of war. The only stipulation was that the owners accommodate to the specifications set down by the Admiralty.

109. Simpson, *The Lusitania*, 25–28.

110. Kenneth MacLeish, "Was There A Gun?" *Sports Illustrated*, December 24, 1962, 44. The photographs were taken by American diver and cameraman John Light during three years of dives in a private attempt to solve the mystery.

111. The *Titanic* sank on the night of April 4, 1912, on her maiden voyage from England to the United States, 1,522 passengers and crew perishing. The formal British investigation into the ship's loss, headed by Lord Mersey, promptly exonerated both the ship's captain and the British Board of Trade. Wyn Craig Wade's book *The Titanic* (New York: Penguin, 1979) quotes a contemporary critic who called the British report "a vague, contradictory and a revolting example of official whitewash" (287). Three years later, Mersey again headed a formal board of inquiry into the loss of the *Lusitania*. England was then at war, and Mersey unquestionably saw his first duty was as that of a patriot. The final report was again a "whitewash," but this time with much graver implications.

112. Patrick Beesley, *Room 40: British Naval Intelligence 1914–18* (New York: Harcourt Brace Jovanovich, 1982), 113.

113. Ibid., 114. A July 29 telegram from Cunard in New York to Liverpool pinpointed the location of the munitions on the liner's last voyage as "in the trunkway of meat boxes and 2 baggage deck." This trunkway was just below the bridge where *U-20*'s torpedo struck, and immediately forward of the first boiler-room bulkhead. Ibid. Light claimed he discovered in his dives that the shells were filled, but not fused. However, a telegram to Liverpool from Cunard's general manager in New York following the *Lusitania*'s previous eastbound voyage had described "Special shipments, Bethlehem, 18 cases fuses, 1466 cases shrapnel shells filled" and stowed in the same space as the fuses, which consisted of fulminate of mercury, a highly explosive substance. It is a fair assumption that on the *Lusitania*'s next eastbound voyage fuses would again have been stowed in the same location. Ibid. Beesley also points out that, while there were survivors from all of the boiler rooms, "none of them mentioned any explosion and some of them reported that water had first entered No. 1 Boiler Room through the bulkhead at its forward end. None of them were called to give evidence. A large proportion of the liner's seamen were working in the passengers' luggage store, just above where the ammunition was stored. Not surprisingly, not a man survived" (115).

114. Robert D. Ballard, *Exploring the Lusitania* (New York: Warner, 1995), 194.

115. Ibid., 195.

116. Beesley, *Room 40*, 91.

117. Simpson, *Lusitania*, 240–241.

118. Patrick Beesly wrote that, based on all the evidence that was available to him at the time of publication of his book in 1982, he was "reluctantly driven to the conclusion that there *was* a conspiracy deliberately to put the *Lusitania* at risk in the hopes that even an abortive attack on her would bring the United States into the war." *Room 40*, 122. Samuel Flagg Bemis in *A Diplomatic History of the United States* (New York: Holt, Rinehart & Winston, 1936) also wondered if the British had not purposely imperiled the *Lusitania*: "This same exposure, possibly deliberate, was true in the case of the unarmed cross-channel passenger boat *Sussex*. ... It was lumbering along, without escort, through a sea littered with the wreckage of recently torpedoed vessels" (610).

119. Diary, May 7, 1915. Edward Mandell House Papers, Manuscripts and Archives, Yale University Library.

120. Ibid., May 8.

121. Author's collection. Printed by Robert & Leete Ltd., London, W 2464/448.

122. *The Letters and Journal of Brand Whitlock: The Journal* (New York: Appleton-Century, 1936), 222.

123. Rowland Ryder, *Edith Cavell* (New York: Stein & Day, 1975), 237–238.

124. The first two of these German nurses were executed under substantially the same circumstances as Cavell. Lasswell reported that there was "not a murmur in the German Press" and discussed a conversation between an American journalist and the German officer in charge of propaganda for the General Staff: "Why don't you do something to counteract the British pro-

paganda in America?" "Why, what do you mean?" "Raise the devil about those nurses the French shot the other day." "What? Protest? The French had a perfect right to shoot them!" *Propaganda Technique*, 32.

125. Trevor Wilson, *The Myriad Faces of War: Britain and the Great War, 1914–1918* (Cambridge: Polity Press, 1986), 744.

126. Ryder, *Edith Cavell*, 237–238.

127. Leonard Stein, *The Balfour Declaration* (New York: Simon & Schuster, 1961), 546.

128. J.L. Hammond, *C. P. Scott of the Manchester Guardian* (New York: Harcourt Brace, 1934), 197.

129. Diary, December 17, 1915. House Papers.

130. Sir Arthur Willert, *Washington and Other Memories* (Boston: Houghton Mifflin, 1972), 53, 79.

131. Stephen Gwynn, ed. *The Letters and Friendships of Sir Cecil Spring Rice: A Record* (New York: Houghton Mifflin, 1929), 2 vols.

132. Historian Arthur Walworth recorded during an interview with Willert in 1959: "U.S. officials asked Spring-Rice who the Intelligence Chief was in the U.S. and he denied there was any. But the British Government thought it best to tell the truth to the State Department, so Sir William Wiseman was instructed to reveal his identity to [State Department counselor] Polk. He said to Polk: 'I understand you wish to see the Chief of British Intelligence in the United States.' When Polk replied affirmatively, Wiseman said, 'You can see him right before you.'" Arthur Walworth Papers, Manuscripts and Archives, Yale University Library.

133. Seymour, *House Papers*, 2:244.

134. Guy Gaunt, *The Yield of the Years* (London: Hutchinson, 1940), 137–138.

135. Gaunt never quite accommodated to Wiseman as head of British intelligence in the United States. The title page of Gaunt's memoir unambiguously refers to the author as "Naval Attaché and Chief of the British Intelligence Service in the United States, 1914–1918." In his retrospective, Gaunt recalled that he had "read in the *Saturday Evening Post* not so long ago that at a dinner party where everybody took me for the head of the British Intelligence, Wiseman was grinning quietly to himself while Gaunt 'squirmed under his eye.' The fact is that Wiseman played a very small part under me, and then only at intervals." *Yield of the Years*, 172.

136. Interview by Arthur Walworth at Wiseman's home, 988 Fifth Avenue, New York City, September 28, 1959. Walworth Papers.

137. He was taken to lunch by Sir Eyre Crowe, a veteran model diplomat of the old school, and told that there was really no need for the services of any information or publicity officer in the staid old Foreign Office, which had a long-standing rule that only laconic formal releases were given out and no questions answered. Arthur Walworth to author.

138. Willert Papers.

139. Ibid.

140. Ibid.

141. Willert to Dawson, October 22, 1914. Ibid.

142. Ibid.

143. Von Mach, *Germany's Point of View* (Chicago: A.C. McClurg, 1915), 216.

144. The famous telegram read: "I send you my sincere congratulations on having, without any appeal to friendly powers, succeeded through the energy of your own people in opposing the armed raiders who have invaded your territory as disturbers of the peace, in restoring tranquility, and in upholding the independence of your country in the face of alien aggression." Emil Ludwig, *Wilhelm Hohenzollern: The Last of the Kaisers* (New York: G.P. Putnam's Sons, 1927), 198–199.

145. Quoted in Paul Ferris, *The House of Northcliffe: A Biography of an Empire* (New York: World, 1972), 103–104.

146. Willert Papers.

147. Ibid. Ian Beith, also known as Ian Hay, was Captain John Hay Beith, a British novelist of modest achievement. His most recent book had been *The First Hundred Thousand*, about "Kitchener's army." After 11 months in France, he arrived in the United States in October 1916 and told reporters that during his stay he would manage the British section of the Allied bazaars and lecture on his experiences at the front.

148. Willert to Dawson, February 13, 1917. Willert Papers. In a conversation in 1959 with

Arthur Walworth, Willert, who obviously cherished his wartime relationship with Wiseman, told him he had written *The Road to Safety* "mainly to put Sir William Wiseman on the map." Ibid.

149. Willert Papers.

150. Ibid. Among the "purposes" of the Vigilantes, as spelled out on their letterhead: "To work vigorously for preparedness, mental, moral and physical; To work with especial vigor for Universal Military Training and Service under exclusive Federal control, as a basic principle of American democracy."

151. Creel Papers. Creel responded that he thought it "wise" to withdraw the book from sale: "Frankly, there is nothing pro–German in any of its pages, but I have no doubt a criticism will be directed against many pages in which a friendly spirit is manifested toward certain individual Germans. All this may seem foolish, and it is foolish to me, but we are dealing with an excited frame of mind that regards everything as pro–German that is not violently anti–German." Ibid.

152. Willert Papers.

153. Ibid.

154. Sir Arthur Willert, *The Road to Safety: A Study in Anglo-American Relations* (New York: Frederick Praeger, 1953), 83.

155. W.B. Fowler, in the annotated bibliography of his biography of Wiseman, *British–American Relations, 1917–1918: The Role of Sir William Wiseman* (Princeton: Princeton University Press, 1969), referring to Wiseman's papers in Yale University Library, wrote: "The files were culled by Wiseman and contain very little related to his intelligence work" (301). In his *The Road to Safety*, Willert defensively rejects any notion of Wiseman as a propagandist before America entered the war, contradicting his own statements in his correspondence with Dawson at the time: "As for the allegation that, as Great Britain's super-propagandist, he directed a propaganda organization in the United States during the neutrality period, it is exploded by the fact that there was then no British propaganda or publicity there for him to direct" (84).

156. Arthur Walworth to author.

157. Charles Seymour, ed., *The Intimate Papers of Colonel House* (New York: Houghton Mifflin, 1926), 2:400.

158. January 26, 1917. House Papers.

159. Diary, June 22, 1917. Gordon Auchincloss Papers, Manuscripts and Archives, Yale University Library.

160. Willert Papers.

161. Fowler, *British–American Relations*, 17.

162. April 3, 1917, House to Wilson, House Papers.

163. Seymour, *Papers of Colonel House*, 3:86–87. Wiseman, too, understood the power residing in the office of the president. He wrote to London: "The essential fact to be grasped is that for the purpose of the War the Government of the United States means the personal decisions of President Wilson. The President of the United States is executively almost an autocrat for the period of his term in office, and such a crisis as War considerably increases his power." Fowler, *British–American Relations*, 247.

164. Wiseman Papers.

165. Willert Papers.

166. Fowler, *British–American Relations*, 237. Another indication of the scope and depth of Wiseman's unique diplomatic role is given in the voluminous index entries on his activities in Seymour's *Intimate Papers of Colonel House*, vol. 3 (*Into the World War*) and vol. 4 (*The Ending of the War*). Under "Wiseman, Sir William," are the following headings: "British chief of secret service; Memorandum on American cooperation; describes arrangements for frank interchange of opinions between British and Americans; his Memorandum upon conference with President on ship-building programme; helps Northcliffe; on importance of America as ally; his financial commission to Washington; comment of, on Lord Robert Cecil's cable to House; Memorandum of, on Wilsonian war policy; in special confidence to Balfour; his Memorandum on the Inquiry; reports on accomplishments of Reading; emphasizes the 'America first' attitude of United States; his Memorandum on Inter-allied Cooperation; insistent that House shall define his appointment to War Commission as temporary; at Reading dinner; work for coordination; comment of, on cable of House to Wilson; explains considerations on which United States joined Supreme War Council; cables Balfour on Wilson's views as to use to be made of American troops; his com-

ments on House's interests in early plans for League; Memorandum of, on Wilson's visit to Magnolia; cables Lord Reading concerning Wilson's view about publishing League plans; on Wilson's fear of Allied policy toward Germany; cables on American attitudes toward economic policy of Allies; on dislike of Allies for Fourteen Points; in discussion of Fourteen Points; opposed to Wilson's sitting in Peace Congress; agrees with House on need of Committees of Peace Conference; liaison officer between Americans and British; helps draft letter on League resolutions; Memorandum of, on mandates; advises George to work with President through House; incident connected with League drafts described by; his account of conversation with Wilson," 4:552.

167. Ted Morgan, *Maugham* (New York: Simon & Schuster, 1980), 186. At the outbreak of war, Maugham was 40 and, at five feet six inches, four inches too short too serve. By October 1914, enlistees were accepted in the British army at five-five. A month later, after the 30,000 casualties at Mons and Aisne, five feet three inches became the standard. By 1918 conscription covered all healthy males to age 50.

168. Maugham's team comprised Emanuel V. Voska, a Bohemian-American striving for Czechoslovakian independence and the most effective intriguer of the lot; Joseph Martinek, editor of a Czech-language newspaper; Vac Svarc, attorney for the Slovak League; and the Rev. Alois Koikol, a New York City minister. Emanuel V. Voska and Will Irwin, *Spy and Counter-Spy* (New York: Doubleday, Doran, 1940), 214–215.

169. Wiseman Papers.

170. H. Montgomery Hyde, *Room 3603: The Story of the British Intelligence Center in New York during World War II* (New York: Farrar, Straus, 1962), 63, 77.

171. F. J. P. Veale, "The Wicked Kaiser Myth—Demonstrating the Unreliability of Unanimous Verdict of Public Opinion," *Social Justice Review*, April 1960, 11.

172. Ibid., 10, 12.

173. Willert, *Road to Safety*, 4.

174. Ibid., 13.

175. Ibid., 14.

Chapter 3–The Germans

1. U-boats early in the war carried experienced maritime officers and pilots to help submarine commanders identify merchant ships. *U-20* had a pilot on board on Schwieger's fateful war patrol. The submarine undoubtedly also carried a current issue of *Jane's Fighting Ships*, which included photographs, plan and elevation drawings, pertinent specifications, and silhouettes of nearly all the men-of-war of the world's navies. The 1914 edition of *Jane's* (London: Sampson Low Marston) included two pages of large-size silhouettes of "British Liners of 18 kts. or over," in a scale of 160 feet=1 inch. The *Lusitania*, "Cunard, 25 kts.," was shown next to its sister ships, the *Mauretania* and the larger *Olympic*. The same edition also had a comprehensive "Index of Merchant Ships" listing tonnage and speeds for all merchantmen 5,000 tons and larger. Schwieger was probably also issued a copy of *Lloyd's Register*, with details (but no silhouettes) of the world's merchant, passenger, and cable-laying ships down to 100 tons in displacement.

2. Beginning in 1916, merchantmen were "defensively" armed with small cannons, as much to compel German submarine commanders to violate cruiser rules as to sink submarines. In fact, few U-boats were sunk by merchant-ship gunfire. Minefields were laid and steel-chain nets floated just under the surface in the waterways along known submarine routes to and from their stations. Decoy "Q-ships" were fitted out with hidden guns to plod along as tempting targets and lure unsuspecting submarines to the surface. Rudimentary hydrophones were developed in vain attempts to track submarines under water and depth charges were developed to destroy them. However, it was the convoy system of escorting merchant ships with destroyers and a new breed of small, agile subchasers, forced on a reluctant Admiralty by incoming Prime Minister David Lloyd George in December 1916, that finally turned the tide against the German undersea menace to England's lifeline.

3. If the German fleet were to sally forth in strength, the plan was to engage it and defeat it decisively in one great naval battle. Such a battle was ardently wished for by the British Admiralty, but never came. The Battle of Jutland of May 31, 1916, was declared a victory by both navies.

While the *Hochseeflotte* achieved a numerical superiority in the number and tonnage of Royal Navy ships sunk, and its gunnery and capital-ship design proved the better, the German surface fleet never again left its harbors to challenge the British surface-fleet's numerical supremacy.

4. A passenger aboard the *Lusitania*, who went on deck just before 1 P.M., reported: "It was a beautiful day then, light wind, a smooth sea, and bright sunshine. I thought to myself that if a German submarine really meant business, she would have to wait weeks for a more ideal chance than the present weather conditions." Charles E. Lauriat, Jr., *The Lusitania's Last Voyage, Being a Narrative of the Torpedoing and Sinking of the R.M.S. Lusitania by a German Submarine off the Irish Coast, May 7, 1915* (New York: Houghton Mifflin, 1915), 70.

5. Schwieger's log (in German time, one hour later than the Greenwich Mean Time observed aboard the *Lusitania*), from the Bundesarchiv, Coblenz, is the translation from Thomas A. Bailey, "German Documents Relating to the Lusitania," *Journal of Modern History*, September 1936, 335–336.

6. Edward M. House was aboard the *Lusitania* on February 5, 1915, when the American flag was run up the jack staff as the ship approached the Irish coast. His diary of the following day reported: "I found ... that Captain Dow had been greatly alarmed the night before. ...He expected to be torpedoed, and that was the reason for raising the American flag. I can see many possible complications arising from this incident. Every newspaper in London has asked me about it, but, fortunately, I was not an eye-witness to it and have been able to say that I only knew it from hearsay." Charles Seymour, ed., *The Intimate Papers of Colonel House* (New York: Houghton Mifflin, 1926), 1:361.

7. Charles E. Lauriat, Jr., who had crossed the Atlantic 23 times and was one of the American survivors, wrote this: "Going along the passage (on deck B [promenade deck]) I looked down some of the cross passages that led to the staterooms, and at the bottom of the ones I passed I saw that the portholes were open and that the water could not have been more than a few feet from them. Here let me state that I consider it most extraordinary that the portholes on the lower decks should not have been closed and sealed as we steamed through the war zone. At luncheon the portholes in the dining saloon on deck D [upper deck] were open, and so I doubt not that all the others on that deck were open. I cannot speak with certainty in regard to the portholes on deck E [main deck]. ...I swam about 100 feet away from the ship. ...The Lusitania did not go down anything like head first: she had, rather, settled along her whole water line. This convinces me that practically all the ports must have been open, even those as far down as deck E." During the Mersey hearings, the *Lusitania*'s master, Captain William Turner, testified to the contrary. He said he stated that he had taken "precautions" when his ship entered the "Danger Zone," namely, "the waters in which enemy submarines might be expected." He had ordered all lifeboats under davits swung out and all bulkhead doors between compartments closed, except those required for the working of the ship, adding, "The portholes were also closed." (*The Lusitania's Last Voyage*, 14–15, 18–19, 136–137).

8. Thomas A. Bailey and Paul B. Ryan in *The Lusitania Disaster* (New York: Free Press, 1975), suggest that this reference of Schwieger's may have been a "late addition" to the *U-20*'s log (158–159). After Schwieger had returned to base and learned of the hysterical press reaction in most countries to his naval victory, he may have been prompted—or ordered—to add such a mollifying reference as a public-relations gesture for future historians. If he had doctored his log, Schwieger would not be the last U-boat commander to have done so. Historian Michael Gannon has documented two similar instances of U-boat logs being altered during World War II in his *Operation Drumbeat* (New York: Harper & Row, 1990), 52–53.

9. *U-20* under Schwieger's command ran aground in fog off the coast of Denmark in November 1915, and was scuttled. Schwieger was given command of *U-88*, which never returned from a war patrol in 1916. It is presumed *U-88* struck a mine and was sunk with all hands. At the end of the war, Schwieger's record ranked in the top ten among U-boat commanders in number of enemy ships sunk. Bailey and Ryan, *Lusitania Disaster*, 161–162.

10. Quoted in Charles Callan Tansill, *America Goes to War* (Boston: Little, Brown, 1938), 277–279.

11. Ibid.

12. Ibid. On May 9, the influential *Frankfurter Zeitung* editorially responded rationally: "The Lusitania carried passengers! In truth we should have been infinitely better pleased if the ship, which for many months has been of aid to the enemy and has done us harm, could have

been destroyed without the necessity of this catastrophe befalling its passengers. ... And if any-one complains and feels doubt about the justification of our war methods, we should ask him what he thinks about England's war of starvation against Germany, and whether he imagines perhaps that it is our purpose to be starved to submission without acting in self-defense? And we shall also ask him what he thinks about the shipment of thousands of millions worth of arms and munitions from America, an assistance by which alone, generally speaking, during the past months, the continued participation in the war has been made possible for the English and French." Lauriat, *Lusitania's Last Voyage*, 101–111.

13. Tansill, *America Goes to War*, 277–279.

14. Ibid.

15. Von Bernstorff, *My Three Years in America*, 35.

16. On April 13, 1918, the ten-foot-high, 1,400-pound statue was quietly removed from its pedestal on the terrace in front of the War College and put away "in seclusion in a cold, damp storeroom" in the basement of the building, reportedly at the behest of Woodrow Wilson. *New York Times*, April 14, 1918.

17. *Memoirs of Count Bernstorff* (New York: Random House, 1936), 99. In his 1920 book, *My Three Years in America*, von Bernstorff recorded that in addition to promoting goodwill, Chancellor Bernard von Bulow had told him, as he was leaving on his new assignment, that he "must without fail bring the negotiations about an Arbitration Treaty with the United States, which had been left unfinished owing to the death of my predecessor, to a satisfactory conclusion." Germany, alone among the great powers, had refused to sign the protocols. Von Bernstorff reflected that "the effect upon the American mind of our obstruction in this matter should not be under-estimated. It helped not a little to convince public opinion in the United States of the alleged warlike intentions of the German people" (24).

18. Clara Eve Schieber, *The Transformation of American Sentiment Toward Germany, 1870–1914* (New York: Cornhill, 1923), 136. The author capped her simplistic analysis by includ-ing the results of a questionnaire she had mailed after the war to "leading citizens of the United States" (university and college presidents, teachers, ministers, doctors, lawyers, prominent busi-nessmen, government officials and diplomats, newspaper editors, and writers) to establish their attitudes toward Germany in 1914. Acknowledging the survey's limitations—"Passions were still warm and an expression of regard for Germany was viewed as savoring of treason"—the author concluded that "the U.S. was more suspicious of, and unfriendly towards, Germany than towards any other European state" (263–264). Another conclusion was that the feeling of fear and sus-picion was largely due to "the increasingly arrogant, saber-rattling, swash-buckling attitude of German officials and the growing militaristic tendency of the German government" (284). Wal-ter Millis, in *The Martial Spirit: A Study of Our War with Spain* (New York: Literary Guild of America, 1931), added another interpretation of the Dewey–von Diederichs confrontation: "Admiral von Diederichs ... was extremely irritating. He got in the way of Admiral Dewey's patrols, resented his blockade regulations, annoyed him with searchlights at night, carried on com-munications with the Spaniards, and behaved in other ways with exasperating provocativeness. ...Our own press was cheerfully convinced of the nefariousness of the German intentions, and was cartooning the still youthful Kaiser with a ferocity which was to be prophetic" (331).

19. Thomas A. Bailey, "Dewey and the Germans at Manila Bay," *American Historical Review*, 15 no. 6 (70).

20. Ibid., 71.

21. "He was generally known as the recluse of the White House. He only received people with whom he had political business to settle. Particularly from diplomats and other foreigners Mr. Wilson kept very aloof...." Von Bernstorff, *My Three Years in America*, 61.

22. Robert Lansing, *War Memoirs of Robert Lansing* (New York: Bobbs-Merrill, 1935), 356–358.

23. Von Bernstorff was supported in these views by embassy First Counselor Eduard Haniel von Haimhausen. In a November 10, 1916, report dealing with American public opinion, von Haimhausen emphasized that the key element in friendly relations between Germany and America was the issue of the submarine: "There is one point on which we must be absolutely clear. A withdrawal from, or even a material limitation of, the exercise of the so-called conces-sion which we made to the United States this spring in connection with the U-boat war, means war with the United States." Quoted in Charles Seymour, *American Neutrality, 1914–1917: Essays*

on the Causes of American Intervention in the World War (New Haven: Yale University Press, 1935), 156.

24. Von Bernstorff, *My Three Years in America*, 50.

25. Ibid., 36.

26. Von Bernstorff, *Memoirs of Count Bernstorff*, 138.

27. Carl Wittke, *German-Americans and the World War (with Special Emphasis on Ohio's German-Language Press)* (Columbus: Ohio State Archeological and Historical Society, 1936), 7.

28. Hugo Muensterberg, *The War and America* (Columbus: D. Appleton, 1914), 18–19.

29. Quoted in Ray Stannard Baker, *Woodrow Wilson: Life and Letters* (New York: Doubleday, Doran, 1931–35), Muensterberg to Wilson, November 7, 1914, 5:222.

30. Ibid., 5:223.

31. Ibid., 5:223–224.

32. Ibid., 5:225.

33. Ibid., 5:225–226.

34. Edmund von Mach, *Germany's Point of View* (Chicago: A. C. McClurg, 1915), ii.

35. Ibid., i.

36. Edmund von Mach, *Official Diplomatic Documents Relating to the Outbreak of the European War* (New York: Macmillan, 1916), v.

37. John William Burgess, *Reminiscences of an American Scholar: The Beginnings of Columbia University* (New York: Columbia University Press, 1934), 96–97. Burgess's autobiographical reflections end before the outbreak of World War I, as if he were reluctant to play over his obvious disappointments with the antagonistic reactions of his colleagues and his harsh treatment in the press.

38. John William Burgess, *The European War of 1914: Its Causes, Purposes, and Probable Results* (Chicago: A.C. McClurg, 1915), 87.

39. Burgess, *Reminiscences*, 313.

40. Burgess, *The European War of 1914*, iii, iv.

41. Ibid., 192–193.

42. John William Burgess, *America's Relations to the Great War* (Chicago: A.C. McClurg, 1916), 17–19.

43. Frank Harris, *England or Germany?* (New York: Wilmarth Press, 1915), 102.

44. U.S. Senate Subcommittee on the Judiciary, *Brewing and Liquor Interests and German and Bolshevik Propaganda*, Senate Document No. 62, 66th Congress, 1st session, 1919, 102: 1406–1407.

45. Edwin J. Clapp, *Economic Aspects of the War: Neutral Rights, Belligerent Claims and American Commerce in the Years 1914–1915* (New Haven: Yale University Press, 1915), 15.

46. Ibid., 309.

47. Karl J. R. Arndt and May E. Olson, *German-American Newspapers and Periodicals, 1732–1955: History and Bibliography* (Heidelberg: Quelle & Meyer, 1961), 5, 9.

48. Ibid., 46, 131, 313, 427, 501. Other leading states included New York with 58 German-language daily and weekly newspapers; Illinois, 55; Ohio, 50; Pennsylvania, 44; and Iowa, 40—for a nationwide total of about 500 at the outbreak of the Great War.

49. The Rev. Otto Wappler, Monona, Iowa, quoted in the *Official Bulletin of the National German-American Alliance*, January 1916.

50. Clifton James Child, *The German-Americans in Politics, 1914–1917* (New York: Arno Press, 1970; Repr. Univ. of Wisconsin, 1939), 3.

51. Congress ratified the Eighteenth Amendment to the Constitution on January 16, 1919, and prohibition that went into effect one year later. "The prohibitionists might never have been able to gain the necessary vote in the Senate and House of Representatives to gain the passage of the Eighteenth Amendment if they had not had a murderous stroke of luck. Their chance was the Great War. ... Pabst and Busch were German; therefore beer was unpatriotic. Liquor stopped American soldiers from firing straight; therefore liquor was a total evil. Brewing used up eleven million loaves of barley bread a day, which could have fed the starving Allies; therefore the consumption of alcohol was treason. Pretzels were German in name; therefore to defend Old Glory, they were banned from the saloons of Cincinnati." Andrew Sinclair, *Prohibition: The Era of Excess* (Boston: Little, Brown, 1962), 20. The Twenty-first Amendment, effective December 5, 1933, repealed prohibition.

52. Wittke, *German-Americans and the World War*, 10.

53. *New York Times*, March 29, 1918. Was the National German-American Alliance, in fact, directed from Berlin, as was charged during the Senate investigation of the Alliance (February 23–April 13, 1918)—or were the findings of the subcommittee skewed by wartime hatred and hysteria? Child concluded that the proceedings of the investigation "were characterized by a surprising amount of distortion and misapprehension of the German-American position. ...The investigation failed to differentiate properly between evidence based upon the activities of the Alliance before the United States entered the war and after. ...Quotations from its monthly organ were detached from their context and used against it. Evidence in German was presented before the committee in large quantities, and yet some of its members were unable to understand the language." Child, *German-Americans in Politics*, 170–171.

54. The infamous "scrap of paper" reference to the treaty of 1839 originated from Chancellor Theobold von Bethmann-Hollweg during his emotion-filled conversation with the British ambassador to Germany, Sir Edward Goschen, late on August 4, just before England's ultimatum to Germany expired. The sentence from which the phrase came was: "Just for a scrap of paper Great Britain is going to make war on a kindred nation." The German later said that he did not realize he could speak English so fluently. Former chancellor Bernard von Bulow wrote angrily about the chancellor's second momentous indiscretion of the day: "There is no need to be a Machiavelli to understand that if, in a moment of collapse, Bethmann really said these unlucky words, the whole *raison d'État*, the supreme interests of the nation, demanded his instant and formal denial of them. It should have been a case of statement for statement; the 'no' would have weighed equally with the 'yes.' Bethmann had no right to lay on our people the burden of this terrible catchword, systematically, incessantly exploited, as long as the war lasted, by the Allies—and after it, at the Versailles peace conference—no right to brand us as the infamous violators of treaty rights, a nation against which mankind must protect itself." *Memoirs of Prince von Bulow* (Boston: Little, Brown, 1931), 3:196.

55. In December 1914, Dernburg published a pamphlet entitled "The Case of Belgium, in the Light of Official Reports Found in the Secret Archives of the Belgian Government after the Occupation of Brussels." He summarized the incriminating documents this way: "1. The first document is a report of the Chief of the Belgian General Staff, Major-General Ducarme, to the Minister of War, reporting a series of conversations which he had had with the Military Attaché of the British Legation, Lieutenant-Colonel Bernardiston, in Brussels. It discloses that as early as January, 1906, the Belgian Government was in consultation with the British Government over steps to be taken by Belgium, Great Britain and France against Germany. A plan had been fully elaborated for the landing of two British army corps in French ports to be transferred to the point in Belgium necessary for the operations against the Germans. Throughout the conversation the British and Belgian forces were spoken of as 'allied armies'; the British Military Attaché insisted on discussing the question of the chief command and he urged the establishment, in the meantime, of a Belgian spy system in Germany. 2. When in the year 1912 Lieutenant-Colonel Bernardiston had been succeeded by Lieutenant-Colonel Bridges as British Military Attaché in Brussels, and the Chief of the Belgian General Staff, Major-General Ducarme, had been succeeded by General Jungbluth as Chief of the Belgian General Staff, the conversations proceeded between the two latter officials. That is to say, these were not casual conversations between individuals, but a series of official conversations between representatives of their respective governments, in pursuance of a well-considered policy on the part of both governments. 3. The above documents are given additional significance by a report made in 1911 by Baron Greindl, Belgian Minister in Berlin to the Belgian Minister for Foreign Affairs, from which it appears that this representative of the Belgian Government in Berlin was familiar with the plans above set forth and protested against them, asking why like preparations had not been made with Germany to repel invasion by the French and English. Taken together, these documents show that *the British Government had the intention, in case of a Franco-German war, of sending troops into Belgium immediately—that is, of doing the very thing which, done by Germany, was used by England as pretext for declaring war on Germany.* They show also that the Belgian Government, in agreement with the English General Staff, took military precautions against a hypothetical German invasion of Belgium. On the other hand, the Belgian Government never made the slightest attempt to take military precautions, in agreement with the German Government, against an Anglo-French invasion of Belgium, though fully informed that it was the purpose of the British Government to

land and dispatch, across French territory into Belgium, 160,000 troops, without asking Belgium's permission, on the first outbreak of the European war. *This clearly demonstrates that the Belgian Government was determined from the outset to join Germany's enemies.*" (Emphasis in the original.)

56. Von Bernhardi fought back by defending his view of war as Darwinian "survival of the fittest." In a short book directed specifically at Americans, *Germany and England* (New York: G.W. Dillingham, 1915) he said that his detractors claimed he frivolously argued for war, and that he "pictured war, and especially war of conquest, as a necessary, and, indeed, the most reliable, instrument of statesmanship." What he claimed he had said was that war was justified only when "peaceful means fail" (8). How could it be, he asked, that Americans "who won their liberty in a conflict against England, and who achieved the acknowledged sovereignty of the Federal Union only through the heroic struggle which two sincere interpretations of the American Constitution gloriously contended on the battlefields of '61–'65" have other than "a lively understanding of this view?" (10–11). He concluded his book by assuring his readers that, "if victory should come to us," it is certain "that we should never think of assuming an antagonistic attitude toward America, much less dream of questioning the Monroe Doctrine" (84–85).

57. Roland G. Usher, *Pan-Germanism* (New York: Houghton Mifflin, 1913), 1, 4, 11. In 1918 Usher published a sequel, *The Winning of the War*, which was a confusing smorgasbord of fact and fancy.

58. Ibid., 12.

59. Ibid., 312.

60. In 1898, the Pan-German League's official publication, *Alldeutsche Blatter*, listed as its goals the following:

1. Adoption of a bill for reorganization of the navy.
2. Laying of a cable from Kiao-chau to Port Arthur, to connect with the Russian-Siberian cable.
3. Strengthening of the German foothold in Kiao-chau.
4. German coaling and cable stations in the Red Sea, in the West Indies, and near Singapore.
5. Complete possession of Samoa.
6. More subsidized steamship lines to Kiao-chau and Korea.
7. Understanding with France, Spain, Portugal, and the Netherlands about the laying of an independent cable from West Africa through the Congo to German East Africa, Madagascar, Batavia, and Tongking to Kiao-chau.
8. Development of the harbor of Swakopmund and railroads to Windhoek (both in German South-West Africa).
9. Securing of concessions for commerce and industry in Asia Minor.
10. Raising of the fund for German schools in foreign countries to 500,000 marks (it had been 150,000 marks), and a division in the Foreign Office to be created to deal with these schools; creation of pension fund for their teachers; standard German textbooks to be supplied to these schools.
11. Further endowment of the Colonization Commission by 100 million marks, the Polish Commission to be under the general commission.
12. Transference to the west of all local and other officials and military men of Polish "race."
13. Guarantee of an increase of pay to the German officials in the Polish parts of the East Province.
14. Acquisition of imperial holdings on the French border in Alsace-Lorraine and of Prussian royal holdings on the Danish border in Schleswig.
15. Employment of only German labor in imperial and state possessions and domains.
16. Prohibition of immigration of "less worthy elements" into the German Empire.
17. Possession of German citizenship by all Germans from the empire in foreign countries.
18. Taxation of foreign language–speaking firms, projects, and advertisements.
19. Prohibition of the use of foreign languages in clubs and meetings.
20. Germanization of all foreign place-names in the German Empire.
21. Establishment of a German consulate general for Bohemia in a German town in Bohemia.

22. Increase in the number of German commercial consuls in the Levant, Far East, South Africa, and Central and South America.

23. Increase in the number of German public libraries in the eastern provinces, in Schleswig, and in Alsace-Lorraine, to be supported by state and imperial subsidies.

24. Setting aside of a sum of money in the Colonial Office treasury to be used to pay for the attendance of the sons of Germans living in foreign countries at German schools in the fatherland.

25. A lessening of the obligation to military service of Germans living in foreign lands.

26. Germanization of foreign words in official language.

Mildred S. Werthheimer, *The Pan-German League, 1890–1914* (New York: Columbia University, 1924), 106–108.

61. Peter Chalmers Mitchell, *Report on the Propaganda Library in the Intelligence Division of the War Office* (London: H.M. Stationery Office, 1917), i.

62. Ibid., 3.

63. Ibid., 13.

64. In October 1915, the German Embassy released affidavits to the American press that purported to prove that on the previous August 19, British naval personnel from the *Baralong* had brutally slain survivors of the crew of *U-27*. The sworn statements included those of four American crewmen from the British muleship *Nicosian*, which had been attacked by the submarine. Before beginning to shell the muleship, *U-27* had forced the crew into the lifeboats. Another merchantman then arrived on the scene, flying the American flag. The unsuspecting submarine allowed the "neutral" ship to close on the action, presuming it would pick up the survivors. Instead, the *Baralong* ran up the British ensign at the moment it dropped its false superstructure to expose its guns, and promptly sank the U-boat. Six of the survivors, including the captain, were then shot while they were in the water, and six others, who had taken refuge on the abandoned *Nicosian*, were hunted down and killed. There was a later British response that explained away the shootings as a justifiable act of war. Then, in 1922, at the annual meeting of the Grotius Society, one speaker "openly regretted that 'on our side we have not brought the officer who was guilty of the crime of the *Baralong* before a court martial.'" James Morgan Read, *Atrocity Propaganda*, 127–130.

65. Yet another myth of German "inhumanity" would be purposefully created at the Paris peace conference by England and France as justification for their takeovers of Germany's colonies. Their delegates contended that Germany was uniquely morally unfit to govern native populations, claims based on exaggerated "evidence" of German maladministration, oppression, and cruelties. The exact opposite was true, according to one observer. Germany's West African colony of Togo was so successfully administered during the 14 years of German control that "up to 1914 both France and Britain cast admiring eyes on Togo, which the Germans called their model colony. ...The first president of independent Togo [in 1960] ... declared that Germany was 'the first country to bring us the benefits of modern life; she opened up the first roads, laid down our railways, and brought the first remedies of science to sickness and epidemics which were decimating our people; she built our first schools and carried us into the main stream of world affairs.' ...The German record, in Togo, at least, was one that not only stood comparison with the French and British record in West Africa before the war, but indeed showed up the deficiencies in their own development policies." Michael Crowder, *West Africa Under Colonial Rule* (Evanston, Ill.: Northwestern University Press, 1968), 242.

66. *New York Times*, August 23, 1914.

67. *New York Times Magazine*, May 28, 1916. The interview took place on April 12, and was sent to the United States by three different routes; the only copy arriving was the personal copy the reporter brought home.

68. George Sylvester Viereck Papers, Library of Congress, Manuscript Division.

69. Ibid.

70. Karl Alexander Fuehr, *The Neutrality of Belgium* (New York: Funk & Wagnalls, 1915). The book included in its appendixes a copy of the French plan of campaign that clearly established Belgium's belligerent role in a continental war against Germany; facsimiles of the well-publicized "Brussels documents"; and newly discovered "military guide-books" edited by the British general army staff entitled *Belgium, Road and River Reports*, which could not have been

prepared "without ready and far-reaching assistance on the part of the Belgian government and military authorities."

71. Compared to *The Fatherland*'s intended audience of the better educated and well informed, *Issues and Events* targeted the lesser educated and those who preferred looking at pictures to reading. One issue even carried a half-page advertisement headlined "NAVAL WAR TOY: A Most Exciting and Interesting Toy. A Realistic Destruction of a Dreadnought by a Submarine. Harmless Amusement for Young and Old." Under sketches showing a wooden toy battleship exploding after being struck by a torpedo fired by a wooden toy submarine was the following text: "You pull the trigger on the submarine, which discharges the torpedo. If your aim is good and you hit the red target, you will behold a most realistic view of blowing up a battleship." The advertisement suggested the toy was "lots of fun for young and old." It cost 50 cents.

72. In July 1918, Dr. Edward A. Rumely, publisher of New York's *Evening Mail*, was arrested with much fanfare and charged with perjury for his assertions that the paper was American-owned. The Federal government had evidence that Rumley had bought the newspaper for $735,000 with money from Dr. Albert; the Germans then had to plow an additional $626,000 into the paper to cover its growing losses. *New York Times*, July 9, 1918.

73. Franz von Papen, *Memoirs* (New York: E. P. Dutton, 1952), 35. Sir Roger David Casement, a fiery Irish nationalist, became a martyr to the cause of Irish separatism. At the turn of the century he had served as British consul in the Congo. He returned to England to write a damning report on the brutal workings of King Leopold's system. Later he was knighted for his investigation of the Anglo-Peruvian Amazon Co. In 1914, Casement fought participation of Irishmen in the war, visiting both Germany and the United States to promote his cause. He tried unsuccessfully to enlist Germany in a military expedition to Ireland. In 1916, returning to Ireland from a German submarine intending to lead what was later called the "Easter uprising," he was captured. Casement was tried, convicted, and hanged as a traitor in London on August 3, 1916. Earlier he had been stripped of his knighthood.

74. Mitchell, *Report on the Propaganda Library*, 7.

75. U.S. Senate Subcommittee, *Brewing and Liquor Interests*, 2:1542–1543.

76. Seymour, *Papers of Colonel House*, 2:374.

77. *New York Times*, September 21, 1917.

78. Ibid., November 24, 1917.

79. Von Bernstorff, *My Three Years in America*, 41.

80. "Pan-Germanism in the United States," *The World's Work*, March 1915.

81. Willert to Dawson, October 22, 1914. Sir Arthur Willert Papers, Manuscripts and Archives, Yale University Library.

82. Oswald Garrison Villard, *Germany Embattled: An American Interpretation* (New York: Charles Scribner's Sons, 1915), 85.

83. "Pan-Germanism in the United States," 135. Dernburg was also an experienced writer, a frequent contributor of articles to the prestigious *Berliner Tageblatt*, and a published author.

84. *New York Times*, December 20, 1914.

85. Indeed, the Germans hated! Ernest Poole, American newspaper correspondent in Germany in 1914 and 1915, recalled in his autobiography *The Bridge: My Own Story* (New York: Macmillan, 1940) that in Berlin's Beethoven Hall he once listened to a famous actor reciting war poems. The actor climaxed his readings with Ernst Lissauer's "The Chant of Hate," in which each verse closed with "We have one foe and one foe alone—England!" Poole wrote that "then those German men and women rose like one man from their seats; there burst forth a fury of cries which set the air to quivering! And looking on those faces, I wondered how many long years it would take for such a passion of hatred to die?" (221–222).

86. U.S. Senate Subcommittee, *Brewing and Liquor Interests*, 1:11–12.

87. *New York Times*, May 9, 1915.

88. Ibid., May 10, 1915.

89. Von Bernstorff, *My Three Years in America*, 145–146.

90. *New York Times*, May 10, 1915.

91. Ibid.

92. David F. Houston, *Eight Years with Wilson's Cabinet, 1913 to 1920* (New York: Doubleday, Page, 1926), 132.

93. *New York Times*, June 14, 1915.

94. "The intricate German propaganda system in America appeared to radiate from Dr. Heinrich F. Albert. ... He had no visible occupation, yet he seemed to be enormously busy. By intercepting wireless messages, sent in code from Germany to Dr. Albert through the radio station at Sayville, on Long Island, we learned that he was receiving large sums of money. This money was deposited in New York banks to his credit, and no one appeared to know what he did with it. After this country went to war, the government got hold of Dr. Albert's account-books. They revealed the fact that he had received from Germany more than twenty-seven million dollars in all, but the records did not show how he had expended this fortune." William Gibbs McAdoo, *Crowded Years* (New York: Houghton Mifflin, 1931), 324. Reports from U.S. Secret Service agents supposedly established that Franz Rintelen von Kleist, a self-proclaimed German saboteur, together with von Papen and Boy-Ed, had spent the $27 million total prior to December 1915. The total was broken down as follows: $12 million to promote a Huerta-Villa counterrevolution in Mexico against Carranza; $5 million for the Bridgeport Projectile Co., created to tie up Allied war orders; $3 million for lecturers' expenses, foreign-language publications, and press activities; $3 million for detective work; two and one half million for supplies for German warships; and one and one half million for miscellaneous activities.

95. Von Papen, *Memoirs*, 38.

96. Von Bernstorff, *My Three Years in America*, 96.

97. U.S. Senate Subcommittee, *Brewing and Liquor Interests*, 2:1628.

98. Quoted in McAdoo, *Crowded Years*, 325. Subsequent quotations from Burke's report, ibid., 325–327.

99. Years later, Flynn, who had been wartime chief of the U.S. Secret Service, exposed another flagrant example of America's militant non-neutrality in a magazine article called "Tapped Wires": "In 1915 ... the United States Secret Service tapped the telephone wires of the German and Austrian embassies in Washington. Thereafter I received each night a stenographic report of every conversation, trivial and important, of the previous twenty-four hours. ...Using leads supplied by official wire tappers, the Secret Service was able to keep a close watch on the German government's prewar activities. Some of the information that came over tapped wires contributed as much as any other factor to our ultimate breaks with Germany and Austria. ...Ordinarily, it is against the law to tap telephone wires and you can be sent to jail for doing it. The Secret Service got government authority to tap the wires. ...The procedure was approved by the State Department and carried out by the best telephone men in America. It was no crude job of climbing telephone poles at midnight. ...I don't know whether President Wilson was shown any of the reports, but he knew they were being made." *Liberty*, June 2, 1928, 19–20.

100. McAdoo, *Crowded Years*, 328.

101. "Author Fox" was German-leaning U.S. journalist Edward Lyell Fox, who had earlier been in Europe with the German armies in Belgium and France. He had written *Behind the Scenes in Warring Germany*, which painted a rosy, exaggerated picture of Germans and the German army. Fox also wrote fictitious atrocity propaganda.

102. George Sylvester Viereck, *Spreading Germs of Hate* (New York: Horace Liveright, 1930), 73.

103. "Why German-Americans Oppose Prohibition," booklet in English published by "Voice of the Liberty-Loving Teutonic Spirit." Elmer Gertz Papers, Manuscript Division, Library of Congress.

104. Letter, Alfred Lau to Elmer Gertz, undated Gertz Papers.

105. *The Story of The Fatherland*, a promotional booklet published by the Fatherland Corporation, 1915. Gertz Papers.

106. Elmer Gertz, *Odyssey of a Barbarian: The Biography of George Sylvester Viereck* (Buffalo, Prometheus Books, 1978), 121–124.

107. While the editorial policy of his publication remained fixed throughout the war years, Viereck adjusted its name to fit the changing climate of public opinion in the country. Following America's severance of diplomatic relations with Germany in February 1917 and as war loomed, *The Fatherland* became *Viereck's New World: The American Weekly*. Then, two issues later, its name was shortened to *Viereck's: The American Weekly*, and its masthead carried a new slogan: "My Country, Right or Wrong; If Right to Be Kept Right, If Wrong, to Be Set Right." By August 1918, with circulation dropping fast, the publication became a monthly as an economy move, and again was retitled, to *The American Monthly*, with a new slogan, "America First and

America Only." Viereck continued to publish *The American Monthly* until 1929, when he renamed it yet again, as *American Monthly and Germanic Review*. This magazine was run with its title unchanged until 1933, when Viereck stopped publication to devote himself to Nazi Germany's cause in America.

108. *New York Times*, July 26, 1918.

109. Quoted in "Pan-Germanism in the United States," *The World's Work*, March 1915, 135. Such unrestrained language, of course, was not appreciated in official American circles. In his postwar memoir, Robert Lansing said that "Of all the pro–German publications in this country none was so contemptible as a New York weekly named The Fatherland which was published in English. The fulminations of its editor against President Wilson and his policies were couched in language insulting and vituperative to the last degree. That many of his assertions were untrue did not appear to trouble him in the least. Possibly of course he believed them, for no one can be sure of the mental processes of such a man." Lansing, *War Memoirs of Robert Lansing*, 77.

110. Alfred Lau came to disagree sharply with Viereck's editorial policies: "I retained a great affection for the magazine, until later on I could not agree with Viereck's policies any longer. I think the *Fatherland* defeated itself when Viereck became more German than the Kaiser, more Austrian than the Emperor and more Turkish than the Sultan. There was nothing that the German side did that Viereck did not applaud. Even when the Central Powers apologized for some action, Viereck vigorously applauded. There was no sense to it anymore." Letter, Lau to Gertz, undated, Gertz Papers.

111. Viereck, *Spreading Germs of Hate*, 61–63. The book subsequently was given high marks for accuracy and objectivity across a broad spectrum of opinion, private and public. Among those who commented favorably were von Bernstorff, U.S. Admiral William S. Sims, Upton Sinclair, and Colonel House, who wrote the book's Foreword. George Sylvester Viereck Papers, Manuscripts and Archives, Yale University Library.

112. Following the meeting, Viereck recalled, he "rushed to his desk" and prepared an editorial for the next issue of *The Fatherland* that included these ominous sentences: "The *Gulflight*, carrying contraband through a war zone, paid the penalty of her foolhardiness. Before long, a large passenger ship like the *Lusitania*, carrying implements of murder to Great Britain, will meet with a similar fate." Viereck, *Spreading Germs of Hate*, 64–65.

113. It is unclear how many newspapers carried the advertisement. According to Judge Julius M. Mayer, who presided over a federal court hearing into the *Lusitania* sinking, the advertisement appeared in only five New York City newspapers: the *Times*, the *World*, the *Sun*, the *Herald*, and the *Tribune*. Viereck casually stated, in *Spreading Germs of Hate*, that the advertisement was inserted in newspapers "throughout the country" (64). The German Embassy, in a May 12 announcement in the *New York Times* that it was discontinuing the advertisement, referred to "newspapers in all of the larger cities of the United States."

114. Hale's interview with the Kaiser was explosive. The loquacious Wilhelm told Hale he esteemed Roosevelt, but other matters he discussed were more newsworthy. The Kaiser railed against the Catholic Church, heaped abuse on England and King Edward VII, damned Japan as "the Yellow Peril" and condemned the recently concluded Anglo-Japanese treaty, presciently predicted a world war, and suggested that America would be forced to fight Japan in ten years. The few on the *New York Times* staff who privately read Hale's cabled interview judged it so inflammatory that, if published, it might endanger the fragile peace among Europe's great powers. Publisher Adolph Ochs elected not to print it, after submitting it to President Roosevelt for his views. Later, when an abridged version of the interview had already been printed for the December 1908 issue of *The Century*, but not yet bound, the German Foreign Office pressed successfully to stop its distribution. The German government rightly considered the interview so potentially damaging to their international relations that they sent the cruiser *Bremen* to New York City to pick up the printed forms and burn them in the ship's boilers at sea. In December 1917, Hale's article was resurrected, with emphasis on the Kaiser's warlike utterances, his prediction of war, and Germany's military readiness. The Kaiser's unfriendly comments about the Catholic Church and the Sultan of Turkey were also used for Allied propaganda. *New York Times* Archives.

115. William Bayard Hale, *Woodrow Wilson: The Story of his Life* (Garden City, N.Y.: Doubleday, Page, 1912), 214, 219–221.

116. William Bayard Hale Papers, Manuscripts and Archives, Yale University Library.

117. Ibid.
118. Ibid.
119. Woodrow Wilson, *The New Freedom* (Garden City, N.Y.: Doubleday, Page, 1913), vii.
120. Hale Papers.
121. Ibid.
122. Cited in *Memoirs of Count Bernstorff*, 163.
123. Hale papers.
124. Hale, *Woodrow Wilson*, 225.
125. William Bayard Hale, *Woodrow Wilson: The Story of a Style* (New York: B.W. Huebsch, 1920), 242.
126. Von Bernstorff, *My Three Years in America*, 42–43.
127. Gertz, *Odyssey of a Barbarian*, 178.

Chapter 4–America's Non-Neutrality

1. *New York Times*, April 3, 1917.
2. See Edwin J. Clapp, *Economic Aspects of the War: Neutral Rights, Belligerent Claims, and American Commerce in the Years 1914–1915* (New Haven: Yale University Press, 1915); Charles Seymour, *American Neutrality, 1914–1917* (New Haven: Yale University Press, 1936); Edwin Borchard and William Potter Lage, *Neutrality for the United States* (New Haven: Yale University Press, 1937); Charles C. Tansill, *America Goes to War* (Boston: Little, Brown, 1938); Alice M. Morrissey, *The American Defense of Neutral Rights, 1914–1917* (Cambridge: Harvard University Press, 1939).
3. In a discussion in 1932 with Ray Stannard Baker, Wilson's authorized biographer, George Creel, chairman of the Committee on Public Information, said that use of the slogan had made Wilson "furious" and that his campaign speeches in St. Louis and Indianapolis had "said just the contrary." Creel remarked that "people do not read; they are governed by slogans." George Creel papers, Manuscript Division, Library of Congress.
4. Seymour, *Papers of Colonel House*, 1:355.
5. Ibid., 1:413–414.
6. *American Machinist*, May 6, 1915.
7. James W. Gerard, *Face to Face with Kaiserism* (New York: George H. Doran, 1918), 69.
8. Remarkably, a similar set of circumstances prevailed in 1939–41, when America waged an undeclared and unpublicized war with Germany in the Atlantic Ocean. This time, on orders from its commander-in-chief, the U.S. Navy harassed, depth-charged, and radioed locations of U-boats to the Royal Navy, and convoyed Allied shipping. The destroyer-bases deal with England and Lend-Lease were also flagrant violations of internationally accepted neutrality norms. Adolf Hitler, remembering the dangers of a war with America, swallowed hard and bided his time. On December 11, 1941, when Germany declared war on the United States, he unleashed his submarines. One of the reasons for the declaration of war was America's provocative non-neutrality.
9. Charles Seymour, *Woodrow Wilson and the World War: A Chronicle of Our Own Times* (New Haven: Yale University Press, 1921), 27–28.
10. In 1936, House acknowledged to an interviewer that he was "a paper colonel. I tried to get rid of the title, but I couldn't. It persisted, and I soon found a certain usefulness in it." Gertz, *Odyssey of a Barbarian*, 205.
11. Seymour, *Papers of Colonel House*, 1:38.
12. Letter, House to Sidney E. Mezes, November 25, 1911. Seymour, *Papers of Colonel House*, 1:46.
13. January 25, 1915. House diary, Edward Mandell House Papers, Manuscripts and Archives, Yale University Library.
14. Wilson's most celebrated anti–Bryan comment was in a letter he had written five years earlier that had been made public. It suggested that Democrats "do something at once dignified and effective to knock Mr. Bryan once and for all into a cocked hat!" Wilson wrote the letter on

April 29, 1907, to Adrian Joline, president of the Missouri, Kansas and Texas Railway. Party opponents to his candidacy had the letter published in the *New York Sun* on January 6, 1912. As early as 1904, Wilson had publicly called for Bryan and his supporters to be thrown out of Democratic counsels. In 1908, when Wilson learned that Bryan would be present at a Democratic dinner, he withdrew his acceptance of the invitation to address the meeting.

15. February 8, 1918, House diary. As House's biographer, Charles Seymour, wrote, "Every evening, with rare exceptions and during eight years, Colonel House dictated to [Miss Frances B. Denton, an assistant who was more collaborator than confidential secretary] his resume of the events of the day. Definitely and objectively, he related his conversations with, often the very words of, his political associates, and he was associated with the men who made the history of the decade." *Intimate Papers of Colonel House,* 1:3. Presumably, the next morning, a refreshed reviewer with a chance to reflect made changes to the transcribed draft not only to smooth its presentation but to make the memorandum worthy of the author's sense of its future historical importance.

16. Seymour, *Papers of Colonel House,* 1:358.

17. Ibid., 1:357–358.

18. January 30, 1915, House diary. House Papers.

19. Seymour, *Papers of Colonel House,* 1:242–243.

20. Ibid., 1:247.

21. Ibid., 1:249. The "militarism run stark mad" reference could only refer to Germany, for House had yet to stop in France or England. He had not yet been exposed to the German military splendors of the *Schrippenfest* feast, where he would meet the Kaiser two days later. During the formal affair, House would be purposefully seated between two high-ranking army officers, the better to discuss issues of common interest, so his attentive hosts thought. The source of House's statement "Whenever England consents ..." remains a mystery.

22. Ibid., 1:254.

23. Ibid., 1:255–257.

24. Viscount Grey of Fallodin, *Twenty-Five Years. 1892–1916* (New York: Frederick A. Stokes, 1925), 2:124–125.

25. Seymour, *Papers of Colonel House,* 1:262. Reading his letters and his diary, one cannot avoid the impression that House was being completely dominated, just as Page was, by British diplomacy, by the sheer persuasiveness and charm of the British statesman at his best—a best that is without equal in this world." Ray Stannard Baker, *Woodrow Wilson, Life and Letters* (Garden City, N.Y.: Doubleday, Doran, 1935), 5:315.

26. Ibid., 1:434.

27. Ibid., 2:90.

28. Quoted in Millis, *Road to War,* 230.

29. Seymour, *Papers of Colonel House,* 2:90–91.

30. Ibid., 2:90.

31. As early as the second cabinet meeting, the president made this clear to at least one cabinet member, Secretary of Agriculture David F. Houston, who interpreted Wilson's reading of a statement assessing the then-volatile Latin American situation: "I do not know to what extent the President had consulted Bryan, but Bryan had not presented the matter and the President did the reading. Bryan listened with a smile on his face and nodded approval as the President read." Houston, *Eight Years with Wilson's Cabinet* (Garden City, N.Y.: Doubleday, Page, 1926), 1:44.

32. Bryan summarized his scheme to prevent wars as follows: "1. Investigation is to follow in all cases where diplomacy fails. 2. The contracting parties reserve the right to act independently after the investigation. 3. There is to be no appeal to force until after the investigation. 4. The commission of investigation is to consist of five members: one chosen for each country by its citizens; one chosen by each country from another country; one chosen by agreement of the two countries. 5. The investigation must be made and reported upon within a year, unless the contracting parties agree to extend the time." Paxton Hibben, *The Peerless Leader: William Jennings Bryan* (New York: Farrar & Rinehart, 1929), 326.

33. Cited in Baker, *Woodrow Wilson,* 5:176.

34. The Declaration of London was the result of a conference among the leading maritime powers in London, December 4, 1908, to February 26, 1909. The British had called the confer-

ence to resolve "divergent views and practices" related to maritime war. Specifically, it was hoped that agreement could be reached concerning such controversial questions as the nature of contraband of war, the legality of certain kinds of blockades, and the relation of the doctrine of continuous voyage to both contraband and blockade. Although the conference did not reach agreement on all questions, a proposed code was concluded. The British government, however, did not ratify the agreement; opponents regarded the declaration as a menace to the Royal Navy's traditional control of the seas. In the British view, loosely defined principles of maritime war were advantageous to a nation with a superior navy.

35. William Jennings Bryan and Mary Baird Bryan, *The Memoirs of William Jennings Bryan* (Philadelphia: John C. Winston, 1925), 396.

36. Baker, *Woodrow Wilson*, 5:333.

37. Hibben, *Peerless Leader*, 344.

38. Quoted in Houston, *Eight Years with Wilson's Cabinet*, 1:146.

39. Arthur S. Link, *Woodrow Wilson and the Progressive Era* (New York: Harper & Brothers, 1954), 27.

40. Memorandum dated July 11, 1915. Robert Lansing, *War Memoirs of Robert Lansing* (New York: Bobbs-Merrill, 1935), 19–21.

41. Gaddis Smith, *Britain's Clandestine Submarines, 1914–1915* (New Haven: Yale University Press, 1964), 36.

42. The *Alabama* had been bought in England by the Confederacy in 1862, fitted with guns in the Azores, and then had begun its voyage of destruction of Union shipping. The United States had protested the ship's departure and then formally held the British government responsible for all damages caused by the raider. A Geneva tribunal convened in 1872 to judge the validity of American claims awarded $15.5 million to the United States.

43. Cited in Smith, *Britain's Clandestine Submarines*, 45–46.

44. Ibid., 28.

45. *New York Times*, February 20, 1915.

46. Cited in Baker, *Woodrow Wilson*, 5:178.

47. Ibid., 5:228.

48. Von Bernstorff, *My Three Years in America*, 76–77.

49. Cited in Charles A. Tansill, *America Goes to War*, 64.

50. Ron Chernow, *The House of Morgan: An American Banking Dynasty and the Rise of Modern Finance* (New York: Atlantic Monthly Press, 1990), 188.

51. Ibid., 195.

52. Letter, McAdoo to Wilson, August 21, 1915, cited in Baker, *Woodrow Wilson*, 5:380–381.

53. Letter, Wilson to Lansing, August 26, 1915, cited in Tansill, *America Goes to War*, 104.

54. Letter, Lansing to Wilson, September 6, 1915, cited in Tansill, *America Goes to War*, 104–105.

55. Alexander Noyes, *The War Period of American Finance, 1908–1925* (New York: G. P. Putnam's Sons, 1926), 96. As late as February 1915, total shipments of munitions—guns, explosives, ammunition, barbed wire, etc.—were less than double the shipments in February 1914. But by May 1915, when David Lloyd George was named Britain's minister of munitions and instituted a crash program, gigantic orders had begun to pour in to American manufacturers. Bethlehem Steel Co., the nation's largest arms manufacturer, recorded a May order for $100 million for shells and shrapnel. The company had reported unfilled orders at the end of 1914 of $46.5 million; at the end of 1915, the figure would be $174.4 million (113–114).

56. Millis, *Road to War*, 221.

57. Cited in Chernow, *House of Morgan*, 200.

58. In his self-serving testimony, Morgan said on January 7, 1936: "When in 1914 the war was begun by Germany by the unexpected and criminal invasion of Belgium in violation of a treaty which had been respected for eighty years, we were deeply shocked. ...From that moment we in common with many others realized that if the Germans should obtain a quick and easy victory the freedom of the rest of the world would be lost. ...We agreed that we should do all that was lawfully within our power to help the Allies win the war as soon as possible. That thought was the fundamental idea underlying everything that we did from the beginning of the struggle till the armistice in November, 1918." *New York Times*, January 8, 1936.

59. Lamont publicly purchased the *New York Evening Post* in July 1918 and put the paper

into a trust, expressing "no intention of taking active part in its direction or of making it the expression of my personal views." All evidence points to his having followed both the letter and the spirit of his pledge. In September 1918 the *Evening Post* was one of the few papers to editorially question the validity of the "Sisson Papers." Lamont vigorously defended his paper's independence in a letter to George Creel on October 14 in response to the CPI chairman's letter of October 8 accusing the *Evening Post* of disloyalty. Thomas W. Lamont Papers, Baker Library, Harvard University.

60. Lamont to Henry P. Davison, June 24, 1912. Lamont Papers.

61. "In 1917, on the floor of Congress it was charged that as early as March, 1915, the Morgan interests had organized and financed a huge propaganda machine, including 12 influential publishers and 197 newspapers, for the purpose of 'persuading' the American people to join the Allies." H.C. Englebrecht and F.C. Hanighen, *Merchants of Death: A Study of the International Armament Industry* (London: George Routledge & Sons, 1934), 176.

62. Von Bernstorff, *Memoirs of Count Bernstorff*, 131–132. Francophile Herrick showed where his sympathies lay in the opening days of the conflict when he talked with young Americans in Paris anxious to enlist in the French army: "There were no protestations, no speeches; they merely wanted to fight, and they asked me if they had a right to do so, if it was legal. ...I wanted to take those boys to my heart and cry, 'God bless you! Go!' But I was held back from doing so by the fact that I was an ambassador. ...It was more than flesh and blood could stand, and catching fire myself from their eagerness, I brought my fist down on the table saying, 'That is the law, boys but if I was young and stood in your shoes, by God I know right well what I would do.'" Col. T. Bentley Mott, *Myron T. Herrick, Friend of France: An Autobiographical Biography* (Garden City, N.Y.: Doubleday, Doran, 1929), 144.

63. Cited in Tertius van Dyke, *Henry van Dyke: A Biography* (New York: Harper & Brothers, 1935), 329–330.

64. August 20, 1914. Allan Nevins, ed., *The Letters and Journal of Brand Whitlock* (New York: D. Appleton-Century, 1936), 2:41–42.

65. Burton J. Hendrick, *The Life and Letters of Walter Hines Page* (New York: Doubleday, Page, 1922), 1:325.

66. Ibid., 1:325–326.

67. Ibid., 1:328.

68. Ibid., 2:69.

69. Viscount Grey of Fallodon, *Twenty-Five Years, 1892–1916* (New York: Frederick A. Stokes, 1925), 2:110.

70. Hendrick, 1:394–395.

71. Ibid., 1:362.

72. Ibid., 2:10.

73. Ibid., 2:25–26.

74. Ibid., 2:269–270.

75. Quoted in Baker, *Woodrow Wilson*, 5:200.

76. Ibid., 5:210.

77. Hendrick, *Walter Hines Page*, 2:23–24.

78. Baker, *Woodrow Wilson*, 8:488.

79. John Terrain, *The Great War, 1914–1918* (New York: Macmillan, 1965), viii.

80. Henry F. Pringle, *Theodore Roosevelt: A Biography* (New York: Harcourt, Brace, 1931), 166–167.

81. Ibid., 579.

82. Ibid., 581.

83. The Lodge-Roosevelt correspondence ceased on May 23, 1914, and did not resume again until December 7, 1914. Bishop, Roosevelt's official biographer, published nothing until October 3, 1914. Ibid., 580.

84. Ibid., 581.

85. Hermann Hagedorn, *Leonard Wood: A Biography*, vol. 2 (New York: Harper & Brothers, 1931), 126.

86. Millis, *Road to War*, 258.

87. Theodore Roosevelt, *America and the World War* (New York: Charles Scribner's Sons, 1915), ix, xiv.

88. *New York Times*, June 15, 1915.

89. Quoted in Pringle, *Theodore Roosevelt*, 349.

90. Theodore Roosevelt, *Roosevelt in the Kansas City Star: War-Time Editorials by Theodore Roosevelt* (New York: Houghton Mifflin, 1921) passim. Roosevelt dictated his last editorial on January 3, the Friday before his death on January 6, 1919.

91. Cited in Millis, *Road to War*, 388.

92. Joseph P. Tumulty, *Woodrow Wilson as I Know Him* (Garden City, N.Y.: Garden City Publishing, 1921), 285.

93. Quoted in John J. Leary, Jr., *Talks with T.R., from the Diaries of John J. Leary, Jr.* (New York: Houghton Mifflin, 1920), cited in Pringle, *Theodore Roosevelt*, 93–99.

94. Arthur Walworth, *Woodrow Wilson* (New York: W.W. Norton, 1958), 2:104.

95. Millis, *Road to War*, 94.

96. Ibid., 95.

97. Leonard Wood, *Our Military History: Its Facts and Fallacies* (Chicago, Reilly & Britton, 1916), 173.

98. Ibid., 178.

99. Frederic Louis Huidekoper, *The Military Unpreparedness of the United States: A History of American Land Forces from Colonial Times until June 1, 1915* (New York: Macmillan, 1915), 31.

100. George Creel, *The World, the War, and Wilson* (New York: Harper Brothers, 1920), 90.

101. Walter Lippmann, *New Republic*, March 17, 1920, 78–79.

102. Cited in Grattan, *Why We Fought*, 119.

103. America had its own Navy League and a 1904 issue of its official journal listed 18 men and one corporation as founders. The lone company was the Midvale Steel Co., which had sold the U.S. government some $20 million in armor plate. Among the individual founders were Colonel Robert M. Thompson, a West Point graduate and chairman of the International Nickel Co., smelter of the metal vital for high-strength steel; Benjamin F. Tracy, former secretary of the navy and attorney for the Carnegie Steel Co.; Charles M. Schwab then president of the U.S. Steel Corporation; and the ubiquitous but very discreet heavy donor to numerous special causes, banker J.P. Morgan, senior. Engelbrecht and Hanighen, *Merchants of Death*, 2.

104. *New York Times*, August 6, 1917.

105. Ibid., July 12, 1917.

106. George T. Blakey, *Historians on the Homefront: American Propagandists for the Great War* (Lexington: University Press of Kentucky, 1970), 148.

107. Hudson Maxim, *Defenseless America* (New York: Hearst's International Library, 1915), v.

108. Michael T. Isenberg, *War on Film: The American Cinema and World War I, 1914–1941* (East Brunswick, N.J.: Associated University Presses, 1981), 101.

109. Cited in ibid., 192.

110. *Motion Picture Magazine*, September 1915, 122–123.

111. Quoted in Isenberg, *War on Film*, 103.

112. James M. Beck, *The Evidence in the Case: A Discussion of the Moral Responsibility for the War of 1914, as Disclosed by the Diplomatic Records of England, Germany, Russia, France, Austria, Italy, and Belgium* (New York: Grosset & Dunlap, 1914), 250–251.

113. *New York Times*, April 19, 1915.

114. Parker, "The United States and the War," 528.

115. Owen Wister, *The Pentecost of Calamity* (New York: Macmillan, 1915), 15, 22–23.

116. Ibid., 23–24, 28.

117. Reverend C. H. Parkhurst, *My Forty Years in New York* (New York: Macmillan, 1923), 116.

118. Newell Dwight Hillis, *German Atrocities—Their Nature and Philosophy: Studies in Belgium and France During July and August of 1917* (New York: Fleming H. Revell, 1918), 106.

119. Ibid., 122.

120. Ibid., 126.

121. Ibid., 138.

122. Ibid., 139–140.

123. Ibid., 16.

124. Ibid., 55–56.

125. Ibid., 75–76.

126. Newell Dwight Hillis, *The Blot on the Kaiser's 'Scutcheon* (New York: Fleming H. Revell, 1918), 58–59.

127. Quoted in Granville Hicks, "The Parsons and the War," *American Mercury*, February 1927, 135.

128. Ibid., 135–136.

129. *Unity*, December 20, 1923, cited in Ray H. Abrams, *Preachers Present Arms* (New York: Round Table Press, 1933), 236.

130. Harry Emerson Fosdick, introduction to *War: Its Causes, Consequences, and Cure*, by Kirby Page (1923), 2–3.

131. Cited in Abrams, *Preachers Present Arms*, 235.

132. Ibid., 237. Some important religious groups were not included in the survey: Roman Catholics, Jews, Lutherans, Southern Baptists, and Southern Methodists. According to the publication, "The total number of clergy in the country exceeds 100,000, and it was necessary on the grounds of expense to limit the inquiry to 53,000."

133. *New York Herald Tribune*, April 18, 1932, cited in Abrams, *Preachers Present Arms*, 236.

134. *American Newspaper Annual and Directory* (Philadelphia: N.W. Ayer & Son, 1914).

135 Frank Luther Mott, *American Journalism: A History, 1690–1960* (New York: Macmillan, 1962), 546.

136. "American Sympathies in the War," *The Literary Digest*, November 14, 1914, 939. In a dispatch to Berlin in December 1916, von Bernstorff listed what he considered to be the most important American newspapers "under British or French influence": the *New York Times*, the *New York Herald*, the *New York Evening Telegram*, the *Philadelphia Public Ledger*, the *Chicago Herald*, and the *Providence Journal*. Less influential or less biased (or, as von Bernstorff referred to them, "other sworn partisans of the Entente Powers") were the *New York Tribune*, the *New York Sun* and the *Evening Sun*, the *New York Evening Post*, the *New York Journal of Commerce*, the *New York Globe*, the *Brooklyn Daily Eagle*, the *Boston Evening Transcript*, and the *Philadelphia Inquirer*. Von Bernstorff, *My Three Years in America*, 335–336.

137. Cited in Paul Ferris, *The House of Northcliffe: A Biography of an Empire* (New York: World, 1972), 155.

138. Meyer Berger, *The Story of The New York Times, 1851–1951* (New York: Simon & Schuster, 1951), 208.

139. *New York Times*, November 6, 1918.

140. Ralph Otto Nafziger, "The American Press and Public Opinion During the World War, 1914 to April 1917 ("Ph.D. diss., University of Wisconsin, 1936). The author also studied other large-city papers across the country: "The Boston *Transcript* ... was favorably disposed toward the Allies, but not so passionately as were the *Times* and the *World*. The *Christian Science Monitor* was generally more fair-minded in its approach to the war issues. ...The Atlanta *Constitution* ... staunchly defended Mr. Wilson's policies; it was not conspicuously partial in its attitude toward the warring nations. The Chicago *Tribune* ... definitely changed its viewpoint as the war progressed. It often reproved the Allies and refrained from vitriolic criticism of Germany until the *Lusitania* was sunk. ...The Kansas City *Star* gave a very inadequate picture of the war issues during the early days of the conflict. It was never conspicuously partial until in 1917 it joined the rest of the press in strong support of any action which the government proposed to take against Germany. The Portland *Oregonian* was annoyed by the war in the early days. It opposed strongly the German submarine campaign, but was not passionately pro-ally in any sense. The San Francisco *Chronicle* attempted conscientiously to be impartial and to present both sides of the conflict as generously as the available news permitted."

141. Gay Talese, *The Kingdom and the Power* (New York: World, 1966), 168. "The chief public service of the *Times* in the war was that from the very beginning it understood where the rights and wrongs of the conflict lay, it was able to justify its position by sound argument, and it never ceased to maintain that position with all the vigor which its editors were able to command. The furious hostility toward the paper which the Germans and their sympathizers soon displayed is the best measure of its success in performing this duty." Elmer Davis, *History of the New York Times, 1851–1921* (New York: New York Times, 1921), 335–336. "Mr. Ochs, I have no doubt whatever, sincerely believes that when he says his is an 'independent newspaper' that 'tolerates no tam-

pering with the news, no colouring, no deception,' and that it has attained a high reputation 'for the fullness, trustworthiness, and impartiality of its news service,' he paints a just picture of his daily. It would be pleasant to be able to agree with him, but the truth lies elsewhere. No journal has exceeded it in disseminating falsehoods, misrepresentations, and half truths during the unparalleled era of wholesale lying in which the world has lived since 1914." Oswald Garrison Villard, *Some Newspapers and Newspaper-Men* (New York: Alfred A. Knopf, 1926), 7–8.

142. Charles Edward Russell, *Pearson's Magazine*, April 1914, 30.

143. June 14, 1917. Woodrow Wilson, *In Our First Year of War* (New York: Harper & Brothers, 1918), 65–66.

144. Seymour, *Papers of Colonel House*, 1:299.

145. Henry Landau, *The Enemy Within: The Inside Story of German Sabotage in America* (New York: G. P. Putnam's Sons, 1937), 305–310. There is not one supporting reference in the book to the many statements made and quotations used. Indeed, the dust-jacket copy gives ironic testimony to the book's true nature: "The book is 100 detective stories rolled into one, a tale so wild, so fantastic, so filled with adventure, villainy, melodrama that one would believe it sprang from the mind of a fiction writer and a lurid one at that." Earlier the same year, Landau published *All's Fair: The Story of the British Secret Service Behind the German Lines*, a melodramatic tale of his personal espionage activities in Holland as a captain in the Special Intelligence Section of the British War Office.

146. Jules Witcover, *Sabotage at Black Tom: Imperial Germany's Secret War in America, 1914–1917* (Chapel Hill, N.C.: Algonquin Books of Chapel Hill, 1989), ix. Two enormous munitions explosions close to New York City in 1917—at Black Tom and Kingsland—continue to be identified with German perfidy. Both of these disasters figured prominently in the postwar legal sparring between the United States and Germany in the Mixed Claims Commission set up on August 10, 1922, as part of the U.S.-German peace treaty, to adjudicate claims for damages. Most of the over 20,000 different claims were settled promptly, but those relating to Black Tom and Kingsland required proof of alleged German sabotage. It was not until October 30, 1939, with World War II underway, that the Commission finally concluded its deliberations. Awards were made to the principal litigants in both explosions. Nevertheless, Nazi Germany's final acceptance of fiscal responsibility for the wartime actions of individuals of quite another government more than two decades before was not necessarily an admission of guilt. It could be chalked up to Germany's need to placate American public opinion at modest cost.

147. *New York Times*, September 11, 1915.

148. Ibid., September 6, 1915. The Liebau Labor Relief Bureau was headquartered in New York City, with branches in Bridgeport, Philadelphia, Pittsburgh, Cleveland, Chicago, and Cincinnati. Its announced function was to help Germans, Austrians, and Hungarians who had been pushed, ostensibly by moral compulsion, to quit their jobs voluntarily in factories supplying the Allies. In fact, coercion was used in the form of threats of imprisonment for subjects who, after working in such plants, returned to their native lands. A report from the German Embassy to the Foreign Office on March 24, 1916, pointed out that after being in operation for six months, the Liebau Bureau had received over 8,000 applications and had filled 4,466 positions permanently." U.S. Senate Subcommittee on the Judiciary, *Brewing and Liquor Interests and German and Bolshevik Propaganda*. Report and Hearings, 3 vols. Senate Document No. 62, 66th Congress, 1st session 1919: 2:1549–1563.

149. Ibid., September 10, 1915. On September 23, a mocking limerick appeared in the *Boston Post*:

> Constantin Theodor Dumba,
> You've roused Uncle Sam from his slumba;
> That letter you wrote,
> Got the old fellow's goat—
> Now his path you'll no longer encumba.

150. Landau, *Enemy Within*, 5–6.

151. *New York Times*, February 26, 1915.

152. Von Papen, *Memoirs*, 34.

153. *New York Times*, November 26, 1915.

154. Seymour, *Papers of Colonel House*, 2:47.

155. *New York Times*, December 9, 1915.

156. Ibid., December 22, 1915.

157. Von Papen, *Memoirs*, 29.

158. *New York Times*, December 29, 1915.

159. This time von Papen's papers were picked up by the English because he was forced to hurriedly flee from an invading British army. After the war, von Papen resigned his army commission, bought a controlling interest in a political journal, and entered politics. Far more successful in this new career than formerly as a military attaché, he was the last chancellor of the Weimar Republic in 1933. He became an enthusiastic Nazi and as vice-chancellor helped to pave the way for Hitler's *Anschluss* in Austria. Von Papen's final diplomatic post was as ambassador to Turkey, in 1944. A year later, von Papen surrendered to American troops and was one of the 21 high-level Nazi officials indicted by the Nuremburg war crimes tribunal. Von Papen was charged with "conspiracy to wage aggressive war." Following the 284-day trial, which ended in October 1946, von Papen, along with Dr. Hjalmar Schacht and Colonel-General Werner von Fritzscke, was acquitted.

160. November 16, 1915, as cited by Bernstorff, *My Three Years in America*, 110.

161. French Strother, "The Providence Journal Will Say This Morning," *The World's Work*, January 1918, 154.

162. Ibid., 153.

163. *New York Times*, January 20, 1918.

164. But see Jerold S. Auerbach, "Woodrow Wilson's 'Prediction' to Frank Cobb: Words Historians Should Doubt Ever Got Spoken," *Journal of American History*, December 1967, 608–617.

165. John L. Heaton, *Cobb of The World* (New York: E. P. Dutton, 1924), 268–270. The book's foreword, by Lindsay Denison, includes a glowing biographical sketch of Cobb. In it, Denison quotes what he calls the "last words dictated by Woodrow Wilson," xi: "I have known no man whose sturdiness of character and clear vision of duty impressed me more than those of Frank I. Cobb. He completely won my confidence and affection and I recognized in him a peculiar genius for giving direct and effective expression to the enlightened opinions which he held. I consider his death an irreparable loss to journalism and to the liberal political policies which are necessary to liberate mankind from the errors of the past and the partisan selfishness of the present. His death leaves a vacancy in the ranks of liberal thinkers which some one should press forward to fill if the impulse of progress is not to be stayed" (v).

Chapter 5—America at War

1. Irwin Hood Hoover Papers, Manuscript Division, Library of Congress.

2. George Creel, in a note dated March 21, 1931, transferring his scrapbooks to his son, George Bates Creel, wrote, "Here and there you will notice matter prepared by me and submitted to him [Woodrow Wilson] for his signature. He was one of the few presidents who wrote his own state papers." George Creel Papers, Manuscript Division, Library of Congress.

3. *New York Times*, April 5, 1917.

4. Ibid., April 5, 1917.

5. Ibid.

6. Ibid.

7. Ibid., April 7, 1917.

8. Cited in Charles Callan Tansill, *America Goes to War*, 650.

9. Creel Papers, Manuscript Division, Library of Congress. The full text of the Lansing-Baker-Daniels letter is as follows: "Even though the cooperation of the press has been generous and patriotic, there is a steadily developing need for some authoritative agency to assure the publication of all the vital facts of national defense. Premature or ill-advised announcements of policies, plans, and specific activities, whether innocent or otherwise, would constitute a source of danger. While there is much that is properly secret in connection with the departments, the total is small compared to the vast amount of information that it is right and proper for the people to have. America's great present needs are confidence, enthusiasm, and service, and these needs

will not be met completely unless every citizen is given the feeling of partnership that comes with full, frank statements concerning the conduct of the public business. It is our opinion that the two functions—censorship and publicity—can be joined in honesty and with profit, and we recommend the creation of a Committee on Public Information. The chairman should be a civilian, preferably some writer of proved courage, ability, and vision, able to gain the understanding of the press and at the same time rally the authors of the country to a work of service. Other members would be the Secretary of State, the Secretary of War, and the Secretary of the Navy, or an officer or officers detailed to the work by them. We believe you have undoubted authority to create this Committee on Public Information without waiting for further legislation, and because of the importance of the task, and its pressing necessity, we trust that you will see fit to do so. The committee, upon appointment, can proceed to the framing of regulations and the creation of machinery that will safeguard all information of value to an enemy, and at the same time open every department of government to the inspection of the people as far as possible. Such regulations and such machinery will, of course, be submitted for your approval before becoming effective."

10. In his printed handout, "Preliminary Statement to the Press of the United States," on May 28, 1917, Creel included these comments on the name of the committee: "The Committee on Public Information was given its name in no spirit of subterfuge, but as an honest announcement of purpose. There is the conviction that its negative functions—censorship—will be increasingly subordinated to the positive function—information," 20. The name was subsequently registered as a U.S. trademark.

11. Among them, Walton E. Bean, "George Creel and His Critics: A Study of the Attacks on the Committee on Public Information, 1917–1919" (Ph.D. diss., University of California, 1941); James R. Mock and Cedric Larson, *Words That Won the War: The Story of the Committee on Public Information, 1917–1919* (Princeton: Princeton University Press, 1939).

12. March 19, 1917. Josephus Daniels Papers, Manuscript Division, Library of Congress.

13. March 28, 1917. Daniels Papers.

14. Melville E. Stone, *Fifty Years a Journalist* (New York: Doubleday, Page, 1921), 326. Stone, who had become executive officer of the Associated Press in 1898, added that Creel had "later assured me that Mr. Hearst had offered him some fabulous salary to enter his service. A great many complications resulted from the appointment of Creel."

15. *The Democratic Observer* (California campaign "newspaper"), 1934. Creel Papers.

16. Memorandum of an interview with Creel, May 23, 1932. Ray Stannard Baker Papers, Manuscripts and Archives, Yale University Library.

17. David M. Kennedy, *Over Here: The First World War and American Society* (New York: Oxford University Press, 1980), 59.

18. Josephus Daniels, *The Wilson Era, Years of War and After—1917–1923* (Chapel Hill: University of North Carolina Press, 1946), 222.

19. January 22, 1917. House Papers.

20. Walter Lippmann Papers, Manuscripts and Archives, Yale University Library.

21. House Papers. Henry Seidel Canby was then a professor of English at Yale and editor of the *Yale Review*. He later became editor of the *Saturday Review of Literature*.

22. Lippmann Papers.

23. House Papers.

24. Lippmann Papers.

25. *New Republic*, February 20, 1915, 60–61.

26. Lippmann and Creel later worked together on New York's woman suffrage campaign. When Creel asked Lippmann to serve on that organization's publicity committee, Lippmann admitted that it was he who had authored the highly critical editorial. It closed, preposterously, "I hope we can be friends and I hope we can work together in this equal suffrage campaign." Creel's reply spurned Lippmann's olive branch: "I could not denounce a man as reckless, brutal, stupid, incompetent, and of a low quality of mind, without hating and loathing him for these qualities. Friendship with such a man would be as impossible as inconceivable. ...I am glad that you will help in the work of the publicity committee. I have never yet failed to keep my personal likes and dislikes entirely separate from my devotion to causes." Lippmann, always insisting on the last word, sent a follow-up letter, that defended his editorial attack. On the occasion of Lippmann's marriage in May 1917, Creel sent a card addressed "My dear Walter," offering his con-

gratulations and wishing the bride and groom "all happiness." Lippmann Papers. There is no record of further correspondence between the two men.

27. Lippmann Papers.

28. After Lippmann quit "The Inquiry" (a secret committee of elite U.S. historians, economists, geographers, and acamedicians appointed by House to develop strategies for the forthcoming peace conference) in June 1918, and with the support of House, who himself was discreetly critical of the CPI and was always looking for private sources of information, he got a captain's commission in the propaganda section of the Army Intelligence. Lippmann's "mission" in England and France was ostensibly to gather information for "The Inquiry"; more important, he was to report back to House about CPI activities in those countries. In three long and typically patronizing cables to House, Lippmann, as might be expected, pulled no punches. On August 9 he wrote, "To do the work effectively over here we shall need to create a real center of political information. Unless the men who are writing and directing propaganda are in close touch with political developments they cannot of course do anything effective. They should be in very close touch with our foreign policy as of course the most important propaganda are diplomatic acts themselves." On August 15: "I should like to say quite for yourself, that the condition we have found existing in the work of the Committee on Public Information in London is very bad. There has been constant change of men in charge of the work; the men sent do not know England, or English journalism, or European affairs, and the reputation of the committee among the English is very low. ...If America is to do anything effective in propaganda in Germany and Austria, it will be necessary to create a new expert organization independent of the Creel Committee." On September 2, listing five "essentials" of successful American propaganda plus "general confidential comments" about European propaganda chiefs who were "high in the councils of their governments," Lippmann took more careful aim at Creel: "American propaganda is either confined to advertising our war effort and distributing the President's speeches, or it becomes the personal views of an unauthorized individual." Wilson reacted to the sum of Lippmann's comments by writing House that Lippmann's judgment was "most unsound, and therefore unserviceable" in matters of propaganda. In turn, House cabled Lippmann on September 6 that "all copies of cables that come through the State Department are sent to the President, and in this way your criticism of propaganda work in Europe reaches those concerned with its direction. They have consequently caused some feeling. I want to caution you now about talking or cabling anything of a critical character. It is difficult to appreciate how careful one must be these days when people are living so largely on their nerves." Lippmann Papers.

29. Letter, Daniels to Larson, June 30, 1938, cited in Cedric Larson and James R. Mock, "The Lost Files of the Creel Committee of 1917–19," *Public Opinion Quarterly*, 10.

30. As the new Secretary of the Navy, Daniels had purchased British armor plate and had tried to use the Federal government to develop oil deposits. In his attempts to make the Navy more democratic, he had opened the Naval Academy to enlisted men. The act that subjected him to the loudest ridicule was his prohibition of alcoholic drinks aboard U.S. warships as well as in Navy facilities on shore; he entertained foreign missions with grape juice rather than wine.

31. George Creel, *Wilson and the Issues* (New York: Century, 1916), 88–89.

32. "Creel: An Announcement," *Everybody's Magazine*, January 1919, cited in Larson and Mock, "Lost Files," January 1939, 38.

33. George Creel, *Rebel at Large: Recollections of Fifty Crowded Years* (New York: G. P. Putnam's Sons, 1947), 38.

34. James Kerney, *The Political Education of Woodrow Wilson* (New York: Century, 1926), 473. Creel also maintained a cordial, long-term relationship with Edith Bolling Wilson following her husband's death in 1923. In Creel's papers is an invitation dated April 12, 1945, in which Mrs. Wilson asks Creel and his second wife to lunch.

35. *War Memoirs of Robert Lansing* (New York: Bobbs-Merrill, 1935), 322–323. Undoubtedly under pressure to convince detractors such as employees that his organization was "loyal, "Creel asked Military Intelligence, on April 10, 1918, to investigate CPI employees "with a view to ascertaining their fitness for employment by the Government during the present critical period." A subsequent M.I. 4–5 report was sent to Creel. Among its conclusions: "The total personnel of the committee is 395, nearly all of whom seem to be sincerely loyal. ...Suspicion of one sort or another has been cast on 14. ... The percentage of those against whom anybody has expressed a doubt is less than four per-cent. ...With these exceptions, the committee should be

given a clean bill of health." Documents of the Committee on Public Information, National Archives.

36. Creel Papers.

37. Daniels, *The Wilson Era*, 222, 227.

38. In Frederick Palmer's biography of Baker (*Newton D. Baker: America at War*, 1931), there is not a single reference to either George Creel or the CPI; Daniels, in his autobiography (*Tar Heel Editor*, 1939), never mentions Creel's name; and in Creel's own nearly 500-page record of the CPI (*How We Advertised America*, 1920), neither Baker's nor Daniels's name ever appears. The frontispiece of Creel's book, however, consists of photographs of the four CPI officials, and Creel elected to include as the foreword to his book "Baker's informal address" at a dinner in Creel's honor in Washington on November 29, 1918.

39. In February 1918, responding to a letter from the secretary of the Smithsonian Institution about his typewriter for display in the museum, Wilson wrote: "Evidently you have been reading some more of the fiction that constantly appears about my typewriting machine. I have been several times represented as pounding away on a worn-out machine that is an interesting antique, when, as a matter of fact, I have a perfectly able-bodied machine of recent manufacture ... and I am not by any means through with it." Baker, *Wilson*, 7:571.

40. According to the diary of Head Usher Irwin Hood Hoover, Creel met at the White House with Wilson 43 times, from April 20, 1917, to November 7, 1918. Irwin Hood Hoover Papers, Manuscript Division, Library of Congress.

41. Head Usher Hoover's diary records that Wilson had Creel as his guest for two meals in the White House, once for lunch and once for dinner. On one occasion, Wilson walked over to CPI headquarters for a short meeting with Creel. Hoover Papers. Creel kept no diary. In his memoir, Creel deprecated House's kind of diary keeping. He called it a worse addiction than "even opium, heroin, or cocaine" in causing "insidious disintegration of character." Soon after he took office as CPI chairman, Creel related, "a very wise old bird gave me a piece of advice: 'Don't start a diary. When you sit down at night to record the events of the day, in spite of honest resolves you'll soon be giving yourself the best of it in every conversation. ...When you feel the craving, my boy, yell for friends and have them tie your hands behind you.'" *Rebel at Large: Recollections of Fifty Crowded Years* (New York: G.P. Putnam's Sons, 1947), 245.

42. Creel's 300-page "Complete Report" to the president summarized the immense scope of the CPI's wartime and immediate postwar activities. Among the domestic divisions and subdivisions covered were: "Division of News, Division of Civic and Educational Cooperation, Division of Production and Distribution, Four Minute Men, Speaking Division, Advertising Division, Division of Films, Bureau of War Expositions, Bureau of War Photographs, Official Bulletin, Service Bureau, Exhibits at State Fairs, Division of Syndicate Features, Division of Women's War Work, Bureau of Cartoons, Division of Business Management, Division of Work among the Foreign Born, Fourth of July Demonstration, Scandinavian Bureau, Polish Bureau, Ukranian Bureau, German Bureau, Hungarian Bureau, Italian Bureau, Russian Bureau, and Jugoslav Bureau." *Complete Report of the Chairman of the Committee on Public Information, 1917:1918:1919* (Washington, D.C.: Government Printing Office, 1920).

43. Mock and Larson, *Words That Won the War*, 67.

44. Creel Papers.

45. Creel, *Preliminary Statement to the Press of the United States*, 11–12.

46. Letters, Creel to P. F. Collier & Son, October 10, 1918, and Creel to Francis J. Reynolds, October 22, 1918. Documents of the Committee on Public Information, National Archives.

47. Larson and Mock, "Lost Files," 20–21.

48. Letter, Creel to Polk, January 14, 1918. Frank Polk Papers, Manuscripts and Archives, Yale University Library.

49. Letter, Creel to Polk, January 15, 1918. Ibid.

50. Letter, Creel to Polk, August 5, 1918. Ibid.

51. George T. Blakey, *Historians on the Homefront: American Propagandists for the Great War* (Lexington: University Press of Kentucky, 1970).

52. Creel Papers.

53. Creel, *How We Advertised America*, 72–73.

54. All news releases, booklets, and advertisements cited in this chapter are in *Documents of the Committee on Public Information*, National Archives.

55. Creel, *How We Advertised America*, 83.

56. Letter, Wilson to Creel, December 31, 1917. Wilson Papers.

57. Wilson apparently had always been fascinated by the idea of an official government daily. In 1885, he wrote in his *Congressional Government* that privately owned newspapers had more power to control public opinion than the government itself. In 1908, Wilson wrote in his *Constitutional Government in the United States* that a "national newspaper" would serve to offset the provincialism he considered typical of local newspapers in the United States.

58. Wilson Papers.

59. Creel, *Complete Report*, 18.

60. Creel, *How We Advertised America*, 107.

61. A postmaster wrote to Creel asking to see a CPI booklet describing the way "that the Germans have bombed hospitals, killed Red Cross workers, raped Belgian women and girls," a newspaper editor demanded that the CPI revive "the news value of the older atrocities." Documents of the Committee on Public Information, as cited by Blakey, *Historians on the Homefront*, 48.

62. Creel, *Complete Report*, 18. In the report Creel boasted that "we sought the verdict of mankind by truth telling. We did not call it 'propaganda,' for that word, in German hands, had come to be associated with lies and corruptions. Our work was educational and informative only, for we had such confidence in our case as to feel that only fair presentation of its facts was needed" (1).

63. "Red, White, and Blue Series." 1. *How the War Came to America* (5,428,048 copies printed); 2. *National Service Handbook* (454,848); 3. *The Battle Line of Democracy* (94,848); 4. *The President's Flag Day Address, with Evidence of Germany's Plans* (6,813,340); 5. *Conquest and Kultur: Aims of the Germans in Their Own Words* (1,203,607) 6. *German War Practices: Treatment of Civilians* (1,592,801); 7. *The War Cyclopedia* (195,231); 8. *German War Practices: Treatment of Conquered Territory* (720,848); 9. *War, Labor, and Peace* (584,027) 10. *German War Plots and Intrigues in the United States during the Period of Our Neutrality* (127,153).

"War Information Series": 1. *The War Message and the Facts Behind It* (2,499,903); 2. *The Nation in Arms* (1,666,231); 3. *The Government of Germany* (1,798,155); 4. *The Great War from Spectator to Participant* (1,581,903); 5. *A War of Self-Defense* (721,944); 6. *American Loyalty by Citizens of German Descent* (702,598); 7. *Amerikanische Burgertreue von Burgern deutscher Abkunft* (564,787); 8. *American Interest in Popular Government Abroad* (596,533); 9. *Home Reading Course for Citizen Soldiers* (361,000); 10. *First Session of War Congress* (608,950); 11. *The German War Code* (514,452); 12. *American and Allied Ideals: An Appeal to Those Who Are Neither Hot nor Cold* (228,986); 13. *German Militarism* (303,600); 14. *The War for Peace: The Present War as Viewed by Friends of Peace* (302,370); 15. *Why America Fights Germany* (725,345); 16. *The Study of the Great War* (678,929); 17. *The Activities of the Committee on Public Information* (23,800); 18. *Lieber and Schurz* (26,360); 19. *The German-Bolshevik Conspiracy* (137,000+); 20. *America's War Aims and Peace Terms* (719,315).

"Loyalty Leaflets": 1. *Friendly Words to the Foreign Born* (570,543); 2. *The Prussian System* (571,036); 3. *Labor and the War* (509,550); 4. *A War Message to the Farmer* (546,911); 5. *Plain Issues of the War* (112,492); 6. *Ways to Serve the Nation* (568,907); 7. *What Really Matters* (574,502). Also, *The Kaiserite in America* (5,550,521); *Germany's Confession* (324,935); *The German Whisper* (437,484); *National School Service* (4,251,570).

64. Blakey, *Historians on the Homefront*, 45.

65. Twenty-seven years later, in his memoir, *Rebel at Large*, Creel was far less reticent. There was an entire chapter titled "The German-Bolshevik Conspiracy." The Cold War was as its height in the late forties, and the versatile Creel, by then a staunch anti–Communist, put an amazing new spin on the old documents: "The 'Sisson documents,' he wrote, "still have a heavy content of interest despite the years that have passed. Not only do they throw light on the methods by which Lenin and Trotsky rose to supreme power, but their publication brought about the first direct interference in our domestic affairs by Communist agents. The technique used then is much the same as that employed ever since: bold attack on whatever is said or done against them and the unceasing repetition of lies until they take on the look of truth" (179). As for verification of the authenticity of the documents, Creel also uncovered brand-new tests, agencies, and experts

to fit his agenda: "For three months the documents were submitted to every known test by various agencies of government, experts on ink, paper, and typewriter type faces being called in" (183).

66. William Appleman Williams, *American Russian Relations, 1781–1947* (New York: Rinehart, 1952), 170.

67. Arthur Walworth, *Woodrow Wilson*, 2:263.

68. Letter, Creel to Rollo Ogden, September 30, 1918. Albert Sydney Burleson Papers, Manuscript Division, Library of Congress. Creel indicated at the bottom of the letter that a copy had gone to Postmaster General Burleson, implying possible loss of franking privileges. According to Arthur Willert, Creel attributed the *Evening Post*'s editorial stance to Thomas W. Lamont, the new owner of the paper, because Lamont was the friend of a "pro–Bolshevist." Letter, Willert to Dawson, September 20, 1918. Willert Papers. Creel also had a run-in with the *New Yorker Volkszeitung*, which also editorially doubted the veracity of the Sisson documents. When the newspaper's editor chose not to back down and stoutly defended the integrity of Lenin and Trotsky in a letter to Creel, Creel sent a copy of the letter to Burleson saying, "I enclose you a most amazing letter for such action as you deem appropriate. This paper baldly charged that the Bolsheviki documents released by the Governments [sic] were forgeries." Letter, Creel to Burleson, October 5, 1918, with copy of letter, Verin Schlueter to Creel, October 9, 1918. *Documents of the Committee on Public Information*.

69. Willert Papers.

70. Creel Papers.

71. September 20, 1918, cited in Mock and Larson, *Words That Won the War*, 317–320.

72. Review of *Russia's Ruin*, E.H. Wilcox (New York: Charles Scribner's Sons, 1920), in the *New Republic*, January 21, 1920, 242.

73. Frederick L. Schuman, *American Policy toward Russia Since 1917* (New York: International, 1928), 152.

74. Edgar Sisson, *One Hundred Red Days: A Personal Chronicle of the Bolshevik Revolution (25 November 1917–4 March 1918)* (New Haven: Yale University Press, 1931), v–vi.

75. George F. Kennan, "The Sisson Documents," *Journal of Modern History*, June 1956, 153–154.

76. The name should have been Four-Minute Men (hyphenated), a surprising error considering the many professional writers and English professors who were CPI advisors. The name was, nevertheless, copyrighted by CPI in 1918 as Four Minute Men.

77. Creel, *How We Advertised America*, 84.

78. Ibid., 84–85.

79. Wayne Alfred Nicholas, "Crossroads Oratory: A Study of the Four Minute Men of World War I" (Ph.D. diss., Columbia University, 1954). By 1947, in *Rebel at Large*, Creel had doubled the numbers: "Before the year [1917] was out, 150,000 trained men were delivering the government's message to the people every week" (162).

80. 1917: "Universal Service by Selective Draft," May 12–21; "First Liberty Loan," May 22–June 15; "Red Cross," June 18–25; "Food Conservation," July 1–14; "Why We Are Fighting," July 23–August 5; "The Nation in Arms," August 6–26; "The Importance of Speed," August 19–26; "What Our Enemy Really Is," August 27–September 23; "Unmasking German Propaganda," August 27–September 23; "Onward to Victory," September 24–October 7; "Second Liberty Loan," October 8–28; "Food Pledge," October 29–November 4; "Maintaining Morals and Morale," November 12–25; "Carrying the Message," November 26–December 22.

1918: "War Savings Stamps," January 2–19; "The Shipbuilder–Man of the Hour," January 28–February 9; "Eyes for the Navy," February 11–16; "The Danger to Democracy," February 18–March 10; "Lincoln's Birthday Address," February 12; "The Income Tax," March 11–16; "Farm and Garden," March 25–30; "President Wilson's Letter to the Theaters," March 31–April 5; "Third Liberty Loan," April 6–May 4; "Second Red Cross Campaign," May 13–25; "Danger to America," May 27–June 12; "Second War Savings Campaign," June 24–28; "The Meaning of America," June 29–July 27; "Mobilizing America's Man Power," July 29–August 17; "Where Did You Get Your Facts?" August 25–September 7; "Certificates to Theater Members," September 9–14; "Register!" September 5–12; "Fourth Liberty Loan," September 38–October 19; "Fire Prevention," October 27–November 2; "United War Work Campaign," November 3–18; "Red Cross Home Service," December 7; "What Have We Won?" December 8–14; "Red Cross Christmas Roll Call," December 15–23; "A Tribute to the Allies," December 24.

81. *Four Minute Men General Bulletin 7A*, April 23, 1918.

82. Documents of the Committee on Public Information, National Archives.

83. George Jones, *Final Report of the State Council of Defense*, Illinois. Documents of the Committee on Public Information.

84. *General Bulletin 7A*.

85. *Four Minute Men News*, Edition F. Documents of the Committee on Public Information.

86. *School Bulletin No. 3*, September 18, 1918. Documents of the Committee on Public Information.

87. Nicholas, "Crossroads Oratory."

88. Creel, *Complete Report*, 29–30.

89. Ibid., 44.

90. Walton Rawls, *Wake Up, America! World War I and The American Poster* (New York: Abbeville Press, 1988) and Yale University Library, World War I Posters Collection.

91. James W. Gerard, *My Four Years in Germany* (New York: George H. Doran, 1917), xii.

92. Ibid., 432.

93. Ibid.

94. Ibid., 57, 269.

95. James W. Gerard, *Face to Face with Kaiserism* (New York: George H. Doran, 1918), 43, 46.

96. Ibid., 58.

97. Ibid., 130–131.

98. Ibid., 169.

99. *Moving Picture World*, March 30, 1918, cited by Isenberg, *War on Film*, 152.

100. James W. Gerard, *My First Eighty-Three Years in America: The Memoirs of James W. Gerard* (Garden City, N.Y.: Doubleday, 1951), 192–193.

101. Ibid., 195.

102. Ibid., 285.

103. Henry Morgenthau, *Ambassador Morgenthau's Story* (Garden City, N.J.: Doubleday, Page, 1918), vii. Like Gerard, Morgenthau was anxious to have his book turned into a motion picture, perhaps as much for vanity's sake as for propaganda purposes. Morgenthau, unlike Gerard, was a wealthy man, and the monetary rewards of a film were not likely to have influenced him. In mid–June 1918, Wilson responded to his suggestion that a movie be made of his book, saying that "I must frankly say that I hope you will not consent to this." He went on to criticize Gerard: "I have been very much distressed that Mr. Gerard should have put his narrative into that form, and personally I believe that we have gone quite far enough in that direction. It is not merely a matter of taste ... but it is also partly a matter of principle. Movies I have seen recently have portrayed so many horrors that I think their effect is far from stimulating and that it does not ... suggest the right attitude of mind or the right national action." Letter, Wilson to Morgenthau, June 14, 1918, cited in Baker, *Woodrow Wilson*, 8:213.

104. Henry Morgenthau, with French Strother, *All in a Life-Time* (New York: Doubleday, Page, 1922), 160.

105. Ibid., 234.

106. Ibid., 84.

107. Ibid., 84–85.

108. Ibid., 86–87.

109. Ibid., 85–86.

110. Sidney Bradshaw Fay, *The Origins of the World War: After Sarajevo* (New York: Macmillan, 1929), 2:169–170.

111. Ibid., 175.

112. Ibid., 176.

113. Ibid., 178.

114. Ibid., 181–182.

115. Cited in Mock and Larson, *Words That Won the War*, 129.

116. Wesley Frost, *German Submarine Warfare: A Study of Its Methods and Spirit* (New York: D. Appleton, 1918), 12–17.

117. Ibid., 29–30.

118. Ibid., 57–59.

119. Ibid., 102.

120. Ibid., 130.

121. Ibid., 203, 227.

122. Rear Admiral William Sowden Sims, "The Truth about the German Submarine Atrocities," *Current History Magazine*, June 1923, 357. Adding powerful credence to the statements of Canadian-born Sims was the fact that he was a dedicated Anglophile. In 1910, as captain of the battleship *Minnesota*, he had visited England and given a speech at the Guildhall that "was purely the inspiration of the moment; it came from the heart, not from the head; probably the evidences that Germany was stealthily preparing her great blow had something to do with my outburst. ... 'If the time should ever come,' I said, 'when the British Empire is menaced by a European coalition, Great Britain can rely upon the last ship, the last dollar, the last man, and the last drop of blood of her kindred beyond the seas.'" Sims, *The Victory at Sea* (New York: Doubleday, Page, 1920), 78–79.

123. Ibid., 362.

124. *Official Bulletin*, July 11, 1918; also cited in Baker, *Woodrow Wilson*, 8:274. Baker included his own footnoted retrospective view of atrocities and a sagacious prediction for the future: "Newspapers and magazines of the period were filled with similar stories of enemy—always enemy—'atrocities.' Harrowing as is such reading in time of peace, it is a necessary part and parcel of war. With marvelously improved methods, not only of killing but of broadcasting the details, the next war should produce a new literature besides which that of the World War will appear insignificant."

125. Cited in Isenberg, *War on Film*, 149.

126. Ibid., 149, 151.

127. Ibid., 148.

128. Ibid.

129. Film Archives Department, Museum of Modern Art.

130. Ibid.

131. Creighton Peet, "Hollywood at War, 1915–1918: A Little Reminder of What the Movies Could Do in the Days of the Beast of Berlin," *Esquire*, September 1936, 109.

132. Kennedy, *Over Here*, 75.

133. Espionage Act of 1917, Section 3, Title I. It was Section 3, Title I of the Espionage Act that was used to convict Eugene V. Debs, Victor L. Berger, William "Big Bill" Haywood and 92 others in the mass trial of the Industrial Workers of the World. Judges imposed sentences of five, ten, and 20 years. However, only the shortest of the sentences were served to completion. President Warren Harding pardoned many of those jailed, and successor President Calvin Coolidge released the last of the political prisoners just before Christmas in 1923. Overall, the Justice Department prosecuted more than 2,000 cases under provisions of the Espionage Act, and over 1,000 defendents were convicted.

134. Albert S. Burleson Papers, Manuscript Division, Library of Congress.

135. Norman Thomas Memoir, Columbia University Oral History Collection, cited by Kennedy, *Over Here*, 76.

136. Zechariah Chafee, Jr., *Free Speech in the United States* (Cambridge: Harvard University Press, 1941), 98–99.

137. Letter, Wilson to Burleson, October 11, 1917, cited in Baker, *Woodrow Wilson*, 7:301.

138. Letter, Wilson to Burleson, October 18, 1917, ibid., 312–313.

139. Letter, Creel to James R. Mock, November 2, 1939. Creel Papers.

140. French Strother, *Fighting Germany's Spies* (Garden City, N.Y.: Doubleday Page, 1918), 199, 202.

141. Ibid., 199–200

142. Letter, Gregory to Francis H. Weston, August 10, 1917, cited in Kennedy, *Over Here*, 82.

143. Ibid., 82.

144. Strother, *Fighting Germany's Spies*, 206–207.

145. Cited in ibid., 215–216.

146. Creel took with him back to private endeavors a sparkling letter of recommendation

from his former boss that both revealed Wilson's close involvement in CPI activities as well as his warm relationship with the chairman. Letter, Wilson to Creel, March 20, 1919 (from Paris): "My dear Creel: I wanted to tell you in person, but find I must now tell you by letter, how deeply I have appreciated the work you have done as Chairman of the Committee on Public Information. The work has been well done, admirably well done, and your inspiration and guidance have been the chief motive power in it all. I have followed what you have done throughout and have approved it, and I want you to know how truly grateful I am. Your personal consideration of myself and your constant thoughtfulness have been a source of pleasure to me all the way through, and I feel I now know beyond peradventure the high motives by which you are governed. It is with real emotion, therefore, that I sign myself, Your sincere friend." Wilson Papers.

147. Letter, Creel to Davis, August 4, 1942. Creel Papers.

148. George Creel, *War Criminals and Punishment* (New York: Robert M. McBride, 1944). In 1920, Creel had published *The War, the World and Wilson* and *How We Advertised America*; and in 1922, *Uncle Henry*. He also published five history books aimed at juvenile readers: *Ireland's Fight for Freedom: Setting Forth the High Lights of Irish History* (1919), *The People Next Door: An Interpretive History of Mexico and the Mexicans* (1926), *Sons of the Eagle: Soaring Figures from America's Past* (1927), *Colossus in Buckskin* (1928), and *Tom Paine: Liberty Bell* (1932). After *War Criminals and Punishment*, Creel wrote two more political books in the 1940s: *White House Physician*, in collaboration with Vice Admiral Ross T. McIntyre (1946), and *Russia's Race for Asia* (1949). In 1947, he wrote his memoir, *Rebel at Large*.

149. *New York Times*, November 25, 1918.

150. Ibid., January 26, 1919.

151. U.S. Senate Subcommittee on the Judiciary, *Brewing and Liquor Interests*, 1:v.

152. Ibid., 1:662.

153. Ibid., 2:2139.

154. Ibid., 2:1602.

155. Ibid., 2:1603.

156. Ibid., 2:1604.

157. Ibid., 2:2517.

158. Ibid., 2:2519.

159. Ibid., 2:2520.

160. *New York Times*, February 11, 1919.

Epilogue

1. *New York Times*, January 23, 1919.

2. U.S. Senate Subcommittee on the Judiciary, *Brewing and Liquor Interests*, 3:114, 123, 146–147.

3. Ibid., 3:251.

4. Ibid., 3:469.

5. Ibid., 3:465.

6. Ibid., 3:941–942.

7. Ibid., 3:946–947.

8. Ibid., 3:974.

BIBLIOGRAPHY

Manuscript Repositories and Library Collections

Baker Library, Harvard University: Thomas W. Lamont Papers.
Film Archives Department, Museum of Modern Art, New York.
Franklin D. Roosevelt Library, Hyde Park: Franklin D. Roosevelt Papers.
Library of Congress, Manuscript Division: Albert Sydney Burleson Papers; George Creel Papers; Josephus Daniels Papers; Elmer Gertz Papers; Irwin Hood Hoover Papers; William S. Sims Papers; George Sylvester Viereck Papers; Edith Bolling Wilson Papers; Woodrow Wilson Papers.
National Archives, Judicial and Fiscal Branch: Documents of the Committee on Public Information.
New York Public Library, World War I Propaganda Pamphlets (BTZE p.v.).
Seeley G. Mudd Manuscript Library, Princeton University: Ivy Ledbetter Lee Papers.
Yale University Library, Manuscripts and Archives: Gordon Auchincloss Papers; Ray Stannard Baker Papers; Edward Mandell House Papers; Sidney E. Mezes Papers; Frank L. Polk Papers; George Sylvester Viereck Papers; Arthur Walworth Papers; Sir Arthur Willert Papers; Sir William Wiseman Papers; World War I Documents Collection; World War I Posters Collection.

Newspapers

New York Times, August 1914 through December 1918, including archives.
New York World, August 1915.
Providence Journal, January 1915 through September 1918.

Books, Articles, Dissertations

Abbott, Wilbur C. "Germany and the Prussian Propaganda." *Yale Review*, July 1915.
Abrams, Ray H. *Preachers Present Arms*. New York: Round Table Press, 1933.
Adler, Selig. "The War-Guilt Question and American Disillusionment, 1918–1928." *The Journal of Modern History*, March 1951.
Albertini, Luigi. *The Origins of the War of 1914*. 3 vols. London: Oxford University Press, 1952.
Allen, H.C. *Great Britain and the United States: A History of Anglo-American Relations, 1783–1952*. London: Odhams Press, 1954.
Allen, William C. *War! Behind the Smoke Screen*. Philadelphia: John C. Winston, 1929.
Angell, Norman. *The Great Illusion, 1933*. New York: G.P. Putnam's Sons, 1933.
_____. *The Public Mind*. London: Unwin Brothers, 1926.
Arndt, Karl J.R., and May E. Olson. *German-American Newspapers and Periodicals, 1732–1955: History and Bibliography*. Heidelberg, Germany: Quelle & Meyer, 1961.
Arthur, Sir George. *George V*. New York: Jonathan Cape & Harrison Smith, 1930.

323

Asinof, Eliot. *1919: America's Loss of Innocence*. New York: Donald I. Fine, 1990.
Aston, Sir George. *Secret Service*. New York: Cosmopolitan Book, 1930.
Auerbach, Jerold S. "Woodrow Wilson's 'Prediction' to Frank Cobb: Words Historians Should Doubt Ever Got Spoken." *Journal of American History*. December 1967.
Bailey, Thomas A. "German Documents Relating to the *Lusitania*." *Journal of Modern History*, September 1936.
_____. *Woodrow Wilson and the Lost Peace*. New York: Macmillan, 1944.
_____, and Paul B. Ryan. *Hitler vs. Roosevelt: The Undeclared Naval War*. New York: Free Press, 1979.
_____, and _____. *The Lusitania Disaster*. New York: Free Press, 1975.
Baker, Newton D. *Why We Went to War*. New York: Harper & Brothers, 1936.
Baker, Ray Stannard. *American Chronicle*. New York: Charles Scribner's Sons, 1945.
_____. *What Wilson Did at Paris*. New York: Doubleday, Page, 1919.
_____. *Woodrow Wilson and World Settlement*, vol. 1. New York: Doubleday, Page, 1922.
_____. *Woodrow Wilson, Life and Letters*. Vol. 4, *President, 1913-1914*; vol. 5, *Neutrality, 1914-1915*; vol. 6, *Facing War, 1915-1917*; vol. 7, *War Leader, April 6, 1917-February 28, 1918*; vol. 8, *Armistice, March 1–November 11, 1918*. Garden City, N.Y.: Doubleday, Doran, 1931-39.
Balfour, Michael. *The Kaiser and His Times*. Boston: Houghton Mifflin, 1964.
Ballard, Robert D. *Exploring the Lusitania*. New York: Warner, 1995.
Bang, J P. *Hurrah and Hallelujah: The Teaching of Germany's Poets, Prophets, Professors, and Teachers: A Documentation*. New York: George H. Doran, 1917.
Bannister, Robert C., Jr. *Ray Stannard Baker—The Mind and Thought of a Progressive*. New Haven: Yale University Press, 1966.
Barnes, Harry Elmer. *The Genesis of the World War*. New York: Alfred A. Knopf, 1929.
_____. *In Quest of Truth and Justice: De-bunking the War-Guilt Myth*. Chicago: National Historical Society, 1928.
_____. "Revisionism and the Promotion of Peace." *Liberation*. July-August, 1958.
_____. "Revisionism Revisited." *Liberation*. July-August, 1959.
Bean, Walton E. "George Creel and His Critics: A Study of the Attacks on the Committee on Public Information, 1917-1919." Ph.D. diss., University of California, 1941.
Beard, Charles A. *The Devil Theory of War*. New York: Vanguard Press, 1936.
_____. *The Rise of American Civilization*. New York: Macmillan, 1935.
Beck, James M. *The Evidence in the Case: A Discussion of the Moral Responsibility for the War of 1914, as Disclosed by the Diplomatic Records of England, Germany, Russia, France, Austria, Italy, and Belgium*. New York: Grosset & Dunlap, 1914.
_____. *The Reckoning: A Discussion of the Moral Aspects of the Peace Problem, and of Retributive Justice as an Indispensable Element*. New York: G.P. Putnam's Sons, 1918.
Beesley, Patrick. *Room 40: British Naval Intelligence 1914–18*. New York: Harcourt Brace Jovanovich, 1982.
Bemis, Samuel Flagg. *A Diplomatic History of the United States*. New York: Holt, Rinehart & Winston, 1936.
Bennett, E.N., trans. *The German Army in Belgium: The White Book of May 1915*. New York: G.W. Heubsch, 1921.
Berger, Meyer. *The Story of The New York Times, 1851-1951*. New York: Simon & Schuster, 1951.
Berkman, Alexander, and Emma Goldman. *Deportation—Its Meaning and Menace (Last Message to the People of the United States)*. New York: M.E. Fitzgerald, 1919. Pamphlet.
Bernays, Edward L. *Biography of an Idea: Memoirs of Public Relations Counsel Edward L. Bernays*. New York: Simon & Schuster, 1965.
_____. *Propaganda*. New York: Liveright, 1928.
Bernhardi, General Friedrich von. *Germany and England*. New York: G.W. Dillingham, 1915.
_____. *Germany and the Next War*. New York: Chas. E. Eron, 1914.
Bernstorff, Johann Heinrich von. *Memoirs of Count Bernstorff*. Trans. Eric Sutton. New York: Random House, 1936.
_____. *My Three Years in America*. New York: Charles Scribner's Sons, 1920.
Blakey, George T. *Historians on the Homefront: American Propagandists for the Great War*. Lexington: University Press of Kentucky, 1970.
Bland, J.O.P., trans. *Germany's Violations of the Laws of War, 1914–15—Compiled Under the Auspices of the French Ministry of Foreign Affairs*. New York: G.P. Putnam's Sons, 1915.

Blankenhorn, Heber. *Adventures in Propaganda: Letters from an Intelligence Officer in France.* New York: Houghton Mifflin, 1919.

Blum, John M. *Joe Tumulty and the Wilson Era.* Boston: Houghton Mifflin, 1931.

Bonadio, Felice A. "The Failure of German Propaganda in the United States, 1914–1917." *Mid-America.* January 1959.

Borchard, Edwin, and William Potter Lage. *Neutrality for the United States.* New Haven: Yale University Press, 1937.

Borland, Hal. "The Kaiser, Japan and Hitler: An Unpublished Chapter of History Which Throws Light on Today's Events." *The New York Times Magazine,* July 16, 1939.

Bright, Charles. *The Story of the Atlantic Cable.* New York: D. Appleton, 1903.

Brooke, Tucker, and Henry Seidel Canby. *War Aims and Peace Ideals.* New Haven: Yale University Press, 1919.

Bruntz, George S. *Allied Propaganda and the Collapse of the German Empire in 1918.* Arno Press: Reprint, 1972. Original edition issued as no. 13, Hoover Inst. (Palo Alto), 1938.

Bryan, William Jennings, and Mary Baird Bryan. *The Memoirs of William Jennings Bryan,* Philadelphia: John C. Winston, 1925.

Bryce, James. *Neutral Nations and the War.* New York: Macmillan, 1914.

Buchanan, Albert Russell. "European Propaganda and American Public Opinion, 1914–1917." Ph.D. diss., Stanford University, 1935.

Buitenhuis, Peter. *The Great War of Words: British, American, and Canadian Propaganda and Fiction, 1914–1933.* Vancouver: University of British Columbia Press, 1987.

Bullard, Arthur. *The Russian Pendulum: Autocracy-Democracy-Bolshevism.* New York: Macmillan, 1919.

Bulow, Bernard von. *Memoirs of Prince von Bulow.* Vol. 1, *From Secretary of State to Imperial Chancellor, 1897-1903;* vol. 2, *From the Morocco Crisis to Resignation, 1903–1909;* vol. 3, *The World War and Germany's Collapse, 1909-1919,* vol. 4, *Early Years and Diplomatic Service, 1849–1897.* Little, Brown, Boston: 1931–32.

Burgess, John. *America's Relations to the Great War.* Chicago: A.C. McClurg, November 1916.

_____. *The European War of 1914.* Chicago: A.C. McClurg, 1915.

_____. *Reminiscences of an American Scholar: The Beginnings of Columbia University.* New York: Columbia University Press, 1934.

Campbell, Craig W. *Reel America and World War I: A Comprehensive Filmography and History of Motion Pictures in the United States, 1914–1920.* Jefferson, N.C.: McFarland, 1985.

Campbell, Rear Admiral Gordon. *My Mystery Ships.* Garden City, N.Y.: Doubleday, Doran, 1929.

Caridi, Ronald J. *Twentieth Century American Foreign Policy: Security and Self-Interest.* Englewood Cliffs, N.J.: Prentice-Hall, 1974.

Carroll, E. Malcolm. *Germany and the Great Powers, 1866–1914: A Study in Public Opinion and Foreign Policy.* New York: Prentice-Hall, 1938.

Chatterton, E. Keble. *Q-Ships and Their Story.* London: Sidgwick & Jackson, 1923.

Cholmondeley, Alice. *Christine.* New York: Macmillan, 1917.

Choukas, Michael. *Propaganda Comes of Age.* Washington, D.C.: Public Affairs Press, 1965.

Church, S.H. *The American Verdict on the War.* Toledo, Ohio: Norman & Remington, 1915.

Churchill, Winston S. *The World Crisis.* New York: Charles Scribner's Sons, 1923.

Clapp, Edwin J. *Economic Aspects of the War: Neutral Rights, Belligerent Claims and American Commerce in the Years 1914–1915.* New Haven: Yale University Press, 1915.

Cobb, Frank. "Military Training for Our Youth." *The Century Magazine,* May 1916.

_____. "The Press and Public Opinion." *The New Republic,* December 31, 1919.

Cobb, Irvin S. *Paths of Glory: Impressions of War Written at and Near the Front.* New York: George H. Doran, 1915.

Cochran, M.H. *Germany Not Guilty in 1914 (Examining a Much Prized Book)* [*The Coming of the War,* 1914, by Bernadotte E. Schmitt]. Boston: Stratford, 1931.

Cohen, Warren I. *The American Revisionists: The Lessons of Intervention in World War I.* Chicago: University of Chicago Press, 1967.

Complete Report of the Chairman of the Committee on Public Information—1917:1918:1919. Washington, D.C.: Government Printing Office, 1920.

Connors, Michael F. "Dealing in Hate: The Development of Anti-German Propaganda." *Institute for Historical Review*, 1981. Pamphlet.

Cooper, John Milton, Jr. *The Warrior and the Priest: Woodrow Wilson and Theodore Roosevelt.* Cambridge: Harvard University Press, Belknap Press, 1983.

Cornebese, Alfred A. *War as Advertised: The Four Minute Men and America's Crusade, 1917–1918.* Philadelphia: American Philosophical Society, 1984.

Corson, William R. *The Armies of Ignorance.* New York: Dial Press, 1977.

Corzier, Emmet. *American Reporters on the Western Front, 1914–1918.* New York: Oxford University Press, 1959.

Cowles, Virginia. *The Kaiser.* New York: Harper & Row, 1963.

Creel, George. *How We Advertised America: The First Telling of the Amazing Story of the Committee on Public Information That Carried the Gospel of Americanism to Every Corner of the Globe.* New York: Harper & Brothers, June 1920.

––––––. "An Open Letter to Dr. Hillis." *Harper's Weekly*, May 29, 1915.

––––––. "The Preparedness with a Punch: An Adequate Navy and an Adequate Army Backed Up by Social and Moral Readiness." *Hearst's*, April 1916.

––––––. "Propaganda and Morale." *The American Journal of Sociology*, November 1941.

––––––. "Public Opinion in War Time." *Annals of the American Academy of Political and Social Science*, July 1918.

––––––. "Raemaekers: Man and Artist." *The Century Magazine*, June 1917.

––––––. *Rebel at Large: Recollections of Fifty Crowded Years.* New York: G.P. Putnam's Sons, 1947.

––––––. "Why the Peace Treaty Was Not Advertised." *Advertising & Selling*, December 13, 1919.

––––––. *Wilson and the Issues.* New York: Century, 1916.

Cronau, Rudolph. *Do We Need a Third War for Independence?* New York: German American Literary Defense Committee, 1914. Pamphlet.

Crowder, Michael. *West Africa Under Colonial Rule.* Evanston, Ill.: Northwestern University Press, 1968.

Curtin, D. Thomas. *The Land of Deepening Shadow: Germany-at-War.* New York: George H. Doran, 1917.

Daniels, Josephus. *The Life of Woodrow Wilson, 1856–1924.* Chicago: John C. Winston, 1924.

––––––. *The Wilson Era: Years of War and After, 1917–1923.* Chapel Hill: University of North Carolina Press, 1946.

Davis, Arthur N. *The Kaiser as I Know Him.* New York: Harper & Brothers, September 1918.

Davis, Elmer. *History of The New York Times, 1851–1921.* New York: New York Times, 1921.

Davis, Kenneth S. *FDR: The New Deal Years, 1933–1937.* New York: Random House, 1979.

Dernburg, Bernhard. *Search-Lights on the War.* New York: Fatherland, 1915. Pamphlet.

Desmond, Robert W. *The Press and World Affairs.* New York: D. Appleton-Century, 1937.

Devlin, Patrick. *Too Proud to Fight: Woodrow Wilson's Neutrality.* New York: Oxford University Press, 1975.

DeWeerd, Harvey A. *President Wilson Fights His War: World War I and the American Intervention.* New York: Macmillan, 1968.

Dodd, William E., Jr. *Ambassador Dodd's Diary*, ed. Martha Dodd. New York: Harcourt, Brace, 1941.

Doob, Leonard W. *Propaganda: Its Psychology and Technique.* New York: Henry Holt, 1935.

––––––. *Public Opinion and Propaganda.* New York: Henry Holt, 1948.

Dos Passos, John. *Mr. Wilson's War.* New York: Doubleday, 1947.

Dower, John W. *War Without Mercy: Race and Power in the Pacific War.* New York: Pantheon Books, 1986.

Doyle, A. Conan. *Great Britain and the Next War.* Boston: Small, Maynard, 1914.

Dumba, Constantin. *Memoirs of a Diplomat.* Boston: Little, Brown, 1932.

Eliot, Charles W. *The Road toward Peace: A Contribution to the Study of the Causes of the European War and of the Means of Preventing War in the Future.* New York: Houghton Mifflin, April 1915.

Ellul, Jacques. *Propaganda: The Formation of Men's Attitudes.* New York: Alfred A. Knopf, 1965.

Engelbrecht, H.C., and F.C. Hanighen. *Merchants of Death: A Study of the International Armament Industry.* London: George Routledge & Sons, 1934.

Essary, J. Frederick. *Covering Washington: Government Reflected to the Public in the Press, 1822–1926.* New York: Houghton Mifflin, 1927.

Farrar, L.L., Jr. *The Short-War Illusion: German Policy, Strategy, and Domestic Affairs, August–December 1914.* Santa Barbara, Calif.: Clio Press, 1973.

Fay, Sidney Bradshaw. *The Origins of the World War: After Sarajevo.* New York: Macmillan, 1929.

———. *The Origins of the World War: Before Sarajevo.* New York: Macmillan, 1928.

Ferris, Paul. *The House of Northcliffe: A Biography of an Empire.* New York: World Publishing, 1972.

Fischer, Fritz. *Germany's Aims in the First World War.* New York: W.W. Norton, 1967.

———. *World Power or Decline: The Controversy over Germany's Aims in the First World War.* New York: W.W. Norton, 1974.

Fisher, H.A.L. *James Bryce.* New York: Macmillan, 1927.

Fisher, Lord John A. *Memories and Records.* 2 vols. New York: George H. Doran, 1920.

Flynn, William J. "Tapped Wires: 'Listening In' at Washington in the Tense Days of 1916." *Liberty,* June 2, 1928.

Fowler, W.B. *British-American Relations, 1917-1918: The Role of Sir William Wiseman.* Princeton: Princeton University Press, 1969.

Fox, Edward Lyell. *Behind the Scenes in Warring Germany.* New York: McBride, Nast, 1915.

Freud, Sigmund, and William C. Bullitt. *Thomas Woodrow Wilson, Twenty-Eighth President of the United States: A Psychological Study.* Boston: Houghton Mifflin, 1966.

Frost, Wesley. *German Submarine Warfare: A Study of Its Methods and Spirit.* New York: D. Appleton, 1918.

Fuehr, Alexander. *The Neutrality of Belgium: A Study of the Belgian Case Under Its Aspects in Political History and International Law.* New York: Funk & Wagnalls, October 1915.

Fussell, Paul. *The Great War and Modern Memory.* New York: Oxford University Press, 1975.

Gaffney, T. St. John. *Breaking the Silence: England, Ireland, Wilson and the War.* New York: Horace Liveright, 1931.

Gaunt, Admiral Sir Guy. *The Yield of the Years: A Story of Adventure Afloat and Ashore.* London: Hutchinson, 1940.

Geiss, Immanuel, ed. *July 1914—The Outbreak of the First World War: Selected Documents.* New York: Charles Scribner's Sons, 1967.

Gelfand, Lawrence E. *The Inquiry: American Preparation for Peace, 1917–1919.* New Haven: Yale University Press, 1963.

George, Alexander L., and Juliette L. George. *Woodrow Wilson and Colonel House: A Personality Study.* New York: John Day, 1956.

Gerard, James W. *Face to Face with Kaiserism.* New York: George H. Doran, 1918.

———. *My First Eighty-Three Years in America: The Memoirs of James W. Gerard.* Garden City, N.Y.: Doubleday, 1951.

———. *My Four Years in Germany.* New York: George H. Doran, 1917.

Gertz, Elmer. *Odyssey of a Barbarian: The Biography of George Sylvester Viereck.* Buffalo: Prometheus Books, 1978.

Gibbs, Philip. *Now It Can Be Told.* New York: Harper & Brothers, 1920.

Gibson, R.H., and Maurice Prendergast. *The German Submarine War, 1914–1918.* London: Constable, 1931.

Ginger, Ray. *The Bending Cross: A Biography of Eugene Victor Debs.* New Brunswick, N.J.: Rutgers University Press, 1949.

Gooch, G.P. *Recent Revelations of European Diplomacy.* New York: Russell & Russell, 1940.

Grattan, C. Hartley. *The Deadly Parallel.* New York: Stackpole Sons, 1939.

———. "The Historians Cut Loose." *The American Mercury,* August 1927.

———. "The Walter Hines Page Legend." *The American Mercury,* July 1925.

———. *Why We Fought.* New York: Vanguard Press, 1929.

Gray, Edwin A. *The Killing Time: The U-Boat War, 1914–1918.* New York: Charles Scribner's Sons, 1972.

Grenfell, Russell. *Unconditional Hatred—German War Guilt and the Future of Europe.* New York: Devon-Adair, 1953.

Grey, Viscount (of Fallodin, K.G.). *Twenty-Five Years, 1892–1916.* 2 vols. New York: Frederick A. Stokes, 1925.

Gruber, Carol S. *Mars and Minerva: World War I and the Uses of Higher Learning in America*. Baton Rouge: Lousiana State University Press, 1975.

Guedalla, Phillip. *Mr. Churchill*. New York: Reynal & Hitchcock, 1942.

Gwynn, Stephen, ed. *The Letters and Friendships of Sir Cecil Spring Rice: A Record*. 2 vols. Boston: Houghton Mifflin, 1929.

Hagedorn, Hermann. *Leonard Wood*. 2 vols. New York: Harper & Brothers, 1931.

_____. *Where Do You Stand? An Appeal to Americans of German Origin*. New York: Macmillan, March 1918.

Hale, William Bayard. *The Story of a Style*. New York: B.W. Huebsch, 1920.

_____. *Woodrow Wilson: The Story of His Life*. Garden City, N.Y.: Doubleday, Page, 1912.

Hale, William Harlan. "Adventures of a Document: The Strange Sequel to the Kaiser Interview." *The Atlantic Monthly*, June 1934.

_____. "Thus Spoke the Kaiser: The Lost Interview Which Solves an International Mystery." *The Atlantic Monthly*, May 1934.

Hamlin, C.H. *The War Myth in United States History*. New York: Vanguard Press, with Association to Abolish War, 1927.

Harris, Frank. *England or Germany?* New York: Wilmarth Press, 1915.

Hart, Albert Bushnell. *America at War: A Handbook of Patriotic Education References*. New York: National Security League Committee on Patriotism through Education, with George H. Doran, 1918.

Heaton, John L. *Cobb of "The World": A Leader in Liberalism*. Freeport, N.Y.: Books for Libraries Press, 1924.

Hecht, George J. *The War in Cartoons: A History of the War in 100 Cartoons by 27 of the Most Prominent American Cartoonists*. New York: E.P. Dutton, 1919.

Hendrick, Burton J. *The Life and Letters of Walter H. Page*. 3 vols. Garden City, N.Y.: Doubleday, Page, 1922.

Hibben, Paxton. *The Peerless Leader: William Jennings Bryan*. New York: Farrar & Rinehart, 1929.

Hicks, Granville. "The Parsons and the War." *The American Mercury*, February 1927.

Hiebert, Ray Eldon. *Courtier to the Crowd: The Story of Ivy Lee and the Development of Public Relations*. Ames: Iowa State University Press, 1966.

Hill, David Jayne. *Impressions of the Kaiser*. New York: Harper & Brothers, November 1918.

Hillis, Newell Dwight. *The Blot on the Kaiser's 'Scutcheon*. New York: Fleming H. Revell, 1918.

_____. *German Atrocities — Their Nature and Philosophy: Studies in Belgium and France During July and August of 1917*. New York: Fleming H. Revell, 1918.

_____. *Studies of the Great War: What Each Nation Has at Stake*. New York: Fleming H. Revell, 1915.

Hitler, Adolph. *Mein Kampf*. Unexpurgated ed. trans. New York: Stackpole, 1939.

Hoover, Herbert. *The Ordeal of Woodrow Wilson*. New York: McGraw-Hill, 1958.

Hough, Emerson. *The Web: The Authorized History of the American Protective League*. Chicago: Reilly & Lee, 1919.

House, Edward Mandell. *What Really Happened at Paris: The Story of the Peace Conference, 1918-1919*. Ed. Charles Seymour. New York: Charles Scribner's Sons, 1921.

Houston, David H. *Eight Years with Wilson's Cabinet, 1913 to 1920*. 2 vols. New York: Doubleday, Page, 1926.

Hungerford, Edward. "The Peace Treaty: A Failure in Advertising." *Advertising & Selling*, November 29, 1919.

Irwin, Will. *Propaganda and the News*. 1936. Reprint, Westport, Conn.: Greenwood Press, 1970.

Isenberg, Michael T. *War on Film: The American Cinema and World War I, 1914–1941*. East Brunswick, N.J.: Associated University Presses, 1981.

Jameson, William. *The Most Formidable Thing*. London: Rupert Hart-Davis, 1965.

Jedell, Hugh. "Why German Propaganda Failed." Review of *Weltkreig Ohne Waffen (World War Without Arms)* by J.G. Cotte. *New York Times Book Review*, September 3, 1932.

Johnson, Neil M. *George Sylvester Viereck: German-American Propagandist*. Chicago: University of Illinois Press, 1972.

Johnston, Winifred. *Memo on the Movies: War Propaganda, 1914–1939*. Norman, Okla.: Cooperative Books, 1939.

Juergens, George. *News from the White House: The Presidential-Press Relationship in the Progressive Era*. Chicago: University of Chicago Press, 1981.

Kaplan, Justin. *Lincoln Steffens: A Biography*. New York: Simon & Schuster, 1974.

Keegan, John. *The Face of Battle*. New York: Viking Press, 1976.

Keim, Jeannette. *Forty Years of German-American Political Relations*. Philadelphia: William J. Dornan, 1919.

Kenez, Peter. *The Birth of the Propaganda State: Soviet Methods of Mass Mobilization, 1917–1929*. Cambridge: Cambridge University Press, 1985.

Kennan, George F. *The Fateful Alliance: France, Russia, and the Coming of the First World War*. New York: Pantheon Books, 1984.

_____. "The Sisson Papers." *Journal of Modern History*, June 1956.

_____. *Soviet-American Relations, 1917–1920*. Vol. 1, *Russia Leaves the War*, 1958; vol. 2, *The Decision to Intervene*. New York: W.W. Norton, 1956.

Kennedy, David M. *Over Here: The First World War and American Society*. New York: Oxford University Press, 1980.

Kennedy, Paul. *The Rise and Fall of the Great Powers*. New York: Random House, 1987.

_____. *The Samoan Tangle: A Study in Anglo-German-American Relations, 1878–1900*. Dublin: Irish University Press, 1974.

_____. *The War Plans of the Great Powers, 1880-1914*. London: George Allen & Unwin, 1979.

Kerney, James. *The Political Education of Woodrow Wilson*. New York: Century, 1926.

Krock, Arthur. *Memoirs: Sixty Years on the Firing Line*. New York: Funk & Wagnalls, 1968.

Landau, Captain Henry. *The Enemy Within: The Inside Story of German Sabotage in America*. New York: G.P. Putnam's Sons, 1937.

Lansing, Robert. *The Peace Negotiations: A Personal Narrative*. New York: Houghton Mifflin, 1921.

_____. *War Memoirs of Robert Lansing*. New York: Bobbs-Merrill, 1935.

Larson, Cedric, and James R. Mock. "The Lost Files of the Creel Committee." *The Public Opinion Quarterly*, January 1939.

Lasswell, Harold D. *Propaganda Technique in the World War*. New York: Alfred A. Knopf, 1927.

Lauriat, Charles E., Jr. *The Lusitania's Last Voyage: Being a Narrative of the Torpedoing and Sinking of the R.M.S. Lusitania by a German Submarine off the Irish Coast, May 7, 1915*. New York: Houghton Mifflin, 1915.

Lavine, Harold, and James Wechsler. *War Propaganda and the United States*. New Haven: Yale University Press, 1940.

Lawrence, David. *The True Story of Woodrow Wilson*. New York: George H. Doran, 1924.

Lea, Homer. *The Day of the Saxon*. New York: Harper & Brothers, 1912.

Link, Arthur S. *World War I and the Progressive Era, 1910–1917*. New York: Harper & Brothers, 1954.

Linn, James Weber. *Jane Addams: A Biography*. New York: D. Appleton-Century, 1935.

Lippmann, Walter. *Public Opinion*. New York: Macmillan, 1922.

_____, and Charles Merz. "A Test of the News." *New Republic*, August 4 and 11, 1920.

Longworth, Alice Roosevelt. *Crowded Hours*. New York: Charles Scribner's Sons, 1933.

Louis, William Roger. *Great Britain and Germany's Lost Colonies*. Oxford: Clarendon Press, 1967.

Lowenthal, Max. *The Federal Bureau of Investigation*. New York: William Sloane Associates, 1950.

Ludendorff, Erich von. *Ludendorff's Own Story, August 1914–November 1918: The Great War from the Siege of Liège to the Signing of the Armistice, As Viewed from the Grand Headquarters of the Germany Army*. 2 vols. New York: Harper & Brothers, 1919.

Ludwig, Emil. *July '14*. New York: G.P. Putnam's Sons, 1929.

_____. *Wilhelm Hohenzollern: The Last of the Kaisers*. Trans. E.C. Mayne. New York: G.P. Putnam's Sons, 1927.

Luebke, Frederick C. *Bonds of Loyalty: German-Americans and World War I*. DeKalb: Northern Illinois University Press, 1974.

Lumley, Frederick E. *The Propaganda Menace*. New York: Century, 1933.

Lutz, Ralph Haswell. "Bibliographical Articles: Studies of World War Propaganda, 1914–1933." *Journal of Modern History*, December 1933.

McAdoo, William Gibbs. *Crowded Years*. New York: Houghton Mifflin, 1931.

McAnn, Richard Dyer. *The People's Films*. New York: Hastings House, 1973.

McGuire, James K. *The King, the Kaiser and Irish Freedom*. New York: Devin-Adair, 1915.

Mach, Edmond von. *Germany's Point of View*. Chicago: A.C. McClurg, 1915.

_____. *Official Diplomatic Documents Relating to the Outbreak of the European War.* New York: Macmillan, 1916.

_____. *What Germany Wants.* Boston: Little, Brown, 1914.

MacLeish, Kenneth. "Was There a Gun?" *Sports Illustrated.* December 24, 1962.

Manchester, William. *The Arms of Krupp, 1587–1968.* Boston: Little, Brown, 1964.

March, Francis A. *History of the World War: An Authentic Narrative of the World's Greatest War.* Chicago: United Publishers of the United States and Canada, 1919.

Marder, Arthur J. *From the Dreadnought to Scapa Flow: The Royal Navy in the Fisher Era, 1904–1919.* Vol. 2, *The War Years: To the Eve of Jutland.* London: Oxford University Press, 1965.

Margutti, Lieutenant-General Baron von. *The Emperor Francis Joseph and His Times.* New York: George H. Doran, 1921.

Marshall, Logan, ed. *Hindenburg's March into London.* Philadelphia: John C. Winston, 1916.

Martin, E.S. *The Diary of a Nation: The War and How We Got into It.* New York: Doubleday, Page, 1917.

Masterman, Lucy. *C.F.G. Masterman: A Biography.* London: Frank Cass, 1939.

Masters, David. *The Submarine War.* New York: Henry Holt, 1935.

Maxim, Hudson. *Defenseless America.* New York: Hearst's International Library, 1915.

Menken, S. Stanwood. "Raemaekers, a Mainspring of Armed Force." *Century Magazine,* February 1918.

Miller, John C. *Sam Adams: Pioneer in Propaganda.* Stanford: Stanford University Press, 1936.

Millis, Walter. *Arms and Men: A Study in American Military History.* New York: G.P. Putnam's Sons, 1956.

_____. *The Martial Spirit: A Study of Our War with Spain.* New York: Literary Guild of America, 1931.

_____. "1939 Is Not 1914." *Life,* November 6, 1939.

_____. *Road to War: America 1914–1917.* New York: Houghton Mifflin, 1935.

Mitchell, Peter Chalmers. *Report on the Propaganda Library in the Intelligence Division of the War Office.* London: H.M. Stationery Office, 1917.

Mock, James R. *Censorship 1917.* Princeton: Princeton University Press, 1941.

_____, and Cedric Larson. *Words That Won the War: The Story of the Committee on Public Information, 1917–1919.* Princeton: Princeton University Press, 1939.

Morel, Edmund Dene. *Red Rubber: The Story of the Rubber Slave Trade Flourishing on the Congo in the Year of Grace 1906.* New York: The Nassau Print, 1907.

_____. *Truth and the War. 1916.* Reprint, New York: Garland, 1972.

Morgan, Ted. *Maugham.* New York: Simon & Schuster, 1980.

Morgenthau, Henry. *All in a Life-Time.* New York: Doubleday, Page, 1922.

_____. *Ambassador Morgenthau's Story.* New York: Doubleday, Page, 1918.

Morrissey, Alice M. *The American Defense of Neutral Rights, 1914–1917.* Cambridge: Harvard University Press, 1939.

Mott, Frank Luther. *American Journalism: A History: 1690–1960.* New York: Macmillan, 1962.

_____. *A History of American Magazines.* New York: D. Appleton, 1938.

Mueller-Meiningen, Ernst. *Who Are the Huns? The Law of Nations and Its Breakers.* Berlin: George Reimer, 1915.

Muensterberg, Hugo. *The War and America.* New York: D. Appleton, 1914.

Murray, Gilbert. *Faith, War and Policy: Addresses and Essays on the European War.* New York: Houghton Mifflin, 1917.

Nafziger, Ralph Otto. "The American Press and Public Opinion During the World War, 1914 to April 1917." Ph.D. diss., University of Wisconsin, 1936.

Nevins, Allan. "Propaganda: An Explosive Word Analyzed." *New York Times Magazine,* October 29, 1939.

_____, ed. *The Letters and Journal of Brand Whitlock.* 2 vols. New York: D. Appleton-Century, 1936.

Nicholas, Wayne Alfred. "Crossroads Oratory: A Study of the Four Minute Men of World War I." Ph.D. diss., Columbia University, 1954.

Nicolson, Harold. *Peacemaking. 1919: Being Reminiscences of the Paris Peace Conference.* New York: Houghton Mifflin, 1933.

Nicolson, Ivor. "An Aspect of British Official Wartime Propaganda." *Cornhill Magazine,* May 1931.

Notter, Harley. *The Origins of the Foreign Policy of Woodrow Wilson.* Baltimore: Johns Hopkins Press, 1937.

Noyes, Alexander D. *The War Period of American Finance, 1908–1925.* New York: G.P. Putnam's Sons, 1926.

Ohlinger, Gustavus. "German Propaganda in the United States." *Atlantic Monthly*, April 1916.

O'Toole, G.J.A. *The Spanish War.* New York: W.W. Norton, 1984.

Padfield, Peter. *The Great Naval Race: Anglo-German Naval Rivalry, 1900–1914.* New York: David McKay, 1974.

Page, Kirby. *War: Causes, Consequences and Cure.* New York: George H. Doran, 1923.

Palmer, Frederick. *With My Own Eyes: A Personal Story of Battle Years.* Indianapolis: Bobbs-Merrill, 1932.

_____, and Newton D. Baker. *America at War.* Vol. 1. New York: Dodd, Mead, 1931.

Papen, Franz von. *Memoirs.* New York: E.P. Dutton, 1952.

Parker, Sir Gilbert. "The United States and the War." *Harper's Monthly Magazine*, March 1918.

Peckelsheim, Baron Spiegel von und zu. *The Adventures of the U-202.* New York: Century, 1917.

Peet, Creighton. "Hollywood at War, 1915-1918: A Little Reminder of What the Movies Could Do in the Days of the Beast of Berlin." *Esquire*, September 1936.

Perry, Ralph Barton. *The Plattsburg Movement—A Chapter of America's Participation in the World War.* New York: E.P. Dutton, 1921.

Pessen, Edward. *Losing Our Souls: The American Experience in the Cold War.* Chicago: Ivan R. Dee, 1993.

Peterson, H.C. *Propaganda for War. 1939.* Reprint, Port Washington, N.Y.: Kennikat Press, 1968.

_____, and Gilbert C. Fite. *Opponents of War, 1917–1918.* Madison: University of Wisconsin Press, 1957.

Playne, Caroline E. *Society at War, 1914–1916.* London: George Allen & Unwin, 1931.

Ponsonby, Arthur. *Falsehood in War-Time.* New York: E.P. Dutton, 1928.

Poole, Ernest. *The Bridge: My Own Story.* New York: Macmillan, 1940.

Pratt, Julius W. *A History of United States Foreign Policy.* New York: Prentice-Hall, 1955.

Pringle, Henry F. *Theodore Roosevelt: A Biography.* New York: Harcourt, Brace, 1931.

Raemaekers, Louis. *America in the War (Each Cartoon Faced with a Page of Comment by a Distinguished American, the Text Forming an Anthology of Patriotic Opinion).* New York: Century, 1918.

_____. *Kultur in Cartoons (with Accompanying Notes by Well-Known English Writers).* New York: Century, 1917.

_____. *Raemaekers' Cartoons (with Accompanying Notes by Well-Known English Writers).* New York: Doubleday, Page, 1916.

Rappaport, Armin. *The British Press and Wilsonian Neutrality.* Stanford: Stanford University Press, 1951.

Rawls, Walton. *Wake Up, America! World War I and the American Poster.* New York: Abbeville Press, 1988.

Read, James Morgan. *Atrocity Propaganda, 1914–1919.* New Haven: Yale University Press, 1941.

Repington, C.C. *The First World War, 1914–1918.* Vol 2. London: Constable, 1920.

Rickards, Maurice. *Posters of the First World War.* New York: Walker, 1968.

Robinson, David. *The History of World Cinema.* New York: Stein & Day, 1973.

Rogerson, Sidney. *Propaganda in the Next War.* London: Geoffrey Bles, 1938.

Roosevelt, Theodore. *America and the World War.* New York: Charles Scribner's Sons, 1915.

_____. *Roosevelt in the Kansas City Star: War-Time Editorials by Theodore Roosevelt.* New York: Houghton Mifflin, 1921.

Rose, Kenneth. *King George V.* New York: Alfred A. Knopf, 1984.

Russell, Bertrand. *Justice in War Time.* Nottingham, England: Bertrand Russell Peace Foundation, 1916.

Ryan, A.P. *Lord Northcliffe.* New York: Macmillan, 1953.

Ryder, Rowland. *Edith Cavell.* New York: Stein & Day, 1975.

Salmon, Lucy Maynard. *The Newspaper and Authority.* New York: Oxford University Press, 1923.

_____. *The Newspaper and the Historian.* New York: Oxford University Press, 1923.

Sanders, M.L., and Philip M. Taylor. *British Propaganda During the First World War, 1914–1918.* London: Macmillan, 1982.

Schactman, Tom. *Edith and Woodrow: A Presidential Romance*. New York: G.P. Putnam's Sons, 1981.

Scheer, Admiral Reinhardt. *Germany's High Sea Fleet in the World War*. New York: Cassell, 1920.

Scheiber, Clara Eve. *The Transformation of American Sentiment Toward Germany, 1870–1914*. New York: Cornhill, 1923.

Schmitt, Bernadotte E. *The Coming of the War, 1914*. 2 vols. New York: Charles Scribner's Sons, 1930.

Schnee, Heinrich. *German Colonization Past and Future: The Truth About the German Colonies*. London: George Allen & Unwin, 1926.

Schreiner, George Abel. *The Craft Sinister: A Diplomatico-Political History of the Great War and Its Causes—Diplomacy and International Politics and Diplomatists as Seen at Close Range by an American Newspaperman Who Served in Central Europe as War and Political Correspondent*. New York: G. Albert Geyer, 1920.

Scott, Jonathan French. *Five Weeks: The Surge of Public Opinion on the Eve of the Great War*. New York: John Day, 1927.

Seitz, Don D. *Joseph Pulitzer: His Life & Letters*. New York: Simon & Schuster, 1924.

Seymour, Charles. *American Neutrality, 1914-1917: Essays on the Causes of American Intervention in the World War*. New Haven: Yale University Press, 1935.

_____. *The Diplomatic Background of the War—1870–1914*. New Haven: Yale University Press, 1916.

_____. *Woodrow Wilson and the World War: A Chronicle of Our Own Times*. New Haven: Yale University Press, 1921.

_____, ed. *The Intimate Papers of Colonel House*. Vol. 1, *Behind the Political Curtain*; vol. 2, *1915–1917*; vol. 3, *Into the World War*; vol. 4, *The Ending of the War*. Cambridge: Houghton Mifflin, 1926-28.

Shaw, Bernard. *What I Really Wrote about the War*. London: Constable, 1930.

Shepherd, William G. "The Free Lance and the Faker: An Inside Story of War Reporting." *Everybody's Magazine*, March 1917.

Simpson, Colin. *The Lusitania*. Boston: Little, Brown, 1972.

Sims, Rear Admiral William Sowden. "The Truth About the German Submarine Atrocities." *Current History Magazine*, June 1923.

_____. *The Victory at Sea*. New York: Doubleday, Page, 1920.

Sinclair, Andrew. *Prohibition: The Era of Excess*. Boston: Little, Brown, 1962.

Sinclair, Upton. *The Brass Check: A Study of American Journalism*. Pasadena, Calif.: privately published, 1920.

Sisson, Edgar. *One Hundred Red Days: A Personal Chronicle of the Bolshevik Revolution (25 November 1917-4 March 1918)*. New Haven: Yale University Press, 1931.

Small, Melvin. "The American Image of Germany, 1906–1914." Ph.D. diss., University of Michigan, 1965.

Smith, Gene. *When the Cheering Stopped: The Last Years of Woodrow Wilson*. New York: William Morrow, 1964.

Solomon, Martha. *Emma Goldman*. Boston: Twayne Publishers, 1987.

Sorokin, Pitrim A. *Social and Cultural Dynamics*. New York: American Book, 1937.

Spencer, Samuel R. *Decision for War, 1917: The Laconia Sinking and the Zimmerman Telegram as Key Factors in the Public Reaction Against Germany*. Peterborough, N.H.: William L. Bauham, 1953.

Squires, James Duane. *British Propaganda at Home and in the United States—From 1914 to 1917*. Cambridge: Harvard University Press, 1935.

Steed, Henry Wickham. *Through Thirty Years*. 2 vols. New York: Doubleday, Page, 1925.

Steel, Ronald. *Walter Lippmann and the American Century*. Boston: Little, Brown, 1980.

Steffens, Lincoln. *Autobiography*. New York: Harcourt, Brace, 1931.

Stein, Leonard. *The Balfour Declaration*. New York: Simon & Schuster, 1961.

Steiner, Zara S. *Britain and the Origins of the First World War*. New York: St. Martin's Press, 1977.

Stephen, S. Ivor. *Neutrality? The Crucifixion of Public Opinion, from the American Point of View*. Chicago: Neutrality Press, 1916.

Stone, Melville E. *Fifty Years a Journalist*. Garden City, N.Y.: Doubleday, Page, 1921.

Strother, French. *Fighting Germany's Spies*. Garden City, N.Y.: Doubleday Page, 1918.

_____. "The Providence Journal Will Say This Morning: An Appreciation of John R. Rathom, the Man Who Exposed the German Plots in This Country, and an Announcement of Mr. Rathom's Own Story, Which Will Be Published in the World's Work." *The World's Work,* January 1918.

Stuart, Sir Campbell. *Secrets of Crewe House.* New York: Hodder & Stoughton, 1920.

Sugrue, Thomas. *Starling of the White House.* New York: Simon & Schuster, 1946.

Sullivan, Mark. *Our Times: The United States, 1900-1925.* Vol. 5, *Over Here, 1914–1918.* New York: Charles Scribner's Sons, 1933.

Swanberg, W.A. *Citizen Hearst.* New York: Charles Scribner's Sons, 1961.

_____. *Norman Thomas: The Last Idealist.* New York: Charles Scribner's Sons, 1976.

_____. *Pulitzer.* New York: Charles Scribner's Sons, 1967.

Talese, Gay. *The Kingdom and the Power.* New York: World Publishing, 1966.

Tansill, Charles Callan. *America Goes to War.* Boston: Little, Brown, 1938.

Taylor, A.J.P. *War By Time-Table: How the First World War Began.* New York: American Heritage, 1969.

Terrain, John. *The U-Boat Wars, 1916–1945.* New York: G.P. Putnam's Sons, 1989.

Thayer, William Roscoe. *Germany vs. Civilization: Notes on the Atrocious War.* New York: Houghton Mifflin, 1916.

Thomas, Norman. *Is Conscience a Crime?* New York: B.W. Huebsch, 1923.

Thwaites, Lieutenant-Col. Norman. *Velvet and Vinegar.* London: Grayson & Grayson, 1932.

Todd, Lewis Paul. *Wartime Relations of the Federal Government and the Public Schools.* New York: Arno Press and *New York Times,* 1971.

Tuchman, Barbara W. *The Guns of August.* New York: Macmillan, 1962.

_____. *The Zimmermann Telegram.* New York: Viking Press, 1958.

Tumulty, Joseph P. *Woodrow Wilson as I Know Him.* Garden City, N.Y.: Garden City Publishing, 1921.

Turner, John Kenneth. *Shall It Be Again?* New York: B.W. Huebsch, 1922.

Turner, L.C.F. *Origins of the First World War.* New York: W.W. Norton, 1970.

Two Thousand Questions and Answers about the War: A Catechism of the Methods of Fighting, Travelling, and Living; of the Armies, Navies, and Air Fleets; of the Personalities, Politics, and Geography of the Warring Countries. New York: Review of Reviews, 1918.

U.S. Senate Subcommittee on the Judiciary, *Brewing and Liquor Interests and German and Bolshevik Propaganda.* Report and Hearings. 3 vols. Senate Document No. 62, 66th Congress, 1st session, 1919.

Usher, Roland G. *Pan-Germanism.* New York: Houghton Mifflin Co., 1913.

_____. *The Winning of the War: A Sequel to "Pan-Germanism."* New York: Harper & Brothers, March 1918.

Vandervelde, Lalla. *Monarchs and Millionaires.* New York: Adelphi, 1925.

Vaughn, Stephen. *Holding Fast the Inner Lines—Democracy, Nationalism, and the Committee on Public Information.* Chapel Hill: University of North Carolina Press, 1980.

Veale, F.J.P. "The Wicked Kaiser Myth: Demonstrating the Unreliability of Unanimous Verdicts of Public Opinion." *Social Justice Review,* April 1960.

Viereck, George Sylvester. *As They Saw Us: Foch, Ludendorff, and Others—Leaders Write Our War History.* New York: Doubleday, Doran, 1919.

_____. *The Kaiser on Trial.* New York: Greystone Press, 1937.

_____. *Spreading Germs of Hate.* New York: Horace Liveright, 1930.

_____. *The Strangest Friendship in History: Woodrow Wilson and Colonel House.* New York: Liveright, 1932.

Villard, Oswald Garrison. *Germany Embattled: An American Interpretation.* New York: Charles Scribner's Sons, 1915.

_____. *Some Newspapers and Newspaper-Men.* New York: Alfred A. Knopf, 1926.

_____. "The True Story of the Lusitania." *The American Mercury,* May 1935.

Voska, Emanuel Victor, and Will Irwin. *Spy and Counterspy.* New York: Doubleday, Doran, 1940.

Walker, J. Bernard. *America Fallen! The Sequel to the European War.* New York: Dodd, Mead, 1915.

Walter, Willard, ed. *War in the Twentieth Century.* New York: Random House, 1940.

Walworth, Arthur. *America's Moment: 1918—American Diplomacy at the End of World War I.* New York: W.W. Norton, 1977.

_____. *Wilson and His Peacemakers: American Diplomacy at the Paris Peace Conference, 1919*. New York: W.W. Norton, 1986.

_____. *Woodrow Wilson*, 2 vols. New York: W.W. Norton, 1958.

Ward, Robert D. "The Origin and Activities of the National Security League, 1914–1919." *The Mississippi Valley Historical Review*, June 1960.

Weinberg, Arthur, and Lila Weinberg. *The Muckrakers*. New York: Simon & Schuster, 1961.

Wells, Herbert George. *In the Fourth Year, Anticipations of a World Peace*. New York: Macmillan, 1918.

_____. *Italy, France and Britain at War*. New York: Macmillan, 1917.

_____. *Mr. Britling Sees It Through*. New York: Macmillan, 1917.

_____. *The War That Will End War*. New York: Duffield, 1914.

_____. *What is Coming?—A European Forecast*. New York: Macmillan, 1916.

_____ (in collaboration with Sir Edward Grey, Lionel Curtis, William Archer, H. Wickham Steed, A.E. Zimmern, J.A. Spender, James Bryce, and Gilbert Murray). *The Idea of a League of Nations*. Boston: Atlantic Monthly Press, 1919.

Wertheimer, Mildred S. *The Pan-German League, 1890–1914*. New York: Longmans, Green, 1924.

Wilkerson, Marcus M. *Public Opinion and the Spanish-American War: A Study in War Propaganda*. Baton Rouge: Louisiana State University Press, 1932.

Willert, Sir Arthur. *The Road to Safety: A Study in Anglo-American Relations*. New York: Frederick A. Praeger, 1953.

_____. "The Vexed Question of Contraband." *The Atlantic Monthly*, March 1915.

_____. *Washington and Other Memories*. Boston: Houghton Mifflin, 1972.

Williams, William Appleman. *American-Russian Relations, 1781–1947*. New York: Rinehart, 1952.

Wilson, Edith Bolling. *My Memoir*. New York: Bobbs-Merrill, 1938.

Wilson, Trevor. "Lord Bryce's Investigation into Alleged German Atrocities in Belgium, 1914–15." *Journal of Contemporary History* 14 (1979).

_____. *The Myriad Faces of War: Britain and the Great War, 1914–1918*. Cambridge: Polity Press, 1986.

Wilson, Woodrow. *In Our First Year of War*. New York: Harper & Brothers, 1918.

_____. "The Road Away from Revolution." *Atlantic Monthly*, August 23, 1923.

Wiltz, John E. *In Search of Peace: The Senate Munitions Inquiry, 1934–36*. Baton Rouge: Louisiana State University Press, 1963.

Winkler, John K. *W.R. Hearst: An American Phenomenon*. New York: Simon & Schuster, 1928.

Wisan, Joseph E. *The Cuban Crisis as Reflected in the New York Press (1895–1898)*. New York: Columbia University Press, 1934.

Wise, Jennings C. *Woodrow Wilson: Disciple of Revolution*. New York: Paisley Press, 1938.

Wister, Owen. *The Pentecost of Calamity*. New York: Macmillan, August 1915.

Wittenberg, Ernest. "The Thrifty Spy on the 6th Avenue El." *American Heritage*, December 1965.

Wittke, Carl. *German-Americans and the World War (with Special Emphasis on Ohio's German-Language Press)*. Columbus: Ohio State Archaeological and Historical Society, 1936.

_____. *The German-Language Press in America*. Lexington: University of Kentucky Press, 1957.

Woehlke, Walter V. "The German-American, I: The Confessions of a Hyphenate." *The Century Magazine*, April 1917.

Wood, Eric Fisher. "Northcliffe." *Century Magazine*, October 1917.

Wood, Leonard. *Our Military History: Its Facts and Fallacies*. Chicago: Reilly & Britton, 1916.

Wrench, John Evelyn. *Geoffrey Dawson and Our Times*. London: Hutchinson, 1955.

Wreszin, Michael. *Oswald Garrison Villard: Pacifist at War*. Bloomington: Indiana University Press, 1965.

Wright, Quincy. *A Study of War*. Chicago: University of Chicago Press, 1942.

Zurier, Rebecca. *Art for the Masses: A Radical Magazine and Its Graphics, 1911–1917*. Philadelphia: Temple University Press, 1988.

INDEX

335

More from ProgressivePress.com at Your Local Bookstore

THE NAZI HYDRA IN AMERICA: Suppressed History of a Century. US corporatists sponsoring fascism over four generations of Bush, Harriman and other dynasties. How they made Hitler, and work towards a world fascist regime today. Ratlines, Paperclip, Nazi Gold, Dulles brothers, Gestapo roots of the CIA. Hugely provocative – and factual. Released January 2009, 700 pages, $19.95.

SEEDS OF DESTRUCTION: The Hidden Agenda of Genetic Manipulation. A crime drama, a frightening vision, and a real one. Science, commerce, agriculture, even seeds – all of our needs – are weapons in the hands of a few global corporations and their corrupt political puppets. To run the world, even sterilize or starve peoples, they only need to control our food production. 360 pages, $24.95.

Skulk! a Post-9/11 Comic Novel. A racy, sophisticated parody of American political reality, a wild ride along a track of ironic twists to a stunning ending. This hilarious vehicle is on a journey into deep truth about things like 9/11 and the powers that be, and aims to lure a lot of riders into new territory. "There is something for almost everyone in this book... Marc Estrin has his finger on the pulse of American madnesses." 180 pp, $14.95

CORPORATISM: The Secret Government of the New World Order by Prof. J. Grupp. Monopolistic mega-corporations control all aspects of life using false-flag terror, brainwashing, vaccines, chemtrails, dumbed-down media, the destruction of nature and society. Their agenda is a Hitlerian global "prison planet" of death camps. 2nd ed., Fall 2008, 412 pages, $15.95.

INSIDE THE GESTAPO: Hitler's Shadow over the World. The fascinating wartime account by a top defector of the ruthlessness, intrigues and curious personalities of the Third Reich. Full of surprises, sardonic wit and tragic endings. "Gestapo tactics" – cunning, cynical in exploiting weaknesses – and murdering anyone in the way. First published in 1940, new reprint 2008. 288 pages, $24.95.

HOW THE WORLD REALLY WORKS. Ten books in one, it ties together the tentacles of the NWO Mega-Conspiracy like no other. The plotting of wars, the bankster elite, social engineering foundations, privatized money power of the "Fed," police statism, globalization and environmental ploys, the drug trade, JFK assassination, Carroll Quigley. Exposure is the cure for the roots of evil. 336 pages, $15.

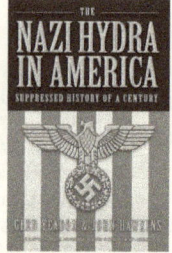

Webster Tarpley Exposes Wall Street Financiers

9/11 Synthetic Terror: Made in USA
The way to stop endless war is to expose the 9/11 plot: a rogue network of moles, patsies, and professional killer cells, covered by corrupt politicians and corporate media. Penetrating insight into history. 512 pages, $17.95.

George Bush: The Unauthorized Biography. Groundbreaking classic exposé of the Bush dynasty and their New World Order. How the Bushes and their Skull & Bones brethren made fortunes on the Nazi death camps. 700 pages, $19.95.

Obama – The Postmodern Coup: Making of a Manchurian Candidate exposes the puppet's handlers as enemies of the people. Foreign policy vizier Brzezinski is gunning for a global showdown with Russia and China. Skull & Bones advisors will plunder the people for Wall Street. The essentials you need to know about US, world politics. 320 pages, $15.95.

Barack H. Obama: The Unauthorized Biography, a massive, devastating exposé. Obama is a creature of the Ford Foundation and the Chicago graft machine. 595 pp., $19.95.

Surviving the Cataclysm, Your Guide through the Greatest Financial Crisis in Human History. The unwinding of the hedge funds and derivatives bubble, and with them, life as we knew it in the USA. Richly detailed history of the financier oligarchy, how they plunder this nation, with solutions to the crisis for individuals and our nation. 668 pages, $29.95.

ProgRESSive

2009: New Releases

Terror on the Tube: Behind the Ve *of 7/7, an Investigation,* by Nic Kollerstrom. First book to compi the clear evidence that all four Mu lim scapegoats were completely inn cent. 7/7 is Bliar's Big Lie and Reich tag Fire, false flag terror as pretext f war and an Orwellian, neo-fasci British police state.

The Complete Patriot's Guide to Ol garchical Collectivism: its Theo1 and Practice by Ethan, an update (Orwell's *1984* for our times. A guid to individual empowerment in th midst of institutional monopolizatio1 and a valuable blueprint for takir ownership of our lives and our world

Global Predator: US Wars for En pire by Stewart Halsey Ross. damning account of the atrocities k US armed forces overseas, since th Cuban-Philippines Wars.

The Telescreen: An Empirical Stuc of the Destruction of Consciousnes by Prof. Jeff Grupp. How the ma: media brainwash us with consume ism, war propaganda, false histor fake news, fake issues, fake reality.

Between a Rock and a Hard Fac(Tales of the Holy City by Sama Jabr. A thoughtful young psychi: trist's perspectives on the plight of th Palestinians under oppression.

Clown Prince Bush the W. A tho oughly tipsy biography of the la resident anti-hero of the White Hous by Kennebunkport reporter Te Cohen. 215 pp, $14.95.

Illuminati: The Cult that Hijacke the World, by Henry Makow. Banl ers stole a monopoly on governmel credit, and took over the world: medi schools, wars, it all. 250 pp, $19.95.

www.ingramcontent.com/pod-product-compliance
Lightning Source LLC
Chambersburg PA
CBHW030043100426
42733CB00040B/78

*9 7 8 1 6 1 5 7 7 1 4 1 7 *